THE CAMBRIDGE COMP/

BRITISH POETRY, 194

The Cambridge Companion to British Poetry, 1945–2010 brings together sixteen essays that explore the full diversity of British poetry since the Second World War, a period of significant achievement in which varied styles and approaches have flourished. As a comprehensive critical, literary-historical and scholarly guide, this *Companion* offers not only new readings of a wide range of poets but a detailed account of the contexts in which their verse was written and received. Focusing on famous and neglected names alike, from Dylan Thomas to John Agard, leading scholars provide readers with insight into the ongoing importance and profundity of post-war poetry.

Edward Larrissy is Emeritus Professor of Poetry in the Queen's University of Belfast. His published works include *Reading Twentieth-Century Poetry: The Language of Gender and Objects*, *Yeats the Poet: The Measures of Difference*, *Blake and Modern Literature* and *The Blind and Blindness in Literature of the Romantic Period*.

A complete list of books in the series is at the back of this book.

THE CAMBRIDGE COMPANION TO BRITISH POETRY, 1945–2010

THE CAMBRIDGE COMPANION TO BRITISH POETRY, 1945–2010

Edited by
EDWARD LARRISSY
Queen's University Belfast

CAMBRIDGE
UNIVERSITY PRESS

32 Avenue of the Americas, New York, NY 10013-2473, USA

Cambridge University Press is part of the University of Cambridge.

It furthers the University's mission by disseminating knowledge in the pursuit of education, learning and research at the highest international levels of excellence.

www.cambridge.org
Information on this title: www.cambridge.org/9781107462847

First published 2016

Printed in the United Kingdom by Clays, St Ives plc.

A catalog record for this publication is available from the British Library.

Library of Congress Cataloging in Publication Data
The Cambridge Companion to British Poetry, 1945–2010 / edited by Edward Larrissy.
pages cm. – (Cambridge companions to literature)
Includes bibliographical references and index.
ISBN 978-1-107-09066-8 (hardback) – ISBN 978-1-107-46284-7 (pbk.)
1. English poetry – 20th century – History and criticism. 2. English poetry – 21st century – History and criticism. I. Larrissy, Edward, editor.
PR601.C36 2015
821′.91409–dc23 2015025685

ISBN 978-1-107-09066-8 Hardback
ISBN 978-1-107-46284-7 Paperback

CONTENTS

NOTES ON CONTRIBUTORS

PETER BARRY is Professor of English at Aberystwyth University. His books on poetry include *New British Poetries* (co-edited with Robert Hampson, 1995), *Contemporary British Poetry and the City* (2000), *Poetry Wars* (2006), *Literature in Contexts* (2007), and *Reading Poetry* (2013). He is also the author of *Beginning Theory* (1995, 3rd edn, 2009, with translated editions in Korean, Hebrew, Ukrainian, Greek, Japanese, and Chinese); and *English in Practice* (2000 and 2nd edn., 2013). He co-edited *English* (the journal of the English Association) for twenty years, and headed the 2012–2015 Leverhulme-funded 'Devolved Voices' project on English-language poetry in Wales since 1997.

PETER BARRY is Professor of English at Aberystwyth University. His books on poetry include *New British Poetries* (co-edited with Robert Hampson, 1995), *Contemporary British Poetry and the City* (2000), *Poetry Wars* (2006), *Literature in Contexts* (2007), and *Reading Poetry* (2013). He is also the author of *Beginning Theory* (1995, 3rd edn, 2009, with translated editions in Korean, Hebrew, Ukrainian, Greek, Japanese, and Chinese); and *English in Practice* (2000 and 2nd edn., 2013). He co-edited *English* (the journal of the English Association) for twenty years, and headed the 2012–2015 Leverhulme-funded 'Devolved Voices' project on English-language poetry in Wales since 1997.

FIONA BECKET lectures in modern and contemporary English literature at the University of Leeds. She is the author of *D. H. Lawrence: The Thinker as Poet* (1997) and *The Complete Critical Guide to D. H. Lawrence* (2002). She has co-edited several volumes including *Culture, Creativity and Environment: New Environmentalist Criticism* with Terry Gifford (2007) and has written articles on modernism and language, the contemporary novel and poetry. She is currently working on a study of post-war experimental poetry and technology in the pre-computer decades, and curating an exhibition of visual poetry. Her principal interests lie in the area of post-war poetics and include eco-poesis.

C. D. BLANTON is associate professor of English at the University of California, Berkeley. He is the author of *Epic Negation: The Dialectical Poetics of Late*

Modernism (2015). He is also the co-editor, with Nigel Alderman, of *A Concise Companion to Postwar British and Irish Poetry* (2009).

FRAN BREARTON is Professor of Modern Poetry at Queen's University Belfast and Director of the Seamus Heaney Centre for Poetry. Her books include *The Great War in Irish Poetry* (2000), *Reading Michael Longley* (2006) and, as co-editor, *Incorrigibly Plural: Louis MacNeice and His Legacy* (2012) and *The Oxford Handbook of Modern Irish Poetry* (2012). She recently edited Robert Graves's war memoir, *Good-bye to All That* for Penguin Classics (2014).

SANDIE BYRNE is University Lecturer in English at the University of Oxford, and Fellow in English of Kellogg College Oxford. She is the author of a number of books and articles on nineteenth- and twentieth-century literature including *Tony Harrison: Loiner* (1997), *H, v. & O: The Poetry of Tony Harrison* (1998), and *The Poetry of Ted Hughes* (2014).

PATRICK DEANE is Professor of English and Cultural Studies at McMaster University, Canada, where he is also President and Vice-Chancellor. His publications include *At Home in Time: Forms of Neo-Augustanism in Modern English Poetry* (1994) and *History in Our Hands: A Critical Anthology of Writings on Literature, Culture and Politics from the 1930s* (1998).

ERIC FALCI is Associate Professor of English at the University of California, Berkeley. He is the author of *Continuity and Change in Irish Poetry, 1966–2010* (2012) and *The Cambridge Introduction to British Poetry, 1945–2010* (2015). He has also published a number of essays on modern British and Irish poetry.

JON GLOVER studied at the University of Leeds from 1962 to 1969. There he met Jon Silkin, Geoffrey Hill, Ken Smith, Peter Redgrove, David Wright, Tony Harrison and Jeffrey Wainwright amongst others. In 1964 he started to help edit Stand of which he is now Managing Editor with John Whale and his wife Elaine. His most recent book of poems is *Glass Is Elastic* (2013). He edited with Kathryn Jenner, *The Complete Poems of Jon Silkin* (2015). He is Professor Emeritus at the University of Bolton and Honorary Fellow of the School of English, University of Leeds.

CORNELIA GRÄBNER lectures in Hispanic Studies and Comparative Literature at Lancaster University. She holds an M.A. in Comparative Literature from the University of Bonn, Germany, and an PhD in Cultural Analysis from the University of Amsterdam, The Netherlands. She has published extensively on performance poetry, on contemporary resistance literature (especially poetry) in Europe and in the Americas, and on the relationship between committed writing, social movements and projects of social and political transformation in the twenty-first century. She is co-editor of an edited collection on performance poetry, and of special issues on the poetics of resistance and poetry in public spaces.

KATIE GRAMICH is a Professor of English Literature at Cardiff University, specialising in the literatures of Wales, women's writing, modern poetry, comparative literature, translation, and travel writing. She is a Fellow of the Learned Society of Wales and a judge for the annual Stephen Spender Poetry in Translation prize. Publications include: *Twentieth Century Women's Writing in Wales: Land, Gender, Belonging* (2007); *Mapping the Territory: Critical Approaches to Welsh Fiction in English* (ed.) (2010); *Feet in Chains,* annotated translation of Kate Roberts' *Traed Mewn Cyffion* (2012); and, co-edited with Kirsti Bohata, *Rediscovering Margiad Evans* (2012).

EDWARD LARRISSY is Emeritus Professor of Poetry at Queen's University, Belfast, where he chaired the Advisory Board of the Seamus Heaney Centre for Poetry. He has also taught at the University of Leeds, where he directed a major project on 'Leeds Poetry: 1950–1980.' His books include *Reading Twentieth Century Poetry: The Language of Gender and Objects, Yeats the Poet: The Measures of Difference, Blake and Modern Literature,* and *The Blind and Blindness in Literature of the Romantic Period.* He has reviewed poetry for the *TLS, Poetry Review, Stand* and *Poetry London.* He is a Member of the Royal Irish Academy.

SARAH LAWSON WELSH is Associate Professor and Reader in English and Postcolonial Literatures at York St John University, York, UK. Her publications include *Grace Nichols* (2007), *Rerouting the Postcolonial: New Directions for a New Millennium* (2011) and *The Routledge Reader in Caribbean Literature* (1996). She is also an editor of the international *Journal of Postcolonial Writing.* Her most recent research focuses on food histories, food cultures and food writing in and from the Caribbean. She is currently writing a monograph entitled *Food, Text and Culture in the Anglophone Caribbean* (2018).

JOHN MATTHIAS is Professor Emeritus at the University of Notre Dame and a Life Member of Clare Hall, Cambridge. He is Editor at Large of *Notre Dame Review.* He has published some thirty books of poetry, criticism, fiction, and scholarship. Shearsman publishes his *Collected Longer* and *Collected Shorter Poems* in three volumes, together with *Trigons*, a book-length poem, and *Different Kinds of Music*, a novel.

JAN MONTEFIORE was born in Cambridge and educated at Oxford University. She is Professor Emerita of the University of Kent, where she worked in the School of English and American Literature from 1978 to 2015. She taught on Kent's pioneering MA in Women's Studies from 1980 to 1992, and in 2007 co-founded the Centre for Gender, Sexuality and Writing with Dr Nicky Hallett. Her books include *Feminism and Poetry* (1987, 1994, 2004), *Men and Women Writers of the 1930s* (1996), *Rudyard Kipling* (2007) and most recently the edited collection *In Time's Eye: Essays on Rudyard Kipling* (2013).

SIMON PERRIL'S poetry publications include *Beneath:a Nekyiad* (2015), *Archilochus on the Moon* (2013), *Newton's Splinter* (2012), *Nitrate* (2010), *A Clutch of Odes* (2009), *Hearing is Itself Suddenly a Kind of Singing* (2004). As a critic he has written widely on contemporary poetry, editing the books *The Salt Companion to John James*, and *Tending the Vortex: The Works of Brian Catling*. He is Reader in Contemporary Poetic Practice at De Montfort University, Leicester.

NATALIE POLLARD is Lecturer in Modernist and Contemporary Literature at the University of Exeter. Her research interests include twentieth- and twenty-first century British poetry and Anglophone fiction, reception theory and philosophy of language. Natalie is the author of *Speaking to You: Poetry and Public Address* (2012), and editor of *Don Paterson: Collected Critical Essays* (2014). She has also recently published on areas including scholarship and stupidity, commerce and literature, the avant-garde and the mainstream, and on the ethics of bickering and rudeness in the South African novelist and scholar J.M. Coetzee.

ALAN RIACH, Professor of Scottish Literature at Glasgow University, is the author of *Hugh MacDiarmid's Epic Poetry* (1991), *Representing Scotland in Literature, Popular Culture and Iconography* and co-author with Alexander Moffat of *Arts of Resistance: Poets, Portraits and Landscapes of Modern Scotland* (2009), described by the *Times Literary Supplement* as 'a landmark book' and *Arts of Independence: The Cultural Argument and Why It Matters Most* (2014), general editor of Hugh MacDiarmid's collected works and co-editor of *The Edinburgh Companion to Twentieth-Century Scottish Literature* (2009) and *Scotlands: Poets and the Nation* (2004). His most recent book of poems is *Homecoming* (2009).

EDWARD LARRISSY

Introduction

A plausible starting point for a volume dealing with British poetry of the latter half of the twentieth century might be the early fifties, with the advent of the 'Movement' announcing a new dry tone, often ironic and sometimes disillusioned, appropriate to a society which had undergone a war that came to the heart of its cities, and to a nation whose empire was vanishing. Yet the Movement cannot be separated from the literary world which preceded it: its critical ideas centred on a reaction against the supposed 'Neo-Romanticism' of the forties; while on the other hand its productions included distinct traces of the poetics it was supposedly erasing. The Romanticism of Larkin's *The North Ship* (1945) persists in subtle and attenuated form in the bleak plangency of his 'less deceived' Movement period. John Wain's early poetic line is palpably indebted to Dylan Thomas. Thom Gunn's loyalty to Reason begins its career in an obviously Byronic mode: this is as true of his leather-clad motorcyclists or his portrayal of Elvis Presley as it is of his sketch of Byron in his sonnet 'Lerici'.[1] And at the same time it is possible to make a balancing point in the other direction. Few would now accept the partisan jibes flung at Thomas, which portray him as a free-associating visionary, drunk on high-sounding verbiage. As William Empson recognised, Thomas believed a poem should go through the head as well as the heart, and he learnt very deliberately from Donne and Eliot.[2] As for W. S. Graham, his contemporary rehabilitation stresses the linguistic self-consciousness and craft which are themselves a major topic of his poems.

Such balanced judgment is essential to the achievement of a more objective view of the poetry of the times, one that is not blinded by the critical war cries which belong more appropriately to the literary history of coteries and movements, but whose descriptive value is innately partial and distorting. Yet the truth which inflects the war cries must also be acknowledged. There is no doubt but that Thomas was a poet who did indeed believe in the Romantic topos of a consciousness enlarged and saved by imagination, and whose most profound poetic debts were to Blake and Wordsworth, not to Donne and Eliot. Poets such as Kathleen Raine, George Barker and John Heath-Stubbs also looked to Romantic models and notions. The forties saw the publication of a major work by an American poet, long resident in London, H. D., whose *Trilogy* was published by Oxford University Press as *The Walls Do Not Fall* (1944), *Tribute to the Angels* (1945) and *The Flowering of the Rod* (1946). While couched in the tough but haunting music of a disciplined free verse, its theme, resolutely and ingeniously pursued, is the ultimate victory of imagination over the destructive spirit of warfare.

Equally, it remains undeniable that Reason was the Movement poets' watchword, and that in its name they fostered a style of clear, rational discursiveness which Donald Davie would sum up as 'urbanity.'[3] And while some may decry the fact, the Movement style has had the most lasting and widely-spread influence on subsequent mainstream poetry, even if it has not had the field to itself. From Derek Mahon to Carol Ann Duffy, and across many points in between (including the point occupied by Tony Harrison) runs a line of lucid craft and rationality which takes its origin in the Movement and which does not have much in common with the Romantic themes and manner which preceded it. Furthermore, the style of poets such as Andrew Motion and Blake Morrison, who attempt to contrast the Movement with the linguistic self-consciousness they claim for themselves, is immediately recognisable as post-Movement. This dominance provides another light by which to comprehend the ascendancy of Larkin, who was incisively and sympathetically commemorated by Motion himself in his biography of the poet.[4]

To note this dominance is to run the risk of turning the publication of the first of Robert Conquest's *New Lines* anthologies (1956) into a moment of revolutionary rupture.[5] However, another balancing point to make is that the Movement poets had obvious ancestors, both immediate and more remote. Among the former, one might note poets such as Alun Lewis or Keith Douglas, both of whom died in the Second World War. Douglas, in particular, had fervent admirers in the years that ensued, among them Ted Hughes. Nor, for many readers of the time – probably the majority – would any revolution have been apparent in any case: revolutions are often noticed or constructed after the event. For a large number of readers, the publication of Auden's *Nones* (New York, 1951; London, 1952) and *The Shield of Achilles* (1955), or of MacNeice's *Autumn Sequel* (1954) and *Visitations* (1957), would have been the most significant events. The works of their Oxford friend John Betjeman constituted cherished reading for many, including those who did not usually keep up with poetry. His *Collected Poems* (1958) was a big seller. While his poems present few major challenges to the reader, their indebtedness to Kipling and Hardy may help to remind us of characteristics they share with the works of 'Movement' poets who incur a similar debt: Kingsley Amis or Larkin.

In any case, there are other ways in which the Movement did not have the field to itself. For those who desired the continuation of Modernist techniques and points of view, the publication of David Jones's *The Anathémata* in 1952 offered an ambitious palimpsest history of Britain, ordered according to Jones's mystical Catholic beliefs, which were fashioned into a principle giving shape also to past mythologies, principally the Celtic, in a manner analogous to what Eliot did. MacDiarmid's *In Memoriam James Joyce* (1955) is open to a range of discourses, scientific, economic and political, which were effectively excluded from poetry by the Movement style. In 1960, the appearance of Basil Bunting's *Briggflatts* confirmed the continuation of the Modernist line, waiting to be picked up by younger poets such as Tom Pickard. Another new Modernist, Charles Tomlinson, castigated the formal banality and narrow horizons, as he saw them, of the Movement poets, whose presiding genius he identified as 'The Middlebrow Muse'.[6] Tomlinson's own poetic debts ranged from Pound and the French Symbolists to the works of George Oppen and of the American Black Mountain school. But his poetry of the fifties and sixties centres on an implicit debate between the contrasting tenets and methods of William Carlos Williams and Wallace Stevens. These were different and more exotic lights from those which guided many of the poets who wrote for the major British publishing houses, though there were others who also sought inspiration beyond the insular – Christopher Middleton and Michael Hamburger, for instance.

What generalisations can one make which could bring together the fifties and the years that follow? There is often a tension either within a poet's oeuvre, or as between one poet and another, between a gesture towards myth-making and a more empirical temper. The myth-makers are attempting something more provisional than might have been tried by the Romantics or the Modernists: there is not much hope of systematising Hughes's *Crow*. But this provisionality may reveal the hidden link between empiricism and myth-making in the search for adequate sense-making. The empirical temper pretends to register a believable world, the myth-maker to endow it with order – but not so ambitiously and schematically that it would run the risk of looking absurd or totalitarian to sceptical contemporary readers. In this provisionality lies one possible use for a word one cannot avoid in this context, 'postmodern' – though not necessarily for the word 'postmodernist.' The latter term tends to come with certain expectations about an ambitious subversion of formal as well as sense-making expectations; the former is easier to see in terms of the governing tone of a whole period: ironic, sceptical and above all conscious of the registers, discourses and dictions which may shape consciousness. But the whole question of giving an account of the world can also be related, among some poets, to the topic of Britain's loss of empire and sense of uncertainty as to the new identity it might gain. Such a claim can be made to sound like a subtopic of vulgar Marxism, but there is sufficient evidence that the Condition of Britain (or is it England?) was self-consciously broached by a number of leading poets. For instance, myth can be rooted in the far past of Britain. This is obviously the case with David Jones. But Hughes thought of Crow in relation to the Celtic god Bran, and Hill's *Mercian Hymns* uses a kind of 'mythic method' to make the Anglian King Offa into an ancestor of English traditions. Bunting's *Briggflatts* looks to the Celtic, Norse and Anglian deep past to find antecedents for a tone and structure of feeling. By contrast with these portentous backgrounds, the more unambitious and ironic style, at least at the inception of the Movement, can be seen as an attempt to shuffle off the vaunting claims of empire along with the dangerous Romantic themes of totalitarianism. Philip Larkin, Kingsley Amis and Donald Davie were quite obviously concerned to present and analyse the distinctive feel of post-war Britain, while in a poem such as 'MCMXIV' Larkin laments the death of an older Britain. A. Alvarez's plea in the foreword to his Penguin anthology, *The New Poetry* (1962, 2nd rev. edn. 1966) that British poets should cast off a disabling 'gentility' can in part be seen as encouragement to rediscover lost confidence. Slightly more recently, a poem such as Iain Sinclair's *Lud Heat* (1975) or his collection *Suicide Bridge* (1979), offered a postmodern (in the sense outlined) and anti-imperial interpretation of London and Britain in terms of Celtic and Blakean mythology. They were published by Sinclair's significantly named 'Albion Village Press.' There are ways of effectively capturing a national spirit which eschew these large and venerable tableaux. Alice Oswald's *Dart* (2002) is sensitive in detail to the particular history of Devon communities, and also to the wildlife and ecology of which they form part. While undeniably English, this landscape is registered as regional and idiosyncratic.

What nation, then, are we talking about? The truth is that in the last paragraph we have been talking mainly about English poets, apart from the Anglo-Welsh David Jones. Even to concede, as one must, that Hughes and Hill are as much concerned with England as with Britain serves as a reminder that poets from Scotland, Wales and Northern Ireland are going to have their own sense of nationality. And here one thinks straight away of the controversy likely to be aroused by including Northern Ireland under the heading of 'Britain'. This was notoriously the case with the Morrison and Motion *Penguin Book of Contemporary British Poetry* (1982). Leaving aside the relevant point that Northern Ireland currently forms part of the United Kingdom and enjoys the connections that come with that fact, a partial response can be framed in empirical terms: many of the poets to come out of Northern Ireland since the mid-sixties were first published by major British publishing houses, and were themselves of a calibre to command the attention and study of British poets and readers. There is another answer, more principled perhaps, but also partial, which would offer a reminder that nationality constitutes no mystical essence. Some Northern Irish poets may espouse an Irish national identity, but if they have become significant agents in a British context, then they cannot be ignored in a volume such as this. The reception of poetry in the Republic of Ireland, by contrast, has created almost a different canon from that which is on offer in the United Kingdom. There Patrick Kavanagh and Thomas Kinsella, say, enjoy a prominence which they deserve to have in Britain, but have demonstrably lacked, at least until recently. In Ireland, poets and readers still remember the names of Thomas MacGreevy, Brian Coffey and Denis Devlin, Irish Modernists largely forgotten in Britain. Seamus Heaney shares with some of his British contemporaries that veering between the empirical (life as it really was on the farm) and the myth-making (the Bog Poems as presided over by a vengeful goddess). But we are dealing with the matter of Ireland, and not so obviously that of Britain. Yet the national questions that affect relationships across our archipelago cannot be so easily shuffled off in the case of Heaney. His learned consciousness of the history of the English language in Ireland is inflected by the wider political and social context of English and Scottish influences in Ireland. This is, in fact, a characteristically Northern Irish perspective, within which his triumphant translation of *Beowulf* (1999) is the statement of a share in the ownership of a tradition. These aspects of Heaney, rather than confirming him as irretrievably different because Irish, help to validate his inclusion, and that of Northern Ireland, in this volume.

There are no cut-and-dried answers to these questions about how to pigeonhole national identity, but the attempt to defer to it in an a priori way can lead to inconsistency. Gerard Carruthers discusses the stance taken by Don Paterson and Charles Simic in *New British Poetry* (2004) as follows:

> When Paterson (and Simic) exclude Ulster poets from the collection, they make the case that most of these self-identify as Irish, and they would not wish to appropriate these writers to Britain or the UK. But what about those they include, such as Paterson's close colleague Robert Crawford, who would primarily self-identify as Scottish?[7]

It seems better to pay heed to the many-faceted and constantly evolving contexts constituted by publishers, readers, reviewers, workshops, universities, performance venues and arts-funding bodies, which allow one to talk, with due caution, in terms of an entity such as 'Britain.' Such caution is nowhere more necessary than when dealing separately with 'Black British Poetry'. It seems clear that due attention should long ago have been accorded to a poet such as John Agard, and not only to him. Yet the sidelining is itself now part of the subject, as is the postcolonial experience which conditions the writing.

Leaving aside national questions, the mythopoeic poetry of the period serves as a reminder that, while it may be true that the Movement has exerted a far-reaching influence on the subsequent history of poetry, this has often been felt as a constraint, for myth was not the Movement thing. Alvarez had castigated the gentility of British poets, and he had the Movement in his sights. Ian Hamilton, as editor first of *The Review* (1962–72) and then *The New Review* (1974–79), encouraged a style in which emotion was concentrated in compact and finely-judged phrasing, and this distilled and chaste lyricism was seen as distinctive. Yet 'control' was one of Hamilton's highest values, and it is open to question how profoundly his own manner and tone should really be differentiated from that of a Movement poet such as Elizabeth Jennings, if one leaves to one side the fact that Jennings tends to rhyme while Hamilton tends not to. Two decades after Alvarez's Penguin anthology, Blake Morrison and Andrew Motion, in their *Penguin Book* (1982), claimed to represent a more politically self-conscious and linguistically adventurous poetry than Alvarez had been able either to promote or to oppose. There is some truth in their claim, but it seems like a decidedly relative matter.

Still, the more thematically and/or linguistically adventurous poetry of the period is saddled with a problem characteristic of poetry in the modern age: the need to find an original poetic language, capable of handling the big questions, while not lapsing into abstraction or generality, or alternatively succumbing to the temptations of irresponsible 'poetic' gesture. This is the more linguistic question which is related to the larger-scale one about veering between empiricism and myth. And it needs to be put in this way, since the terms of debate should pay heed to the formal ruses of poetry and to its transformation of language, and not just to thematic questions. Geoffrey Hill is a salient example of a poet whose sense of the need to grapple with the problem of a responsible and adequate language informs his method and is itself part of the subject matter of his poetry. His 2001 volume, *Speech! Speech!*, foregrounds the topic. David Trotter, in *The Making of the Reader* (1984), recognised the way this question has weighed on modern and contemporary poets, and saw it as modified in the post-war period by the quality of the teaching of poetry in schools and universities.[8] Modernist poets had already been seeking to guide their readers towards an understanding of a particular and innovative array of techniques. In the post-war period, poets are exceptionally aware of the way in which such guidance could be a subject of discussion in the tutorial. According to Trotter, while there is a hot-house tendency towards the gestation of unique and original methods, there has also been a tendency to over-identify poetry with simile (the most obvious figure for novel perception), a tendency he sees as particularly acute in the phenomenon of the 'Metaphor Men' as they came to be known in the early 1980s: Christopher Reid, Craig Raine and David Sweetman.[9] Indeed, contemporary poetry plays itself out on this terrain of ambitious modernist views and ingeniously accurate simile. The reader will note that this could be seen as another way of conceiving the 'myth versus empiricism' couple.

The identification, in the period of the so-called Metaphor Men, of poetry with the striking use of simile was seen by at least one critic in terms of the easy gratification sought by a consumer society.[10] Whether or not this is a valid connection, the claim does not establish that good poetry could not emerge from such a supposedly inauspicious context. The real target of the critique is a supposed superficiality and narrowness: superficiality of the presentation of experience; narrowness of linguistic register and of intellectual and cultural horizons. Questions about the degree to which poetry might be identified with a facile technique and world view may assume added passion when related questions are asked about the proliferation of creative writing courses in universities. It may be an obvious question, but it is well worth investigating: are these courses encouraging the large-scale production of inoffensive but predictable poetry? Whatever the answer to this question, there is no doubt but that universities have become ever more significant as 'singing schools' in the past decade. At their most adventurous, they can support a wide range of interconnected and mutually enhancing activities: the creative writing class, the poetry workshop, the poetry reading, the literary journal or review, links to the literary criticism classes taught elsewhere in the curriculum, and a two-way street to the cultural life of the city outside the university walls. In some cases, a university is drawing upon and developing an honourable tradition of patronage of the arts, and of the formation of poetry workshops on the fringes of university English departments. These drew their membership both from within and from outside academia. This is a story of city and university, and in some cases – Leeds and Belfast, for instance – it begins quite early in our period.

The subject of technical superficiality returns us to our question about how far the language of poetry can address large philosophical or political questions and make these seem to matter to the reader. Recently, Natalie Pollard has made this question the subject of an important book, *Speaking to You: Contemporary Poetry and Public Address*.[11] In relation to the work of Geoffrey Hill, W. S. Graham, C. H. Sisson and Don Paterson, she fastens on one major aspect of this question: the pervasive device of the lyric 'you', which serves as a way of weaving together the public and the subjective registers of poetry. It may also be a way of underlining the situatedness of both poet and reader as speaking subjects in a particular nation, region or community. But the question whether or not British poetry has been able to find a style adequate to serious reflection had been answered in a more sceptical way by some of the poets and critics associated with the 'British Poetry Revival' of the sixties and seventies.[12] A central point in the objection to what some of the critics persisted in calling 'establishment' poetry was the way that, whether making grand imaginative gestures or signalling its accuracy of perception, it defined poetry as having a special language, separate from a range of familiar discourses and even modes of expression. If the dictions of science, economics and sociology were somehow inappropriate, overt expressions of feeling, if not tethered to 'objects', were simply not the done thing. And yet the discourse of intelligent and enquiring people, outside the sphere of poetry, might veer in either or both directions without embarrassment. One of the arguments often made in favour of the early work, at least, of J. H. Prynne is to do with its deployment of a wide range of registers.

Apart from raising questions about the nature of contemporary poetic language, *The Penguin Book of Contemporary British Poetry* initiated a debate about who was in and who was out. Many commentators at the time and since have remarked on the highly selective character of this anthology, which for instance ignored some excellent poetry by black and women writers. A new openness was apparently signalled by an influential anthology from Bloodaxe in 1993: *The New Poetry*, edited by Michael Hulse, David Kennedy and David Morley. In their introduction, the editors announced that 'plurality has flourished'.[13] Yet it might be claimed that the characteristics of the poetry represented therein were not markedly different from those of the poetry in Morrison and Motion – and the same might be said, allowing for a slightly different selection of poets, about *New British Poetry*, edited by Don Paterson and Charles Simic in 2004.[14] Nevertheless, a sense that there have been too many exclusions in British poetry is gaining ground among many readers and in the academy. This sense benefits not only women poets, or black British poets, but also those associated with the avant-garde and experimental, who have sought to extend the formal and thematic scope of poetry by recourse either to American models, or to theories which have made of art an engine of the political remoulding of consciousness. The field of possibility is more open and various than it has been for many years.

NOTES

1 Thom Gunn, *Fighting Terms*, 2nd edn. (London: Faber, 1962), p. 27. (1st edn., Oxford: Fantasy Press, 1954).
2 See Edward Larrissy, 'Languages of Modernism', *Twentieth-Century English Poetry*, ed. Neil Corcoran (Cambridge: Cambridge University Press), p. 137.
3 Donald Davie, *Purity of Diction in English Verse* (London: Chatto and Windus, 1952), p. 133.
4 Andrew Motion, *Philip Larkin: A Writer's Life* (London: Faber, 1993).
5 Robert Conquest, *New Lines: Poets of the 1950s* (London: Macmillan, 1956).
6 Charles Tomlinson, 'The Middlebrow Muse', *Essays in Criticism*, 7:2 (1957), 208–17.
7 Gerard Carruthers, 'Scotland, Britain and the Elsewhere of Poetry', *Don Paterson: Contemporary Critical Essays*, ed. Natalie Pollard (Edinburgh: Edinburgh University Press, 2014), p. 89.
8 David Trotter, *The Making of the Reader: Language and Subjectivity in Modern American, English and Irish Poetry* (Basingstoke: Macmillan, 1984), pp. 2, 242–50.
9 Ibid., pp. 248–50.
10 Andrew Crozier, 'Thrills and Frills: Poetry as Figures of Empirical Lyricism', in *Society and Literature 1945–1979*, ed. Alan Sinfield (London: Methuen, 1983), pp. 199–233.
11 Natalie Pollard, *Speaking to You: Contemporary Poetry and Public Address* (Oxford: Oxford University Press, 2012).
12 Disagreements between 'innovative' poets and those of a more conservative disposition issued in a memorable feud within the Poetry Society, especially about its organ, *Poetry Review*, which for a time in the seventies was edited by Eric Mottram, who was particularly influenced by the Beats and by the American Black Mountain School. See Peter Barry, *The Battle of Earl's Court* (Manchester: Manchester University Press, 2007).
13 Michael Hulse, David Kennedy and David Morley, eds., *The New Poetry* (Newcastle: Bloodaxe, 1993), p. 15.
14 Don Paterson and Charles Simic, eds., *New British Poetry* (St. Paul, MN: Graywolf Press, 2004).

I

C. D. BLANTON

Poets of the Forties and Early Fifties: The Last Romantics?

It is not quite true that the century's second European cataclysm produced no important poetry in English or in Britain. From 1939 to 1945, the poetic generation formed during the First World War found itself caught up once again, but at a distance: T. S. Eliot straining for orthodoxy in London; Ezra Pound spewing propaganda from Rapallo, then returning to verse from a cage near Pisa, largely broken by the experience. A younger generation, formed by the uneasy history of the interwar years, measured its distances too: from self-imposed exile, like W. H. Auden, or somewhere within the civilian bureaucratic apparatus spawned by the war, like most of his comrades. By 1939, older and younger poets alike had been charting war's approach for some time, nervously watching Spain and China and Munich, suggesting that (as a large abstraction at least) the war might be experienced in advance.

It is certainly true, however, that the Second World War somehow failed to offer itself as the substance of lyric experience as easily as the first had once done, somehow preserving lyric itself as the soldier's grim expressive privilege: the vehicle best suited to the otherwise unspeakable facts and symbolic implications of the trench. High modernism's adaptation of French symbolist obliquities to an indirect and allusive style of historical commentary, in W. B. Yeats's strident last work or Eliot's more meditative late style, the Pylon poets' reclamation of a more urgently political style; both unquestionably served, in different ways, to comprehend the war's approach through the 1930s, occasionally to analyse the crises and social contradictions that produced it, but they could do little to express it as an arrived and experienced fact.

And that is, perhaps, the problem. Harder to describe, more difficult to grasp whole, often admitting no gap between civilians and combatants, less measurable *as* individual experience, the second war often seems to reveal a formal inadequacy, some deficit in the available resources of poetic language. Writing during Dunkirk's evacuation, Herbert Read, a poet from the earlier war, recalled his generation's 'resolve | to tell the truth without rhetoric | the truth about war'.[1] Even a refusal of rhetoric is rhetorical, of course, but for poets such as Siegfried Sassoon and Wilfred Owen, the claim had entailed a polemical suspension of communicability as such, an insistence that even a poem telling the truth about war could not be understood by those not fighting it. For those developing a more radical, often cryptic style in years to follow – Eliot, Pound or Yeats, most inescapably – the events of 1914–18 would signify more generally, marking the historical collapse of a culture, leaving poets to sift through signs that seemed to have forgotten their meanings. The difference of the second war, more intense yet also more diffuse, simultaneously cataclysmic and unsurprising, experienced everywhere and nowhere, seems to lie in its demand for the renewal of some public language, some way to secure or assume communication or a meaning in common. If the first war provoked a new poetry, the second posed the subtler question of what poetry might still do at all.

Take for example one of the conflict's more durably wrought pieces: F. T. Prince's 'Soldiers Bathing', written in 1942 and published a year later by an intelligence officer who spent most of the conflict at Bletchley Park.[2] The poem measures its removal from battle immediately, as an officer gazes on a squad 'Of soldiers who belong to me', 'bathing in the sea' (p. 55). 'All's pathos now', it declares, but that pathos is predicated on an incongruity between bodies that are 'gross, | Rank, ravenous, disgusting in the act or in repose, | All fever, filth and sweat' (p. 55) and some higher idea that the poem must extract from such base facts. Classical and cool in tone, almost austere, the poem underscores the same tension formally. Its couplets regularly answer an initially strict pentameter in the first line with a more sprawling refusal of it in the second, only to settle again on simple rhymes that momentarily stay the poem's compulsive enjambment. Prince's largest synoptic gesture, however, lies in his title, with its glance toward Michelangelo's depiction of the Battle of Cascina, fought between Pisa and Florence in 1364. The allusion is comfortably modernist in style, familiarly erudite and evocative, even as it heavily overcodes the scene witnessed, bestowing both historical significance and sensuous force on the anonymous soldierly band. Indeed, Prince redoubles the scholarly effect in the next lines, recalling that Antonio del Pollaiullo later 'Painted a naked battle' (p. 56) too, before turning to moralise a little sententiously on 'a theme | Born out of the experience of war's horrible extreme' (p. 56).

But there is something elusive in the poem's seemingly assured exegetical movements. The problem can be glimpsed in the recollection of Michelangelo's scene, originally designed to face Leonardo's depiction of the later Battle of Anghiari across Florence's Palazzo Vecchio but never completed, known only through students' copies of a lost cartoon. Or in the slight error regarding Pollaiullo's famous engraving *The Battle of the Nudes*, not quite a painting at all, as it happens. In each case, the poem's memory goes slightly awry, filling in or projecting an image, a meaning, neither evident nor sustained by its sources. And in fact, the poem subtly confesses as much when it claims to glimpse 'The *idea* of Michelangelo's cartoon | Of soldiers bathing' rather than the thing itself, or when it thinks 'of the *theme* another found' in Pollaiuolo's print, or again when it acknowledges that, in the vision of the begrimed soldiers, 'my mind towards the *meaning* of it strives' (pp. 55–56, emphases added). Strictly, Prince's poem is less about the soldiers or their war than about the need for a meaning not quite provided in the scene itself, betrayed in the poem's concluding rhetorical bid to discern 'a commentary | on the Crucifixion?' (p. 56). As the question mark (almost) admits, the hope is forced at best, grimly absurd at worst, and the poem's concluding recognition in the sunset of 'a streak of red that might have issued from Christ's breast' (p. 57) marks a kind of hermeneutic failure, trading the soldiers' experience for the thin promise of some symbol that might restore an aesthetic unity not glimpsed in experience or in things as they appear.

In most ways, as we will see, Prince's poem remains atypical of its moment, more remote and dispassionate than the work of younger poets working in spaces both created and abandoned by Eliot and Auden. Maintaining more of the former's orthodox reserve than his contemporaries, and more of the latter's terse formalism, Prince represents no movement in particular. The need to which 'Soldiers Bathing' compulsively confesses, however, for some organizing unity to which the extremities of experience might be submitted and through which they might be rendered poetically legible, is more common, and it offers a way to graph some of the cross pressures of this uncertain, often canonically forgotten moment after modernism, before the Movement. The poem's insistent hermeneutic authorization of embedded details, its nervous reduction of ideas to visible signs, its transcription of natural scenes into (partially) legible texts, all partake of the logic of allegory, labouring to fortify and remediate some expressive power already revealed as insufficient. This is certainly rhetoric of a sort, but almost accidentally so, occasioned by some larger force withdrawn from the surface of the verse, uncertain that anything might be communicated otherwise. The argument might therefore be refined. If the second war did not quite produce poetry as the first had, it did reveal a larger problem of expression much longer in formation, visible even before the war's onset: a difficulty in calibrating poetic language's increasingly frail resources and shallow experiential reservoirs to events of ever expanding scale.

Even the work of Keith Douglas, perhaps the war's best-known poet, committed to a more documentary idiom, a realism even, betrays the same allegorical need for some binding figure capable of vouching a larger premise of meaningfulness beyond the poem's edge. '*Vergissmeinnicht*' refrains from any gesture as large as Prince's sacrificial theology but strains for its thematic resolution no less arduously.[3] Returning weeks later to the scene of a skirmish, a scouting party chances on the remains of a soldier it killed. Douglas juxtaposes the bloated corpse with the pristine weapon that abases it in a strict sequence of quatrains, sentimentally rooting the scene's pathos in the now conventional ironies developed by Sassoon, Owen and Rosenberg ('Rosenberg I only repeat what you were saying', he freely admits in 'Desert Flowers' (p. 108)). But it is also a provisional figure, used only momentarily to establish the poem's larger conceit:

> Look. Here in the gunpit spoil
> the dishonoured picture of his girl
> who has put: *Steffi. Vergissmeinnicht*
> in a copybook gothic script. (p. 118)

Untranslated but maintained as title, Steffi's inscription – 'forget-me-not' – does double work, unheeded at one level only to be recuperated at another. While the German phrase and gothic hand interpose an alienating distance, gesturing toward the lost particularity of the soldier's life, they also enfold his death in a recognizable field of scripted sentimental allusions. Dividing the 'dishonoured picture' against the injunction to remember it bears, the poem thus assumes the task of commemoration itself, summoning a counterfactual image of Steffi to imagine her tears at 'the swart flies' (p. 118) moving across the soldier's skin and to press its final argument: 'here the lover and killer are mingled' (p. 118). It is, in this regard, Steffi's presence that matters most, her power to haunt the scene graphically, thereby securing its reading and claiming her lover's remains at a distance. If Prince must work to discern the meaning inscribed in things, Douglas insists that it is (quite literally) written in the scene already.

To describe this mode as allegorical is not to reduce the poem to some truth known in advance, but rather to specify something irreducible about a formal logic shared by poems otherwise radically different: a distrust of mere appearances, a need to refer interpretation to some second order of reading to which language merely points, some abstraction with which it fails ultimately to coincide. Understood in this way, such poems undertake acts of translation, searching after or laboriously manufacturing an illusion of hermeneutic transparency, even while acknowledging the desire as illusory. This problem of allegory is an ancient one, of course, but the modernism of the interwar years had seemingly rediscovered it at every turn, enshrining the division between poetic figure and its hermeneutic code as a formal inevitability. Eliot suggested as much when he hypothesised a 'dissociation of sensibility', effectively a historical disintegration of experience as such; the critics of the Frankfurt School, writing contemporaneously, located the break with Baudelaire and the systematic emergence of industrial urban capitalism.[4] Under such accounts, the difficulty confronted by 'Soldiers Bathing' and '*Vergissmeinnicht*' begins to appear systematic, as if it had become possible, by the mid century, to suspect that poetry could not be other than allegorical, but impossible not to recognise in that situation an intractable loss of some older idea of poetic language, romantic in origin: expressively dense and phenomenologically self-sufficient, formed in the sphere of a symbol that (in Coleridge's canonical formulation) 'partakes of the Reality which it renders intelligible', that 'enunciates the whole, abides itself as a living part of that Unity, of which it is the representative'.[5]

Paul de Man famously argues that even the romantic symbol of which Coleridge dreamed inevitably finds itself unmade, eventually and predictably lapsing into the overdetermined rhetoric of mere irony or allegory.[6] And it is difficult to argue that the 'new romanticism' that flourished in the 1930s and through the 1940s ever succeeded in evading that fate. But it is also impossible to grasp the poetic ambitions of those years without noticing the persistence of a desire like Coleridge's, recovered in modernism's wake, for a translucent poetic language, somehow able to overcome the gaps stipulated not only by Prince and Douglas but presupposed in a now canonised modernist style. 'We were the last romantics', sighed Yeats in 1931, before concluding (with characteristic drama) that 'all is changed, that high horse riderless'.[7] Yeats was thinking back to the century's turn, acknowledging what had happened in the interim – the avant-gardes, high modernism's studied classicism and the larger history to which both responded – before gesturally disowning the ingenuous enthusiasm for which 'romanticism' provides an encompassing sign. Beneath the familiar modernist polemics, however, the gesture also suggests a fascination that had abided, which figures like Read and John Middleton Murry had always cultivated even within the modernist cultural scene (with D. H. Lawrence usually providing the example). By the decade's end, Read's increasingly committed anarchism had begun to suggest that such isolated inclinations might fuse in a more sustained philosophical tendency, while his editorial position at Routledge opened an alternative to Eliot's Faber, available to younger poets anxious to challenge Yeats's assumption that romanticism had exhausted itself definitively, looking to recover some visionary possibility lost in the interim.[8] Prefacing an anthology (published by Read) of the young Oxford poets (including Douglas and John Heath-Stubbs, but not classmate Philip Larkin) he deemed 'most interesting, most typical, and most hopeful for the future', Sidney Keyes sought to describe their common inclination in the same terms that even Yeats might have recognised: 'we are all ... *Romantic* writers, though by that I mean little more than that our greatest fault is a tendency to floridity; and that we have, on the whole, little sympathy with the Audenian school of poets'.[9]

Like Douglas, Keyes would not survive the war, and his version of a visionary idiom in a florid style – as indebted to the ornate mythologies of Hölderlin and Rilke as the topographical modes of Wordsworth and John Clare – remains partially formed. In a poem like 'The Anti-Symbolist', however, Keyes had already reformulated Coleridge's dream of an immanent poetic unity in a mildly diminished key, confessing uncertainty 'That nature evolved through a zodiac of symbols | Upon an axis of creative mind', before breaking across a stanza to argue 'We should not work that way.'[10] Keyes's *anti*-symbolism accordingly recuperates symbolism as an immanent claim on present experience, in an accumulating profusion of natural images that forswear any prophetic power but strive to suffuse the present with a near equivalent density of meaning: 'Anticipation | Is crooked thinking' (p. 22), he concludes, 'Forward is not our business' (p. 23). The claim thus matches a pose of apparent epistemological modesty with an expansive assertion of the poet's power to penetrate the surrounding world as a succession of charged impressions, partial encounters that need not promise transcendence to achieve 'higher | Reaches' 'mapped | With some small boast of skill and application' (p. 23). If Keyes forswears the symbol's power to grasp things in themselves, he nonetheless insists that their surprising manifestation as scattered images bespeaks a kind of intuitive unity, available to sense if not thought. As Keyes's friend Heath-Stubbs suggested a few years later, seeking to discern romanticism's persistence long after its canonical phase (in the work of figures from George Darley, Thomas Lovell Beddoes and Thomas Hood to the pre-Raphaelites and early Yeats), what began as 'a revolt of the intuitive imagination' accordingly returns as the cultivation of imagination in its practical guise, less a fully developed symbology than 'imagery, symbolically interpreted'.[11]

The difference seems slight, but for the poets of the war years it proved crucial. Reconceived as an underlying immanence, a kind of poetic presupposition rather than a revealed sign, a transfigured version of the symbol might undertake a different work, charting an escape from the hermeneutic demands of allegory imposed by modernist styles and restoring to subjective perception an assumption of underlying coherence, if not transparency. Stripped of its transcendentalising reach, meanwhile, a romantic imagination now etymologically devolved into the worldly presentation of concrete images might test itself in the historical world as well. The resulting assertion of an unabashed romantic style's power against an unsympathetic social order was most loudly made as the war began, in an anthology edited by J. F. Hendry. *The New Apocalypse* addressed itself, in Hendry's phrase, to '[t]he technical problem of how to write organically' – almost identical, he asserted, 'with the human problem of how to act organically'.[12] 'Apocalyptic writing', he continued, 'is therefore concerned with the study of living, the collapse of social forms and the emergence of new and more organic ones' (p. 9). The sliding reference in that sentence catches some of the anthology's confusion, but also frames its ambition. On one side, 'apocalypse' assumes an eschatological connotation, caught in 'the collapse of social forms' (a suggestion underscored by the epigraph from Lawrence's *Apocalypse* that heads the volume's 1941 sequel, *The White Horseman*).[13] Hendry's immediate pivot to 'the emergence of new and more organic ones' points in another direction, however, toward the term's deeper etymology of 'disclosure' or 'uncovering'. The implicit historical reference to ongoing events is thus quickly absorbed in a more mythical register, reclaimed from a social order defined by 'the object-machine, whether state, system or rationalism' and submitted to a natural order felt in the emergence of poetic language.

The volume's ostensible sources waver similarly, oscillating between Marx and myth, swerving from Joyce and Kafka to Cézanne and Picasso, but a separate essay by Henry Treece fixes its stylistic points of reference more securely, juxtaposing Dylan Thomas's early verse with French surrealism, as represented by the group's most prominent English member David Gascoyne.[14] As the mixed genealogy suggests, with Thomas enlisted alongside continental avant-gardes, this self-described 'new romanticism' remains unorthodox and a little mottled, freely mixing scraps of revelation where they can be found. Its anthologies remain similarly heterogeneous, mingling fiction and criticism among selections from the early work of poets such as Nicholas Moore and Norman MacCaig, later Vernon Watkins. G. S. Fraser doubtless overstated its rigor when he labelled the New Apocalypse a derivation from surrealism, even 'a dialectical development of it', embodying 'not only a certain attitude to the technique of writing, but a certain attitude to life in general'.[15] The new romanticism's symbolic diction always owed more to Jung than to Freud, while its notion of an organic layer of being, trapped beneath or forgotten by the normalizing logic of the mechanical age, wrapped vague Heideggerian tones around a 'flexible philosophy' designed to recoil from the limitations of empiricism but 'which hardly dictates to anyone how he is to write or feel' (p. 6).

Despite its apparent eclecticism, however, the insistent doubling of Thomas and surrealism as orienting points is less adventitious than might appear, securing the most important formal element of a recognizable common style. Thomas's singular, often exuberantly bardic voice had first emerged with *18 Poems* (1934), in lyrics that often strain against the limits of semantic sense, leaving pure rhetorical force in its place: 'The force that through the green fuse drives the flower | Drives my green age', or, as the sentence continues, 'that blasts the roots of trees | Is my destroyer'.[16] At its simplest, the statement is an exercise in simple analogy, straining toward metaphor by yoking speaker to natural world, each submitted to a larger natural force – something like that 'common mind' that Keyes could not prove but felt. The poem's work lies not in its predictable, even trite figurative equation, however, but in the dense series of more local effects that coalesce in distinct but overlapping patterns: sonic, prosodic, lexical, grammatical, all at once. The almost excessive alliteration of the first line – five small soundings of *th*, modulating into three larger returns to an *f* – rises into full repetition in the second, as *drives* and *green* seal the first full clause, even while momentarily inverting an iambic into a trochaic cadence. The elision that connects the sentence's subject, *force*, to the second parallel adjectival clause quickens the pace again: *that drives ... that blasts*. The poem's diction is no less tense. Rapid monosyllables relax only in the third truncated line, while apparently uncomplicated words – *fuse*, *blasts* – hesitate between noun and verb or surreptitiously admit archaic natural subtones that unfix their more colloquially modern technological senses. If it is difficult to paraphrase the poem, that is at least partially because there seems little need to do so. Succeeding stanzas recapitulate the same grammar and rhythm to make the same basic point: the same force yokes 'the water through the rocks' and 'my red blood'; moves water and quicksand alike (p. 10), without attaching definitive reference to either, compulsively flattening even Keyes's 'higher reaches' across a single plane. The poem's complexity lies entirely at the surface, as if too much meaning had been pressed onto the senses at once, losing its quality as meaning in the process.

If Thomas's underlying vision of a natural monism requires no particular exegesis, however, the poem still insists on a reckoning of a different sort, generating a catalogue of surface effects moving at cross-purposes. What the poem seems to generate most compulsively is a sequence of stark images, but images that stand as mere markers of a kind of pure intensity, sufficient to derange reading through simple repetitive force – images, as it were, of nothing in particular. To a considerable degree, the often mesmerizing power of Thomas's verse lies in this simultaneous evacuation and reclamation of the image as such, on the poem's capacity to unmoor its elements from their expected conventional senses, only to recombine sound and apparent sense in several countervailing patterns at once. Even a poem like 'Light breaks where no sun shines', built on the progressive complication of an originating paradox (how should one render the sense of *breaks*, after all?), thus manages to reduce declaration to a surfeit of impression: 'Light breaks on secret lots, | On tips of thought where thoughts smell in the rain' (p. 30). As the poem coils to its crescendo, discrete lexical registers fold underneath one another: logics that die, soil that breeds secrets 'through the eye', as 'Above the waste allotments the dawn halts' (p. 30). There is a dry echo of an Eliotic rationality lurking in secret lots and waste allotments, in tips of thought and dying logics. But it is just that suggestion of a determinate intelligible scheme or scaffolding – some allegorical remnant – that the poem resists most fiercely, insisting instead on its own capacity to reduce abstractions to graspable quantities and smells in the rain, to strip meaningful signs into pure conceits. By the 1930s, Thomas's seemingly innocent vision of blood-and-soil might (perhaps should) have summoned a menacing allusion to European fascism, but the deeper point is that his language seems to refuse such assignable reference altogether. Even the insistently Christian imagery of slightly later poems like 'And death shall have no dominion' or the sonnet sequence 'Altarwise by owl-light' revels not in orthodoxy but in programmatic evasions of propositional sense, the capacity to encompass content as pure sound: 'What is the metre of the dictionary? | The size of genesis? the short spark's gender?'; or even the assonant 'shape of Pharaoh's echo?' (p. 81)

By no strict measure, then, could Thomas's work be counted as a mere surrealist annex. As readers like Read and Treece regularly argued (usually with a hint of national pride), its delicate craft owes more to an intricate reworking of English verse than experiments in automatic writing or hypotheses regarding the unconscious, and Thomas himself loudly disowned the association. But its overladen surfaces, formed by smoothing multiple poetic registers onto a single expressive plane, flattening semantic and syntactical elements into purely sonic ones, opened a space for the profusion and regeneration of the image as such, no longer reduced to the pristine simplicity of Poundian Imagism, but instead driven breathlessly into rhetorical inflation. What Thomas shares with surrealism, as well as what he refuses, can be glimpsed in the early work of Gascoyne, who had emerged as the group's primary exponent in English with an array of translations, critical surveys and experiments approaching automatic writing. The concluding poem of *Man's Life Is This Meat* (1936), 'And the Seventh Dream Is the Dream of Isis', condenses several of its definitive effects:

> there is an explosion of geraniums in the ballroom of the hotel
> there is an extremely unpleasant odour of decaying meat

arising from the depetalled flower growing out her ear
her arms are like pieces of sandpaper
or wings of leprous birds in taxis[17]

The poem's extended line ensures an almost prosaic rhythm, slack where Thomas is tense. Its benumbed anaphora ('there is an ex-') seems to impose a strictly conventional stock of images – flowers, flesh, birds – only to dissolve each into scabrous excess or emblems of decomposition. What is most striking about the poem's movement, however, lies in its apparently normal elements: a sedentary grammar that maps each line onto an extended phrase, never quite fully enjambing; a deliberately fatigued reliance on rhetorical figures (metaphor, simile) that remain both thoroughly conventional in structure and provocatively exaggerated, even impossible. Rather than dividing sound against sense, Gascoyne divides sense against structure, as if to excavate the normative force of grammar or figuration itself, littering the poem with images half-twisted out of place, evidence of an unnamed semantic derangement.

Such effects are of course predictable elements of surrealist practice, constructed to register the symptomatic evidence of the unconscious at work. Transposed onto an English graph, however, and stripped of surrealism's informing theoretical substructure, this programmatic juxtaposition of unlike imagistic particles – arms like sandpaper, leprous birds in taxis – also isolates the conjunctively estranging operation of the image itself, laying bare the mechanism through which the poem seeks to distinguish itself from a more ordinary worldly prose. Surrealism's claims to unconscious depths, that is, themselves the product of a species of allegory, are quickly refigured as a conscious power of imagination. It was thus that Read could preface a retrospective of the London International Surrealist Exhibition of 1936, including contributions by Breton and Éluard, with a Coleridgean epigraph on 'the self-power of the imagination' and proceed to name the movement nothing less than 'a reaffirmation of the romantic principle', adducing Blake, Shelley and Swinburne as sympathetic precursors.[18] Writing in the same volume, Hugh Sykes Davies was less expansive but more precise, claiming surrealism as 'a direct continuation of Coleridge's work – we are its prehensile tail' (p. 139). Paradoxically, then, the last of modernism's major avant-gardes also opened the portal through which the rhetoric of imagination might be reclaimed to license an expanded notion of style – no longer merely verbal, but the signature inhabitation of a more general faculty of consciousness itself.

Perhaps not the last romantics, then, but belated ones certainly. If it remains difficult to generalise about the style emergent at the war's end, it is at least partially because its construction of imagination mitigates against the formative collective tropes, either vanguard or corporate, of the Auden generation or the Movement, their committed intimation of a shared practice. What these belated romantics share most deeply, that is, is not merely a mythologizing tendency or an ornate technique verging on opacity, but rather a will to singularity. Prefacing the anthology that launched the Movement in 1956, Robert Conquest pointedly disowned the tendency to traffic in 'great systems of theoretical constructs' and 'agglomerations of unconscious commands', 'to abandon a rational structure and comprehensible language'.[19] But paradoxically, it was just this extreme stylistic variety that would later make a number of its writers available as subterranean influences to later poets attempting to escape Movement orthodoxies, from the mainstream voices of the 1960s New Poetry or, Andrew Duncan has recently argued, the 'unofficial' experimentalism of the British Poetry Revival.[20] To be sure, the 1940s occasionally bent New Apocalyptic exuberance into recognizable shapes. Gascoyne's *Poems 1937–1942*, reprinted after the war, thus turns surrealism to devotional meditation, while *A Vagrant, and Other Poems* (1950) fixes attention on the desolate political field of post-war scarcity. With *Deaths and Entrances* (1946), Thomas retains rich sonic textures, but also adopts more ceremonious tones, again transposing depth into formal surface, but now by way of a stately elegiac mode built on the resistance to consolation: 'A Refusal to Mourn the Death, by Fire, of a Child in London', 'Among Those Killed in the Dawn Raid Was a Man Aged a Hundred', even the series of concrete poems 'Vision and Prayer'. Both poets would ultimately seek (and in Thomas's case, find) a more public language, built on the foundation of a private mythology. More generally, however, imagination's recovery would eventuate in more tightly enclosed systems, esoteric or merely private, premised on the rights of consciousness to impose its own linguistic forms as reflexive meanings in themselves. The classic example of the gesture was made in 1948, with Robert Graves's publication of *The White Goddess*, a self-described 'historical grammar of the language of poetic myth', designed to locate 'the language of true poetry' in a forgotten bedrock of pre-classical cultic ritual.[21] Graves's elaborate system, both idiosyncratic and earnestly meant, seems almost to parody works like Frazer's *Golden Bough*, the tome that catalysed an earlier generation. But oddly, it is just its eccentricity that guarantees a representative quality, found not in any particular anthropological argument, however outlandish, but in the presumption that a poem entails its own private system of meaning.

What links the poets of the post-war moment most firmly, then, lies not in any commonly ascribable style, but rather in the necessity of *inventing* a style, reducible to no other voice, and with it an entire conception of the poetic as such. The effect can be glimpsed in the work of two figures that might otherwise appear simply incomparable. In 1937, George Barker's *Calamiterror* invented a grotesque surrealism of its own, stretched over ten intensely pitched books composed of overstuffed octaves. Nervously aware of events in Spain and Germany, Barker turns not outward but in, discerning harrowing traces of political events as constituents of his own psychological and linguistic space: 'I sense the | Advent of the extraordinary event, the calamiterror, | Turn and encounter the mountain descending upon me.'[22] Even the compulsive repetitions of the internal rhyme – sense, advent, event – reinforce the effect of a more programmatic historical constriction, as though even private fantasy had found itself penetrated by the world formerly outside. But the converse holds equally, suddenly able to license even an inner life as a general fact: 'The moment of terror flashes like dead powder | Revealing the features of the mass as mine' (p. 46). What is most remarkable about Barker's poem, then, in all its uneven excess, is its categorical refusal of allegorical distance, its simple denial of any separation between poetic experience and historical event. Literary history is enfolded in the same way, when 'the figure of Milton frequented my bedroom' (p. 45) or when 'I saw | The figure of William Blake bright and huge | Hung over the Thames at Sonning' (p. 49). When Barker declares that 'I achieved apocalypse' (p. 50), he thereby asserts the force of private revelation upon all of history at once, a gesture renewed in *Lament in Triumph* (1940) when he rewrites Shelley's 'England in 1819' as his own personal vision (pp. 65–75).

In effect, Barker succeeds in mistaking revelation *for* history. But in so doing, he also perversely reinvents the English or romantic ode, continuously (if often bathetically) restaging a voice defined by its absorption of cultural debris: 'The detritus is us' (p. 210), he boasts in *The True Confession of George Barker* (1950). But in the tabloid hint of that title (or of *News of the World*), Barker suggests something else as well, postulating a parodic symbolic unity as the substance of his own degraded experience: 'What's the point of a confession | If you have nothing to confess?' (p. 176). There is, to be sure, little of particular value in the confession: the poet's 'perjuring profession' (p. 176) has been reduced to tradecraft or degraded salesmanship, Barker's own lines to a carnivalesque performance ('one barker to another' (p. 186), he gleefully puns). At stake is an emphatically visionary style, but a degraded one, qualified into a state of near indifference to the actual content of any particular vision. The test of such a style, that is, lies in its ultimate porousness, its readiness to be suffused with any substance or sensation that might congeal as an image.

By contrast, Kathleen Raine seems consciously to refuse both the historical moment and the larger social pressure it bears. Terse where Barker expatiates, guarded where he risks vulgarity, impersonal where he boasts, Raine spent the war years crafting a minimalist voice, seeming indeed to exclude the mundane world entirely. With the poems gathered in *The Pythoness* (1949) and *The Year One* (1952), she often reduces lyric to sheer refrain, uncoiling ritually anaphoric incantations anchored only by an initial predicating thought or particle: 'God in me' in 'Storm'; an incarnated 'Word' in 'Word Made Flesh'; the prepositional relation 'By the' in 'Love Spell'; the simple self-assertion 'I am' in 'The Unloved'; the confessional 'Because I love' in 'Amo Ergo Sum'.[23] Composed of resonant or even prayerful phrases rather than sentences, grammatically simple but mystically complex, such poems eschew both narrative and observation, attempting to resacralise the practice of confession and restore the symbol to its theological ground. For Raine too, then, romanticism's canonical names, from Blake to Coleridge, stand (alongside Yeats) as visionary influences, and later as exhaustive scholarly interests. What each authorises most decisively, however, is not a strict poetic mode, but the syncretic freedom to form a metaphysical system, in Raine's case a hermetic latter-day neoplatonism capable of imbuing present experience with an encompassing ideal force. Like Barker's, though with radically different effect, Raine's system often seems, as Eliot acerbically remarked of Blake 'an ingenious piece of home-made furniture', capable indeed of reincorporating Blake's own.[24] What it shares more deeply, however, is a style of vision irreducible to its simple object, almost indifferent to vision's content, but premised instead on a reflexive system of relations that comes to comprise the substance of a poetic style.

At their most thickly opaque, the tendency of such privatised styles to curl away from readerly engagement risks an intractable isolation verging on epistemological solipsism. If it is true, however, that the poetry first of the war years and then of its aftermath derived its force from the collapse of untenable allegories into a nervously imagistically modulated self-referentiality, from an unwitting constriction of the poem's referential range, then this apparent privatisation of style might be characterised more properly as a belated accession to history's retreat from the range of experience, an acknowledgment that neither war nor its effects can best be thought in verse. Under that suggestion, the assertion of private style might amount to more than a romantic afterthought; might indeed be taken as the continuation of a distinctly different kind of modernist thought: less home-made furniture than home-grown phenomenology. If so, the claim's best evidence would arrive in the poem that seems at once to provide new romanticism's coda and its apotheosis, W. S. Graham's *The Nightfishing*. Published in 1955, as Movement scepticism ascended, Graham's elusive masterpiece bears the formal marks of an apocalyptic mode suddenly in eclipse. But its achievement finally lies elsewhere. Its simple scene – a night on a herring-trawler – silently recalls a set of forebodingly large terms just beyond the poem's range: on one side, the ocean as a sign of nature's implacable force; on the other, the symbolism of the herring catch, a staple of working-class political iconography since the Documentary Film Movement's early days. But Graham's poem transpires beneath the range of such allegorical correspondences, insistently attentive instead to the intricate encounters that configure the poet's moving consciousness as the thought of a place, an occasion, a movement and interaction of those forces (indifferently natural or historical) that conjoin in and summon an 'I' into speech: 'I watch, merged | In this and in a like event', Graham notes, 'and each event speaks through'.[25]

The Nightfishing is a sustained experiment in this mode of speaking through, a poem in which words stand as emanations or encounters rather than signs, 'each a longing | Set out to break', and thus point not to large meanings but rather to discrete elements that together compose an epistemological field: the night bell on the quay, the trawler, the waves, the 'mingling element' (p. 115) in which each is momentarily held. The poet's word carries no particular knowledge here, but its very emergence asserts a diminished kind of meaning: 'Yet in | Its meaning I am' (p. 108). For Graham, then, what the poem can still do, what imagination can achieve, is indeed modest: 'He that | I'm not lies down. Men shout. Words break. I am | My fruitful share' (p. 116). It declares no particular name and achieves no particular voice. But without its predicating power, nothing could be said at all.

NOTES

1 Herbert Read, 'Ode: Written during the Battle of Dunkirk, May, 1940', *Collected Poems* (London: Faber and Faber, 1966), p. 158.
2 F. T. Prince, *Collected Poems, 1935–1992* (Manchester: Carcanet, 2012), pp. 55–57.
3 Keith Douglas, *The Complete Poems*, Third Edition (London: Faber and Faber, 2000), p. 118.
4 Eliot, 'The Metaphysical Poets', *Selected Essays, 1917–1932* (New York: Harcourt, Brace and Company, 1932), p. 247; on allegory more generally, see Walter Benjamin, *The Origin of German Tragic Drama*, trans. John Osborne (London: Verso, 2008).
5 S. T. Coleridge, *The Statesman's Manual, or The Bible the Best Guide to Political Skill and Foresight: A Lay Sermon* (London: Gale and Fenner, 1816), p. 37.
6 Paul de Man, 'The Rhetoric of Temporality', *Blindness and Insight*, Second Edition (Minneapolis: University of Minnesota Press, 1983).
7 W. B. Yeats, 'Coole and Ballylee, 1931', *The Collected Poems of W. B. Yeats*, Revised Second Edition, ed. Richard J. Finneran (New York: Scribner, 1996), p. 245.

8 Herbert Read, *Poetry and Anarchism* (London: Faber and Faber, 1938).
9 *Eight Oxford Poets*, ed. Michael Meyer and Sidney Keyes (London: George Routledge & Sons, 1941), p. vii.
10 Sidney Keyes, *Collected Poems*, ed. Michael Meyer (Manchester: Carcanet, 2002), p. 22.
11 John Heath-Stubbs, *The Darkling Plain: A Study of the Later Fortunes of Romanticism in English Poetry from George Darley to W. B. Yeats* (London: Eyre & Spottiswoode, 1950), pp. xii, xv.
12 J. F. Hendry, 'Writers and Apocalypse', *The New Apocalypse: An Anthology of Criticism, Poems, and Stories* (London: The Fortune Press, 1940), p. 9.
13 Hendry and Henry Treece, ed., *The White Horseman: Prose and Verse of the New Apocalypse* (London: Routledge, 1941), p. v.
14 Treece, 'An Apocalyptic Writer and the Surrealists', *The New Apocalypse*, pp. 49–58.
15 Fraser, 'Apocalypse in Poetry', *The White Horseman*, p. 3.
16 Dylan Thomas, *Collected Poems, 1934–1952* (New York: New Directions, 1971), p. 10.
17 David Gascoyne, *New Collected Poems, 1929–1995*, ed. Roger Scott (London: Enitharmon Press, 2014), p. 69.
18 *Surrealism*, ed. Herbert Read (London: Faber and Faber, 1936), pp. 18, 28.
19 *New Lines: An Anthology*, ed. Robert Conquest (London: Macmillan and Co., 1956), p. xv.
20 Andrew Duncan, *Origins of the Underground* (Cambridge: Salt, 2008), p. 1.
21 Robert Graves, *The White Goddess: A Historical Grammar of Poetic Myth* (New York: Farrar, Straus and Giroux, 2013), pp. 5, 6.
22 George Barker, *Collected Poems*, ed. Robert Fraser (London: Faber and Faber, 1987), p. 46.
23 Kathleen Raine, *Collected Poems* (Ipswich: Golgonzoola Press, 2008), pp. 43, 45, 69–70, 75–76, 76–77.
24 Eliot, 'William Blake', *Selected Essays*, p. 279.
25 W. S. Graham, *New Collected Poems*, ed. Matthew Francis (London: Faber and Faber, 2004), p. 108.

2

PATRICK DEANE

The Movement: Poetry and the Reading Public

Accepting the Shakespeare Prize in 1976, Philip Larkin noted that poets 'go their own ways without reference or resemblance to each other'.[1] Even if one suspects it might not be entirely true, that is a consoling thought for any reader who comes to the Movement – that heterodox, piebald and loose literary association of which Larkin is the most famous member – seeking to understand the 'certain unity of approach' which Robert Conquest in 1956 argued could be found in it.[2] Having just proposed that there was a family resemblance sufficient to distinguish the poetry of the 1950s from its predecessors, even Conquest was forced to concede that 'what they do have in common is perhaps, at its lowest, little more than a negative determination to avoid bad principles.'[3] Because the writers of that period submit 'to no great systems of theoretical constructs nor agglomerations of unconscious commands', critics ever since have struggled to define what exactly the Movement was, or even *if* it was. Ian Hamilton famously labelled the emergence of the Movement as a 'P.R. job', initiated in the pages of the *Spectator*.[4]

While asserting that poets go their own ways, Larkin did note a persisting ground of unity between them. 'Every age has its own particular image of poetry', he wrote, 'and its own conditions under which poets operate'.[5] Writers of the Movement are often said to be anti-Romantic, and this statement provides an interesting and instructive example of that tendency: poets and poetry, Larkin seems to be saying, do not transcend their historic moment but are instead shaped or even constrained by it. Dylan Thomas's work he implies was the worse for this ('I don't think he always kept … [the public and the private] operations as separate as they should be'), but Shakespeare's was probably better for it: 'if we speculate what his plays would have been like if he hadn't had to please … [his audiences], it is hard to avoid the conclusion that they wouldn't have been as good'.[6] Larkin deliberately puts aside the notion of the poet as inspired individual – indeed, he becomes excited at the thought of Shakespeare's complete anonymity when his plays were performed in renaissance Germany – and focuses on what he calls 'the fundamental nexus between poet and audience, which is something he has to struggle for in the same way that he struggles with his medium of words'.[7]

Neil Corcoran has noted that the emergence of the Movement 'clearly owed a great deal to the skilful use of a metropolitan publicity machine in the creation of audience expectation and taste'.[8] But even if it was not a *mere* 'P.R. job', Larkin's comments suggest nevertheless that the Movement does need to be understood in those terms: that 'fundamental nexus' between poet and audience, between the art and its moment, will help us to account for the rather inexplicable success and influence of a group of writers remembered largely for being 'anti-phoney' and 'anti-wet', 'skeptical, robust, ironic, prepared to be as comfortable as possible in a wicked, commercial, threatened world'.[9] Impatient though they may have been of 'poetic sensibility', especially poetic sensibility about 'the writer and society', they were in many respects the movement that their age and their culture at that point demanded.

'In the 1940s', wrote Robert Conquest in his Introduction to *New Lines*, the 1956 anthology that defined the Movement, 'the mistake was made of giving the Id, a sound player on the percussion side under a strict conductor, too much of a say in the doings of the orchestra as a whole'.[10] By way of explanation he approvingly cites a somewhat disturbing passage from Aldous Huxley's *Texts and Pretexts* which in his view captures 'the sort of corruption which has affected the general attitude to poetry in the last decade'. Huxley rails against people who 'love music, not wisely, but too well ... whose passion for music is such, that it robs them of their judgement.... One can love music gluttonously and voluptuously (and I have known people whose appetite for sweet sounds was positively hoggish), or one can love it with heart, soul and mind, as a complete and fully developed human being'.[11]

This is a version of Larkin's complaint that Dylan Thomas somehow failed to achieve an appropriate balance between the public and the private, that in his desire to satisfy the 'hoggish' appetites of himself and his audience Thomas compromised – by overemphasizing musicality and subjectivity in his work – the 'fully developed human being', or as Larkin put it, the 'fundamental nexus' between the poet, his medium and his audience. Clearly Dylan Thomas is in Conquest's mind as he writes the Introduction to *New Lines*, but not Thomas alone. An entire field of poetic practice is the object of this demurrer:

> In this indiscriminating atmosphere other types of vicious taste, too, began to be catered for. The debilitating theory that poetry *must* be metaphorical gained wide acceptance. Poets were encouraged to produce diffuse and

> sentimental verbiage, or hollow technical pirouettes: praise even went to writers whose verse seemed to have been put together from the snippets in the 'Towards More Picturesque Speech' page of the *Reader's Digest*. Residual nuisances like the Social-realists, the Lallans-mongers, the church-furnishers and the neo-Georgians were able to sustain themselves.[12]

All of this activity in the 1940s – it is difficult to think of any poet who could not be swept into such a broad malediction – led, according to Conquest, 'to a rapid collapse of public taste, from which [in 1956] we have not yet recovered'.[13] The indictment of Dylan Thomas is that he was the kind of neo-Romantic who courted and debased public taste by allowing the Id to play too freely; yet another kind of neo-Romantic might be indifferent to public taste, or even (like Ezra Pound) wish to antagonize it, *épater la bourgeoisie*. As we have already seen in Larkin's reflections upon this issue, the Movement approach seeks neither to indulge nor to repudiate the poetic values of its audience. 'The complete and fully developed human being' recognizes that the nexus between poet and audience will be profoundly influential on the quality of what gets written; but more than that, he or she understands that there is a pragmatic, economic dimension to the relationship, without an understanding of which even the best work is unlikely to see the light of day.

That last point is interestingly made in a little-noticed section of Conquest's Introduction. Having observed that 'at any time a great deal of dubious verse is published, and no great harm comes of this since the good and new usually gets published too, and almost as easily', he goes on to notice that at that moment in the mid-fifties 'publication of poetry, particularly in books, but also in magazines, is severely limited'.[14] It is certainly true that although many wartime shortages had begun to ease by that time and the post-war economy was gaining traction, some industries – in particular, those without a mass market or peripheral to the consumerist drive to replace austerity with material affluence – remained on more or less the same footing as in 1945.

In such circumstances, according to Conquest, 'poems more in accord with the general taste have been all that publishers could afford'. Certainly, if we exempt T. S. Eliot because of his personal role in shaping the list at Faber and Faber, the dominant poetic presence in mainstream publishing in the early fifties was Dylan Thomas, whose *Collected Poems* appeared in 1952. W. H. Auden – the third member of this group that according to Larkin had 'altered the face of poetry'[15] – had by then been in the United States more than a decade, and was not only supported by the more vital publishing industry in that country, but had like Dylan Thomas begun to build a popular profile by giving readings with reasonably broad appeal.

When he notes that writers of this sort found resonance 'with the general taste', Conquest does not necessarily disparage them; on the contrary, if, as Larkin said, poetry is to be 'more entertaining' and 'should keep the child from its television set and the old man from his pub',[16] some sort of popular appeal would be essential. What concerns Conquest rather is that in a climate in which publishers are unwilling to take risks, established writers easily make their way into print while 'the good and new' tend to be overlooked. Despite that, he makes the point that many of the writers collected in *New Lines* 'have already wrested reasonable recognition from middleman and public even in these conditions' – largely due to the good offices, however, of small presses willing to run off pamphlets and limited editions.

The period of *New Lines* was indeed one in which small presses and magazines had begun to burgeon. Fortune Press in London issued Kingsley Amis's *Bright November* in 1947; The Fantasy Press at Swinford in Oxfordshire published Larkin's *The North Ship* in 1945, Elizabeth Jennings's *Poems* in 1953, Thom Gunn's *Fighting Terms* in 1954, and Donald Davie's *Brides of Reason* in 1955; The Marvell Press published Larkin's *The Less Deceived* that same year and John Holloway's *The Minute and Longer Poems* in 1956. But the real opening-up of the poetry publishing market did not occur until four or five years after the appearance of *New Lines*.

Larkin's 'Annus Mirabilis' identifies 1963 as a critical year in a period of decisive cultural change – it was the year in which 'Sexual intercourse began . . ./Between the end of the *Chatterley* ban/ And the Beatles' first LP'. Other things in that time 'began' anew as well: an efflorescence of poetry publishing in England was interwoven intriguingly with the advent of the sexual revolution. The point of connection is *Lady Chatterley's Lover*, which was cleared for publication and sale after charges of obscenity brought against Penguin Books were finally dismissed in November 1960. As John Sutherland noted on the fiftieth anniversary of the case, the decision to sell the book in paperback at a price of 3/6d (12.5p), rather than in hardback for 25/- (£1.25) 'triggered the "paperback revolution". Lady Chat sold 2m in a year, 7m in a decade. Allen Lane's Penguin got rich, and the British reading public got a whole lot better-read.'[17]

British poetry in particular was an immediate beneficiary. William Wootten has observed that as the financial benefits of *Lady Chatterley* began to accrue to Penguin, and before the advent of the Beatles ensured that 'the new and relevant would be more culturally synonymous with Pop than with Lawrentian intensities and critical seriousness,' 'contemporary poetry began'[18] – with Penguin's anthology *The New Poetry*, edited by A. Alvarez in 1962, and the first two volumes of *Penguin Modern Poets*, which included work by Kingsley Amis, Lawrence Durrell, Elizabeth Jennings and R. S. Thomas. Tony Godwin had joined the senior editorial group at Penguin in 1960, just as the *Lady Chatterley* ban was being lifted; and rising quickly to chief editor, he found himself able to drive design and editorial change and to initiate bold new projects.[19]

Penguin Modern Poets was indeed bold, and effected precisely the transformation of poetry publishing that Conquest had called for in his introduction to *New Lines*. April 1962 was the moment, Wootten tells us,

> when poetry reached the many, and in a form that encouraged readers to confer authority on to themselves. The Penguin Modern Poets series took the context-free principles of practical criticism, remade and rebranded them to create a model of consumer democracy. The format of each paperback volume – three poets, thirty poems per poet, no biographical material or critical apparatus – encouraged readers to sample widely and deeply and to compare the merits of the poetries on display.[20]

These were books very different from *New Lines*, which in its introduction had sought to 'sweep the stage' of 'dubious verse', which provided the reader with a condensed history and pointed critique of poetry since the twenties, and which looked at everything from the conditions of contemporary publishing to poetic influences – all of this before purportedly letting the poems collected 'speak for themselves'. It was – and remains – difficult to hear what they might have had to say, left to themselves in the manner of *Penguin Modern Poets*.

Wootten notes that 'societal changes, not least the Butler Education Act [1944], had created an appetite for affordable new poetry', and the extraordinary sales of *The New Poetry* and the first two volumes of *Penguin Modern Poets* bear this out: the initial run for the former was 30,000 copies, while both volumes of *PMP* sold out and had to be reprinted.[21] As more volumes in the series were issued it became clear that in addition to changes in the culture, the unprogrammatic nature – the eclecticism – of *Penguin Modern Poets* was key to its success. The diversity of taste in the reading public to which that was Tony Godwin's inspired response arguably continues to this day: not since *New Lines* and *The New Poetry* has there been a 'manifesto' anthology of British poetry that purported, plausibly, to define the mainstream. *The Penguin Book of Contemporary British Poetry*, edited by Blake Morrison and Andrew Motion in 1982 could only vaguely gesture towards extending the 'imaginative franchise' of poetry; and *The New British Poetry 1968–88*, edited by Gillian Allnutt and others in 1988, was intended to document an 'alternative' poetry and implicitly to contest the existence or desirability of a normative poetic.

It might seem as if the emergence of a broader audience for poetry, linked to a mechanism intended to facilitate publication of a wider range of work, would be exactly the change in conditions Conquest was hoping for in 1956. Unfortunately for the Movement, however, the first manifestation of the new, post–*Chatterley* poetic-economic order – the first collection to achieve mass distribution, thereby shaping the market in its own image – was *The New Poetry*, a volume which included a number of the *New Lines* poets but which nevertheless demurred at the defining Movement ethos. Alvarez's now famous introductory essay, 'The New Poetry or Beyond the Gentility Principle', identified *New Lines* and the Movement as a reaction against the 'wild, loose emotion' of the forties – as an overreaction, in fact, which had produced work characterized by a 'unity of flatness'. The new poetry, if Alvarez was to be believed, wished to move 'Beyond the Gentility Principle', beyond the 'belief that life is always more or less orderly, people always more or less polite, their emotions and habits more or less decent and more or less controllable; that God, in short, is more or less good.'[22]

Two world wars had called that belief into question, had challenged what Alvarez calls English 'insulation', and now demanded that 'genuine poetry' be allowed to filter through the various forms of personal and cultural defence which, in the late fifties and early sixties, were in the process of being reconstructed: Robert Graves's 'elaborate barricade of White Goddesses and classicizing' must give way, George Orwell must 'purge himself of his governing-class upbringing by deliberately plunging into the abjectest poverty and pain', and the example of D. H. Lawrence – 'the only English writer who was able to face the more uncompromising forces at work in our time' – must be embraced.[23] Apparently the fortunes of the new poetry were tied to Lawrence's work and thought by a good deal more than the economics of publishing.

'Uncompromising forces' puts it mildly, however. Taking an approach that would find much more eloquent articulation five years later in George Steiner's *Language and Silence*, Alvarez notes that war and cruelty in the twentieth century cannot be ignored, and that mass exterminations and death factories command an entirely new kind of literary response – if not absolute silence, then at least 'a new seriousness,' in which the poet is willing and able 'to face the full range of his experience with his full intelligence'. To 'walk naked' is a metaphor for this kind of engagement with the world, and not surprisingly Alvarez concludes, despite recognizing that 'At Grass' is 'elegant and unpretentious and rather beautiful in its gentle way', that Philip Larkin does not walk naked. That poem is 'a nostalgic re-creation of the Platonic (or *New Yorker*) idea of the English scene, part pastoral, part sporting'. Nostalgia is a form of psychological clothing allegedly absent in Ted Hughes's 'A Dream of Horses', where the horses 'have a violent, impending presence … [and] through the sharp details which bring them so threateningly to life, ... reach back, as in a dream, into a nexus of fear and sensation'. We are reminded again of Lawrence and of the 'strange savage horses which terrorize Ursula Brangwen at the end of *The Rainbow*'.[24]

However uncompromising is Alvarez's polemic against gentility, it is not overly prescriptive of what kinds of poem should be the result of walking naked. 'I am not suggesting', he writes, 'that English poetry, to be really modern, must be concerned with psychoanalysis or with the concentration camps or with the hydrogen bomb or with any other of the modern horrors. I am not suggesting, in fact, that it *must* be anything'.[25] Not surprisingly, then, the poems which follow Alvarez's introduction are an eclectic lot, although as Wootten points out they do give prominence 'to a darker, more violent and psychically tortured, and ... masculinist poetry': 'Most provocatively, *The New Poetry* broke the rules and opened a nominally British selection with the Americans Robert Lowell and John Berryman as reproachful examples of an expressive, personal, yet controlled poetry that could bear witness to inner and outer turmoil'.[26]

The anti-Movement bias of the volume was articulated in the introductory essay but even more vividly revealed in the poems chosen. Wootten is correct to observe that it was in the decision to include twenty-two poems by Ted Hughes and only eight by Larkin that Alvarez appeared most willful, although one reason for this was that Larkin and his publisher charged unusually high fees – further evidence that literary reputations are influenced not only by aesthetics and taste but economics as well. What is perhaps most significant about the partiality of *The New Poetry*, however, is that it proscribed the work of only one 'school' – the Movement – while in the spirit of the paperback poetry revolution being open to multiple new voices and approaches.

Ironically given Robert Conquest's plea for a new openness in publishing, Alvarez's anthology had the effect of fossilizing the Movement less than a decade after it had first been announced by J. D. Scott in *The Spectator*. A number of *New Lines* poets were included in *The New Poetry*, as I have noted, and several went on to be included in *Penguin Modern Poets*, all of which is to say that individual voices found an audience and positive regard long after the Movement as an artistic and critical construct had been relegated to the museum of literary history, where it has continued to be identified with the fifties – a period that began with the optimistic, reconstructive and forward-looking Festival of Britain in 1951, saw a chastening of the national spirit in the Suez crisis of 1956, in the first mass rally for nuclear disarmament and in the Notting Hill riots of 1958, and which ended with Harold Macmillan's famous 'Wind of Change' speech, given in Cape Town in February, 1960, just a month before the Sharpeville Massacre.

For the Movement it was an unpromising coincidence that *New Lines*, with its quietly proud insularity, emerged in the same year as the Suez crisis. Given other world events, it is furthermore little wonder that by 1962 the 'gentility principle' was looking simply quaint. In that phrase Alvarez had captured an ethic, attractive because it was intuitively felt to be connected to the English character and history, which was then perceived to have been overtaken by events. In retrospect, that mid-century confutation of gentility was decisive, and neither the Movement nor any of its possible avatars could imaginably assume cultural dominance today – except perhaps through the medium of nostalgic popular culture, as in *Downton Abbey*, *Jeeves and Wooster* or *Brideshead Revisited*. But while the Movement, *qua* movement, may be impossible to imagine outside of its very limited coordinates in twentieth-century British history, the individual writers associated with it have proven to be remarkably enduring in their appeal and standing – indomitable, even, in facing the wind of poetic change.

The fortunes of the Movement poets after 1962 testify to the truth of Larkin's assertion that writers 'go their own ways'. Blake Morrison's chapter on the group after 1956 is called 'Divergent Lines', and even though he argues firmly that 'the view that the Movement was a journalistic invention or agreed fiction can no longer be allowed to stand', his extensive study makes clear that the 'Movement consensus'[27] was not programmatic, did not involve submission by its members to what Conquest called 'great systems of theoretical constructs' and was arrived at without any of its proponents having to relinquish their individual directions. Larkin, Kingsley Amis, Donald Davie, D. J. Enright, Thom Gunn, John Wain and Elizabeth Jennings: they were each 'going their own way' even if for several years in the fifties they appeared to be following the same directions. That is what has made the Movement a challenge for critics to describe, especially those who focus primarily on poetic style and content – two areas in which the Movement always surprises readers with its diversity.

We must remember Larkin's point that poetry is always shaped by two things: by poets as well as by 'the conditions' under which they operate. The 'Movement consensus' was in that sense both the creation of the individuals involved and a conception arising in complex ways from their historical moment. That last observation means that in some way the Movement came into existence because consensus was what the age demanded – a possibly confounding thought, but one that has been intelligently explored by a number of critics. Daniel Weston, for example, has rejected the 'simple reflectionist argument' that Larkin's shift away from a 'poetics of consensus' represents 'the underlying presence of wider societal shifts towards a post-consensus society'; but he does not rule out – and in fact brilliantly expatiates upon – a much more complex articulation between Larkin's poetry and reputation, on the one hand, and societal change on the other. Writing in particular about the oscillation in Larkin's work between 'an empirical pessimism and a more hopeful symbolist element', he notes that 'A changing historical context has determined both the balance of these two elements in the poetry, and the degree to which each aspect has received more attention in the development of a body of criticism'.[28]

Weston is talking about that 'fundamental nexus' between poet and audience – contemporary and subsequent – which Larkin argued was central to both the project of writing and the question of its critical appraisal. Take up the invitation to further theorize that nexus and you are rapidly on the edge of an abyss of infinite regressions, having to conclude with Auden that a poem is always and perpetually 'a way of happening, a mouth', its author having become 'his admirers',[29] Larkin irritably dismissed such rarefied considerations – 'Oh, for Christ's sake, one doesn't *study* poets! You *read* them' he retorted to a question from Robert Phillips[30] – but he understood poetry in a very similar way to Auden: 'Some years ago I came to the conclusion that to write a poem was to construct a verbal device that would preserve an experience indefinitely by reproducing it in whoever read the poem'.[31] 'Reproducing': the word indicates either extraordinary naïveté regarding the relationship between texts and the context in which they are read, or a determination to keep things simple, to keep art aligned with 'the pleasure principle' from which Larkin argued in 1957 poetry had become estranged. One result of modernist experimentation, he implied, is that the 'modern poetic audience, when it is not taking in its own washing, is a *student* audience', and a poet should seek to regain 'the only audience worth having' – 'the pleasure-seeking audience he has lost'.[32]

This very straightforward approach to his readership – and Larkin's skill in realizing it – has had predictable results. In 2003 he was voted 'the nation's best-loved poet' in a survey by the Poetry Book Society – this despite his taste for pornography, his racism and his increasing conservatism all being widely known after publication of Anthony Thwaite's edition of his letters[33] and Andrew Motion's *Philip Larkin: A Writer's Life*.[34] In 2008 he was named by *The Times* the greatest British post-war writer, and extracts from Larkin's poems were painted on buses in Hull in July 2010.[35]

All of this is evidence of a remarkably, perhaps uniquely, durable reputation for a poet whose voice emerged in the 1950s and whose ideological and temperamental affinities remained in that decade. It also raises some very significant questions, especially in the context of the massive transformation that few would deny has occurred in British life and culture since the Wind of Change began to blow in the late fifties. Is the ongoing love of Larkin evidence that in some way the values of post–World War II reconstruction persist into the second decade of the twenty-first century? Or, more worryingly, did his reputation survive the revelations of racism and sexism because there, by coincidence, he gave voice to attitudes latent in the culture of the early nineties? Or do the continuing accolades tell us less about British taste and society at large than about who remains in control in the establishing of curricula, the shaping of publishers' lists and the adjudication of awards?

That last question represents a corrosive challenge to the not uncommon assertion that Larkin – and to a lesser extent the whole of the Movement – in some way 'captured' the essence of Englishness in the period of post-war consolidation, or that he is the 'archetypal English poet' and therefore has an appeal that transcends time and endures through cultural change.[36] Donald Davie, Larkin's colleague in the Movement, did much to advance this view in *Thomas Hardy and British Poetry* of 1972, a book which argued that the example of Hardy had enabled British poetry to deflect the powerful influence of literary Modernism and to maintain its continuity with its own history. After he had cast off the influence of W. B. Yeats and consciously adopted Hardy as a model, Larkin emerged as Hardy's natural heir in the twentieth century and the leading voice of the native tradition: thus Davie's view of Larkin's career and of the intractable resistance of a British poetic to wholesale annexation by 'foreign' Modernism. Larkin's *obiter dicta* – such as his comments on the pleasure principle, his observation that 'deep down I think foreign languages irrelevant' and his remark that 'the chromatic scale is what you use to give the effect of drinking a quinine martini and having an enema simultaneously'[37] – capture perfectly the droll hostility to all things alien and experimental that define this allegedly 'archetypal' voice.

As a critic, Davie engaged very readily with both the 'foreign' and the avant-garde, but as a poet he did not – or at least not in any way that would indicate modernist influence. In 'Homage to William Cowper' he describes himself as 'a pasticheur of late-Augustan styles',[38] and indeed, his poetry has from its beginning been concerned to seek its effect less through 'apt and memorable metaphor' – the stock-in-trade of the Symbolists, Imagists and Modernist mainstream – than through the 'purity of diction' which as early as 1952 he identified in English poets of the eighteenth century.[39] In 'Poem as Abstract', written at about that time, he puts it this way: 'A poem is less an orange than a grid;/ It hoists a charge; it does not ooze a juice'; and at the end he emphasizes syntax as a source of affect, pondering what should be a 'poet's gait' if 'poems make a style, a way of walking/ With enterprise'.[40]

Perhaps it was Davie's critical articulation of this issue that gave rise to the *New Lines* repudiation of 'the debilitating theory that poetry *must* be metaphorical'. His ongoing exploration of a discursive style, seeking poetic effect through 'economy in metaphor' was nevertheless undogmatic: even as he framed this approach in 1952 he could acknowledge that, 'suitably qualified', it was still his belief that 'poetic greatness' had something to do with the ability to organize experience in metaphorical terms.

Davie is a poet whose preoccupations were reflected in Robert Conquest's manifesto for the Movement, but never circumscribed by it. *Six Epistles to Eva Hesse*,[41] which he published in 1970, wittily brings together his poetry and criticism and represents an interesting point in his significant, serious and intellectually complex engagement with the principles and legacy of literary modernism. In her *New Approaches to Ezra* Pound (1969), Hesse had written that in Pound's ideogrammic method poetry 'breaks away from the thin-blooded progressions of occidental syllogization.... Syntax yields to parataxis.... The grammatical link becomes irrelevant.'[42] To this Modernist rejection of 'dumb clockwork Time' in favour of temporal plasticity, Davie observes of Time that 'some of it seems resistant stuff/ Still, and linear enough'.[43] Linearity was critical in his early definition of poetry as 'walking/ With enterprise', and the same pragmatic view asserts itself as he comments to Hesse, 'No, Madam, Pound's a splendid poet/ But a sucker, and we know it'.[44]

Davie's critique of Modernist preoccupations is no less effective than Larkin's for all that it 'hoists a charge' through the syntactical ranginess of an eighteenth-century epistolary style, and is 'economical' with dramatic metaphor. He makes no mention of either quinine martinis or enemas, but he does contest the claims of the Modernist enterprise and in that regard is one with the Movement as a whole. His interest in defining and exploring the contemporary potential of inherited British poetic forms also confirms his membership, but despite this there is no hint in his work of xenophobia or racism.

If we move beyond Davie to the work of other poets associated with the Movement – Thom Gunn, Elizabeth Jennings and Kingsley Amis, say – it is possible to identify many versions of the Larkinesque: Gunn's self-regarding transgressiveness in 'La Prisonnière' with its deliberately shocking declaration that even if a woman shut 'in a box/ With massive sides and a lid that locks' were to end up as a heap of bones, 'Too dry to simper, too dry to whine – ', she would still be 'mine and only mine'[45]; Jennings's sad resignation, in poem after poem, to the inevitable frustration of love; and Amis's iconoclastic deprecation of high art, as in 'Mightier than the Pen' where we are told that 'Fussing with flash and tripod's fun,/ But bang's the way to get things done.'[46]

It is Larkin, though, of whom Davie said 'there has been the widest possible agreement, over most of this period, that [he] ... is for good or ill, the effective unofficial laureate of post-1945 England',[47] presumably because in his work these Movement attitudes and themes were integrated in a manner uniquely resonant with the post-war reading public. Davie goes on to declare that 'what Larkin says is true' and 'the England in his poems is the England we have inhabited.'[48] That last point has been fiercely contested by Davie's student, Charles Tomlinson, perhaps the most trenchant and articulate critic of the Movement; but the broader resonance of Larkin's work Tomlinson implicitly acknowledged when he wrote in 1956 that 'with Larkin poetry is on its way back to the middle-brow public'.[49] And angered by the parochialism, 'the horribly common style, ... that "man-of-the-world" off-handedness, [and] that rather rootless wit,'[50] Tomlinson has fiercely disputed any suggestion that the author of 'Church Going' – surely one of the most widely read and loved poems of the twentieth century – is the authentic voice of modern England.

The truth of that claim is really beside the point. Obviously, so long as there is no agreement about what constitutes 'modern England', there can be no meaningful competition to judge which is the more 'authentic' voice. If we are to grasp the nation through the work of its poets, the range of options extends infinitely far beyond Larkin and Tomlinson. Does Tony Harrison's *v*, or his 'School of Eloquence' sonnets qualify him as an 'authentic' voice? Or Linton Kwesi Johnson's dub poetry? Carol Ann Duffy has been Poet Laureate since 2009, so does she have a special claim? Is modern Britain as we can infer it from her work, the real thing? The answer is obvious: it is and it is not. That the laureateship is not the One Ring to Rule Them All is something Larkin knew full well in 1984 when he rejected the honour.

The important point, though, is not that Larkin or any of his colleagues has consciously claimed to be the authentic voice of modern Britain, but that the Movement ethos and its literary products undoubtedly did strike a chord with the reading public, 'middle-brow' though it largely was and continues to be. Larkin and the Movement poets, whether because of their commitment to the 'pleasure principle', to accessibility, to being 'entertaining' or to appearing bluff and human, did achieve popularity and a place in the broader culture that was denied to writers catering to that 'humbler squad, whose aim is not pleasure but self-improvement', to what Larkin identified as the 'student audience'.[51]

NOTES

1 'Subsidizing Poetry', *Required Writing: Miscellaneous Pieces 1955–1982* (London: Faber and Faber, 1983), p. 87.

2 *New Lines*, ed. Robert Conquest (1956; London: Macmillan, 1967), p. xiv.

3 *New Lines*, p. xv.
4 'The Making of the Movement', *A Poetry Chronicle* (London: Faber and Faber, 1973), p. 129.
5 'Subsidizing Poetry', p. 87.
6 'Subsidizing Poetry', p. 91.
7 'Subsidizing Poetry', p. 92.
8 *English Poetry since 1940* (London: Longman, 1993), p. 81.
9 Anon. [J. D. Scott], 'Poets of the Fifties' (*Spectator*, 27 August 1954), 260–61.
10 *New Lines*, p. xi.
11 *New Lines*, p. xii.
12 *New Lines*, p. xii.
13 *New Lines*, p. xi.
14 *New Lines*, p. xiii.
15 Letter to Patsy Strang, 10 December 1953. *Selected Letters of Philip Larkin, 1940–1985*, ed. Anthony Thwaite (London: Faber and Faber, 1992), p. 220.
16 Quoted by Richard Murphy in 'The Art of Debunkery', *The New York Review of Books* 15 May 1975. Found at www.nybooks.com/articles/archives/1975/may/15/the-art-of-debunkery/.
17 'Lady Chatterley's Legacy,' http://www.theguardian.com/books,booksblog/2010/oct/29/lady-chatterley-legacy-john-sutherland.
18 William Wootten, *Times Literary Supplement*, 25 April 2012. http://www.the-tls.co.uk/tls/public/article1024506.ece. 1. Quoted in David Kynaston, *Modernity Britain: A Shake of the Dice. 1959–1962* (London: Bloomsbury, 2014), pp. 373–74.
19 See Kynaston, p. 374.
20 Wootten, p. 2.
21 Wootten, p. 2.
22 A. Alvarez, *The New Poetry*, 1962; Revised Edition (Harmondsworth: Penguin Books, 1965), pp. 24–25.
23 *The New Poetry*, pp. 25–26.
24 *The New Poetry*, p. 31.
25 *The New Poetry*, p. 27.
26 Wootten, p. 2.
27 *The Movement: English Poetry and Fiction of the 1950s* (1980; London: Methuen, 1986), p. 6.
28 Daniel Weston (2010) A Sustained Movement: Philip Larkin's poetics of consensus, *Textual Practice*, 24:2, 313–30, DOI:10.1080/09502361003595071, 328 and 313.
29 'In Memory of W.B. Yeats'. *Collected Poems*, ed. Edward Mendelson (New York: Vintage, 1991), pp. 247–48.
30 *Required Writing*, p. 67.
31 *Required Writing*, p. 83.
32 *Required Writing*, pp. 81–82.
33 *Selected Letters of Philip Larkin 1940–1985* (London: Faber and Faber, 1992).
34 London: Faber and Faber, 1993.
35 'Hull buses display Larkin's words in tribute to poet' (http://news.bbc.co.uk/2/hi/england/humberside/10538324.stm). *BBC News Online* (BBC) 7 July 2010. Retrieved 14 July 2010. Cited http://en.wikipedia.org/wiki/Philip_Larkin.

36 Here see Leo Cox's review of *High Windows*, *The English Review*, 1 February, 2001.
37 *Required Writing*, pp. 69, 72.
38 *Collected Poems* (Chicago: University of Chicago Press, 1990), p. 17.
39 *Purity of Diction in English Verse* (London: Chatto and Windus, 1952), Introduction.
40 *Collected Poems*, pp. 24–25.
41 *Collected Poems*, pp. 209–41.
42 *New Approaches to Ezra Pound: A Co-ordinated Investigation of Pound's Poetry and Ideas* (Berkeley and Los Angeles: University of California Press, 1969), p. 48. See 'Donald Davie's Quarrel with Modernism' in Patrick Deane, *At Home in Time: Forms of Neo-Augustanism in Modern English Poetry* (Montreal and Kingston: McGill-Queen's University Press, 1994), pp. 161–202. Discussion of this passage from Hesse, p. 177.
43 *Collected Poems*, p. 209.
44 *Collected Poems*, p. 210.
45 *Collected Poems*, p. 14.
46 *Collected Poems 1944–1979*, p. 66.
47 *Thomas Hardy and British Poetry*, p. 64.
48 *Thomas Hardy and British Poetry*, p. 64.
49 'The Middlebrow Muse', 209.
50 Peter Orr, ed., *The Poet Speaks: Interviews With Contemporary Poets* (London: Routledge and Kegan Paul, 1966), p. 252. For a discussion of these comments, see Brian John, *The World as Event: The Poetry of Charles Tomlinson* (Montreal and Kingston: McGill-Queen's University Press, 1989), p. 23.
51 *Required Writing*, p. 81.

3

JOHN MATTHIAS

Survivors from before the War: Late Modernists and Poets of the 1930s

In April of 1945, W. H. Auden had just put on the uniform of a U.S. Army major to take part in a 'Strategic Bombing Survey' in Germany. Because he spoke German and had lived in Germany for some time during the 1930s, the Pentagon felt his knowledge would be useful and had asked him to participate in an attempt to discover how American bombing had affected the morale and the lives of German civilians (as if such a thing could be in doubt). He had been in America since January 1939, when he arrived with his friend and collaborator, the novelist Christopher Isherwood. Louis MacNeice, Benjamin Britten and Peter Pears soon followed, but by 1945 Isherwood was in Los Angeles, and Britten, Pears and MacNeice back in England. Dylan Thomas had not yet begun his American reading tours, but they were soon enough to set off fireworks displays all across the continent. Stephen Spender's post-war sojourns were less electrifying, but very regular. Basil Bunting had tried America briefly before the war and would come again to give readings after the publication of *Briggflatts*, but he was now in England and would soon return to Persia, where he had been in the military, as chief of political intelligence at the British Embassy in Teheran. David Jones, who knew more than any of them what falling explosives felt like from his years in the trenches of World War I, lived in a series of small rooms – 'dugouts', as Kathleen Raine called them – or sometimes with friends in London. As Auden left for Germany, much of his re-invention of himself as a New Yorker and as a poet standing on rapidly shifting ideological sands was already behind him. He had written three major long poems – *New Year Letter, For the Time Being* and *The Sea and the Mirror*. As he left for a devastated Europe, his recent shorter poems were about to appear with the three longer ones in the Random House *Collected Poetry of W. H. Auden* (1945). He was still under forty, and the collected volume, which had a lot missing, was about 470 pages long.

A lot was missing in two senses.[1] First of all, there were no poems by Auden about the London blitz because the poet had not been in London to write them. When the war broke out he was famously 'in one of the dives / On Fifty-Second Street / Uncertain and afraid'. But any reader looking for the poet's resolve in 'September 1, 1939' to undo with his voice 'the folded lie / the romantic lie in the brain / of the sensual man on the street or the lie of Authority / whose buildings grope the sky', would not have found the stanza in which those lines occur and which concludes: 'We must love one another or die'. Nor would he have found entire poems like the seventeenth from *Look, Stranger!*, 'Here on the cropped grass of the narrow ridge I stand', much despised by defenders of Auden's later judgment against his early work,[2] but providing nonetheless more autobiographical and social context for his poems from the 1930s than any other save perhaps the epistolary poem to Christopher Isherwood from the same book, number XXXIV, 'August for the people and their favorite islands', which was also missing from the *Collected*, along with its resolve to emulate the virtues of Isherwood's 'strict and adult pen' and 'make action urgent and its nature clear'. One poem, the 'Commentary' to the sonnet sequence 'In Time of War', had a conclusion which substituted for its original hope that forces of the will might be gathered to let loose upon the earth a 'human justice' a new desire that we should 'follow / the clear instructions of that Justice, in the shadow / Of Whose uplifting, loving, and constraining power / All human reasons do rejoice and operate'. Many readers thought they saw a great poet of history in the process of erasing his own. The coherent sequence of numbered poems from *Poems*, *Look, Stranger!*, and *Another Time* acquired (sometimes ridiculous or self-mocking) titles and appeared in the alphabetical order of the first word in their first lines, with no dates of composition. Some poems seemed to say the opposite of what they originally said, especially the poem from *Look, Stranger!*, eventually called 'A Summer Night', which, through the omission of several stanzas about bourgeois class guilt managed to produce the 'vision of Agape' that became in many ways the key event in the central poem in Auden's transition from a Freudian/Marxist humanist to a Christian religious poet for major scholars of Auden's work, like Edward Mendelson, his executor and editor, and John Fuller, author of the reference work, *W. H. Auden: A Commentary*, which everyone writing about the poet has on his desk.[3] But in 1945, readers familiar with the books from which the *Collected* drew its contents might have been surprised to find the political flood 'for which we dread to lose our privacy' and which derives 'from intentions not our own' revised to celebrate 'This privacy' and 'delights we dread to lose'. Most of all perhaps, the unique Auden Country that had mystified but also delighted readers of the earliest *Poems* which, read in numbered sequence and taken as a whole (including *Paid on Both Sides*), created what Randall Jarrell, the harshest critic of Auden's later work, called 'a picture of a world ... far more effective than any selection of the best poems' from those works.[4]

Even the jacket blurb was a bit strange. It quotes *Time* magazine from September 11, 1944 saying, 'In 1936 [W. H. Auden] married Thomas Mann's eldest daughter, an exiled anti-Nazi playwright deprived of her nationality by Hitler'.[5] Why did Auden (or Random House) want to make a fuss about Auden's 'marriage'? True enough, Auden had legally married Erika Mann to obtain the necessary papers to insure her safety. But everyone in the literary community knew perfectly well by this point that Auden considered himself married to Chester Kallman, the young New Yorker who introduced him to opera and collaborated with him on several of his most important post-war projects. Auden was a *Double Man* indeed at the time the book of that title was published in 1941. Four years later, on the way back to the Germany of his youth wearing an American officer's uniform, he left with his publishers a book that obscured in various ways poems selected from the volume (*Look, Stranger!*) that had been dedicated to Erika Mann out of the kind of disciplined social love, midway between Eros and Agape, and celebrated in that book – 'What can truth treasure, or heart bless, / But a narrow strictness'[6] – and now found their justification or otherwise in one dedicated to Christopher Isherwood, Auden's former lover and collaborator, and Chester Kallman: 'The truth is one and incapable of contradiction; / All knowledge that conflicts with itself is Poetic Fiction'.[7]

Looking back to discover what new readers of Auden might have made of these things, one discovers mainly statistics. According to Auden biographer Humphrey Carpenter, the 1945 *Collected* sold 15,000 copies in its first year of publication.[8] The reactions of readers already familiar with Auden's work, most of whom already knew what they liked – 1930s Auden – and wanted more of it, got their views into the record. But my guess is that the majority of the 15,000, not to mention the 52,000 readers who bought the book in the years before it was replaced by the *Collected Shorter* and *Collected Longer* volumes of the 1960s, simply read with appreciation what was offered in the order it appeared. Although a reader familiar with Auden's original single volumes might have been surprised, even annoyed, to find the very recent 'Musée des Beaux Arts' leading off the shorter poems simply because its first line began with ab ('About suffering they were never wrong, the old masters'), my guess is that the new reader found that first poem compelling and read on. What he found, if he kept reading until the end, was some of the best poetry written in the previous twenty years, high points being perhaps the great elegies of Auden's middle phase – poems for Yeats, Freud, James and, in the context of *New Year Letter*, even Marx – along with the very effectively grouped 'songs and other musical pieces' and the long poems *The Sea and the Mirror* and *For the Time Being* at the end. Even the surprising pluckings-out of two virtuoso prose pieces – 'Letter to a Wound' and 'Depravity: A Sermon' – from their contexts in *The Orators* and *The Dog beneath the Skin* made aesthetic sense in their anticipation of 'Caliban to the Audience' in *The Sea and the Mirror*, the work that Auden said in his later years was the best he had ever written, although it too is in prose.[9]

Auden didn't really defend the structure or selections in his 1945 *Collected* until the 1967 *Collected Shorter* volume appeared. At that point, though poems like 'Spain' and 'September 1st' disappeared entirely, the poems were re-configured more or less chronologically and Auden explained a little of what he had felt obliged to do in 1945. He said that when he first collected his poems he was 'still too young to have any sure sense of the direction in which [he] was moving, and ... did not wish critics to waste their time, and mislead readers, making guesses about it which would certainly turn out to be wrong'.[10] But no 'guessing' was necessary. It was clear enough from the poems at the end of the 1945 *Collected* that Auden was now a Christian poet with a fully developed poetics – this is achieved in 'Caliban to the Audience' – and a system of belief approximating that of his pious mother to whom *For the Time Being* was dedicated *in memoriam* with an epigraph from Romans VI: 'What shall we say then? Shall we continue in sin, that grace may abound? God forbid'.[11] All of Auden's dedications are important, and the dedicatory texts or epigraphs would make a fascinating study all on their own.

Although older readers of Auden's work continued to regret the omission of poems like 'Sir, No Man's Enemy', 'September 1st', 'Spain' and others from Auden's subsequent collected and selected volumes, and to find rather absurd his claims in the 1967 *Collected Shorter* that his celebration of 'new kinds of architecture' was 'dishonest' because he really preferred 'old styles', and that 'History to the defeated / may say alas but cannot help nor pardon' was to 'equate goodness with success',[12] it is difficult to argue with Edward Mendelson's position, loyally representing Auden's own, in the most recent *Selected Poems*, the book from which most new readers have, since Auden's death, first encountered the work beyond selections in anthologies.

> Critics who find [Auden's revisions] deplorable generally argue, in effect, that a poet loses his right to revise or reject his work after he publishes it – as if the skill with which he brought his poems from their early drafts to the point of publication somehow left him at the moment they appeared, making him a trespasser on his own work thereafter.... In revising his poems, Auden opened his workshop to the public, and the spectacle proved unsettling, ... Much as Brecht had brought his stagehands into the full view of the audience ... [Auden's] goal

> was to remove the mystery that surrounds works of art, to explode the myth of poetic inspiration, and to deny any special privileges to poetry in the realm of language or artists in the realm of ethics.[13]

Marking the end of the 'long Thirties' that concluded for Auden with major works from the early forties dealing with religion and poetics rather than war, the 1945 *Collected* made clear, if it hadn't been before, that a new 'American' Auden had declared his independence. If the new Auden was rather disliked in Britain, he became in his adopted country not just a poet but also a kind of nineteenth century man of letters. He edited, translated, lectured and dominated the New York poetry scene like a latter-day Sam Johnson, *talk* becoming one of his favoured art forms (and recorded brilliantly in, for example, Howard Griffin's little known Boswellian *Conversations with Auden*).[14] Such talk – Peter Pears complained to Benjamin Britten, 'does he *never* stop talking?'[15] – was reflected in his virtuoso syllabics, probably inspired by Marianne Moore, and the informal tone of his essays and reviews. It is quite possible to argue that one of his greatest strengths during his American period was either prose or prosey. He excelled after 1945 at being discursive – whether over drinks and dinner, or in his poems.

Friends and fellow poets were influenced, directly and through his work, by some of the choices Auden made during these years. *Paul Bunyan*, in the operetta Auden wrote with Benjamin Britten, made a parting speech to his loggers, who had extended the range of choice by following necessity, saying: 'America is what you do, / America is I and you, / America is what you choose to make it'.[16] This cheerful paraphrase of the existential commitments of 'Spain' appealed to poets ranging from Stephen Spender to Paul Muldoon, who wrote (in Auden's voice) in '7 Middagh Street' – the address where Auden presided over a ménage including Gypsy Rose Lee, Britten and Pears, Salvador Dali, Carson McCullers, Paul and Jane Bowles and, briefly, Louis MacNeice – 'The roots by which we were once bound // are severed here, in any case, / and we are all now dispossessed ... all equally isolated'.[17] This condition was to be briefly experienced (more than explored) by MacNeice and Dylan Thomas. For Stephen Spender, the American literary-political scene became a preoccupation in books like *The Making of a Poem* (1962), *The Thirties and After* (1975), and *Love-Hate Relations: A Study of Anglo-American Sensibilities* (1974).

Although there is no evidence that Spender and Auden met in Germany – Spender too had an official job to do as of 1944, having volunteered for the Occupying Forces' program of de-Nazification – they did meet in London both before they left and after their official assignments were over and both eventually wrote poems deriving from their respective missions. During the war Spender had co-edited *Horizon*, the major British literary magazine published in those grim days, with Cyril Connelly, and he had written some good poems about the London blitz in pretty much the same personal idiom he had used in his poems about the Spanish Civil War, poems that couldn't have been more different from Auden's 'Spain', which is really about the operation of vast historical forces and the place and time at which individual choice, recognizing necessity, might intervene. Spender had always been an autobiographer, Auden an analytic observer of a world outside himself. But one thing that Spender and Auden had in common was a deep knowledge of and fondness for German literature. They had translated, edited and introduced major German writers from Goethe and Schiller to Rilke and Brecht. Auden had even written some of his earliest poems in German.[18] Unlike the poets of the 1920s, these veterans of the 1930s were not Francophiles but, in spite of the two world wars, essentially Germanophiles. Even Auden's Italian phase, when his summer home was in Ischia, was mediated in part by his translation of Goethe's *Italian Journey*, and his longest poem, *The Age of Anxiety*, is written in Germanic alliterative meters. When Spender published his own Random House *Collected Poems* a decade following Auden's, his translation, with J. B. Leishmann, of Rilke's *Duino Elegies*, had been in print for fifteen years. It is interesting that Spender's most recent editor, Grey Gowry, including translations of Rilke's first and fifth elegies in the Faber *Selected Poems*, argues that Spender's translation of the first elegy 'anticipates the conversational mode of John Ashbery's mature style so completely it is hard not to conjecture that Ashbery knows and loves this version'.[19] Spender's essay 'Immigration in Reverse' imagines – and perhaps fears – that the Brits, even if they are reading and translating German poetry and prose, are going to be over-influenced by the new American world in which they arrive and by the American writers whom they will read.[20] In Auden's case, the question of influence turned out to be complicated. What he took from Marianne Moore, for example, he gave back not only to Ashbery, but also to the entire New York School. American poets in his debt ranged from, to use Robert Lowell's terminology, 'cooked' poets like James Merrill to 'raw' poets like Kenneth Rexroth. Auden was himself becoming, as he said in his elegy for Freud, 'a whole climate' – not exactly 'of opinion', but of something that survives, as he wrote in his elegy for Yeats, 'scattered among a hundred cities'.[21]

When Stephen Spender arrived for the first time in America he came to teach at Sarah Lawrence in the fall of 1947. His last two books, *The Still Centre* (1939) and *Ruins and Visions* (1942) had not been enthusiastically received. Moreover, most of the poems that would appear in *Poems of Dedication* (1947) had already been written; his best work as a poet was behind him. After *The Edge of Being* (1949) was also generally disliked by critics, Spender didn't publish a new book of verse for more than two decades. He did, however, continue writing poems.

Spender characteristically implicated himself in 'Responsibility: The Pilots Who Destroyed Germany in 1945'.[22] For someone who had been a fireman during the blitz, the whole question of outraged revenge – even on a people with whom he had experienced considerable sympathy during the time of his earliest visits, and whose literature he loved – and the internalization of collective guilt is something to be acknowledged: 'Oh, that April morning they carried my will / Exalted expanding singing in their aerial cage. / They carried my will. They dropped it on a German town. / My will exploded. Tall buildings fell down ... And my life, which never paid the price of their wounds / ... Assumes their guilt, honours, repents, prays for them'. Auden delayed writing the poem that seems to have emerged from his own official work with the Strategic Bombing Survey until 1949. The perspective of section I of 'Memorial for the City' is familiar from the poet's earlier work: observed above the fray, as Auden's 1930s hawk might see it, or 'the helmeted airman', although this time a scene of newsreel violence is seen by 'the crow on the crematorium chimney' and a 'roving' camera. Both record 'a space where time has no place. / On the right a village is burning, in a market-town to the left / The soldiers fire, the mayor bursts into tears / The captives are led far away'.

While Stephen Spender's post-war poems are not up to Auden's standard and none are as ambitious as *The Age of Anxiety*, to the composition of which Auden returned after the assignment in Germany, both 'Elegy for Margaret' and 'Returning to Vienna' have considerable interest. The first of these became central to Spender's *Collected Poems* in both the 1955 and the substantially revised 1985 versions, but the latter, like *Vienna*, which the poem revisits, disappeared from his books until Michael Brett edited the posthumous *New Collected Poems* in 2004.[23]

Vienna, despite its flaws, and despite its author's verdict against it, deserves to survive. Spender was one of the few British poets of his generation to write directly out of the boiling cauldron in four contexts: Berlin, Vienna, Spain and London during the blitz. It is a pity that Spender was so mocked and derided by younger poets and critics emerging after the war. (By Thom Gunn, for example: 'I praise the overdogs from Alexander / To those who wouldn't play with Stephen Spender'.[24]) His innocent enjoyment of friendship with famous people and the accusations about his complicity in the CIA funding of *Encounter* magazine,[25] which he co-edited, pretty much ended the serious consideration of his poetry. But his deep engagement of the theme of interpenetrating public and private worlds in many of his poems, and especially in *Vienna*, is important for any consideration of British poetry in the 1930s. If *The Waste Land* had been a political poem, it would have been *Vienna*.

'Returning to Vienna' emerged from a visit Spender made a couple of years after his official duties in Germany to the scene of his relationship with a woman called 'Elizabeth' in his autobiography, *World Within World*, but whose identity became known to many people when Muriel Gardiner published *Code Name 'Mary'* after Lillian Hellman had published *Pentimento*, a 'memoir' that more or less told Gardiner's story of underground work during and after the suppression of Viennese socialists by Dollfuss, Fey and Starhemberg in her third chapter, 'Julia', which also became a popular film.[26] Spender had been drawn into the world of Gardiner's underground activities through his relationship with her, and so inevitably enough the political and personal themes became integrated in the poem he wrote in 1935. The theme of both *Vienna* and its sequel (1947) is stated clearly in the latter: 'I saw there in our gaze what breaks the heart – the tears and bloodshot vein of seeing / the outer world destroy the inner world'.[27] Because I regard *Vienna*, unlike the poet himself in later years and unlike his most recent editors, biographers and basically anyone else, to be Spender's most interesting poem, though not his most successful, I find the sequel –available now only in the 2004 *New Collected Poems* – important as a kind of retrospective gloss. *Vienna* is a prototype for what critics now call 'the pocket epic', thinking of other 'poems including history' by poets like Basil Bunting in *Briggflatts* and Geoffrey Hill in *Mercian Hymns*. The poem of return is moving and candid: 'My own existence dwelling in my body / Seems like an odour sicklied under rubble, / A taste of marrow in the taste of bones / Tormented into apathy by shame – / The shame of what I never was, / That when I lived my life among these dead / I did not live enough –[28]

If 'Returning to Vienna' looks back, 'Elegy for Margaret' (1947) suggests the direction in which Spender's work will move – the political becoming less and less important in his poetry as it was taken up more and more in his prose, and the intimate voice, or even proto-'confessional', coming to dominate his verse. One late direction taken in his writing was the 'diary poem', written in an informal idiom that may have been influenced by the blank verse sonnets that Robert Lowell was writing in the 1960s. In one of these, he remembers Louis MacNeice leaning against a marble chimney piece with 'the superior head slanted back / With dancing eyes summing [him] up'. Re-reading 'Bagpipe Music', Spender realizes that he doesn't know 'how to pronounce / C-e-i-l-i-d-h, nor what it means'.[29] It's another elegy, of course, but too slight to compare with his work from the 1930s,

'Elegy for Margaret', or a few later poems in a more formal idiom such as 'The Generous Days' or 'One More New Botched Beginning'.

Louis MacNeice's wartime visit among the ménage at Auden's 7 Middagh St. address in Brooklyn was brief. By the time he arrived in New York, he had of course known Auden for many years and had collaborated with him on one of the liveliest books of the 1930s, *Letters from Iceland*. As an 'Auden generation' poet, MacNeice was always the most independent of Auden himself. His early eclogues, including the one in the Iceland book, have the feel of short plays by W. B. Yeats, and doubtless led the poet to experiment with full-scale drama, first during the thirties at Group Theatre with *Out of the Picture*, but later and more importantly with many of the plays and scripts he wrote during an extensive career at the BBC which lasted from 1941, following his return from America, until his death in 1963.

MacNeice became one of the pioneering writers and producers for high-brow radio which, despite its intellectual ambitions, easily reached millions who might never have seen a play or heard a poem recited before. His own *The Dark Tower* became a kind of classic of the radio-play genre, and his collaborations with Dylan Thomas led to the even more famous *Under Milkwood* and, indirectly, to Douglas Cleverdon's radio version of David Jones's *In Parenthesis* (with Thomas and Richard Burton in the cast) and, much later, the first instalments of Christopher Logue's versions of the *Iliad*, eventually called *War Music*. Along the way, MacNeice produced a translation of Goethe's *Faust*, edited into six radio instalments, which some believe is the best English version ever made. It is certainly, in a great age of verse translation which contains many masterpieces from Pound to Logue, one of MacNeice's major post-war achievements.

Although MacNeice's influence on poets beginning to publish after 1945 was mostly due either to early poems such as 'Wolves' and 'Snow' or those in his posthumous volume, *The Burning Perch*, *Autumn Sequel* (1954) is important as a work which, like Spender's 'Returning to Vienna', revisits an earlier poem and, in MacNeice's case, aims to replace it and perhaps to compete with Auden on the terms laid down by his own long poems of the 1940s. It is important to remember, however, that *Autumn Sequel* was, like the *Faust* translation, written to be broadcast, at least in part, on the radio. Canto IV actually describes MacNeice the radio producer at work. This is a subject which, as far as I know, had never been treated in verse before, though the connections made with oral epic reach back in the history of poetry as far as it is possible to go. 'Not matching pictures but inventing sound, / Precalculating microphone and knob / In homage to the human voice'. Would the radio play the part of Homer to its audience in MacNeice's terza rima? MacNeice 'agreed / to join this new crusade' as explained by 'Harrap', (A. E. Harding, of the BBC): 'You will have to feed / The tall transmitters with hot news – Dunkirk, / Tobruk or Singapore, you will have to set / Traps for your neutral listeners ... For that is propaganda.... // Thus humbled and exalted day by day/ We scratched among the debris. The war flowed by / In short or medium waves ... / oh when would this / Thing start or that thing stop?[30]

One might well imagine that some of the radio programs that interrupt monologues and dialogues of Auden's characters in *The Age of Anxiety* could have originally been produced by MacNeice himself if it were not for all of the American-derived advertising that accompanies them. These interruptions sit awkwardly with the texture of the verse; they are meant to. The extreme artifice of *Autumn Sequel* (the extended terza rima) parallels as a prosodic challenge Auden's use of Anglo-Saxon alliterative meter in *The Age of Anxiety*, which Auden had called in his subtitle, no apology intended and combining in a stroke the classical pastoral with the walloping accents of *Piers Plowman*, 'A Baroque Eclogue'. Though published some seven years apart, these poems represented the last attempt by both poets to write long poems. Both works were attacked by the younger critics on the make, A. Alvarez, for example, lumping them both together: '*Autumn Sequel*, like *The Age on Anxiety*, shows that [MacNeice and Auden] have become weary and knowing and bored with it all'.[31] And Randall Jarrell was on record in his 1952 Princeton lectures saying that Auden had, in the long poems of the 1940s, been writing poetry 'as obsessively as a neurotic washes his hands'.[32]

But Auden's *The Age of Anxiety* is better than its present lack of wide attention suggests. It is the poem in which Auden deals most directly with the effects of the war on North Americans, and two of his four speakers, Malin and Emble, are still in the military. The most interesting of the four is clearly Rosetta, to whose apartment the representatives of Jung's four faculties of intuition, feeling, sensation and thought return when the bar where they meet closes for the night on All Souls' Eve. Rosetta represents the faculty of feeling. In earlier sections of the poem she has expressed her Arcadian nostalgia for the England of her youth. Auden had already examined the Arcadian form of delusion in that part of 'Caliban to the Audience' beginning 'Carry me back ... to the cathedral town where the canons run through the water meadows with butterfly nets and the old women keep sweetshops in the cobbled side streets ...'.[33] Rosetta's longing is similar, and similar as well to the Arcadian's confrontation with the Utopian in the 'Vespers' section of 'Horae Canonicae' (1952) where Auden's representative, the Arcadian, arouses the contempt of his anti-type ('between my Eden and his New Jerusalem, no treaty is negotiable'): 'One reason for his contempt is that I have only to close my eyes, cross the iron footbridge to the tow-path, take the barge through the short brick tunnel and // there I stand in Eden again'.[34] Rosetta, however, represents not only feeling and Arcadianism, but also the feminine and Judaism. It is not irrelevant to notice that *The Age of Anxiety* was written a little after Auden's mother had died and during his one known heterosexual relationship, with the Jewish Rhoda Jaffe. Before his conversion to Christianity, he had considered converting to Judaism. And, like Benjamin Britten, he had found a kind of surrogate mother in Elizabeth Mayer to whom *New Year Letter* had been dedicated and with whom he translated Goethe's *Italian Journey*. Auden sometimes maintained that his homosexuality was a 'sin' for which God would forgive him. He also may have felt that way about his Arcadianism. But the tone of the various Arcadian passages in his work usually manifests what Yvor Winters called 'compensatory irony'. Although it is clear that the reader is meant to be critical of these nostalgias, the longing of the speakers is unabated and contagious.[35]

Rosetta's favoured landscapes are the same as Auden's. As he wrote in *The Dyer's Hand*, his Eden would be set in 'limestone uplands like the Pennines plus a small region of igneous rocks with at least one extinct volcano'. It would also contain 'a precipitous and indented sea-coast'.[36] Rosetta's first long monologue speaks of 'Undulant land / [that] rose layer by layer till at last the sea / Far away flashed; from fretted uplands / That lay to the north, from limestone heights'. Malin had already warned that 'The greenest arcadias have ghosts too', and he later declares that man 'pines for some / Nameless Eden where he never was / But where in his wishes once again / On hollowed acres … the children play'. This is Rosetta's 'besieged island … where my home once was'.[37] The visionary writing of David Jones in *The Anathémata* and certain fragments in *The Sleeping Lord* evoke a deeply feminine feeling for place that is not unlike Rosetta's own, though not undercut by 'compensatory ironies' or an interrupting voice like Malin's. For Basil Bunting, a childhood Eden appears at once in the Northumbrian landscape of *Briggflatts*, then seems to be lost by the adult poet and wanderer, but is finally returned to him at the end, not only to be celebrated, but actually inhabited. There is much in common between Jones's mytho-historical Wales and Bunting's mytho-historical Northumbria (and, before *Briggflatts*, in the Persian world of 'The Spoils').

It is difficult to quote adequately from David Jones's work, and it does not offer much to an editor looking for brief anthology selections. He does not write in the traditional meters and stanzas favoured by the generation of poets gaining an audience in the 1950s. His work is more like certain passages of *Finnegans Wake* – certainly more like Joyce than *The Age of Anxiety*, which, consensus notwithstanding, actually recalls Virginia Woolf of *The Waves* – or of Welsh poetry written in the Welsh language. 'Poets like Aneirin', Gwyn Williams writes, 'were not trying to write poems that would read like Greek temples or even gothic cathedrals, but, rather, like stone circles or the contour-following rings of the forts from which they fought, with hidden ways slipping from one ring to another'.[38] At the centre of these circles or forts we often find a figuration of the feminine – from 'The Queen of the Woods' in *In Parenthesis*, to 'The Lady of the Pool' and the Venus of Willendorf in *The Anathémata*, to 'The Tutelar of the Place' in *The Sleeping Lord*. These figures represent or long for the same Arcadian condition that Auden's Rosetta does. Even the hard-boiled Roman Tribune, the leveller, the Imperialist, who speaks in one of the late monologues in *The Sleeping Lord* and claims to believe that 'only the neurotic / look to their beginnings', finds himself growing more candid than he had intended to be, speaking to his men: 'I too could weep / for these Saturnian spells / and for the remembered things. No dying Gaul / figures in the rucked circus sand / his far green valley / more clear than do I figure / from this guard-house door / a little porch below Albanus ... and streams more loved [than Tiber], more loved because more known ... because our mothers' wombs were opened on their margins / and our sisters' shifts / laved in the upper pools'.[39] These passages evoke feelings much like those of Basil Bunting's Macedonian soldiers in the section of *Briggflatts* where they march with Alexander to the mountains of Gog and Magog at the edge of the world where he alone resolves to climb to the top and encounters Israfel, trumpet in hand. All the others now 'desired Macedonia, / the rocky meadows, horses, barley pancakes, incest and familiar games, / to end in our [own] place ... [We] deemed the peak unscaleable'.[40] Even Alexander's most loyal followers, like the Roman Tribune's men, might well end by praying to 'The Tutelar of the Place', David Jones's version of the mother goddess of the loved and remembered hearth:

> In all times of *gleichschaltung* in the days of the central economies, set up the hedges of illusion round some remnant of us, twine the wattles of mist, white-web a Gwydion-hedge ... against the commissioners and assessors bearing the writs of the Ram to square the world floor and number the tribes and write down the secret things and take away the diversities by which we are, by which we call on your name, sweet Jill of the demarcations....[41]

Bunting's autobiographical hero is at this point in *Briggflatts* assimilated to the historical-mythical Alexander as a figure of ambition. When this figure falls from the mountain top of his hubristic climb that extends all the way from 'the fells' late spring' of Part One in which a 'sweet tenor bull' sings by the river Rawthey and a boy and girl touch each other innocently on a 'pricked rug mat' while the slowworm rises both as emblem of place and the boy's phallus, he falls back into the landscape of his youth: 'He lay / on glistening moss by a spring;/ as a woodman dazed by an adder's sting / barely within recall .../ I am neither snake nor lizard, / I am the slowworm'.[42]

In the final section of *Briggflatts*, spring comes to the cold north and the pastoral setting of part one is reconfigured. Fifty years have passed and 'Then is diffused in Now'. The setting is both actual and Arcadian. It is a real place, where Bunting himself returned to live, needing no reminder that *Et in Arcadia ego*; even the sexual play of the children in the poem's first section was accompanied by the sound of the stone carver's mallet: 'Every birth a crime / Every sentence death'.[43] The 'child' to whom the poem is dedicated had to be consulted in order to determine whether or not she would accept the dedication. The poem, as it were, summoned her back into the poet's life. The poet and the old woman met. Their feeling for each other was still alive. A very long journey brought the poet home and his poem became, almost, canonical. But more than canonical (almost), it actually grew to be loved, not just admired and influential – a rare thing for a long and difficult modernist poem – in much the same way that certain lyrics by Hardy, Frost, and Yeats are loved. What better story could be told?

> Fifty years a letter unanswered;
> A visit postponed for fifty years
> She has been with me fifty years.
> Starlight quivers. I had day enough.
> For love uninterrupted night.[44]

NOTES

1 Nearly all serious critics of Auden's work take up the question of the poet's revisions. The major Auden volumes that anyone new to this issue should consult are *Poems* (London: Faber and Faber 1930, 1933), *The Orators* (London: Faber and Faber, 1932); *Look, Stranger!* (London: Faber and Faber, 1936); *Spain* (London: Faber and Faber, 1937); *Letters from Iceland* (London: Faber and Faber, 1937); *Journey to a War* (London: Faber and Faber, 1939); *Another Time* (New York: Random House, 1940); *The Double Man* (New York: Random House, 1941); *The Collected Poetry* (New York: Random House, 1945); *Collected Shorter Poems* (London: Faber and Faber, 1950); *Collected Shorter Poems* (New York: Random House, 1966); *Collected Longer Poems* (New York: Random House, 1967); *The English Auden*, Edward Mendelson, ed. (London: Faber and Faber, 1977); *Collected Poems*, Edward Mendelson, ed. (New York: Modern Library, 1991).

2 Edward Mendelson, *Early Auden* (New York: The Viking Press, 1981), pp. 240–41, 334–35, 336.

3 Mendelson, *Early Auden*, pp. 160–76; John Fuller, *W. H. Auden: A Commentary* (Princeton: Princeton University Press, 1998), pp. 149–50.

4 Randall Jarrell, *Randall Jarrell on W. H. Auden*, ed. Stephen Burt (New York: Columbia University Press, 2005), p. 23.
5 W. H. Auden, *The Collected Poetry* (New York: Random House, 1945), jacket blurb quote from *Time Magazine*, September 11, 1944.
6 W. H. Auden, *Look, Stranger*! (London: Faber and Faber, 1936), Dedication page: 'To Erika Mann'.
7 Auden, *The Collected Poetry*, Dedication Page.
8 Humphrey Carpenter, *W. H. Auden: A Biography* (Boston: Houghton Mifflin, 1981), p. 332.
9 Carpenter, *W. H. Auden: A Biography*, p. 328.
10 W. H. Auden, *Collected Shorter Poems* (New York: Random House, 1966), p. 15.
11 Auden, *Collected Poetry* (1945), p. 405.
12 Auden, *Collected Shorter Poems*, pp. 15–16.
13 W. H. Auden, *Selected Poems*, ed. Edward Mendelson (New York: Random House, 1979), p. xviii.
14 Howard Griffin, *Conversations with Auden* (San Francisco: Gray Fox, 1981).
15 Peter Pears, in conversation with the author, November 1978.
16 W. H. Auden, *Paul Bunyan: The Libretto of the Operetta by Benjamin Britten* (London: Faber and Faber, 1988), p. 71.
17 Paul Muldoon, *Meeting the British* (Winston-Salem: Wake Forest University Press, 1987), p. 46.
18 For both German originals and English translations see David Constantine, 'The German Auden: Six Early Poems' in Kathereine Bucknell and Ncholas Jenkeins (eds.), *W. H. Auden: 'The Map of All My Youth'* (Oxford: Clarendon Press, 1990), pp. 1–15.
19 Stephen Spender, *Selected Poems*, Grey Gowrie (ed.) (London: Faber and Faber, 2009), pp. 115–18.
20 Stephen Spender, *The Making of a Poem* (New York: W. W. Norton, 1962), pp. 193–205.
21 Auden, *Selected Poems*, p. 81.
22 Stephen Spender, *Collected Poems* (London: Faber and Faber, 2004), pp. 247–48.
23 Stephen Spender, *Collected Poems 1928–1955* (New York: Random House, 1986), pp. 113–15; *New Collected Poems* (London: Faber and Faber, 2004), pp. 235–41.
24 Thom Gunn, *The Sense of Movement* (London: Faber and Faber, 1957), p. 30.
25 John Sutherland, *Stephen Spender: A Biography* (Oxford: Oxford University Press, 2005). pp. 389–91.
26 Compare Spender, *World Within World* (London: Hamish Hamilton, 1951) pp. 193 ff., Lillian Hellman, *Pentimento* (Boston: Little, Brown and Co., 1973), pp. 101–47, and Muriel Gardiner, *Code Name 'Mary'* (New Haven: Yale University Press, 1983). The film was *Julia*, directed by Fred Zimmerman, with Jane Fonda, Vanessa Redgrave and Jason Robards, 1977.
27 Spender, *New Collected Poems*, p. 238.
28 Spender, *New Collected Poems*, p. 240.
29 Spender, *New Collected Poems*, p. 322.
30 Muldoon, *The Faber Book of Contemporary Irish Poetry*, pp. 121–27.
31 Jon Stallworthy, *Louis MacNeice: a Biography* (New York: W. W. Norton, 1995), p. 411.

32 Randall Jarrell, *Randall Jarrell on W. H. Auden*, p. 61.
33 Auden, *Selected Poems*, p. 165–64.
34 Auden, *Selected Poems*, p. 228–29.
35 Yvor Winters, *In Defense of Reason* (Denver: Alan Swallow, 1947), pp. 65–74.
36 W. H. Auden, *The Dyer's Hand* (New York: Vintage Books, 1968), p. 6.
37 W. H. Auden, *The Age of Anxiety* (Princeton: Princeton University Press, 2011), pp. 7, 13.
38 John Matthias (ed.), *Introducing David Jones* (London: Faber and Faber, 1980), p. 20.
39 David Jones, *The Sleeping Lord and Other Fragments* (London: Faber and Faber, 1974), pp. 52–53.
40 Bunting, *Briggflatts*, p. 24.
41 Jones, *The Sleeping Lord*, p. 63.
42 Bunting, *Briggflatts*, p. 25.
43 Bunting, Briggflatts, p. 17.
44 Bunting, *Briggflatts*, p. 32.

4

ERIC FALCI

Beyond All This Fiddle: Hughes, Hill, Tomlinson and Fisher

Al Alvarez's 1962 anthology *The New Poetry* is, first and foremost, a response to the poetry of the Movement, and especially to Robert Conquest's *New Lines* (1956). Alvarez's volume, and its 1966 'revised and enlarged edition', aimed to reshuffle the field of British poetry, and most critics have thought about his intervention using his own terms. In 'The New Poetry, *or* Beyond the Gentility Principle', the anthology's famous introduction, Alvarez suggests that 'since about 1930 the machinery of modern English poetry seems to have been controlled by a series of negative feed-backs designed to produce precisely the effect Hardy wanted', which, according to Alvarez, is an eschewal of *vers libre* and a return to traditional English metres and modes.[1] *The New Poetry*, under this reading, constitutes another feedback loop along with the earlier examples that Alvarez catalogues: W. H. Auden and the thirties poets, Dylan Thomas and the neo-Romantic and Apocalyptic poets of the 1940s, and Philip Larkin and the Movement in the 1950s.

Each of these 'negative feed-backs' reverses the energy of the dominant poetic formation of the previous moment, and the kind of poetry that Alvarez endorsed was meant to counter what he saw as the moderate empiricism and limited stakes of Movement poetry. Alvarez's rhetorical stratagems are well known, and, considering how often critics continue to mention them, they have certainly taken hold. To fall into line, I'll spin through them again. He engages in an *ad hominem* attack, suggesting that the tedium of the Movement's 'academic-administrative verse' is inevitable, considering that it is written by six 'university teachers, two librarians, and ... a Civil Servant'.[2] Using the speaker of Larkin's 'Church-Going', he confects a synthetic Movement poet as 'the image of the post-war Welfare State Englishman', someone who is 'just like the man next door – in fact, he probably *is* the man next door'.[3] He produces an oeuvre for this makeshift poet by amalgamating lines from eight of the nine *New Lines* writers into a single marvellously bland lyric in order to demonstrate their lack of originality and distinction. He arranges a joust between the Movement's champion, Larkin, and his own favoured figure, Ted Hughes, and then rigs the match so that Hughes's poem 'A Dream of Horses' defeats Larkin's 'At Grass', because even though 'At Grass' is 'more skillful' than Hughes' poem, it is 'less urgent'.[4] Hughes's poem is 'unquestionably *about* something', even though it verges 'on the pretentious', and it becomes the implicit example of the 'new depth poetry' that Alvarez favours against that 'disease so often found in English culture: gentility'.[5]

We can get a clearer sense of Alvarez's hopes for such 'new depth poetry' by turning briefly to the article that provides this essay's title. In 'Beyond All this Fiddle', which first appeared in the *Times Literary Supplement* in 1967, Alvarez reprises some of the themes of his introduction to *The New Poetry* within a broader cultural context. He offers 'Extremist art' (or, alternately, 'Extremist style') as 'the most courageous response' to the sorts of 'radical and thorough-going' transformations in culture, society and politics that threaten, in particular, traditional arts.[6] Rather than the genteel poetry that he scorns in 'The New Poetry, *or* Beyond the Gentility Principle', or the pop poetry against which he rails in 'Beyond All This Fiddle', Alvarez endorses the boldness of 'Extremist art'. The essay's ultimate definition of 'Extremist art' is itself mild – 'internal confusion transmuted into new kinds of artistic order' – and could stand as a fairly generic definition not of 'extremist art', but of, quite simply, 'art'.[7] However, an earlier comment gets us closer to the nub of Alvarez's polemic: 'a major test of originality is not a question of form but of psychic exploration, not of artifact but of the artist's identity'.[8]

What is clear in both of these essays is that Alvarez is interested primarily not in poems, but in poets – not in artefacts, but in psychic journeys and the artistic identities that ensue. To be fair, Alvarez told his readers this in the very first sentence of the 'Prefatory Note' in the 1962 edition of *The New Poetry*: 'this is a personal anthology'.[9] Most obviously, this means that the book represents Alvarez's own aesthetic tastes. However, it can also be taken to mean that those tastes have everything to do with the 'personal', that is, the *persons* of poets, and the idea of the poetic personality more broadly. This yields an important notion, one that was implicit in a number of the contemporary reviews of his volume: Alvarez's *The New Poetry* is really two anthologies.

Most palpably, *The New Poetry* is a moderately sized volume published by Allen Lane at Penguin Press. The 1966 edition contains the work of twenty-eight poets: four Americans lead off the volume and are followed by twenty-four British poets. Except for the Americans Sylvia Plath and Anne Sexton, all of the poets are men. These selections represent what Alvarez calls in the 'Prefatory Note' to the 1962 edition 'the most significant work of the British poets who began to come into their own in the fifties', as well as what he describes in the preface to the 1966 edition as 'the poems I most liked from the period'.[10] This is the book as it exists on the shelf. The other anthology is virtual, embedded within *The New Poetry* and much more strongly aligned with Alvarez's vision. This shadow anthology consists of the poets who are both represented in the volume *and* who conform to the notion of the poet that Alvarez lays out in the introduction. It is this version of the anthology that has lingered in literary-historical memory. As he writes in the 'Preface to the Revised Edition', his inclusion of Plath and Sexton (who did not appear in the first edition) is entirely tendentious: 'their work, more than anyone else's, makes sense of my introduction'.[11] The shadow anthology is Alvarez's book in its purest form. Along with Lowell, Berryman, Plath and Sexton, the distilled volume would also contain Ted Hughes, Thom Gunn and, less prominently featured, Peter Redgrove and Geoffrey Hill. These are the poets closest to the book's core, taking into account both the arguments Alvarez makes in the introduction and the space that these poets are allotted in comparison to the other twenty poets in the volume.

I am not simply arguing that Alvarez liked some of the poets he included better than others, and so gave his preferred poets more room. Rather, I'm suggesting that the actual anthology and the version of the anthology projected by his introduction are at cross-purposes. Although Alvarez doesn't name the 'fiddle' that he wants to get 'beyond' in the essay that provides my title, we can use the shared phrasing between it and his anthology introduction to pin it down: the 'fiddle' to discard and move beyond is 'the Gentility Principle'. 'The Gentility Principle' is embodied for Alvarez in the Movement poets. They are the 'fiddle'. And yet, the Movement poets are well represented in Alvarez's anthology: six of the nine poets who appear in *New Lines* also appear in *The New Poetry*. And quite a number of the other poets who Alvarez includes would fit quite neatly into Conquest's volume (and several of them did make it into the 1963 sequel, *New Lines II*). It isn't the case that *The New Poetry* gathered a substantively new or different version of British poetry than what had been on offer for the previous decade. His own anthological feedback loop was not entirely negative. It picks up much of the most celebrated poetry of the 1950s even as its polemical introduction positions itself against it: the 'fiddle' that Alvarez means to get beyond is everywhere present in his selection. For the remainder of this essay, I will re-direct his title phrase in two directions. First, I will look at the work Alvarez posed as being beyond the fiddle of the Movement, that which he includes within his anthology and which also accords with the desideratum of his introduction. I will then move beyond this desideratum, looking initially at the poetry he includes in the anthology but that falls outside of his proffered terms, and then briefly at poetry of the period that lies beyond Alvarez's ken.

Along with Thom Gunn, Ted Hughes mediates the two incarnations of Alvarez's anthology, the actual book and its idealized distillation. By the time the first edition of *The New Poetry* was published, Hughes was already a significant figure. His first two volumes, *The Hawk in the Rain* (1957) and *Lupercal* (1960), established Hughes as an anti-Movement paragon: his was an instinctual and earthy poetry to set against the suburban moderations of figures like Larkin and Kingsley Amis. Beginning a pattern that would inflect his entire writing career, Hughes devoted the bulk of his attention to animals, with his numerous creature poems doubling as psychological investigations and parables of civilizational violence. From *The Hawk in the Rain* through *Crow: From the Life and Songs of the Crow* (1970) and well beyond, Hughes's bent is to re-enchant the space of nature by tapping the depths of psyche, 'as if the eye and the head / Were an underworld'.[12] In *Wodwo* (1967) and *Crow* in particular, Hughes uses an array of mythic and folk materials to fashion new lore, what he calls 'a sort of hair and bone wisdom'.[13] Hughes's typical mode of interchange between the human and natural worlds is already established in the title poem that opens his first volume. 'The Hawk in the Rain' inscribes a chiasmus between celestial and terrestrial realms. In the first of the poem's five quatrains, the speaker is stuck in the soaked ground, dragging up 'heel after heel from the swallowing of the earth's mouth'.[14] In contrast, the hawk of the title is the quintessence of power and control, hanging 'steady as a hallucination in the streaming air'.[15] The speaker, a 'morsel in the earth's mouth', strains 'towards the master- / Fulcrum of violence where the hawk hangs still'.[16] The poem pivots on the enjambment, and the conspicuousness of the line break signals the aesthetic will of the poet overcoming the speaker's frailty among the elements. The final line of the penultimate stanza begins to construct an imaginative crossing pattern that envisions the hawk one day getting caught in a storm and crashing to earth. A cacophony of verb tenses mimics the hawk's loss of control, and 'The Hawk in the Rain['s]' final line reroutes its title by picturing the hawk dead on the ground: 'the round angelic eye / Smashed, mix his heart's blood with the mire of the land'.[17] The poem's reversal culminates with the hawk taking the speaker's place as a 'morsel in the earth's mouth' and the speaker now figuratively overlooking the hawk's strewn corpse. The odd juxtaposition of verbs in the final line demonstrates the sacrifice that the poem has forced in order to spur itself into realization: the hawk's eye is described in the past tense – 'smashed' – while the present tense 'mix' reads as an imperative from the poet-self to the rain-walking speaker. 'Mixing' the hawk into the land is both a burial and an instance of authorial power. Proleptically transposing the allegory of aesthetic creation forwarded by Hughes's famous poem 'The Thought-Fox', which appears several pages later in *The Hawk in the Rain* and which ends as the fox of the title moves from the poem's surround into 'the dark hole of the head' and spurs the completion of the text ('The page is printed'), 'The Hawk in the Rain' is catalysed not by the radical joining of speaker and nature but by their estrangement and ultimate substitution.[18]

The dialectic of self and world, and especially of self and animal, drives Hughes's early work. One of the most remarkable instances of this dialectic occurs in 'Pike', in which the ravenous, cannibalistic nature of the fish becomes first the poem's topic and then its metaphorical method. The speaker spends the first seven stanzas describing in vivid detail the three pike 'we kept behind glass, / jungled in weed'.[19] As they grow, they begin to devour each other, until the final two die when one tries to consume the other: 'one jammed past its gills down the other's gullet'.[20] The poem abruptly switches from the deathly scene in the fish tank to the speaker's memory of a pond he once fished, which – he imagines – must contain 'pike too immense to stir'.[21] The pond is certainly a metaphor for the speaker's psyche, filled with treacherous depths and ancient monsters. But it also becomes a metonym for an entire nation and culture: 'Stilled legendary depth: / It was as deep as England'.[22] In such moments we can watch Hughes's seemingly transhistorical vision take on particular historical weight, especially considering that this poem appeared as Britain's imperial width and reach were being drastically reduced. The poem ends with a compound of counterfactual memory and dream, as the speaker claims that he 'dared not cast' into the pond 'past nightfall', but then immediately countermands his own warning by imagining himself, cold and scared, fishing at night. He listens to the sounds of the 'dark pond' and 'owls hushing the floating woods', and the external soundscape is absorbed into a kind of psychic sensorium:

> Frail on my ear against the dream
> Darkness beneath night's darkness had freed,
> That rose slowly towards me, watching.[23]

As with the scumbled verb tenses at the end of 'The Hawk in the Rain', 'Pike' ends in a passage of syntactical lures and snares. The 'frail' sounds of water and owls are placed against the 'dream / darkness', which is placed above 'night's darkness', which, in turn, has 'freed' the 'dream / darkness'. An entire psychic topography is projected, replete with heights, depths and phantasmal actors.

However, the penultimate line's final verb phrase – the past perfect 'had freed' – causes a significant readjustment. Instead of reading 'dream /

darkness' as a noun phrase that contrasts with 'night's darkness', we might think of it as part of a dense nest of relative clauses. In this case, the water and owl sounds are said to be 'frail on my ear' and 'against the dream', a dream that 'darkness beneath night's darkness had freed'. It isn't a 'dream / darkness' that is 'beneath night's darkness', but a dream that had been freed *by* the 'darkness beneath night's darkness'. So, the original binary of darknesses is factored out into a triad: a dream, 'night's darkness', and another darkness that is below that one and that enables the dream to form. The sense of abyssal darknesses, which are by this point in the poem both individual and civilizational, ramifies further with the final line. In one sense, we might say that it is 'the dream' that 'rises slowly towards me, watching'. But it also can be the 'darkness' itself that 'rises', as the demarcation between figure and ground is substantively lost. Either way, we are brought back to the grim emblem of the pike, which, at poem's end, is both internal to the speaker – emerging out of his own dreaming head – and a menacing force watching him as it rises in the dim water. As is clear in 'Pike', more often than not the encounter between the speaker and the environment in Hughes's poetry produces a third term, what we might call myth, or at least an impulse towards mythmaking as a way to both bind and free the multifarious darkness that clusters around human life.

If the third term in Hughes's work – that which both surrounds and goes beyond it – is *myth*, then for Geoffrey Hill the third term between the self and the poem is *history*. Hill's poetry from *For the Unfallen* (1959) to *The Mystery of the Charity of Charles Péguy* (1983) is consumed by, among other topics, the press of history upon the present. His early, tightly torqued poems seek to encode history's full burden within nearly every line while pointing out again and again how they themselves are both complicit in and incommensurate to the historical material that they address. If, as he writes in 'The Distant Fury of Battle', 'the dead maintain their ground', then the space of the poem is always impinged upon by the stuff of a past that it cannot fully represent.[24] The elegy, then, with its tilted dialectic of mourning and renewal, or melancholia and repair, becomes a central – because fundamentally problematic – form. A number of Hill's most well-known early poems are elegies of one sort or another, but unlike other major British elegists of the late twentieth century – Heaney, Dunn, Muldoon, Longley, Riley – many of Hill's early elegies are for people who he does not and cannot know, whether the child who is murdered by the Nazis in 'September Song', the entire European Jewish population in 'Two Formal Elegies', or the executed fifteenth-century English noblemen who are named at the start of his sonnet sequence, 'Funeral Music'. In part, such elegies are catalysed by their own inadequacy, a point Hill makes in the eighth sonnet of the sequence: 'so we bear witness, / Despite ourselves to what is beyond us, / Each distant sphere of harmony forever / Poised, unanswerable'.[25] Hill's Christian vision and his approach to history collapse in an image of ceaseless waiting. The tensed stasis that characterizes this act of witness is both substantive and necessarily incomplete, and it corresponds with the highly pressurized formalism that defines his early volumes, and, in a very different way, the voluble torrent of late career work that has appeared since *Canaan* (1996).

As Hill more adamantly focuses on the historical wreckage of 'Europe, the much-scarred, much-scoured terrain' and, more particularly, of 'coiled entrenched England' in *King Log* (1968), *Mercian Hymns* (1972) and *Tenebrae* (1978), his formal methods stretch beyond the mainly iambic, rhyming quatrains and couplets that comprise *For the Unfallen*.[26] But what remains, whether in the highly wrought sonnet sequence, 'An Apology for the Revival of Christian Architecture in England', or in the thirty textured prose poems that make up the *Mercian Hymns*, is a charged and sceptical lyric density. Hill, to a degree matched only by Prynne among contemporary British poets, forces every word to unspool its idioms and connotations. If the atrocities of history must be continually faced by poetry, then poems are never untrammelled from that history. What Hill names 'the tongue's atrocities' are the historical atrocities that literature must name and those from which it is inextricable.[27] In certain ways, Hill fulfils more than any other poet in *The New Poetry* the 'new seriousness' for which Alvarez calls.[28] However, he fulfils this call on quite different terms. His ardent attention to history, politics, civil society and religion places him at some distance from the sorts of psychological investigations that Alvarez champions and finds more readily in Lowell, Plath and Hughes. Hill's formal shapes are highly wrought and rely on traditional genres and metres, and so his work aligns closely with certain Movement precepts, especially if considered in the context of Donald Davie's critical writings in *Articulate Energy: An Inquiry into the Syntax of English Poetry* (1954), a highly influential study and a text often described as a Movement manifesto (a moderate one, to be sure). But Hill's work moves well beyond the Movement's scope. Similarly, Hill's poetry readily fulfils Alvarez's wishes for poetry, but also expands past their conditions. A similar claim might be made for Charles Tomlinson, who appears in Alvarez's anthology but who is much farther from its polemical nub. Tomlinson is, like Hill, both within and beyond the formations that were most influential in British poetry in the middle decades of the twentieth century.

A student of Davie's at Cambridge, Tomlinson's work resembles that of the Movement poets, but as refracted through the styles of American modernists, primarily Wallace Stevens, William Carlos Williams and Marianne Moore, as well as European and Latin American writers, especially several with whom he was close friends, such as Octavio Paz. For the most part, Tomlinson is focused on limning the external world, its textures, landscapes, vistas and materials. Diametrically opposed to Hughes, for whom the natural world indexes the bleak psyche, Tomlinson keeps his lines trained on exteriors, and a considerable portion of his large body of poetry consists of description and scenery, a project indicated by the title of his second major volume, *Seeing Is Believing* (1958). Many of his poems are occasional, comprising the records of his wide travels, and nearly all of them are guided by stable first-person speakers who recount their journeys. Tomlinson's poetry eschews the psychological storminess of Hughes or the confessional poets, but also the rhetorical and grammatical torsions endemic to Hill's work. Like the Movement poets, Tomlinson's poetry is moderate, and his poem 'Against Extremity' is both a direct rebuttal to Plath and Sexton and a broader signal of his affinities with poets like Larkin and Davie.

Tomlinson is often described as a poet in the Objectivist tradition, and his links to Williams in particular were important and enabling. However, such a comparison doesn't quite catch the degree of visual coherence of Tomlinson's poems, which are painterly in their complex arrangements of figure and ground. Nor does the comparison quite fit Tomlinson's enduring faith in the ability of language to represent adequately the world: 'Word and world rhyme / As the penstrokes might if you drew / The spaciousness reaching down through a valley view'.[29] While he adapts formal structures from Williams and several of the American modernists, his poetry is distinct for its perceptual constancy. Even when a speaker is looking at 'indistinctness', as in 'Mistlines', the poem's view is limpid:

> Watching the mistlines flow slowly in
>   And fill the land's declivities that lay
> Unseen until that indistinctness
>   Had acknowledged them, the eye
> Grasps, at a glance, the mind's own
>   Food and substance.[30]

The alternating pattern of indentation is borrowed in part from Williams, but also derives from Auden's stair-step poems, primarily 'In Praise of Limestone'. The speaker has an unimpeded view of mist entering a valley, and from that vantage point is able to make swift and sure relays ('at a glance') between the scene, the body's visual apparatus, and the brain's manipulation of visual information. 'Mistlines' goes on to query the way that the mind shapes its perceptions, but, at least at the start, nothing is beyond its ken. However, such perceptual sturdiness does not indicate a wholly imperial lyric subject. Rather than the empirical lyric 'I' favoured by Movement tenets, or Hughes's psychologically tormented speaker, or Hill's rhetorically torn subject, Tomlinson's typical 'I' is just a little beside itself. Many of his poems have the feel of free indirect discourse, as though the monologue shuttles between a first and a third person perspective. As in this passage from 'Swimming Chenango Lake', perhaps his most renowned poem, Tomlinson's lyric 'I' is frequently watching himself out of one eye while watching the world with other: 'It is a consistency, the grain of the pulsating flow. / But he has looked long enough, and now / Body must recall the eye to its dependence / As he scissors the waterscape apart / And sways to its tatters'.[31] The initial line replicates its referent – water – by repeatedly overflowing its terms of reference, from *grain* to *pulse* to *flow*, each of which might be said to model quite different forms of 'consistency'. Building upon these subtle estrangements, the next lines turn their gaze inward, watching the swimming protagonist who, considering the intimacy of the perspective and the outlines of the experience described, must also be the speaker. In a reversal of the effortless perceptual relays inscribed in 'Mistlines', the body here has to re-view itself in the water, objectifying its act of looking and then transferring its energy from vision to movement. Along with Christopher Middleton, Michael Hoffman and Hughes himself, Tomlinson is one of the key translators among post-war British poets, and we might say that this passage offers a different sort of translation, from the water's incessant mutability to the body's shifting form. Remaining largely within an aesthetic and stylistic compass that aligns both with the Movement and those figures just beyond it, Tomlinson infuses a subtle phenomenological inquiry into his pictorial verse.

For a more far-reaching and decisive poetic investigation of the paths of perception and the routes of mental and bodily knowledge, we can turn to the work of Roy Fisher. Like Tomlinson, Fisher is indebted to Williams as well as to a range of American poets, and just as Williams is celebrated for *Paterson*, his multi-part poem about a town near his home in New Jersey, so is Fisher best known for writing about his own home city, Birmingham. Beginning with the alternating verse and prose sequence, *City* (1961), and continuing through and beyond his later masterpiece, *A Furnace* (1986), Birmingham has been at the centre of Fisher's work. As he writes in 'Texts for a Film' (1991), 'Birmingham's what I think with'.[32] At the centre of his poetic project is an attempt to map the interface between an individual and the urban environment. His poems are about particular places, but – more importantly – they set themselves in the limen between the concrete realities of a place and the individual subject's experience within that place. Peter

Barry's essay in this volume considers more fully Fisher's urban and suburban poetics, and here I will focus on Fisher's work of as a model of post-war English poetry that largely escapes the dominant terms of the field's unfolding. Neither represented in Alvarez's anthology, nor amenable to his terms, Fisher's forms range widely, from the loco-descriptive poems of *City* to the oddly surreal prose sequence, *A Ship's Orchestra* (1962–63), to the cut-up and collage work in *The Cut Pages* (1970). Toggling between traditional lyric stances and experimental modes, his substantial body of work exhibits a thoroughgoing heterogeneity, a capaciousness encapsulated in one of the *The Cut Pages*' isolated lines: 'there is no process. There are many changes'.[33]

Another line from *The Cut Pages* can serve as both a primer for understanding the compositional structure of that work and as an account of his poetry as a whole. The entirety of the line reads: 'Tumbled. Strewn. Built. Grown. Allowed'.[34] It catches the broader feel of Fisher's project, its simultaneous spontaneity ('Tumbled. Strewn') and constructedness ('Built. Grown'). The primary structural means by which Fisher achieves his multivalent forms is modularity. Fisher's poems most frequently unfold as an accretion of instants, most frequently juxtaposing short passages of visual attention and perceptual process, but rarely subordinating them within an overarching design. In this sense, we might use the final term in the above quotation ('Allowed') to understand the freedoms inherent to Fisher's compositions. Such formal openness affords a mobile and rangy process of reception, wherein a reader at once encounters 'shaggy fragments sailing out of the background' and is able to locate connections between such fragments, which are both discrete and, as Fisher phrases it in 'Matrix', 'inseparable, interfolded'.[35]

The opening passage from Fisher's 'Glenthorne Poems' can help to concretize the texture of Fisher's phenomenological descriptions: 'Straight into the sea fog / the descent / drops / red track / with sudden angles / turn below turn / into the white'.[36] Compared to Tomlinson's 'Mistlines', Fisher's vista is radically de-centred. The short lines tumble downward, tracking the eye as it seeks to follow the wash of fog, sea and wave. The passage provides neither setting nor speaker, and any line of sight that appears is fleeting and detached from a perceptual locus. Rather than a coherent speaker or 'I', Fisher's poems provide zones of perception and phenomenological response that are leveraged by what John Kerrigan calls 'a receptiveness fed by detachment'.[37] In a brief poem titled 'It Is Writing', Fisher declares, 'I mistrust the poem in its hour of success', and a good deal of his formal project is committed to sustaining a poem's processual momentum while remaining attuned to the material and social realities of the world.[38]

The major instance of this project is his book-length poem, *A Furnace* (1986), which is one of the central long poems in the modern British canon, a late entry in a line that includes T. S. Eliot's *The Waste Land* (1922), David Jones's *The Anathémata* (1952) and Basil Bunting's *Briggflatts* (1966). As with much of his work, *A Furnace* takes place primarily in Birmingham and environs, as he suggests in his 'Preface': 'I have, indeed, set one landscape to work with another in this poem, more by way of superimposition than comparison: Birmingham, where I was born in a district that had not long since been annexed from the southern edge of the old county of Staffordshire, and the stretch of hill country around the northern tip of the same county where I have been living recently; about the same size as Birmingham, and, in its way, equally complex'.[39] Unlike many of Fisher's poems, *A Furnace* also has a global reach, and over the course of its seven sections it moves beyond Staffordshire and touches down briefly in Wales, Brittany, Paris, the Orkneys, Trier in Germany (Marx's birthplace) and, finally, Ampurias, an ancient Greek town on the Catalan coast.

A Furnace is a dense and compendious poem, what Fisher describes as 'an engine devised, like a cauldron, or a still, or a blast-furnace, to invoke and assist natural processes of change; to persuade obstinate substances to alter their condition and show relativities which would otherwise remain hidden by their concreteness'.[40] It is heavily visual, but compounded into Fisher's typical descriptions and oblique emplacements are broader considerations of industrial history, economics and politics, both within the specific context of Birmingham and more widely conceived. Fisher spends substantial time in the poem critiquing the politics of contemporary England and the conditions of late capitalism generally, and on the whole *A Furnace* is a deeply materialist poem, in nearly every sense of that word. It is also, at certain moments and from certain angles, a gothic text, a large-scale elegy, and an occasionally mystical and science-fictional text that draws on the idiosyncratic vision of its dedicatee, John Cowper Powys. Clair Wills offers a concise description of the poem's double impulse: '*A Furnace* straddles the dividing line between world as a place of mystery (the domain of fetishes, folklore and religion) and world as a set of processes to be explained (the domain of realism, enlightenment and natural science)'.[41]

As is clear, *A Furnace* is a difficult and many-minded text, and anything like a full reading of it is well out of my scope here. It moves constantly between descriptive passages, second-order reflections on the conditions of perception and description, more abstract philosophical speculations and moments that verge on the mystical or supernatural. But this passage from the opening section, titled 'Introit' and dated '12 November 1958', indicates the text's basic mechanism: 'Whatever / approaches my passive taking-in, / then surrounds me and goes by / will have itself understood only / phase upon phase / by separate involuntary / strokes of my mind'.[42] The 'Introit' describes a commute by trolley in mid-century Birmingham, and sets in motion the poem's tendency to spiral between perception, observation, reflection and abstraction.[43] *A Furnace* condenses empirical and phenomenological impulses, while simultaneously digging deeply into the material conditions of late twentieth-century England. It also provides a rich and sceptical investigation into the ideologies of myth and history. Finally, *A Furnace* continually seeks to move beyond its own conditions, a feature of the poem most powerfully seen in its strange and stunning conclusion, which concentrates on the so-called 'snails of Ampurias' as they ascend the ruins of the town and 'infest / the wild fennel / that infests the verges of the road'.[44] The snails become Fisher's final emblem of transformative spiralling, with the concluding lines describing their quasi-religious ascension as they 'rasp[] their way round / together, and upward; tight and seraphic'.[45] In quite a number of ways, however, this concluding image, for all of its strange luminosity, exceeds the poem's overall terms. The final module in a complex mesh of lyric writing, the snail passage that ends *A Furnace* is connected to the rest of the poem mainly by way of a loose association. The text's primary materials and geographical coordinates are abandoned in this oddly one-off moment on the coast of the Mediterranean. We might read this concluding moment as a deliberate act of counter-programming on Fisher's part. Instead of his typical themes and textures, we get a finale that compounds, one might say, the styles or concerns of the three poets who have preceded him in this essay: the creaturely (Hughes), the attention to distant places (Tomlinson), and the religious (Hill). While such a reading is much too neat to stand, it does give a sense in which Fisher's poetry – and *A Furnace* in particular – indexes the formal and substantive possibilities at work in British poetry in the middle and latter decades of the twentieth century, even as the concluding gambit of his long poem escapes its orbit.

I have spent much of this essay refashioning Alvarez's quite generative phrase – 'beyond all this fiddle' – in order to account for several key patterns in post-war British poetry. Alvarez shows what is beyond the Movement. Hill and Tomlinson show what exceeds Alvarez's introductory argument but remains within the orbit of his anthological reach. And Fisher shows a kind of poetry emerging in the 1960s that was beyond both Alvarez's polemic and the terms of his intervention. Much remains outside of this essay's own ken, but will come into view in subsequent chapters: the vitalization of performance poetry in the 1960s; the broad impact of post-war American poetry in Britain – especially as presented in Donald Allen's *The New American Poetry* (1960) – beyond the small cache of figures favoured by Alvarez;

and the importance of the activities and innovations that emerged from the British Poetry Revival. Other aspects of British poetry from the 1950s through 1970s remain occluded or still just beyond our view. As Andrew Duncan and others have shown, our overall literary-historical picture of British poetry in the several decades after the end of the war still has a number of blind spots. It is crucial, then, to move beyond the terms established by Conquest and Alvarez, which, although more than half a century old, still have sway. What I have aimed to provide here, albeit quite briefly, are several interpretive paths that we might take in order to rebuff, or at least disrupt, a narrow literary history that presents the period as merely toggling between two versions of the mainstream, most readily emblematized by the figures of Larkin and Hughes. Much remains to see beyond that partial vista.

NOTES

1 A. Alvarez, 'The New Poetry, *or* Beyond the Gentility Principle', *The New Poetry*, rev. ed. (London: Penguin Books, 1966), pp. 21–32, at 21.
2 Ibid., p. 23.
3 Ibid., pp. 24–25.
4 Ibid., p. 30.
5 Ibid., p. 32.
6 A. Alvarez, *Beyond All This Fiddle: Essays 1955–1967* (London: Allen Lane, The Penguin Press, 1968), p. 21.
7 Ibid., p. 21.
8 Ibid., pp. 5–6.
9 Alvarez, *The New Poetry*, p. 17.
10 Ibid., p. 17.
11 Ibid., p. 18.
12 Ted Hughes, *Collected Poems*, ed. Paul Keegan (New York: Farrar, Straus and Giroux, 2003), p. 67.
13 Ibid., p. 88.
14 Ibid., p. 19.
15 Ibid., p. 19.
16 Ibid., p. 19.
17 Ibid., p. 19.
18 Ibid., p. 21.
19 Ibid., p. 85.
20 Ibid., p. 85.
21 Ibid., p. 85.
22 Ibid., p. 85.
23 Ibid., pp. 85–86.
24 Geoffrey Hill, *Broken Hierarchies: Poems 1952–2012*, ed. Kenneth Haynes (Oxford: Oxford University Press, 2013), p. 13.
25 Ibid., p. 54.
26 Ibid., pp. 28, 102.
27 Ibid., p. 61.

28 Alvarez, *The New Poetry*, p. 28.
29 Charles Tomlinson, *New Collected Poems* (Manchester: Carcanet Press, 2009), p. 299.
30 Ibid., p. 245.
31 Ibid., p. 159.
32 Roy Fisher, *The Long and the Short of It: Poems 1955–2005* (Northumberland: Bloodaxe Books, 2005), p. 285.
33 Fisher, *The Long and the Short of It*, p. 102.
34 Ibid., p. 89.
35 Ibid., pp. 93, 280.
36 Ibid., p. 295.
37 John Kerrigan, 'Roy Fisher on Location', in John Kerrigan and Peter Robinson (eds.), *The Thing About Roy Fisher: Critical Studies* (Liverpool: Liverpool University Press, 2000), pp. 16–46, at 39.
38 Fisher, *The Long and the Short of It*, p. 221.
39 Roy Fisher, *A Furnace* (Oxford: Oxford University Press, 1986), p. vii. This preface is not reprinted in Fisher's 1996 selected volume, *The Dow Low Drop*, nor in his 2005 collected volume.
40 Ibid., pp. vii–viii.
41 Clair Wills, '*A Furnace* and the Life of the Dead', in *The Thing about Roy Fisher: Critical Studies*, pp. 257–74, at 273.
42 Fisher, *The Long and the Short of It*, p. 52.
43 In his original preface to *A Furnace*, Fisher describes the text's structure as spiral-like, and an image of a spiral appears on the cover of the 1986 Oxford University Press edition.
44 Fisher, *The Long and the Short of It*, p. 85.
45 Ibid., p. 85.

5

CORNELIA GRÄBNER

Poetry and Performance: The Mersey Poets, the International Poetry Incarnation and Performance Poetry

The public reception of poetry in Britain – as in many other countries of the Global North – has always relied on diverse media. Poetry performances were crucial to folk and oral traditions, and often intersected and intermingled with music. Recitals of written or printed poets were important ways of sharing poetry in a collective setting throughout the nineteenth and twentieth century. In the early twentieth century, the availability of new technologies led poets and artists to experiment with the intermedial potential of poetry, including its visual and its sonic dimensions, often during specifically organized events. In the post-war period, during the 1950s and 1960s, another major shift occurred in the ways in which poetry was shared and performed publicly. During that time, existing cultural hierarchies were questioned by broad sectors of the population, and poetry was once again transformed, this time alongside the emerging British counterculture. Out of this process, which starts in the early 1960s and lasts into the 1970s, emerged the currents we today call 'performance poetry'.[1]

Poetry, art and music were crucial to British counterculture in the 1950s and 1960s and to what Andrew Wilson has referred to as its 'poetics of dissent'. Poetry and art were considered potential agents for cultural transformation at a time when neither the state nor grassroots activism seemed to hold the potential for social and political transformation. In the early 1960s it had become clear that as far as the government was concerned, 'any serious attempt to reformulate the relationship of class, value, and culture was passed up in favor of a model of good culture, which meant, in practice a middle-class "high culture"'.[2] Anyone who wanted to profoundly change cultural hierarchies or who wished to express themselves in ways that deviated from the 'good culture' that informed governmental cultural policy, realised that they would have to do this without support from the state and probably, in opposition to it. As a result, autonomous spaces like pirate radio, art galleries, clubs, magazines and bookshops became home to rich and diverse forms of expression in performance art, music and poetry.[3] Moreover, grassroots activism was for many no longer the force that could achieve such a transformation. For artists like Jeff Nuttall, who eventually participated in the 'Poetry Incarnation', this was exemplified in the disintegration of the Campaign for Nuclear Disarmament (CND) and the Aldermaston marches; because grassroots activism could not replace or transform institutionalized political power, former activists decided that culture and forms of expression had to change before institutionalized politics could.[4] Related to this was the international outlook of many performance poets; they looked to the United States for inspiration and conceptualized their own poetics and poetic identity in relation to like-minded individuals and communities in other parts of the Western world. As a result, the emerging scenes in Britain – such as the Liverpool scene, the London Underground or the community that formed around Michael Horovitz's *New Departures* – were locally or regionally based but, importantly, had an international outlook and were often transnationally connected with like-minded communities.

The poetry performance turned out to be a great medium for those who wanted to involve poetry and poetic language into a project of cultural change and transformation. This is due to its five main characteristics, which I will briefly conceptualise so that we can then see them at work of the Mersey poets and in the 'London Poetry Incarnation'. The first characteristic of the poetry performance is its intermediality. Intermediality may involve the interaction of spoken word and music, of voice and musical instruments and the interaction of language patterns that come from conversational speech, with language patterns akin to recitation or oratory; it can draw on the poet's style of dress, body language, pitch of voice and pace of speech, the words of the poem, sounds from or referring to the location, non-verbal sounds, visuals, movement or interventions of the audience. Importantly, the poetry performance interweaves or layers such different elements of signification. Layers of signification can be important to the second element of the poetry performance, the staging of authorship.[5] Different styles of dress can situate the poet within certain communities, or outside of them; the use of the vernacular can emphasize the poet's background or loyalty to a community or class. Poets speaking their own words publicly can be understood as their taking public responsibility for their experience and their way of expressing it, a powerful example being Allen Ginsberg with *Howl*; or the poet can become the spokesperson for a community. The poet can also perform or act in a way that purposefully disconcerts or offends an audience or questions its expectations, as we will see in the examples of Adrian Mitchell's and Gregory Corso's performances at the 'Poetry Incarnation'. In these cases the public performance of authorship can be one way of exploring how the authority of voice is constituted, how poetic public speech is listened and responded to, or which poetic identities are unacceptable or incomprehensible to specific audiences.

The performance of authorship is closely related to the third element of performance poetry, the intersubjective processes that unfold during the performance and the communitarian processes that precede it or of which the poetry performance is a part. Intersubjective processes refer to the ways in which poet and audience members connect or disconnect through the performed poetry. Communitarian processes refer to the ways in which the poetry performance embeds the poem and the author within a community, and they are often – though not always – linked to the relationship between the poetry performance and place. 'Place' can refer to a venue, or to a locally defined community. The dynamics of a poetry performance will differ significantly depending on whether the poets are familiar and comfortable with the venue, or not; whether the venue intervenes through sounds or interruptions, as often happens in bars, cafés or open-air locations, or whether it is a venue that shuts out disturbances. As we will see with regards to the city of Liverpool, place can become a constitutive part of performance poetry for the ways in which elements of its topography or sociality are present in the poetic language, and for the ways in which cultural identities can inform poetic identities.

The fifth characteristic of the poetry performance concerns a collective reflection on poetry itself. Gaston Franssen has theorised this as a 'staging of poeticity'. With this he refers to performed poetry which contradicts and deconstructs existing expectations of what constitutes 'poetry' or 'poetic', and it is this staging of poeticity that, according to Franssen, distinguishes performance poetry from other forms of public poetry recitals which draw on the tradition of oratory.[6] The staging of poeticity spills over from the performance as event into the communitarian processes that surround it. For this reason the 'reproductive labour' carried out by cultural organisers is vital to this element of performance poetry because it is often the work of cultural organisers that articulates new frameworks of reference through which deconstructions of existing expectations can be understood, responded to and built upon.

In what follows I will focus on two very different examples of 1960s performance poetry, the Mersey Poets and the International Poetry Incarnation in London. The work of the Mersey Poets exemplifies performance poetry that emerges alongside music and art and as part of a 'scene'; the 'Poetry Incarnation' exemplifies a large-scale collective poetry event that brings together poets from many different project, and then congeals them into a new 'scene', the London Underground.

'To Create an Environment of One's Own': The Liverpool Poets

The 'Liverpool scene' of the 1960s brought together art, poetry and music on equal footing. Coffee houses, bars and clubs provided autonomous and semi-autonomous spaces for regular or one-off poetry performances and readings, the format of many of which was modelled on one-night acts of musicians or the collective performances of bands. Among the core poetry performers and cultural organizers were Adrian Henri, Roger McGough and Brian Patten. Patten edited the magazine *Underdog* which published poems by Allen Ginsberg, Robert Creeley and Gregory Corso, as well as works by poets from Liverpool. Henri was inspired by the U.S. American performance artist Robert Kaprow. He assembled a group of musicians, poets and painters – among them John Gorman, Roger McGough, Andy Roberts, Mike Hart and Mike McCartney – and organized 'events': 'a mixture of poetry, rock'n'roll and assemblage'.[7] The events premiered in 1962 and 1963 at the Merseyside Arts Festival but quickly became popular across town. Members of the core group then formed the groups *Scaffold* and *The Liverpool Scene*, which released five albums. 1967 saw the publication of three books emerging from the Liverpool scene: Henri's poetry collection *Tonight at Noon*, the best-selling anthology of Henri, McGough and Patten's poetry entitled *The Mersey Sound* which was part of Penguin's well-respected Modern Poets Series, and Edward Lucie-Smith's *The Liverpool Scene*. Lucie-Smith responded from a critical and theoretical perspective to the interaction of layers of signification in performance poetry, by interspersing poems with photographs of the poets, their surroundings and quotations from 'rambling conversations with the machine [tape recorder]', in an attempt 'to establish a kind of texture, both social and verbal, in which the poems take, quite naturally, the predominant place'.[8]

Lucie-Smith's metaphor of a 'texture' emphasizes that the poetics of the Liverpool poets are stitched into the physical, social and cultural context of 'Liverpool', understood as a geographical location as well as a social construct and a cultural identity. The poets maintain a relationship of mutual nurture with both, and this relationship has important implications for their performance of authorship, and their poetic imaginaries and languages. Authorship is always performed in critical loyalty with their environment and its people. This is challenging because, as Murphy and Rees-Jones have pointed out, 'While other cities celebrate the writer as a dissident voice, such dissent in Liverpool is often regarded as a betrayal of class and family. To write is to "get above yourself": it's to break rank, think yourself better than you are. It is to become one of Them instead of Us'.[9] The Liverpool poets respond to this challenge with an ethos that Richard Craig in *New*

Formations has described as a 'fellow-feeling between author and other people',[10] and which Lucie-Smith called 'a real sympathy for their environment, but an even greater loyalty'.[11] This 'fellow feeling' is expressed in the title of *Underdog*, which Stan Smith interprets as a reference to 'the excluded majority who had failed to "make it" to the elite grammar or technical schools' and became known as underdogs,[12] and in the ways in which the speakers of their poem are always embedded in an environment or a community, even when they struggle with it. The implications of this nurturing and loyal relationship for the poets' poetic imagination is expressed by Adrian Henri, when he celebrates that in Liverpool, 'Art could go into the streets, be a political act, take away the barrier between fantasy and reality, affect the quality of daily life, seek inspiration from humble and despised objects, create an environment of its own'.[13] These implications are also expressed in the quiet awareness of 'fragility and transience'[14] of the poems collected in *The Mersey Sound*, which resonates with working class and immigrant populations' experience that they will be the first to be sacrificed during the next political crisis or economic downturn; and in the poets' irreverence towards authorities put in place by somebody else: 'We've got no literary or dramatic heritage. We try out what we're doing, and we test it on people, and people react, and we sort of go on from there. We haven't got people to bow down to'.[15]

The Liverpool poets interweave authorship, place, intersubjectivity, intermediality and poeticity so closely that the listener has to trace each of these threads within the complete texture of the poem, rather than unmaking that texture. I will explore this through a brief analysis of Adrian Henri's poem 'The Entry of Christ into Liverpool'. This poem exists as a textual poem with authorship ascribed to Henri, as a song-poem released under the collective authorship of the Liverpool Scene, and as a painting signed by Henri. The poem is set in the streets of Liverpool and chronicles a walk through the city on a Saturday. Speaker and listener set out in the morning up on the hill and in a side street, they then walk to the city centre where they are drawn into a carnivalesque crowd, and they then walk home in the evening. The sonic, visual and tactile environment is revealed gradually, evoking the pace of the speaker and the listener's traversal of the city. The arrangement of the typeface on the page captures pauses in the enunciation of the poem, changes in rhythm and pace, and shifts in the interaction between spoken word and music. The first and last stanza, which frame the events referred to in the poem, are left-aligned; the middle part of the poem is centred. The first stanza – enunciated a cappella on the recording – evokes the environment of the area in which listener and speaker start out: 'City morning. dandelionseeds blowing from wasteground. / smell of overgrown privethedges. children's voices / in the distance. sounds from the river'.[16] The dandelion seeds, the waste grounds and the overgrown privet hedges emphasize the humble setting, and the appeal to smell and sound locates speaker and listener within the environment. The speaker then takes the listener around the corner into Myrtle Street and down the hill into the city centre, which provides rich sensory stimulation. The centred and capitalised typescript and the onset of music on the LP version initiate an intense visual, aural and tactile experience, initially on the outskirts of the procession – signalled by the textual reference to the sounds of trumpets, of cheering and of shouting heard from a distance – and then, in the following stanza, as part of the crowd. The perspective focuses on the textual equivalent of a visual close-up of masked individuals, and of a physical close-up expressed through awareness of their smell: 'hideous masked Breughel faces of old ladies in the crowd / yellow masks of girls in curlers and headscarves / smelling of factories'. The references to physical contact with strangers intensifies the tactile experience of being part of the crowd, and it is within the visual and the tactile that the speaker verbally manifest his subjectivity through an (albeit indirect) pronoun: 'red masks purple masks pink masks / crushing surging carrying me along'.

Authorship is performed in an understated manner which acknowledges voice and subjectivity without placing the individual centre-stage. The 'me' emerges from and merges into the intersubjective and communitarian processes that take place on three different levels: between the speaker and the listener, among the crowd of which the speaker is a part, and between words and music. Firstly, the speaker assumes the role of guide and guardian of the listener, who trustingly relinquishes control to the speaker. The anonymity of the sound recording intensifies this process because we can hear the speaker's voice but we cannot see him; and at the same time our perception and orientation completely depend on what he tells us. Secondly, the speaker entrusts himself to the crowd which carries him. The trust is part of a mutually reciprocated, typically urban complicity in which people keep each other safe, even when they are strangers encountering one another by chance. This is given a sharp edge by the views expressed on some of the banners described by the speaker: 'Keep Britain White / End the War in Vietnam / God Bless Our Pope'. Those indicate that the conviviality *among* the crowd is not necessarily harmonious and holds potential for conflict and clashes. At this point it also becomes obvious that the speaker is not only male, but most probably white and assumes that the listener can accommodate to his perspective – otherwise he would be more careful about exposing the listener to people who want to keep Britain white. Thirdly, voice and music are engaged in a process of mutually listening to each other. The rhythm of the music synchronises with the pace of enunciation and with the implied pace of the walkers, and pitch and tone of voice constantly interact with the music. In the last stanza, these three levels of intersubjective and communitarian processes quietly fade into a verbal sketch of one of those unspectacularly spectacular northern skies ('thin sickle moon / pale blue sky / flecked with bright orange clouds') and a quietly spoken, a cappella evocation of what it feels like to walk the streets alone at the end of a busy day: 'me / walking home / empty chip-papers drifting round my feet'.[17]

Like those of Henri, the works of McGough and Patten take inspiration from what the establishment disdained and despised, and engage with it without wishing to 'elevate' it. They frequently evoke carnivalesque, transgressive and 'upside-down' situations, and de-link urban everyday life from a 'normality' determined by the status quo. Their autonomous stance towards the literary establishment, cultural hierarchies and poetic conventions got them contempt from some; others, like the editors of the Penguin Modern Poets series, wished to give national recognition to the three poets and their 'sound'. But in so doing, Penguin shoved a poetic licence on the poets that they had consciously decided not to ask for. On the symbolic level this has opened the door to a process that Stan Smith, in an analysis of Brian Patten's more recent work, describes as 'cultural dispossession'. He locates the beginning of this process with the publication of *The Mersey Sound*, a poetry collection, which as he notes, "raised questions about the ultimate ownership of a local identity appropriated and marketed as a commodity, a people's culture cashed in as "pop culture"'.[18] Respondents to performance poetry still need to build ways of appreciating the poetry of those who choose not to comply, who choose to remain autonomous; in other words, of respecting the difference of the environment that they have created.

The International Poetry Incarnation

The 'International Poetry Incarnation' was organized in London by an internationally minded community of artists, cultural organizers and writers who knew each other and shared mutual understandings and appreciations of poetry and art, but had not yet congealed into a 'scene'. They had so far assembled around Alexander Trocchi's project Sigma, and around the bookshop Better Books. Then, in June 1965, a visit by Allen Ginsberg to London provided the opportunity for an 'incarnation' of these connections. Brian Mills in *London Calling* describes how, during an informal gathering after a reading at Better Books the idea was mooted to organize a poetry event with Ginsberg, as well as Lawrence Ferlinghetti and Gregory Corso, who were also in Europe. The U.S. American film director and cultural organizer Barbara

Rubin asked which was the biggest venue for hire and, upon hearing that it was the Royal Albert Hall, picked up the phone and reserved it for a night two weeks ahead. A 'Poet's Cooperative' consisting of John Esam, Dan Richter, Jill Richter, Michael Horovitz and Alexander Trocchi was formed and put in charge of organising this event. Over the following days, a group of poets collectively created a manifesto. John Hopkins took publicity photographs and managed to attract the interest of mainstream newspapers, and the BBC interviewed Ginsberg before he headed up north for a visit to Liverpool.[19]

The 'International Poetry Incarnation' took place on 11 June 1965. It featured Pete Brown, Gregory Corso, John Esam, Harry Fainlight, Lawrence Ferlinghetti, Allen Ginsberg, Spike Hawkins, Anselm Hollo, Michael Horovitz, Ernst Jandl, Paul Leonni, Christopher Logue, George Macbeth, Tom McGrath, Adrian Mitchell, Daniel Richter, Alexander Trocchi and Simon Vinkenoog. They performed their poetry before an audience of 7,000 people in a sold-out venue. The event was recorded by the BBC, and thirty-three minutes of it were preserved by Peter Whitehead in his documentary film *Wholly Communion*.[20] The intermedial concept included folk music played by Davy Graham, papier-mâché robots created by Bruce Lacey, a taped reading by William Burroughs and a happening to be carried out by Jeff Nuttall and John Latham.

The poetry performances themselves mostly gravitated around the question of 'what it means to be a poet' (Middleton). The performances of authorship indicate diverse views on this matter, and I will here refer to just a few. Many of the U.S. American poets performed unity of the author and the speaking voice in the poem. The event started out with a performance by Lawrence Ferlinghetti, who projected his poetry into the audience in the style of Charles Olson's 'Projective Verse', and confidently and humorously challenged and ridiculed social conventions and political authorities. Gregory Corso was less accommodating of the audience's expectations. Daniel Kane argues that through Corso's choice of clothing (a blazer) and his body language (he sat down as he recited), he enacted a critique of the 'easily replicated antiestablishment postures' of some of the poets present. Kane also notes that Corso's thick New York working class accent contrasted with the Oxford English accent of the poet who had performed just before him, and I would add that the environment of the Royal Albert Hall exacerbated this effect. Moreover, Corso did not project his voice into the audience but instead challenged the audience to accompany him on an emotionally complex and experientially liminal internal journey through his poem 'Mutations of the Spirit'.[21] Corso's performance can be interpreted as subtly reminding the audience that the American poets in the room were descendants of those who had left behind the injustices and constraints of racist and classist Europe, or who had been forced or compelled to leave, and that his performance was no homecoming on the terms of those who had stayed.

Harry Fainlight also violated the expectations for the performance of authorship, though he did so unintentionally. He read his poem 'The Spider', about a bad LSD trip in New York. Though Fainlight's nervous and self-conscious performance style was appropriate to the subject matter, it did not recommend him as a guide for a transgressive journey into what was to many audience members an unfamiliar and unknown experience. Moreover, Simon Vinkenoog (who had taken mescaline before the event) responded to themes such as lack of connectivity and inner turmoil by interrupting the poem with repeated and insistent chants of 'Love!Love! Love!' This caused commotion in the audience, and Fainlight's performance fizzled out into an altercation between himself and master of ceremonies Trocchi. The comparison between Corso's and Fainlight's performances shows that expectations can be violated if done in an authoritative way; a shy performance, in contrast, is considered unacceptable even when it is appropriate to the subject matter.

Adrian Mitchell in his performance of 'To Whom It May Concern' occupies the space of the live poetry performance to appeal to the audience's ability to critique. The title of the poem enacts what Jonathan Culler has termed 'the search for a You' by inviting the audience members to constitute themselves as 'concerned'. However, Mitchell makes it impossible for them to express their 'concern' by identification with the poem's lyric, or the author. The lyric I immerses himself ever deeper into a denial of the terrible news about the Vietnam War, engaging into increasingly long-winded excuses for his own disengagement and self-deception. Mitchell himself clearly does not identify with the poem's speaker but, at the same time, does not provide an alternative stance that audience members could adopt. Thus, the audience members, if they are truly concerned, have to renounce the process of identification and 'communion' that is so often expected from a poetry performance and instead think critically and find their own solution to the staged dilemma.

Both Brian Mills and Andrew Wilson, from different analytical perspectives, identify the 'Poetry Incarnation' as a cataclysmic event for the emergence of the London Underground. The live event created a space and a stance in which people could recognize their affinities, and people then acted on this recognition.[22] Hopkins and Mills set up Lovebooks Limited, which specialised in poetry magazines and spoken word records and became the first British publisher dedicated specifically to what later came to be called 'performance poetry'. Better Books continued to provide and create spaces for poetry readings and performances under the management of Bob Cobbing, who eventually founded the mimeograph poetry publisher Writers' Forum. Brian Mills left Better Books and founded Indica Gallery. Michael Horovitz, one of the main organizers of the 'Poetry Incarnation' and a participating poet, preserved some of the poetry in print in the anthology *Children of Albion* (1969), which also included poems from other poets – men and women – associated with the 'London Underground'. Over the following decades, London became one of the best-organised centres of performance poetry in the United Kingdom with a variety of state-sponsored, corporate and autonomous spaces, and with organisations like the Poetry Café or Apples and Snakes, which have organised a wide range of poetry performances.

Listening Differently: Opportunities Passed Up and Taken On

Performance poetry has opened up new spaces for a performative exploration of the speaking subject, and the focus on the poet's self-expression has increased the capacity of audiences to hear and understand liminal or deviant poetic languages. However, the importance of silences and of listening have not been fostered with quite the same dedication, though these are crucial to the fifth characteristic of the poetry performance, the critical engagement with staged poeticity. During the performance the audience spends much time in the equivalent of what Tillie Olsen described as 'natural silences', 'that necessary time for renewal, lying fallow, gestation, in the natural cycle of creation' and, I would add, for finding the appropriate response to what has not been said before quite in this way.[23] Moreover, during collective events poets listen to other poets, and good performers are attentive to the inarticulate, intangible shifts of energy among their listeners. However, when listeners pass up the opportunity of listening differently during the natural silences of the performance, the resulting lack of response creates 'unnatural silences', which are the result of 'the unnatural thwarting of what struggles to come into being, but cannot'.[24] One such silence is the absence of women's voices from the two case studies discussed above.

Libby Houston – together with Frances Horovitz, Anna Lovell, Tina Morris and Carlyle Reedy – is one of the few women whose poetry was included in *Children of Albion*, and the only woman to perform regularly in the 1960s with the male poets associated with the 'Poetry Incarnation'. Her first poetry collection *A Stained Glass Raree Show* was published in 1967, the same year as *The Mersey Sound*, *The Liverpool Scene* and Henri's first poetry collection. Her reflections on the 1960s and 1970s in her essay 'On Being a Woman Poet' are permeated by the sense that even though she spoke and wrote, her poetic voice got lost in the black holes of nonresponse or negative response. The first instance in which her voice gets lost is related to the intersections of class and gender. Houston was brought up in a middle-class family, and her desire to write and to be a public figure was encouraged from an early age. She then went to Oxford, where the opportunity to study Anglo-Saxon poetry gave her a profound appreciation for oral poetry, especially pace, which, as she points out, 'is almost impossible to indicate in print'.[25] However, in her male-dominated poetic environment, a middle-class background was frowned upon, and her male companions did not seem to understand that for many women, higher education was not necessarily a way of accessing the equivalent of male or class privilege, but the only way of accessing knowledge and understanding that would have otherwise been foreclosed to them because of their gender. As a result, Houston herself took a long time to embrace what had nurtured her poetic voice and sensibility. Secondly, Houston's poetic sensibility was inextricably linked to the experiences of child-rearing, social isolation and living on a council estate where many people did not speak English. The traces of her lived experiences in her poetic language were met with what Claire Buck has described as a social and cultural 'hostility to women's experience'.[26] This manifested itself in the academic and critical dismissal and denigration of her use of style, of pace and of the rhythm and poeticity of the non-hierarchical conversational speech (often maligned as 'chattiness') characteristic of storytelling and often located in the intimacy of private spaces. During the 1970s women poets started to build their own, autonomous structures to create other listening spaces, often focusing on the experimental dimensions of language and, in so doing, tackling the underpinnings of the dismissal and disdain.[27] Linda McKinnahan has discussed the work of some of them – Caroline Bergvall, Hazel Smith, Geraldine Monk, Paula Claire, Denise Riley, Maggie O'Sullivan – specifically in the context of experimental poetry.

Since the 1990s especially, the importance of authorship has been emphasised in the ways in which performance poetry has been conceptualised, understood and marketed. Across the Western world this has led to a shift away from the communitarian and intersubjective processes in poetry performances, towards a consumer-orientated celebration of individualistic authorship. At the same time, many dedicated smaller spaces – Apples & Snakes in London, the Contact Theatre in Manchester, the Bluecoat in Liverpool, to mention only a few – have been working hard at maintaining the socially engaged dimension of performance poetry while also encouraging its experimental dimensions. Some poets who started to perform in the 1960s – Libby Houston, Pete Brown, the late Adrian Mitchell and

Adrian Henri – have worked actively with community projects and with children, thus preserving the spirit of performance poetry as an art form that does not take for granted what it means to be a poet, that is committed to open-mindedness and curiosity about poetic languages and about the type of poetic expression that emerges from liminal, deviant or unusual experiences, and that does not impose poetry and poetic language on a social or spatial environment but explores them – and sometimes, creates them – within an environment.

NOTES

1 I have elsewhere argued that performance poetry draws on four strands or currents. One originates from the avant-garde of the 1920s and 1930s, especially Surrealism and Dadaism; one builds on the folk and oral tradition; one emerges from the cultural encounter between the (often oral) cultures of immigrant populations and the Western poetic tradition and the fourth is countercultural. Those four currents, despite their differences, share their opposition to the imposition of a hegemonic Western poetic tradition, and their appreciation of a diversity of oral and written poetic cultures. See Cornelia Gräbner, 'Public Poetry Performances of the 1970s and 1980s: Reconsiderations of Poetic Licence', Margalida Pons, ed., *Lírica i deslírica. Anàlisis i propostes de la poesia d'experimentació* (Palma de Mallorca: University of the Balearic Islands Press, 2012).

2 Claire Buck, 'Poetry and the Women's Movement in Britain', James Acheson and Romana Huck, eds., *Contemporary British Poetry: Essays in Theory and Criticism* (New York: State University of New York Press, 1996), p. 101.

3 In *London Calling: Countercultural History of London*, Brian Mills traces the emergence of pirate radio, art galleries, journals and *zines*, clubs and, importantly, bookshops like Better Books. Mark Donnelly highlights the importance of this alternative cultural infrastructure, including 'small, cheap, and experimental' literary magazines that were edited across the country: *New Departure* (edited by Michael Horovitz in Oxford), *Migrant* (Gael Turnbull and Michael Shayer, Worcester), *Tree* (Brian Miles, Cheltenham), *Poetmeat* (Dave Cunliffe, Blackpool), *Underdog* (Liverpool), *Sidewalk* (Edinburgh) and *Outburst* (London). Better Books maintained close links with the City Lights bookshop in San Francisco, which included a barter arrangement in which Better Books sent old Penguin titles and received in return publications from City Lights. Individuals, journals and books travelled across the Atlantic.

4 Jeff Nuttall makes this point, and elaborates on it, in *Bomb Culture*.

5 Some of these characteristics were developed in close dialogue with the work of Peter Middleton, especially his points on authorship. He argues that the staging of authorship and the exploration of what it means to be a poet is one of the most important elements of the poetry performance. See Peter Middleton, 'How to Read a Reading of a Written Poem', *Oral Tradition*, 20:1 (2005), p. 23.

6 Franssen develops these reflections through an analysis of 'Poëzie en Carré', an event inspired by the 'International Poetry Incarnation' and organized by Simon Vinkenoog – one of the poets who had performed in London – on 28 February 1966 in the Carré Theatre in Amsterdam. See Franssen p. 35

7 Adrian Henri, *Environments and Happenings* (London: Thames and Hudson, 1974), p. 117.

8 Edward Lucie-Smith, ed., *The Liverpool Scene: Recorded Live along the Mersey Beat* (London: Donald Carroll, 1967), p. 3. Lucie-Smith's metaphor of the text as texture resonates with Jacques Derrida's conceptualization of the text as texture in *L'écriture et la différance*, published in the same year.

9 Michael Murphy and Deryn Rees-Jones, ed., *Writing Liverpool* (Liverpool: Liverpool University Press, 2007), p. 25.

10 David Craig, *The Real Foundations: Literature and Social Change* (London: Chatto & Windus, 1973), p. 259.

11 Edward Lucie-Smith, ed., *The Liverpool Scene: Recorded Live along the Mersey Beat* (London: Donald Carroll, 1967), p. 6.

12 Stan Smith, '"Every Time a Thing Is Possessed, It Vanishes": The Poetry of Brian Patten', in Michael Murphy and Deryn Rees-Jones, ed., *Writing Liverpool* (Liverpool: Liverpool University Press, 2007), p. 119.

13 Adrian Henri, *Environments and Happenings* (London: Thames and Hudson, 1974), p. 27.

14 Stan Smith, '"Every Time a Thing Is Possessed, It Vanishes": The Poetry of Brian Patten', p. 120.

15 McGough in Lucie-Smith (1967: 23).

16 Adrian Henri, 'The Entry of Christ Into Liverpool', http://www.adrianhenri.com/writer-poems-entrychrist.html.

17 Adrian Henri, 'The Entry of Christ Into Liverpool'.

18 Stan Smith, '"Every Time a Thing Is Possessed, It Vanishes", p. 123.

19 Liverpool had been recommended to Ginsberg by Robert Creeley, and it was home to The Beatles, with whom Ginsberg was infatuated. During his stay in Liverpool, Ginsberg stayed at the homes of Brian Patten and Adrian Henri. He did one reading (together with Michael Horovitz and Pete Brown) in a packed small bookshop and apart from that relaxed and enjoyed himself. The Liverpool poets appreciated Ginsberg's unassuming attitude, his considerate behaviour, and his enthusiasm for their city. Ginsberg, in turn, grew fond of the city, the cultural scene and the people, which led to his frequently quoted statement that Liverpool was the centre of the creative universe. His visit to the Liverpool Art Gallery with Adrian Henri while tripping on LSD found a poetic testament in Henri's 'Mrs Albion You Have a Lovely Daughter'. For a full account of the visit see Simon Warner, 'Raising the Consciousness? Re-Visiting Allen Ginsberg's Liverpool Trip in 1965', in Christoph Grunenberg & Robert Knifton, ed., *Centre of the Creative Universe: Liverpool & the Avant-Garde* (Liverpool: Liverpool University Press, 2007), pp. 95–108.

20 *Wholly Communion* is one of the first example of films – documentary and fiction – that explore the intersection of cinema and performance poetry. It was awarded a gold medal at the Mannheim Film Festival in 1966. In 2011 it was the subject of a special edition of the journal *Framework: The Journal of Cinema and Media.*

21 Daniel Kane, 'Wholly Communion, Literary Nationalism, and the Sorrows of the Counterculture', *Framework: The Journal of Cinema and Media*, 52:1 (Spring 2011), p. 115.

22 See Andrew Wilson, 'A Poetics of Dissent: Notes on a Developing Counterculture in London in the Early Sixties', in Chris Stephens & Katharine Stout, eds., *Art & The 60s: This Was Tomorrow* (London: Tate Publishing, 2004), p. 93, and John Hopkins quoted in Brian Mills, *London Calling: A Countercultural History of London Since 1945* (London: Atlantic Books, 2010), p. 151.
23 Tillie Olsen, *Silences* (New York: The Feminist Press at the City University of New York), p. 6.
24 Olsen, Tillie, *Silences*, p. 6.
25 Libby Houston, 'On Being a Woman Poet', Michelène Wandor, ed., *On Gender and Writing* (London: Pandora Press, 1983), p. 45.
26 Claire Buck, 'Poetry and the Women's Movement in Britain', James Acheson and Romana Huk, eds., *Contemporary British Poetry: Essays in Theory and Criticism* (New York: State University of New York Press, 1996), pp. 81–111.
27 See Linda Kinnahan, 'Feminism's Experimental "Work at the Language-Face"', Jane Dowson, ed., *The Cambridge Companion to Twentieth-Century British and Irish Women's Poetry* (Cambridge: Cambridge University Press, 2011), pp. 154–78.

6

SIMON PERRIL

High Late-Modernists or Postmodernists? Vanguard and Linguistically Innovative British Poetries since 1960

Permissions

Recounting a two-day visit in 1956 to Worcester to visit poet Gael Turnbull, Roy Fisher lists modernist luminaries and associates of the New American Poetry he was suddenly exposed to, and explains 'I'd never seen poetry used as these people were, in their various ways, using it, nor had I seen it treated as so vital an activity. These people were behaving with all the freedom and artistic optimism of painters. Decidedly un-English'.[1] Fisher's sense of the abiding importance of *permission* as the force that underwrites creative endeavour is a salient alternative to more vexed models of influence. And yet the drive to figure innovation as a question solely of modernist heritage is too simplistic. The binary options within the question 'high late-modernists or postmodernists'? ignores so many of the English tributaries that swell contemporary vanguard practice: Maggie O'Sullivan's debt to the material-yet-visionary nature of John Clare and a much earlier Celtic heritage, the reconfigured syntax Bill Griffiths shapes from his immersion in Old English, the sonic licence Geraldine Monk takes from Hopkins, Allen Fisher and Iain Sinclair's debt to the autodidactic mythological 'systems' of Blake, Barry MacSweeney's fascination with the faux-medievalism of Chatterton, Sean Bonney's appropriation of the apocalyptical egalitarianism of ranters like Abiezer Coppe, Keston Sutherland's re-contextualisation of vanguard language use through Pope's eighteenth century figuring of bathos. Indeed, such is the scope of British poetry since the 'mimeograph revolution' of the 1960s that attempts to contain it within labels that have academic currency is to risk acts of reductionist positioning. The anthology *Cusp* is a very useful counter to such tendencies. Its editor, Geraldine Monk, dubs it a 'collective autobiography'[2] that sets out to explore the nature of 'the poetic insurgence that began in the 1950s/60s' as a 'provincial one emanating from the industrial cities of the North and Midlands' rather than the exclusive preserve of 'those two strongholds of poetic power … London and Cambridge'.[3] Monk invited upwards of twenty poets to write about their journey into poetic activity, noting 'it would take a social historian to explain why so many young, working-class people took to poetry at this time, especially the more experimental areas of expression' in an era witnessing 'the after-effects of two world wars … and the Cold War hotting up'.[4] What emerges in the recollections Monk gathers is how the 'very real difficulty of finding kindred spirits in small provincial towns' was mitigated by the 'small press publishing network and the alternative or specialist bookshops'.[5] The latter might be in decline as I write this, but the former is still very much the life pulse of the area of poetry being discussed here.

The Challenge of the Long Poem

American long poems such as Williams's *Paterson*, Pound's *Cantos*, Zukofsky's *A* and Olson's *Maximus Poems* form a major legacy for British poets. Bunting's *Briggflatts* defined the British Poetry Revival of the 1960s, but since the 1970s UK poets have reached for other formal logics for the assemblage of long poems. In his 1973 collection *Act* Tom Raworth posed a significant question: 'The connections (or connectives) no longer work – so how to build the long poem everyone is straining for'?[6] His answer in the mid to late 1970s is exemplified in poems like *Ace* and *Writing* that unfold in very short lines that resemble the outpourings of a ticker-tape machine. Where the New American Poetry privileged measure propelled by breath, Raworth explored a dislocatory syntax ambiguating the relationships between lines with a kinetic dynamism that far outpaced projective verse. Elsewhere I have written of how Raworth's short poems 'often gesture to a world beyond the grasp of the poem' whereas his long poems 'seem more concerned to enter into the pattern of a world whose wider design is acknowledged to be inaccessible'.[7] By the time of *West Wind*, written during Margaret Thatcher's Falklands war, the poetry dramatises a scepticism towards the reader's urge to establish a pattern: 'later fragments / we assume / are one with those before / a sad dance'.[8] And yet the sadness of this dance relates to the imposition of more politically dubious imperial narratives upon the nation as 'puffs of unrelated news / restore / our former glory / which apparently / was a global servant class / too poor / to see the crown jewels' (Raworth, 1988, p. 127).

Geraldine Monk's work offers an ongoing interrogation of the 'emotional geography of place', most especially her native Lancashire. Her habitats are haunted by a sense of inequalities and injustices that the landscape has preserved as its own memory, and that charge the language with both neologistic verve and a sense of regional historical witness. The long poem *Interregnum* manages to fuse place and character in its exploration of the so-called Pendle Witches, ten women tried and hung in East Lancashire in 1612. It closes with an incantatory occupation of the nine-year-old Jennett Device's 'possession': 'I weird sang. / High trilled and skirled … / Rhymed thing with thing with string /… Word buntings. / Wildways'.[9] Monk reinvents language to re-orient her relationship to place and history in ways that calls upon her working class heritage of 'playing … on cobbled streets, us girls doing our handstands and crab walking and our endless reciting of rhymes & chants … Political satirical rhymes turned nonsense playground chant'.[10] Her sequence 'Hidden Cities' was a performance work commissioned by the Ruskin School of Fine Art as part of a series of 'alternative' bus tours around five English cities. She was allotted Manchester, and takes a less-than-scenic route through the fluidity and menace of 'Funchester … Gunchester … Madchester'.[11] On this trip we are 'X-ing territorial membranes. // Unseenable'. Through a punning discourse we witness the ghostliness of the hidden city, its 'Unguest terrors. / Hexing. Unguessed traces'.

Robert Sheppard's *Twentieth Century Blues* is a long poem that has learnt from the politicised discontinuities of Raworth and the polyvocality of Monk. Sheppard was part of the London poetry scene in the 1980s and co-edited, with Adrian Clarke, an important anthology *Floating Capital*. It gathered work from a generation of 'linguistically innovative' poets embarking upon work subtly different from the 'Open Field' poetry of the seventies, and the afterword noted 'if there was less evidence of varieties of overtly utopian poetics through the 80s, there was an expanded range of critical strategies in texts whose writers have relinquished claims to proprietorial control of meaning'.[12] Written between 1989 and 2000, *Twentieth Century Blues* is a vast 'network' of poems built around a sense that 'Bunting was right, that the world changes too quickly in the twentieth century for a long poem. All that can be sketched out in advance are generative schema'.[13] Despite its page-based publication, the formal logic is closer to the multi-linearity of digital hypertext work. Sheppard not only conceived the work as time-based, designed to end with the century, but in the final 'complete' edition of the poem he also gives individual pieces a complex numbering which allows such pieces to belong to several 'strands' at once; a simultaneity that enables and urges the reader to chart different paths through the collection rather than necessarily opt for a linear 'chronological' path. As he explains it 'The long poem's ambition towards inclusiveness, its grasping for totality, with all its attendant drifts into dogmatism as well as stale repetition, has been, at least in this [20th] century, its most negative condition' (Sheppard, 2008, p. 84).

Agoraphobia and the Tyranny of Labels

It would be easy to reproduce here what Roy Fisher has called an 'idiot bipartite map' of mainstream versus modernist/postmodernist/experimental poetry (Fisher, 2000, p. 121). A more nuanced account can be found in Drew Milne's 'Neo-Modernism and Avant-Garde Orientations', and David and Christine Kennedy's 'Terms of Engagement: Experimental Poetry and Its Others'. Milne stresses that what is meant by modernism is less a movement, or canon, more 'an experimental orientation developed through cosmopolitan networks'.[14] The Kennedys quote Chris Hamilton-Emery's sense that bipartite distinctions between vanguard and mainstream no longer function as 'what we have now is a multiplicity of practices and readerships and no real framework for understanding their trajectories, outside of consumption'.[15] The applicability of postmodernism is no less contested; the phrase 'postmoderns' is already tainted with caricature in the wake of Don Paterson's ill-tempered preface to the *New British Poetry*.[16] And this is far from the only objection to the term. When, in 2004, Rod Mengham and John Kinsella edited an impressively geographically diverse anthology, *Vanishing Points*, it was explicitly subtitled *New Modernist Poems*; and claimed the writers gathered have 'stayed in touch with the agendas of modernism; they are not postmodernist, but late modernist writers'.[17] Fundamental to Mengham's assertion of a 'late' modernism is a need to separate the poets in question from the 'postmodernist ideology' of 'language' writing. The reasons for such a distinction will be addressed later.[18]

An earlier Milne essay from the nineties admitted 'Someone trying to approach the fragments of the British avant-garde over the last 25 years will look in vain for helpful and easily available manifestos for contemporary poetry.'[19] This article was originally delivered as a paper at the Cambridge Conference of Contemporary Poetry on the theme of '21st century poetry' and addresses a 'conspiracy of expertise', Milne's summary phrase for how the perceived cultural marginality of poetry has left the small-press poetry scene with a sense of heritage that 'becomes almost theological in the depth of assumed knowledges, and hermetic in its collectivity' (Milne 1993, p. 26). His final topic, agoraphobia, points to these writers' reluctance to make public declarations in the form of manifestos. Milne prods at this reluctance in a bid to 'develop a different social basis for a poetry which is both public and private, while transforming the terms of such an opposition' (Ibid., p. 29). His talk is salient for its hunger for a conception of poetry as a 'collective mediation', and I shall attend to two historical moments that feed such hunger.

Two Utopian Episodes

Milne directly refers to the first moment by closing his discussion with a lengthy quotation from *The English Intelligencer*[20] about the push towards poetry 'as to whatever extent a communal activity' (38). *TEI* was a 'worksheet' begun in 1965 and passed on, in the form of photocopies, to a pre-selected list of people presumed to have an interest. It was not available in any commercial sense, and not susceptible to any external economic or distributive pressures. The pressures it did seek were social, communal. The contributors were united through their interest in the New American Poetry and poetics of the 1950s and 1960s, and *TEI* first appeared with a bold declaration: 'The Intelligencer is for the Island and its language, to circulate as quickly as needs be'. Initially, Andrew Crozier's editorship was virtually invisible, printing all material sent. But this led to problems with some contributors mistaking the space on offer as being that of a conventional publication with no attendant obligation towards dialogical engagement and participation. Crozier intervened in 1967 to explain 'The Intelligencer is hardly a magazine, and I've never regarded what has circulated in it as published'.[21] This solicited responses from Peter Riley about the 'need to share something more than private correspondence can cope with' and how '... the language we can use has to be worked out in common, among however many will allow themselves to trust, respond, risk, REACT, move outside their private worlds' (Ibid., p. 207). A second series of *TEI* began in April 1967, under Riley's new editorship, with an 'announcement' prompted by a summary of the achievements of recent American poetry (particularly Charles Olson) and its relevance for British poetry. The poem was defined as 'physiological presence + cosmological range', the latter concept initiating a complex debate about what conclusions could be drawn from pre-history in order to understand the present landscape condition of humankind. Such a vast project was a conscious determination to push poetry into a scope so extensive that it could be maintained only by a communal venture. The ramifications of the project – both its hopes and failures – certainly reverberate through Riley and Prynne's lengthy oeuvre. Over a decade after the waning of the *Intelligencer* project, Riley was still occupying an interrogatory mode intent upon undermining the primacy of the 'poet occupying his own private world of language and experience' (Ibid., p. 35). *Lines on the Liver*, from 1981, states, 'I don't anyway see how any person / Could hope to attain to a greater degree / Of sufficiency compaction and cleverness / Than a brown berry fallen in the grass'. We are invited to 'Look at it sitting there with its maps / And its charts and its migratory tables: / It settles its fate before it starts / To a plain contingency – / It waits to be eaten'.[22]

The second moment is the reverse to that of *TEI*, and concerns a period in the mid-1970s when poets associated with the British Poetry Revival of the 1960s and its network of magazines and small presses found themselves with access to the most public institution in British Poetry, the Poetry Society, and its journal *Poetry Review*. Eric Mottram, a poet, critic and lecturer at King's College in London, played a crucial role in this moment when 'a small group of 'radical' or 'experimental' poets took over the Poetry Society ... for a period of six years, from 1971 to 1977'.[23] Peter Barry's account of this episode of *Poetry Wars* is an exhaustive documentary of this period, and also constitutes what he regards as 'a case study of the inevitable frictions and tactical struggles between an avant-garde and a 'mainstream'[24] (Ibid., p. 2). Mottram's 'revival' (he coined the term) centred upon a sense that 'The parameters of poetry and poetics were recognised afresh as geology, geography, etymology, history and the erotic' with an accompanying belief in 'the discovery of coherences and locations for a renewal of civic poetry in the culture'.[25] It is a tale of poets infiltrating the General Council of the Society, conflict with the Arts Council, boycotts and eventual resignations. But, as with *TEI*, this episode reverberates beyond its historical moment, and informs the poetic work of later generations and the questions they interrogate. Not least of these questions concerns the capabilities and culpabilities of language itself, and the degree to which it can bear communal endeavour.

Prynne's experiences of the *Intelligencer* years of the sixties provoked poems (featured in *TEI*) suspicious of the designs they might have upon a collective: 'we/you/they, all the / pronouns by now know how to make a sentence work with *ought to*'.[26] Ken Edwards, a London poet in the 1980s (and editor of the important *Reality Studios* magazine, and subsequent Reality Street Editions press) was working within vanguard networks in the capital after the *Poetry Review* debacle, when the then prime minister Margaret Thatcher infamously claimed 'there is no such thing as society'. In *Intensive Care* he writes 'No public language that is / fit for such a time'.[27] The sequence in question is titled 'Their Daily Island Life', and its gentle restatement of the phrase 'behind the wire' builds in its intense sense of socioeconomic division, just as the title's third person plural pronoun posits the poem's distance from any attainable collective sense of belonging. Lines like 'I have tried (he wrote) / to knit fragments to make / coherence' log Eliot's Modernist shoring of fragments against personal ruin, but neither ironises nor endorses it. The poem works in a recombinatory fashion, revisiting key phrases like 'There was a country' and 'I have known people' in ways that make their simple decontextualised statements an index to values lost to a ruthlessly monetarist agenda. Suspicion is cast upon those to whom access to a public language is part of their class privilege: 'I have known people / whose language is public & pursues / or attains coherence. / Their house is too hot & is full / of beautiful things' (Ibid., p. 69), and the close of the poem moves towards a specific people; the marginalised poor, the sick, and the immigrant. And yet it admits 'there is a thing about them /I can't tell' (Ibid., p. 70). The poem manages to gesture towards what it cannot 'tell' in the absence of a public language that shares, and enshrines, communitarian values. During the period immediately after *Intensive Care*, Edwards would take these poetic concerns and focus them upon his own communal milieu. In the auspicious year 1984, he gave a talk called 'The We Expression'. Robert Sheppard explains that 'This was a singular London excursion into the American language poetry mode of the 'talk" and emphasises how 'Discussion of poetics was rare in this London avant-garde and Edwards's gesture to sacrifice a poetry reading to public thinking was a revolutionary one'.[28] The substance of his talk was later published as 'Grasping the plural'[29]; an interrogation of the nuances of the collective pronoun 'we' that Margaret Thatcher infamously co-opted as a 'first person plural,' after ten years in power, in the phrase 'We have become a grandmother' (Ibid., p. 21).

In/Adequate Language

For all the connotations poetry has as an art of accomplished language use, vanguard British poetry is often ambivalent towards its very materials, and suspicious of such a sense of mastery (with all the gendered politics that implies). Raworth's careful line break in 'Stag Skull Mounted' slices into this ambivalence with both humour and scepticism: 'in/adequate language/ i love you'.[30] An early Denise Riley poem, 'A note on sex and 'the reclaiming of language" plays with Renaissance tropes that align the discovery of new lands with the virgin land of the female body in need of conquering. 'She' is figured as a 'Savage' who returns from the 'New Country' only to weep at the airport being 'asked to by wood carvings, which represent herself' as exotic other.[31] Riley, a feminist critic with several monographs to her name – including *Am I That Name* which disputes the validity of the category 'woman' – offers a subtle interrogation of how female identity is colonised through interpellation. She carefully places 'the reclaiming of language' in scare quotes in anxious meditation that resistance to the generic pronoun 'He' will force her to occupy a female pronoun no less distant from a sense of individual agency. Instead, the poem offers 'The work is / e.g. to write 'she' and for that to be a statement / of fact only and not a strong image / of everything that is not-you, which sees you'. A later poem, 'Milk Ink', casts a sceptical eye upon the essentialist French feminist vision of an écriture feminine that writes the body. It opens with the injunction 'Don't read this as white ink flow, pressed out /Of retractable nipples. No, / Black as his is mine' (Ibid., p. 104). In much of her work there is a continuation of W. S. Graham's sense of the autonomy of a language that won't be tamed by the author's intentions. Graham's *Malcolm Mooney's Land* both posits and creates an arctic landscape whereby the male poet-adventurer crosses a frozen landscape that is also a representation of the white expanse of the page, with print figured as footprints: writing-as-journey-into-uncharted territory. In Riley's 'A Shortened Set' the Scottish poet's 'Grammarsow' and 'word-louse' have become her 'animals of unease' critically eating into her manuscripts (Ibid., p. 40).

Robert Duncan, an American poet with affiliations to both Black Mountain and the San Francisco Renaissance, proclaimed himself a 'derivative' poet, explaining 'I'm a development in a language, but I certainly didn't develop the language ... and at the same time I am the only place where that derivation can happen'.[32] Duncan's discussion was informed by an understanding of DNA, and this biological account of language has certainly been influential, for example, upon Allen Fisher – a poet to whom he bears little stylistic affinity. In a public talk from the late 1970s, Fisher quotes from Robert Kelly's *Against the Code* to usher in an important sense that 'through the manipulation and derangement of ordinary language the conditioned world is changed, weakened, in its associated links, its power to hold an unconscious world-view together'.[33] Fisher uses this quotation in a talk about his long poem *Place*, in some sense a misunderstood work because its title is too easily assimilated into a post-Olsonian vision of the 'open form' epic.[34] As Olson dug into the history of Gloucester, so Fisher delves into London, and the many tributaries of the Thames buried beneath the streets of the city. Peter Barry developed the term 'content-specific' for poetry 'which explores highly specific materials and data with heuristic intent and as implicit metaphor'[35] and yet, as shown in his chosen Kelly quotation, Fisher has other preoccupations too. The Kelly quote nods towards Russian Formalist interests in the necessity of cultivating linguistic strangeness, defamiliarisation, in order to alter our perceptions (and the structures they uphold) in order to 'make the stone *stony*'[36] and reconnect ourselves with the material conditions of daily life. But the quote also stresses the importance of extending that disruption and strangeness to the idea of associated links. Fisher's work, in *Place* and beyond, is a complex dance between pattern and pattern disruption. Olson's 'Projective Verse' expounds an organic sense that 'ONE PERCEPTION MUST IMMEDIATELY AND DIRECTLY LEAD TO A FURTHER PERCEPTION'. Fisher mistrusts the resulting sense of an overarching master narrative, and yet Olson is also the source of his suspicion. Olson's Gloucester epic has Maximus as its central pivot, but his *Special View of History* cites Keats's idea of negative capability as the desirable capacity 'of being in uncertainties, mysteries, doubts, without any irritable reaching after fact and reason'.[37] Olson recognised this as a precursor to Heisenberg's Uncertainty Principle whereby 'a methodology becomes the object of its attention' and the observer always effects what is observed.[38] Fisher's work takes from this a prompt to rethink the validity of stable models: 'What we're looking for in a model is coherence. What I'm saying is, that's no longer enough. That's far too much of a summarising exclusory activity' (Fisher 2013, p. 116). He has also interrogated Olson's notion of 'Proprioception', taking its conception into directions that might stand for a useful distinction between the American-informed British Poetry Revival of the 1960s and vanguard British poetic practice since the 1970s. Olson's 'Proprioception' is a brief piece, partly in his urgent 'notes' format, that acknowledges 'the data of depth sensibility / the "body" of us as object which spontaneously or of its own order produces experience of ... SENSIBILITY WITHIN THE ORGANISM BY MOVEMENT OF ITS OWN TISSUES'.[39] Fisher appropriates the idea to produce a summary of a poetics that foregrounds the notion of a 'multiple text' open to giving the reader many 'performance-options'.[40] As he has it 'Proprioception encourages the compositional paradigm that allows you to situate yourself, through discriminating performance or narration, as part of the process of aesthetic participation'.[41]

Like Fisher, J. H. Prynne's work since the sixties has developed a distinctive response to language that incorporates an astonishing range of specialist discourses into its poetry. Early Prynne, in the *TEI* years, is replete with remorse at the casual violence of expression: 'I draw blood whenever I open my stupid mouth',[42] and this ethical concern with damage and wounded utterance has never left his work. And yet by the end of the seventies, *Down Where Changed* took distinctly pessimistic steps away from the moral urgency of his earlier work, into a profound sense of the incapacities and culpabilities of language. The book ends with quandary ('What do you say then / Well yes and no / About four times a day') edging into resignation: 'Sick and nonplussed / By the thought of less / You say stuff it'.[43]

The aesthetic Allen Fisher describes in his extension of Olson's proprioception into the realm of readerly reception is the locus of nuanced debate within contemporary poetics, especially in the light of the American Language poets. The influential journal *L=A=N=G=U=A=G=E* began the year before *Down Where Changed*, showcasing a generation of 'language-centred' writers informed by Marxist and poststructuralist philosophy. Accompanied by Robert Grenier's famous pronouncement 'I HATE SPEECH', such writers offered a materialist critique of the expressivist tendencies of the New

American poetry. Charles Bernstein was concerned with 'seeing language not as a transparency, not as something which simply dissolves as you get a picture of the world in focus, so that, in reading a text you are hardly aware of the language at all'.[44] Resisting the 'referential fallacy', and keeping the reader's focus upon the texture and materiality of the language, were seen as redefining hierarchical reader-writer relations. A Marxist sense of being made passive consumers of language as a commodity fetishized for its illusion of transparency led to a call for the readerly act of 'repossessing the sign through close attention to, and active participation in, its production'.[45] American 'language centred' emphasis upon the liberatory 'freedom' the reader is offered by the text that 'resists' reference differs from its UK counterpart. In a document first published in a spoof magazine, Prynne balked at the claims being made; not because he disagreed with the politicised account of commodified language, but because he refused to see the poem as immune from such forces. Since early poems such as 'Sketch for a Financial Theory of the Self' Prynne has utilised the model of market economics precisely because its scope encompasses the commodification of both freedom and dissent. His 'Letter to Steve McCaffery' is suspicious of the 'open text' and any proposed readerly freedom to produce meaning. It asks 'Isn't it the classic freedom to eat cake, to diversify an assumed leisure and to choose out of a diversity which is precisely the commodity-spectacle of a pre-disposed array, clearwrapped in unitised portion control?'[46] A later letter to Allen Fisher confirms how Prynne's emphasis varies from the Language poets, and confirms the direction his increasingly impacted and fractured practice has taken since the aforementioned *Down Where Changed*: 'The reader's freedom was to be constantly interfered with, as an invidious commodity; pretending that there had been no immunity to the violence and yet also noticing that pretense as just that'.[47]

Immunity and Inoculation: A Contemporary War Poetry

Milne's 'Agoraphobia' piece from the 1990s contains a statement that certainly pre-empts the emergence of a younger generation of vanguard poets in the next decade: 'The most important modernist manifesto is Marx's Communist Manifesto'.[48] Articulations such as Prynne's above on the complexity of poetry's complicity in capitalist structures have had a profound effect on a younger generation of poets forging a sense of collective endeavour since the mid-nineties in magazines such as *Object Permanence*, *Quid*, *Onedit*, *High Zero*, *Hix Eros*; small presses such as Barque, Bad Press, Yt Communications, Crater Press, and in online journals such as *Glossator* and seminal blogs like Sean Bonney's *Abandonedbuildings*. Indeed, *Complicities* is the title of a collection of essays devoted to poetry and criticism that 'knows language to be profoundly complicit across the board in the extension of acts of domination, from the preparation for and execution of war, to the composition of the suicide note, from the overt corrupting of the democratic franchise, to cold calling's interpellation of the human subject as consumer-in-waiting'.[49]

It has been a little observed fact that British vanguard poetry since the eighties has offered some of the most insightful and adventurous war poetry of the twentieth and twenty-first centuries. A roll call would have to include Tom Raworth's Falklands-conflict era 'West Wind', Denise Riley's negotiation of the ethnic conflicts in the former Yugoslavia in 'Laibach Lyrik', John Wilkinson's *The Nile* on the first Gulf War, and *Iphigenia* on the second, Robert Sheppard's examination of the war on terror, *Warrant Error*, and Carol Watts's punning adoption of George Bush's dominant verbalizing of 'I-raq' in the news in *Wrack*. Poets such as Bonney, Keston Sutherland, Andrea Brady, Peter Manson and Marianne Morris have been profoundly shaped by emerging as writers into a 'global war on terror' ushered in by the 9/11 attacks that prompted George W. Bush to controversially state 'This crusade – this War on Terrorism – is going to take a while'. Sam Ladkin and Robin Purves, young critics both heavily active in the editing and publishing of poetry within the small press scenes, edited *Complicities* and a special British Poetry issue for *Chicago Review*. The introduction to this issue unites the poets in question through 'concern with consumption in all its forms, and especially the co-implication of digestive, commercial, military, and information economies'.[50] There is an intensity and rigour to the engagement with such concerns that seems markedly different in emphasis from the politicisation of poetic form as argued for by the language poets. Whereas language writing rejected lyric modes, these poets have interrogated them precisely because they are a site of conflict, and precisely because the 'purity' of lyric address cannot be granted immunity. Prynne theorised this conflict early, in the 1980s, in a letter to the poet Andrew Duncan[51] that diagnoses Prynne's sense of a 'privilege of exemption' within the lyric stance in its 'readiness to claim the privilege of an autonomous occasion which covertly it exploits'.[52] He questions the capacity of such lyric identification to offer critique and transcendence: 'How can you give, unless you are to present merely symptomatic malnutrition, what you claim to have taken away'.[53]

Andrea Brady's poetry has absorbed these questions into its very skin. *Cold Calling's* title simultaneously blends a sense of the detached rigour of poetic vocation and the invasive unsolicited telesales pitch in complicit combination. Recent work has found her more attuned to the risks of occupying a rhetoric of politicised outrage. It is perhaps a risk that the female poet is more attuned to, having less 'natural' right to occupy a public voice. Denise Riley's poem 'Problems of Horror' offers a gendered critique of the allure of outrage in which a male pronoun, 'He,' has 'tailored a cadence out of disgust, and spins to see its hang on him'.[54] The sense of dubious display extends to the poet being 'privately faint at heart' as he pirouettes 'sporting a lapel nausea carnation', knowing 'this smooth emulsion is truly-felt revulsion'.[55] The poem's opening question, 'Through perfectly heat-sealed lyric, how to breathe'? might summarise Brady's suspicions over her own facility with a poetry of occasion. Such concerns drove her to the verse essay as a 'forensic' form whose 'structure could accommodate an excess of social information'.[56] This marks a conscious attempt to decentralise her lyric practice, and the choice of subject matter assists with this. *Wildfire* is further proof of the versatility of British vanguard war poetry. It is a book-length poem concerned with 'the history of incendiary devices, of the evolution of Greek fire from a divine secret which could sustain or destroy empires, into white phosphorous and napalm'.[57] The book's subtitle, 'a verse essay on Obscurity and Illumination', is there to keep in check the allure of the pyrotechnics of poetic outrage. It makes the poem additionally 'an interrogation of writing practices which fume as much as they enlighten'.[58] When such matters are addressed, it is Prynne's critique of the politics of lyric address that shines through in her observation 'I was tired of trying to position "us" on the ground, like actors in real carnage, where being "implicated" is also a way of sharing the spoils'.[59] This makes for a nuanced poetry that urges 'Remember I am / on fire / cannot be trusted'.[60]

In the last fifteen years, Keston Sutherland has engaged in the most sustained tracking of the implications of Prynne's position. At the turn of the twenty-first century, Sutherland returned to the eighteenth century for a model of the attitudes towards language applicable to 'innovative poetry', suggesting that the new century constitutes 'the crest' of a 'mythic triumph of liberalization' begun in an earlier historical moment of parallel 'massive financial upheaval'. It is the point at which Pope introduced the word and concept of 'Bathos,' 'the Bottom, the End, the Central Point, the *non plus ultra* of true Modern Poesie'.[61] Pope intended such a category as a means of ridiculing corrupt language, Sutherland notes how these debased and corrupt features of language use are precisely those celebrated in contemporary vanguard practice. He grasps for a poetry of affirmatory bathos that 'tends not to regret, but to celebrate the idea of its inadequacy, and to reject the desire for moral rectitude which seems implicit in the very idea that language might be adequate.'[62] Prynne is the model, and a later essay focuses upon the turn in his later poetry, noting it 'was not from its beginning condemned to be the moral anthropology of the consumerism of suffering'.[63] Sutherland's first book of critical writing furthers his examination of bathos by revisiting Marx as a satirist of consumption whose very style is 'the concentrated literary exposure of social contradiction'.[64] He discloses that previous accounts of Marx have ignored his 'risks in style, his seizure, infiltration and parodic recycling of what he called 'the jargon of Political Economy',[65] qualities that make *Das Kapital* a work of 'internal generic disintegration ... a difficult collage of the poetic, the scientific and the jargonist within individual sentences and ideas'.[66] This prompts a revisitation of one of the most influential tenets of Marxist thought, the concept of the abstraction of human labour. Sutherland takes Marx back to the original German, and finds that human beings are reduced to the word *Gallerte*. It is not the supposed abstract noun indicating a process of congelation, but a specific commodity: concentrated glue that all animals yield when industrially boiled down. As such, Sutherland uncovers Marx's vivid sense that 'social existence under capitalism is thus gruesomely savage and primitivistic ... in the still more disgusting sense that our most routine, unavoidable and everyday act, the act of consumption of use value – that is, first of all, purchase – is in every case an act of cannibalism'.[67] Sutherland's poetry spares us none of this barbarism. Instead it gleefully serves it with ballistic force in the opening to 'Torture Lite': 'Candied *faits divers* in frosted crackling, hurl myself / myself-mud immaterially scoffing up my fig / leaf face in a panto breakfast of hallucinations'.[68]

Sean Bonney's resolutely urban work has frequently touched base with nineteenth-century French poetry closest to the tremors of social revolution: the Baudelaire Benjamin celebrated as 'a Lyric poet in an era of high capitalism', whom he has 'translated' into spikey missives of post-concrete poetry; and Rimbaud who he has partly ventriloquized, partly reconstituted, as a poet of the Paris Commune, in *Happiness*. Bonney first found his poetic direction in the collection *Poisons, their antidotes*. The title gives a flavour of its concerns with the tensions in poetic language between the need to utter critique, and the degree to which such language can inoculate itself from the poisons it would swallow in order to spit out. Tony Blair is a particularly vivid target: 'blair is / personal / cannot reconsider the / salt in my face is / real is / bitter'.[69] Since such work, Bonney has shown himself on a quest 'to wake up this morning / and wake up this morning'[70] unembarrassed at occupying a sense of the visionary. Writing about Geraldine Monk, he praises her poetry for its consideration 'of what language, song and spell might mean'[71] and for being 'a part of the historical heretical current, opposed to the official version of reality'.[72] *Document* asserts a singular vision that also taps into the forces at work in other younger British vanguard poets: 'There is no refuge to be had in the separation of artistic, social and sexual desires, or a stone to soak up the groaning protein interference. We are condemned to speak by the same causes that drive the world into war, to determine which ideas are taken to market: radio waves, muscle, crotch split'.[73] Bonney's poetry is emblematic of so much of the excitements of contemporary British poetry in its call for 'the taste of waking strange with new speech circuits'.[74]

NOTES

1 Roy Fisher, *Interviews Through Time and Selected Prose* (Kentisbeare: Shearsman, 2000), p. 31.
2 Geraldine Monk, ed. *Cusp: Recollections of Poetry in Transition* (Bristol: Shear sman: 2012), p. 7.
3 Ibid., p. 8.
4 Ibid., p. 12.
5 Ibid., p. 8.
6 Tom Raworth, *Tottering State: Selected Poems 1963–1987* (London: Paladin, 1988), p. 91.
7 Simon Perril, '"What Rhymes with Cow / and Starts with N": Tom Raworth's Time and Motion Studies', in Nate Dorward ed. *Removed for Further Study: The Poetry of Tom Raworth* (Toronto: The Gig, 2003), p. 126.
8 Tom Raworth, *Collected Poems* (Manchester: Carcanet, 2003), p. 358.
9 Geraldine Monk, *Selected Poems* (Cambridge: Salt, 2003), p. 163.
10 Monk 2012, p. 183.
11 Geraldine Monk, *Noctivagations* (Sheffield: West House, 2001), p. 63.
12 Adrian Clarke, Robert Sheppard, eds., *Floating Capital: New Poets from London* (Elmwood: Potes and Poets Press 21, 1991), p. 123.
13 Robert Sheppard, *Complete Twentieth Century Blues* (Great Wilbraham: Salt, 2008), p. 332.
14 Drew Milne, 'Neo-Modernism and Avant-Garde Orientations' in Nigel Alderman, C. D. Blanton, eds., *A Concise Companion to Postwar British and Irish Poetry* (Chichester: Wiley-Blackwell, 2009), p. 160.
15 David Kennedy, Christine Kennedy, *Women's Experimental Poetry in Britain 1970–2010: Body, Time & Locale* (Liverpool: Liverpool University Press, 2013), p. 20.
16 Paterson's preface is to the American anthology *New British Poetry*, an outburst occasioned by Keith Tuma's Oxford *Anthology of Twentieth-Century British and Irish Poetry* which has overt modernist leanings, and reinstates the significance of an Irish Modernist heritage through the inclusion of Brian Coffey and Denis Devlin alongside contemporary poets such as Trevor Joyce, Maurice Scully and Randolph Healy. For a riposte to Paterson, see Andrea Brady, '"Meagrely Provided": A Response to Don Paterson', *Chicago Review*, 49.3/4 and 50.1 (Summer 2004), 396–402. For a more positive use of the term postmodernism see Peter Brooker, 'Postmodern Postpoetry: Tom Raworth's *Tottering State*' in Anthony Easthope, John O. Thompson, eds. *Contemporary Poetry Meets Modern Theory* (Toronto, Buffalo and London: University of Toronto Press, 1991) pp. 153–65.

17 Rod Mengham, John Kinsella, eds. *Vanishing Points: New Modernist Poems* (Cambridge: Salt, 2004), p. xviii.
18 For a more detailed sense of the complexity of UK poetry's relationship to 'language writing', see Robert Sheppard's chapter, 'Beyond Anxiety: Legacy or Miscegenation' in *When Bad Times Made for Good Poetry*. The book also engages with the emergence of the label 'Linguistically Innovative' as a further designation, again sometimes contested, for the poetry discussed here.
19 Drew Milne, 'Agoraphobia, and the Embarrassment of Manifestos: Notes towards a Community of Risk'. *Parataxis: Modernism and Modern Writing*, no.3, Spring 1993, p. 33.
20 Given that Milne's piece points to the parlous and confusing state of *TEI* manuscripts in academic libraries, we are grateful for a recent, intelligently edited anthology: Neil Pattison, Reitha Pattison, Luke Roberts, eds. *Certain Prose of the English Intelligencer*. (Cambridge: Mountain, 2012, second revised edition 2014).
21 Neil Pattison, Reitha Pattison, Luke Roberts, eds. *Certain Prose of the English Intelligencer* (Cambridge: Mountain, 2012, second revised edition 2014), p. 204.
22 Peter Riley, *Lines on the Liver* (London: Ferry Press, 1981) unpaginated.
23 Peter Barry, *Poetry Wars: British Poetry of the 1970s and the Battle of Earls Court* (Cambridge: Salt, 2006), p. 1.
24 Ibid., p. 2.
25 Eric Mottram, 'The British Poetry Revival, 1960–75', in Peter Barry, Robert Hampson, eds., *New British Poetries: the Scope of the Possible* (Manchester: Manchester University Press, 1993) pp. 15–50, pp. 28–29.
26 J. H. Prynne, *Poems* (Newcastle Upon Tyne, South Freemantle: Bloodaxe / Folio / Freemantle Arts Centre Press, 1997), p. 112.
27 Ken Edwards, *No Public Language: Selected Poems 1975–1995* (Exeter: Shearsman, 2006), p. 68.
28 Robert Sheppard, *When Bad Times Made for Good Poetry: Episodes in the History of the Poetics of Innovation* (Exeter: Shearsman, 2011), p. 101.
29 Ken Edwards,'Grasping the Plural', in Denise Riley, ed. *Poets on Writing: Britain, 1970–1991* (Houndmills: Macmillan, 1992), pp. 21–29.
30 Raworth 2003, p. 79.
31 Denise Riley, *Selected Poems* (London: Reality Street Editions, 2000), p. 11.
32 Quoted in Stephen Collis, Graham Lyons, eds., *Reading Duncan Reading: Robert Duncan and the Poetics of Derivation* (Iowa City: University of Iowa Press, 2012), p. 29.
33 Allen Fisher, *The Marvels of Lambeth: Interviews & Statements by Allen Fisher*, ed. Andrew Duncan (Bristol: Shearsman Books, 2013), p. 51.
34 For a detailed account of the trajectory of Fisher's work across his two long poem projects *Place* and *Gravity as a Consequence of Shape*, see Robert Sheppard's 'Allen Fisher's Apocalypse Then: Between *Place* and Gravity – Technique and Technology', and 'Fracture and Fracture: Resisting the Total in Allen Fisher's *Gravity as a Consequence of Shape*' both in his *When Bad Times Made for Good Poetry*.
35 Peter Barry, 'Allen Fisher and "Content-Specific" Poetry', in Peter Barry, Robert Hampson, eds., *New British Poetries: the Scope of the Possible* (Manchester: Manchester University Press, 1993), p. 201.

36 The phrase 'make the stony *stony*' comes from Victor Shklovsky's seminal essay called 'Art as Technique' (1917). See Rick Rylance, ed., *Debating Texts* (Open University Press, 1987), pp. 48–49.
37 Charles Olson, *The Special View of History*, ed. Ann Charters (Berkeley: Oyez, 1970), p. 14.
38 Ibid., pp. 41–42.
39 Charles Olson, *Collected Prose*, eds. Donald Allen, Benjamin Friedlander (Berkeley: University of California Press, 1997), p. 181.
40 Allen Fisher, 'Notes for the Conference Contemporary Poetry and Performance', *Fragmente* 7, 1997, p. 111.
41 Ibid., p. 111.
42 J. H. Prynne, *Poems* (Newcastle Upon Tyne, South Freemantle: Bloodaxe / Folio / Freemantle Arts Centre Press, 1997), p. 82.
43 Ibid., p. 310.
44 Quoted from Bruce Andrews, Charles Bernstein, 'The Pacifica Interview', *L=A=N=G=U=A=G=E* 3, Oct. 1981. Unpaginated.
45 Bruce Andrews, Charles Bernstein, eds. *The L=A=N=G=U=A=G=E Book* (Carbondale: Southern Illinois University Press, 1984), p. x.
46 J. H. Prynne, 'Letter to Steve McCaffery', *The Gig* 7, 2000 pp. 40–46 (p. 41).
47 J. H. Prynne, 'A Letter to Allen Fisher', *Parataxis* 8/9, pp. 157–58.
48 Milne 1993, p. 30.
49 Back cover blurb to Sam Ladkin, Robin Purves, eds. *Complicities: British Poetry 1945–2007* (Prague: Literaria Pragensia, 2007).
50 Sam Ladkin, Robin Purves, eds. *Chicago Review* 53:1 Spring 2007. British Poetry Issue, pp. 1–8.
51 Andrew Duncan edits the important journal *Angel Exhaust* and has published many poetry collections, as well as two monographs: *The Failure of Conservatism in Modern British Poetry* (Salt 2003) and *The Council of Heresy: a Primer of Poetry in a Balkanised Terrain* (Shearsman 2009).
52 J. H. Prynne, 'A Letter to Andrew Duncan', *Grosseteste Review* 15, 1983–84, 105.
53 Ibid., p. 105.
54 Denise Riley 2000, p. 103.
55 Ibid., p. 103.
56 Andrea Brady, *Wildfire: A Verse Essay on Obscurity and Illumination* (San Francisco: Krupskaya, 2010), p. 71.
57 Ibid., p. 71.
58 Ibid., p. 71.
59 Ibid., p. 71.
60 Ibid., p. 13.
61 Keston Sutherland, 'The Trade in Bathos' *Jacket*. 15 (2001). http://jacketmagazine.com/15/sutherland-bathos.html accessed 25 Feb. 2015.
62 Ibid.
63 Keston Sutherland, 'X L Prynne', in Ian Brinton, ed. *A Manner of Utterance: the Poetry of J. H. Prynne* (Exeter: Shearsman, 2009), p. 109.
64 Keston Sutherland, *Stupefaction: A Radical Anatomy of Phantoms* (London, Calcutta: Seagull Books, 2011), p. 47.
65 Ibid., pp. 38–39.
66 Ibid., p. 39.

67 Ibid., p. 49.
68 Keston Sutherland, *Neocosis* (London: Barque, 2005), p. 17.
69 Sean Bonney, *Poisons, Their Antidotes* (Sheffield: West House Books, 2003). Unpaginated.
70 Sean Bonney, *Document: Poems, Diagrams, Manifestos July 7th 2005-June 27th 2007* (London: Barque Press, 2009), p. 10.
71 Sean Bonney, 'What the Tourists Never See: the Social Poetics of Geraldine Monk', in Scott Thurston, ed. *The Salt Companion to Geraldine Monk* (Cambridge: Salt, 2007), pp. 62–78 (p. 68).
72 Ibid., p. 73.
73 Bonney 2009, p. 17.
74 Ibid., p. 19.

7

NATALIE POLLARD

Stretching the Lyric: The Anthology Wars, Martianism and After

Andrew Motion's poetic and editorial work has repeatedly turned its eye on negotiations of literary status and valuation in post-war British poetry. In a 2006 review, he interprets an earlier moment in the English lyric tradition in terms of the politics of reception:

> The picture of John Donne 'in the pose of a melancholy lover' ... bought by the National Portrait Gallery in the summer of 2006, has fixed a particular image of the poet in the public mind ... soulful and amorous (the folded hands and sensual mouth), theatrical (the wide-brimmed black hat) ... and enigmatic (the deep background shadows).[1]

Such remarks draw attention to the poet's need to project a 'particular image' in public. For Motion, the display of a 'soulful' artistic internality is integral to success with one's audience, both in Donne's age and his own. At the same time, the writer preserves 'enigma' at the heart of the performance, balancing the sincere with the staged. 'Donne's sickbed is a stage, and we admire the patient as if we were looking at him across footlights', he writes of *Devotions*: 'all his great writing ... is a performance, which means it holds us at arm's length' (126–27).

It is an analysis that corresponds, of course, with the contemporary poet-editor's own history of influential literary wheelings and dealings. Motion's canny negotiations of the poetry industry are visible at least from 1982, the year his and Blake Morrison's co-edited anthology, *The Penguin Book of Contemporary British Poetry*, was published.[2] Assembling a poetical cast that would establish (they hoped) the tenets of a new poetical value system, the book asserted itself against its poetic and editorial forebears. As anthologisers are wont to do, Motion and Morrison gathered and promoted poetry that conformed to their tastes, which they argued was characteristic of a much-needed change of direction in late twentieth-century poetry. They also hoped to give futurity – and community – to the kind of poetry they were themselves writing.

What were the qualities of this 'new' poetry? Motion and Morrison's introduction praises writing that achieves its effects through irregularity: 'a delight ... to twist and mix language in order to revive' (*M&M* 18). Rendering strange the language of what a previous generation of readers – largely of Movement poetry – conceived as super-typical reality, the editors champion work that surprises and startles. They delight in unsettling habituated perceptions. Perhaps most notably, they gather authors identified with the 'Martian' poetry of Craig Raine (a moniker that caught on after being wittily adapted – by James Fenton – from the title of Raine's 1979 collection *A Martian Sends a Postcard Home*).[3] Reviewing Raine's volume for the *London Review of Books*, Fenton had characterised the Martian style as using a 'twist and mix' of language that, through unusual metaphors and similes, crystallises and compacts experiences, rendering the familiar strange.[4]

Here is the beginning of the title poem from Raine's volume:

> Caxtons are mechanical birds with many wings
> and some are treasured for their markings –
>
> they cause the eyes to melt (*Postcard* 1)

A few lines later, this metaphor between bird and book is pressed still further: 'I have never seen one fly, but / sometimes they perch on the hand' (1). As if anticipating audience confusion about what is flying and perching, the Martian gaze guides our reading, by homing in on everyday objects and domestic practices. Raine's poem shows how watching television, telling the time, reading books, and looking at the English weather exhibit overlooked idiosyncrasies and oddities: 'time is tied to the wrist / or kept in a box, ticking with impatience', 'Rain is when the earth is television. / It has the property of making colours darker' (1). These metaphors and similes transform domestic space into a site of altered lyric visions and object relations. The book is a bird 'perch[ed] on the hand' that holds it, and pages are seen as 'wings'. The physical book appears more animate than the reader, as if it had agency over her, and were posing flightily on her hand. The lines emphasise how easily, in reading, one peers *within* – at the interior 'markings' – and misses the sense of the book as a tangible thing, that might be held, ruffled or discarded.

The success of such work, however richly deserved, was dependent on the social standing of its supporters. Martianism was first publicly identified and championed in 1978 by Fenton, in an article entitled 'Of the Martian School'. (It was published in the *New Statesman*, where he was then editorial assistant.) Pivotal in propelling Reid and Raine to fame in the eyes of their contemporaries, Fenton's piece announced the pair as joint winners of the Prudence Farmer award for the best poems published in that magazine the previous year. In simultaneously declaring them the advocates of a new school of poetry, which 'ought to be noticed, since it has enrolled two of the best poets writing in England today', he prompted broad-scale publicity for a hitherto unknown (indeed, nonexistent) aesthetic, 'which always insists on presenting the familiar at its most strange'. Cleverly playing on late twentieth-century journalistic desires to announce and debate the rise of so-called new literary movements, the piece spurred the London press's enthusiastic contestation of the merits and demerits of an up-and-coming Martianism.

Fenton's poetry too often implemented metaphorical 'strangeness' and situational bizarrerie. His literary success owed as much as Reid and Raine did to the proponents of these techniques during the late 1970s and 1980s. Although different in kind from the pithy compactness of Martianism, Fenton's narrative-based poetry was lauded by its advocates. An extended *Poetry Review* interview between Motion and Fenton was calculated to coincide with the latter's publication of *The Memory of War*, and put him in the public eye at a key moment in his career. A few months later, *M&M* featured Fenton's work, and placed him again as part of a new generation's 'reformation of poetic taste'. Such assertions promoted two kinds of writing in the period: 'new narrative' and Martian poetry. Whilst the latter involved lyric crystallisations of a moment in time, achieving perspectival change through tightly-structured patternings of metaphor and simile, the former was more plot-driven. It emphasised the hidden instabilities of familiar places, voices and histories, used shape-shifting speakers, produced a sense of complicity with violent narrators, and often incorporated a hyperbolic social satire that both lampooned its rivals and seemed oddly self-accusatory.

Fenton's twenty-five stanza poem, 'A Staffordshire Murderer', is a good example. The piece reworks reassuringly commonplace events, objects and shared values, such as a 'stroll to the carpark', attention to '[a]n ornamental pond', and familiar address: 'would you care for a boiled sweet?'. It transforms them into the material of violent fantasy, where '[e]very fear is a desire' and '[e]very desire is fear', and: 'The cigarettes are burning under the trees / Where the Staffordshire murderers wait for their accomplices / And victims. Every victim is an accomplice' (*M&M* 112). Fenton's lines associate creativity with fear and guilt, envisaging the narrating victim as a homicidal accomplice. Instead of a sympathetic figure, the poem produces a murderously focalising 'I' spinning out his story. Fenton emphasises the peculiarity and otherness of storytelling, as the voice slips between murderer and murdered. 'Surely these preachers are poisoners, these martyrs murderers?', 'Surely this is all a gigantic mistake?' But no: 'You have come as an anchorite to kneel at your funeral'. Self-estrangement is linked to the narrative voice's confused distance from others. This poetry trades on, as *M&M* puts it, 'the difficulties and strategies involved in retelling', given a writing self's contradictory and perverse impulses (12). Such narratives offer 'a radical departure from the mimetic mode' by revealing how 'the poem is an invention' that is not to be trusted (12; 19). The writer is praised for virtuously reminding readers of 'the artifice and autonomy of his text' (19). We should trust neither these tales nor their tellers.

What these pro-alienation anthologisers want is to bring about a change in audience taste. John Redmond thinks they encourage the reading public to turn against 'the doleful resignation, the narrowed horizons, that one found in Larkin's work', by promoting its own dynamic and ludic perceptions.[5] This writing hopes to startle reader and writer out of the reassuring, apparently stable lyric world of a Larkin or Gunn poem, and to exchange 'the received idea of the poet as the person-next-door, or knowing insider, for the attitude of the anthropologist or alien invader or remembering exile' (*M&M* 12).

This self-promotional determination to alter audience values is also seen in the style and form of the poetry. A not-unfriendly competitiveness characterises Reid's and Raine's parallel development of surprise tactics in the late 1970s and early eighties. Reid was taught by Raine during postgraduate study at Oxford, and the early collections of both bear traces of playful, metaphorical one-upmanship, as if each was egging the other on to produce increasingly 'outrageous' similes and connections between objects. Reid's early volumes, *Arcadia* (1979) and *Pea Soup* (1982), showcase a desire for fresh sensory gratification, such as in the title poem of his 1982 collection: 'A wriggling, long-tailed kite leaps like a sperm / at the sun, its blurry ovum' (*M&M* 185). Raine's first collection, *The Onion, Memory* (1978), riffs off exaggerated forms of the gluttonously comparative imagination: a butcher presides over 'the slap and trickle / of blood', and his 'striped apron / gets as dirty as the mattress in a brothel' (*M&M* 171).

A key point of similarity is their shape-shifting personae. Readers glimpse the careful image-management of the writer, who leads his 'I's and 'you's through a succession of nonhuman guises. Reid's 1979 poem 'Baldanders' is a good example. It takes its title from a mythical protean creature, conceived of by Hans Sachs. (The term means 'soon-another', and has been used as a symbol of continual societal and natural change.) Reid redeploys the mythical beast as a figure for an imagined weightlifter; a would-be world champion whom the poem makes pirouette through simile upon simile: 'squat as an armchair', '[g]lazed, like a mantlepiece frog', a 'prima donna', and '[h]uman [t]elephone'. Whilst Reid tells us to: 'Pity the poor weightlifter / alone on his catasta', he also encourages us to find humour in a comparison between the 'pregnant belly' he carries in his 'leotard' and 'a melon wedged in a shopping-bag ...', and to discover 'domestic parody' in his 'Japanese muscularity'.

Reid ends with a surreptitious implication that the Baldanders is analogous to a familiar kind of champion's (lyric) exertions:

> he strains to become
>
> the World Champion (somebody, answer it!)
> Human Telephone.

These final comparisons actively appeal to 'somebody' to perceive them. The delicate humour of Reid's parenthesised request is also a parting shot: a striking command to the audience ('answer it!'). If that is an admission of the need for others, in spite of literal or metaphorical strength, it is also an injunction to 'you' to respond to the poem's shrilly ringing stimuli.

Raine's surprising association of unlikely sensations shows a comparable desire to enchant and discombobulate. The poem 'Floods', from the 1979 *Postcard*, begins by showing us how:

> Bright as meringues, the swans sweep
> sideways down the passionate water. (*Postcard* 7)

It then goes on to celebrate a flood that 'shines like Occam's razor', a 'bank of froth' that has 'thrown in the sponge', and a compelling 'torrent'. Always ensuring that his lyric phenomena keep attention trained on his linguistic pyrotechnics, Raine keeps his birds 'bright as meringues' and his 'punts ... magnetized'. Even his 'rain scores a bull's-eye every time'. Persuading us to admire the ingenuities of water, 'Floods' makes fluidity manifest as *linguistic* 'brilliance' and lucid design. 'The slow digressions' of the floods 'are part of an overall argument' in which '[e]very quibble returns to the torrent'. That '[t]hey cover all the points' points out how adeptly language gives form to 'passionate water'. Raine finally stages a fantasy of praise and reward from others:

> What single-minded brilliance,
>
> what logic!
> Not one of us can look away. (*Postcard* 7)

It is a dream of rapt, exclamatory admiration that casts the poet, too, as one of 'us' – caught up, with the audience, in witnessing the natural world's spellbinding 'brilliance'. But the lines also set out to harness these eyes for their own agenda: Raine prompts readers not to look away from the poem's 'single-minded' ingenuities, and to bestow similar praise on its fluid accomplishments.

For John Bayley, such poetry is problematically self-delighting. Its precocious strategies to win admiration suggest anxieties about securing a place in the English post-war tradition, and about being seen as both innovative and comprehensible.[6] Certainly, the desire to make a language and an art 'smaller and clearer' (articulated by Philip Larkin in the mid-1950s in 'Lines on a Young Lady's Photograph Album') bears resemblance to the Martian determination to 'say only a little but to say it memorably', as Bayley puts it.[7] Fearful that Martianism insufficiently marks itself out from its forebears, its poets often assertively render the world strange, whilst dropping hints about their admirable gift for making that departure. Such work, Bayley thinks, 'composes itself into too precise a satisfaction with itself' (233).

More obliquely self-promotional strategies manifest in the 'new narrative' poetry celebrated by *M&M*. Besides James Fenton, Motion and Morrison, a number of esteemed poets of the 1980s deploy narrative, including Jeffrey Wainwright, Peter Reading, and David Sweetman. Each plays out, in the fabulatory vein, a sense of skewed, psychotic or nightmarish reality.[8] Linguistic eccentricity and role-changing often evoke an ordinariness gone to seed. Such work favours unreliable and protean storytellers. 'I explode – out of this narrow house, / My mind lips hands skin my whole body', writes one of Wainwright's volatile narrators.[9] '*This is not / A vision*', another voice continues, before we switch to the perspective of 'maggots' who plead for response: 'Why is this happening to us? / Forgive us Forgive us'. Not only is such writing more self-admonishing than self-congratulatory ('Forgive us'), its succession of first-person pronouns tunes in to a jumble of voices – rather than a text 'brilliantly' mastered by a single author-figure.

Associations of personal instability and narrative guilt emerge repeatedly in the longer sequences of the period. Motion's 'Dangerous Play' laments that: 'I am guessing / *There must be some evidence here*' but 'I can scarcely be sure which footprints / are innocent: which ones are mine / which yours, and which, … / belong to the killer' (*SP* 50). Comparably, in Fenton's 'A Staffordshire Murderer', a sense of criminality in the narrating self reveals uncanny parallels between its self-admiring artist and its proud homicidal subject. 'This murder is yours', writes Fenton. This accusation is directed at the victim (the poet-figure), but also indirectly at the audience, for whose benefit the speaker produces the narrative: 'You see? he has thought of everything', 'He speaks of his victims as a sexual braggart / With a tradesman's emphasis on the word "satisfaction"' (*M&M* 114–15). In such work, a storyteller's propensity to boast is akin to the determined genius of the murderer.

Although these narrative selves are primed for instability, 'I' is rarely so various as to be incapable of 'single-minded' action. 'Precarious' first-person voices parade themselves, by turns, as paranoidly self-denunciatory ('the killer' that might be 'myself') and proudly masterful: 'braggart', 'emphasis on the word "satisfaction"'. Comparably, in 'Death of an Actor', Hugo Williams deploys a compellingly retrospective, grieving 'I', who keeps reiterating his existence in the 'Now' of writing. He insistently asserts the immediacy of his narrative, even as his memories can be seen scripting the present: 'Now that I am grown', 'Now that he is gone', 'Now that we have seen' ...[10] Williams's engaging persona appears able *only* to enact his identity in the moment of utterance. It is a performance that requires the conjuring of ghosts and doubles – in particular, the endlessly refracting images of his father, who keeps sliding out of the frame and re-emerging in different guises: as soldier, actor, family man. 'I hold him up like a mirror / To look over my shoulder', says our narrator, but he disappears 'again / Leaving me no wiser'. Yet like his ingeniously recalled spectre, Williams's 'I' enacts a succession of impressively Baldanderic alterations that skilfully command attention through the declarative present: 'I'm sitting here like an actor / Waiting to go on', 'I'm given to wondering / What manner of man I might be'.

In such poetry, fluid and uncertain selves situate themselves through energetic performance. 'I' don't know '[w]hat manner of man I might be', but it's possible that you, the audience, will. A narrator will make use of an attention-grabbing declamatory voice, as if inviting dialogue. So too in Martianism. Reid, for instance, employs a didactic author- and ringmaster-figure, who gives instructions for how the page should be read, and answers his or her own questions: 'But wait: can mirrors / be said to have memories? / Yes'.[11] The staginess reminds readers not to be taken in: this work is less confounded than we might think (hence its deft affirmative). Similarly, Morrison and Motion show a penchant for fast-paced slippages between narrators, which the poet organises assertively as part of the literary performance.

The latter, in particular, compose narrative selves from public idioms, drawing on reportage, social and political commentary, and the rhetoric and form of local interest stories, newspaper headlines, legal cases and eyewitness accounts. 'This were the nub o t'court case: / were Peter reet or mad?' writes Morrison, observing the case of the Yorkshire Ripper from the perspective of a local male. The poem not only uses the first person for the Ripper himself ('"Ah were carrying out God's mission"', '"Ah were putty in is ands"'), it also directly taps into the accusatory voices of the prosecution: 'Cos why, if e were loopy', 'An why, if e weren't no sadist'. We also hear laddish debate about the Ripper, and women's angry responses: 'Listen to your beer-talk – / "hammer", "poke" and "screw", / ... / that's what the Ripper does'.[12] The editorial introduction proclaims that such polyvocality strikingly unsettles audience expectations of coherent selfhood – although one suspects this would be the case for only the most naïve readers.

Despite their soundbites about 'arrest', these poets do not expect audiences to be so baffled by surface 'haphazardness' that they miss the poetry's crafted play of voices. Nor its careful juggling of recognisable social contexts and idioms. An example is Motion's 1994 poetic sequence, 'Joe Soap'. This account of a protean Everyman – who is killed in the First World War and reborn in changeable guises through the twentieth century – ranges between testimony, quotation and adaptation of (imagined) historical persons, newspaper reports, recorded statements and lyric address. The poem recreates, seemingly verbatim, the textual apparatus of articles from 'the *Birmingham Post*, 3 February 1918', 'TRAGIC ACCIDENT', as well as professional eyewitness accounts:

> Date: 4 January 1918
>
> *Statement taken by*: PC 407 Smith
> *From*: Joseph Soap (Captain)[13]

Motion's snippets of pseudo-historical verity appear in a narrative ragbag of ontological slippages, evasions, fabricated histories and half-truths. His shape-shifting everyman, Joe Soap, 'might take the wrong way through fog / any time in his life without warning'. But the poem's succession of first personal voicings convey, with perfect lucidity, the Whitmanseque experience of boundless self-diversity:

> I can speak in my voice
> in a hundred tongues ...
> never again as myself'.

At the very moment of claiming 'I' can talk 'never again as myself', the lines proclaim that, indeed, the self 'can speak' and is doing so in a 'hundred tongue[d]' manifestation of itself. Mutable perspective goes hand in hand with the proclaimed desire to be – *and to promote* the modern poet's being – as Reid puts it: 'spacious and adventurous ... that was the lesson we thought we were putting out as we crashed the scene'.[14]

Being adventurous, for a Martian poet, involves the urge to *grip* readers. In late twentieth-century narrative poetry, this effect is often achieved in a parade of speakers and roles; a noisy plurality of interrelating objects and persons. These writers are welcoming (but not subservient) to their reading public. Hence Motion and Morrison, Reid and Raine strike the more genial chords of narratological and metaphorical eccentricity. Here is Raine's 1987 case for the winsome miscreant: 'Martianism is intellectually delinquent ... The tidy given world is leading a double life where things are less tame, even a bit deranged'.[15] Similarly, *M&M* tells us that poetic value isn't about laying one's soul bare, but about making mischief with that notion. Good writing exposes the self's double, if not treble or quadruple, life. Morrison's and Motion's ideal poets are compellingly unmanageable in relation to their audience: 'linguistic[ally] daring', they trade on 'poetic bizarrerie', probing creativity as part of 'the dark force of human history' (12). Such pronouncements set out to capture the public imagination: these authors hope to secure their own reputations, as well as those of their preferred poets, through audacious anthologising. Part of the success with which Motion's works have been traded, then and now, depends on the comprehensibility of his voice, despite its puckish 'delinquency'. He is marketed as accessible: the blurb of his 1998 *Selected Poems 1976–97* praises the 'artistic integrity that insists on ... addressing the reader with maximum clarity'. Reviewers celebrate his ability to share his changing 'public status ... the progress of literary vocation and the formation of the self', and his capacity to 'capture the reader's attention' by keeping us 'guessing little by little'.[16]

These poets show the *hospitable* face of alienation. Hence Motion says convivially that artworks 'welcome us into a narrative' and also flummox the expectations this sets up: such works will 'perplex us, but they also make us feel at home'.[17] In this hyperbolic emphasis on clarity and invitation, slippages of seeing and being are fêted as part of ordinary experience.

'The history of poetry, the making of reputations and movements, is in the hands of a powerful group of contemporaries ... self-consciously ally[ing] themselves to the tradition of myth-making anthologies' observes Adrian Caesar.[18] Critical of the conservativism of anthologies like *M&M*, Caesar considers the text as a preserve of power marketing itself and its values (in this case, verbal pyrotechnics combined with long-admired lyric traits: poise, balanced oppositions and metaphoricity). But Morrison and Motion do not disguise their self-interest: they declare their partisan approach to anthologising. They also select poetry frank about its affiliations and audience negotiations. For these late 1970s and early eighties poets, lyric declarations of literary hobnobbing, group-politicking and marketing *engage* a reading public.

It is an approach that pits itself against those plain-speaking poets of the preceding generation who considered themselves anti-allusive and anti-name-dropping. In 1955, Larkin famously lambasted Eliotic and Poundian literary hob-nobbing in and out of poems 'letting you see they know the right people'.[19] This was itself tactical (though he would not say so), for Larkin's lyrics are often spoken by a lonely, inward-directed poet-figure, not the voice of learned polyphonic historicity, whereas the poetry celebrated by *M&M* is social, assertive and multivocal. It alludes to poetry's promotion in a live, vituperative social scene, and deploys frank, provocative addresses to 'you'. The audience is confronted with wittily competitive notions of poetic engagement.

Fenton's 'Letter to Fuller', for example, attempts to get both Fuller, and his readership, on his side, by satirising literary competitors. Poking fun at a mid-century, rival anthologiser's literary values, it performs a disparaging run-through of its opponent's depiction of poetic success: 'He tells you, in the sombrest notes, / If poets want to get their oats / The first step is to slit their throats'. A parodic run-through of the supposed ingenuities of literary self-destructiveness follows, as Fenton catalogues famous nineteenth- and twentieth-century poets who fit his adversary's bill: 'Hardy and Hopkins hacked off their honkers. / Auden took laudanum in Yonkers. / Yeats ate a fatal plate of conkers'. Fenton then adopts the voice of his caricatured anthologist to make the argument that:

> The way to divide
> The sheep of poetry from the goats
> Is suicide.

Such a poem is reacting specifically against the arguments made by Al Alvarez's 1962 anthology *The New Poetry*.[20] That book had championed post-Movement writing that rejected 'academic-administrative' writing in favour of lyric irrationality, psychic energy, destructive sexuality and mythic violence. Alvarez's assertions of the necessity of poetical 'emotional intensity' – such as might be found in the confessionalism of Sylvia Plath or Robert Lowell, or in the violent corporeality of Ted Hughes – are repudiated by the poetry represented in *M&M* (245). Motion and Morrison argue that Hughes and Lowell were misleadingly described by *The New Poetry* as poets 'dealing with their experience "nakedly"' and writing "in a confessional white heat": they call this a falsely 'therapeutic transaction between writer and reader' (*M&M* 13).

'Letter to Fuller' invites its readers to see, and to become complicit with, the bias of the letter-writer. His partiality is genially revealed to the readers over his shoulder – so that that we and Fuller might take up his view of the better literary camp to join. Here, poetically 'knowing the right people', cattily disapproving of the 'wrong' ones (Alvarez) and using deprecatory black humour to express this, is a form of audience invitation.[21]

Comparably, Fuller's reply, 'To James Fenton' is an insistently congenial demonstration of the politics of poetic allegiance. 'You say that *Oxford* has no marrow, / Sucked dry by *Trevor-Roper, Sparrow*,' the 'Muse is / A sensible girl. / Even some antics of *Ted Hughes's* / Make her hair curl', 'I'm glad, of course, that you're with *Secker* / And not with *Fulcrum*'.[22] Fuller's and Fenton's negotiations of reputation trade on the 'I's unabashedness about others witnessing his poetic shoptalk. They display personal bugbears and a view of the professional wranglings of the zeitgeist. The letter-writer delivers sharp insights into the work of his contemporaries, as well as passing judgement on the vituperative anthologising, promoting, publishing and reviewing circuits. We hear a tongue-in-cheek account of how to 'divide / The sheep ... from the goats' so that poets 'get their oats'.

Backbiting self-promotional tactics perhaps unduly preoccupied these poet-editors, but this is by no means a new trait. (One thinks again of Donne's portrait. Or the embattled relations between the 'Satanic School' and 'Lake School' in the 1820s to 1830s. Or Ezra Pound taking up the voices of 'gagged reviewers' and angry professors in his 'Salutation' poems: '"Is this," they say, "the nonsense / that we expect of poets?"').[23] What comes to the fore in the factionality of *M&M* is its participation in an age-old struggle to persuade audiences of the superiority of one literary value system over others.

Subsequent poets and anthologisers have found facets of Martianism and its proponents objectionable. '[E]specially since Raine's editorship at Faber, unusual metaphor has too often become the definition of poetry, reducing valued writing to issues of perception and alienation', writes Peter Childs, observing the litany of critical complaints about the poetries celebrated during Raine's 1981–91 stint.[24] Another notable accusant is David Trotter, who, in *The Making of the Reader*, argues against the privileging of metaphorical power over all other forms of poetic skill.[25] For Trotter, the dangers of the view that '[p]oems are, in the first instance, metaphors or similes' can be seen in that 'set of 'skill[s] defined and over-defined by the work of Raine and Reid ... which has become in our society a sign for the entire scope and value of poetry', rather than one available marker of value (243–46). By these lights, those whose anthologising and promotional practices encourage audiences only to value a poetry adept at 'comparing things' (and not at all at, say, 'handling genre or rhythm or argument') abnegate their cultural duty: 'it is the responsibility of criticism to sustain a plurality of readerships, if necessary against the monopoly power of any institution or rhetoric' (249–50). When Raine is accused by later editors of exerting a restrictive influence over the scope of the British poetry scene (an influence upheld by *M&M*), a comparable narrowness of literary taste is rebuked. Barry and Robert Hampson, for instance, see Morrison and Motion's collection as an unrepresentative sample of the writing being penned in Britain during this period.[26] For them, such editorial politicking is to have knock-on effects on the kinds of work enjoyed by – and familiar to – Penguin and Faber readerships during the nineties and the early twenty-first century, as well as on poets and poetry audiences at large.

They 'advertised a rhetoric of the "new"' writes John Redmond in 2007: they were '[p]reoccupied with branding'.[27] Redmond is speaking about the contemporary poetic group dubbed the 'New Generation' – amongst whom Carol Ann Duffy, Simon Armitage and Don Paterson were announced in 1994 – whose work he compares with Martian and narrative poetry.[28] For Redmond, what lies behind the 'New Gen' writers' inveigling of themselves into disconcerting, direct and often buttonholing relations with their audiences, is the influence of those earlier poets that combined 'a man-of-the-people ... accessibility' with the 'uneasy energies' of ominous persuasion and narrative disjunction (246). The work of both groups is haunted by – as well as exploitative of – the language of branding and valuation. They draw on such sources not only in their subject matter (rivals, publishers, blurbs, bookshops and paychecks) but also in their idioms and forms, which often incorporate newspaper headlines, adverts, cliché, found texts.

For instance, in Duffy's 'Poet for Our Times', the first person is used to ventriloquise a figure who 'write[s] the headlines for a Daily Paper' (*NSP* 70). But of course it is not just this speaker who must 'grab attention / with just one phrase as punters rush on by'. Alert to the fact that the readers of her poetry are no strangers to a writer's self-publicising desires for celebrity, Duffy's poem capitalises on the shared ground between author and audience:

> I like to think that I'm a sort of poet
> for our times. My shout. Know what I mean?
> I've got a special talent and I show it (*NSP* 70).

In Duffy, the determination to assume a literary form that can be heard above the rest is so urgently self-interested that writing poetry can be drawn into analogy with penning newspaper headlines.

> The poems of the decade ... *Stuff 'em! Gotcha!*
> The instant tits and bottom line of art.

As the poet-figure both reports on and deploys 'attention'-grabbing diction and typography, the printed tactics that 'INCREASE ... TENSION' are both parodied and paraded. Duffy's text is a critique, from the inside, of a writer's in-your-face verbal strategies.

But it's also a request for the *recipient's* vigilance about her proclivity to be swayed by the consumerist soundbites that infiltrate judgements of aesthetic 'talent': '[t]he poems of the decade', 'special talent'. The poem exhibits anxieties about the misguided valuation of fallen literary registers on *both* sides of the contemporary lyric transaction. Such concerns inflect the way the audience is led through the verbal terrain. A culpable speaker, both engaging and untrustworthy, trades on cliché – but this lexicon has been adopted for the benefit of an assumed audience, for whom truisms are thought necessary to ensure maximum accessibility and popular appeal: 'My shout. Know what I mean?'.

Stan Smith writes that '[m]any of the New Generation poets were clearly fascinated by the media-saturated nature of the universe we inhabit'.[29] They are willing to harness the potentials of literary media and haunted by having exploited their saturation. By the nineties, authorial culpability is being paraded within the poem as a tactic for audience engagement. It is part of what comes to look like the 'honest' – or at least open – acknowledgement of the poet's compromised relationship with the culture industry. Such self-admissions were in place in the poetry championed by *M&M*, though most frequently expressed through a protean clamour of changeable self-promoting voices. Later in the century, they develop into more direct proclamations of a single author's need to perform savvy aesthetic image-management.

In Don Paterson's poem 'A Talking Book', for instance, a warm '[w]elcome' and 'a big hi!' go out to the audience. The book's lines meet and greet 'those undecided' browsers in 'Waterstones / trapped between the promise and the cost', and those 'who have diligently ploughed this far on foot / by way of bastard title, biog note / acknowledgements and prefatory quote'.[30] Paterson's book imagines eyeing its recipients across the named, shared spaces in which it meets them – such as the Waterstones bookstore – in which the 'talking' text will be read, received, judged and traded. Pursued by a guilty sense of complicity with the literary industry, this poem imagines itself in a nightmarish world of trade from which it cannot awake.

In Paterson, bad dreams cut both ways, bothering speaker and reader. The gentle purchaser is at once soothed and encouraged with such comments as: 'Be sure this song is just for you', 'a big hi!', 'we're of one mind now, i.e. yours –'. But this appeal to 'you' is hedged about with all the menace visited upon the far-too-anxious-to-please enunciating 'I'. The book's welcome is not addressed to living readers with freedom to choose their favourite collection, but 'those undecided shades' who are 'trapped' in the shop, and made feverishly to negotiate publishing and marketing lexicons – such as those 'all set to prove the Great Beast lies at slumber / in the ISBN or the barcode number' (26). Reader, speaker and textual object are lost together in this dark literary-commercial hallucination: 'You never meet your underself, other / than in dreams or sickness', 'at the bottom of this escalator / ... a cloven altar / awaits your sacrifice or desecration. / Now shake yourself awake' (29–30).

Such an author-figure is rarely alone in literary nightmare. In Paterson's case, 'I' is here with 'you', the reader, his companion in these fevered journeyings through the commercial lyric underworld. Yet, like a number of his peers, Paterson's narrative poems are simultaneously suspicious of the fellow-travellers they enlist, fearful that the speaking self is being taken over by hostile, invading voices, with their own demons and agendas. '*Someone appears to be using your mouth / to scream through*' he writes in Part III of his long poem, 'The Alexandrian Library'.[31] The poem appears to be 'rising in syllables we did not speak', as the American poet Wallace Stevens puts it: the language world appears to write the subject, rather than the other way round. In Paterson's early twenty-first-century reality, this produces a saleable textual object, over which the ghosts of the literary past, as well as family, friends and the intrusive lexicons of the present, are driven.

Armitage's poetry has also expressed the sense of being culpably scripted by a medley of idioms, transmissions and testimonies – yet here guilt is less purgatorial nightmare than waking trial. In 'The Stuff', in *Zoom!*, a mixture of free indirect speech and parody construct the poem's narrative framework and its moments of individual expression.[32] When 'I' shuffles into the witness box to tell 'the addict's side of the story', we find ourselves in another court case. Here, the voices of poet and poem, narrator and addict are put on trial:

> In court I ambled up and took the oath ...
> I said grapevine, barge pole whirlpool, chloride
> Concrete, bandage, station, story. Honest.

Armitage's juggling of stories and their sides, truths and their permutations, appraises a succession of speaking voices. It also considers whether the work comprised of a web of partial accounts – as opposed to the story of a monologic 'I' – is more or less likely to stand up to scrutiny. 'The Stuff' is poised between speaking for oneself, and speaking for others. The plain-speaking annotative brevity of the speaker's oath (above) at once asserts his verity: 'I said grapevine, barge pole, whirlpool', 'Honest'. But of course the very stockpiling of single-word evidential particulars ('Concrete, bandage, station, story') blunts the assertion of probity: 'Honest'. Rhythmically, the assertion arrives as if just another addition to the 'side of the story' he is delivering: one more exhibited duosyllablic item. At the level of sentence structure, what 'I said' for the jury arrives in a different mode from the narrator's recreation of it for readers: 'The Stuff' remains tongue-in-cheek about the extent to which poetic utterance could ever offer 'proof' of verbal integrity. Armitage's interpenetration of voices and stories – those belonging to the speaker, addict, the poet-figure himself – sets each of its solo voices up for a fall, by insisting on 'honesty' under oath. The narrative texture obliges readers to remain wary about the verity 'I' presents, exposing us to the untrustworthiness of narrative fabulation.

By these lights, we might almost be persuaded that there is a perceptible line of literary influence between New Generation poets and their Martian and New Narrative forebears. Each of these different writers is chary of literary authenticity, exhibits instabilities of voice and emphasises the mediated – and often commercial nature of – poet-audience relations. But I find myself holding back. For these are characteristics of a diverse range of late twentieth-century poetry. They only very weakly indicate a single 'group' or school, or suggest a solitary line of influence. When W. S. Graham says in his poem, 'Language Ah Now you Have Me': 'please speak for me between the social beasts which quick assail me' – or when he writes in another poetic sequence from the late 1970s, that the bad word is the one that 'glamours me' and goes out 'to strut' – I am not inclined to read him as a 'new narrative' poet.[33] Even if he, like Morrison or Fenton, is writing in a fragmentary, late twentieth-century narrative mode. Nor would I read Roy Fisher's *The Ship's Orchestra* or Geoffrey Hill's *Speech! Speech!* under such a banner – in spite of their sharing certain disjunctive effects with Raine, Fenton, Morrison. Even some the poets within *M&M* do not quite fit the bill. However fresh or startling his vocabulary and metaphorical idiom, Seamus Heaney hardly seems readable in terms of Martianism. Nor do we, today, read Anne Stevenson or Tony Harrison or Paul Muldoon as displaying New Narrative propensities.

Each of the poets named in this chapter would perhaps more accurately be understood as participating in a broader literary-historical exploration of the shifting boundaries of personal authority, selfhood, literary trade and narrative guilt. Whilst shape-shifting narration has precedents in (if not before) the dramatic monologues of Robert Browning, the sexual politics of Meredith's 'Modern Love', and the polyvocality of Ezra Pound's 'Hugh Selwyn Mauberley', the tactics of audience engagement and lyric self-promotion can be seen from Siminodes to the Chartists, from the Cockney school to the New Gen. Theoretically, too, alienation and defamiliarisation have affinities with the thought of Viktor Shklovsky and the Russian Formalists.[34] The traits we have seen promoted did not originate with – and are by no means unique to – poetry of the late 1970s and the 1980s. We glean as much from the fact that the terms Martian and New Narrative have very infrequently been taken up to describe the practices of subsequent generations of poets – such as the New Generation – and even less often applied as self-descriptions by these contemporary poets themselves.[35]

NOTES

1 Motion, review of *John Donne: The Reformed Soul*, by John Stubbs (Viking, 2006), in *Ways of Life: On Places, Painters and Poets* (London: Faber, 2008), p. 122.
2 Motion and Morrison, eds., *The Penguin Book of Contemporary British Poetry* (Harmondsworth: Penguin, 1982). Referred to as *M&M*.
3 Craig Raine, *A Martian Sends a Postcard Home* (Oxford: Oxford University Press, 1979), p. 1. Referred to as *Postcard*.
4 Fenton, 'A Martian School of Two or More', *LRB* 1:4 (Dec. 1979): 16.
5 John Redmond, 'Ringmaster', Rev. of *Expanded Universes* by Reid, *LRB* 18:23 (Nov. 1996): 25–26.
6 Bayley, 'Contemporary British Poetry: A Romantic Persistence', *Poetry* 146:4 (Jul. 1985): 227–36.
7 Bayley, 233; Larkin, *Collected Poems* (London: Faber, 2003), p. 43.
8 See Reading's *Ukulele Music*, a narrative pastiche of work-songs, sea shanties, English medieval alliterative poetry, heroic epic and classical forms (Secker & Warburg, 1985).
9 Wainwright, 'Thomas Müntzer', *M&M* 127–29.
10 Williams, *Penguin Modern Poets 11* (Harmondsworth: Penguin, 1997), p. 125.
11 Reid, 'Like a Mirror', *Katerina Brac* (1985), quoted from *Selected Poems* (London: Faber, 2011).
12 Morrison, *The Ballad of the Yorkshire Ripper* (London: Chatto & Windus, 1987), pp. 31–32.
13 Motion, *The Price of Everything* (London: Faber, 1994).
14 See Elisabeth Frost, 'Found in Translation: An Interview with Christopher Reid', *Electronic Poetry Review* 6 (Spring 2003): www.epoetry.org/issues/issue6/text/prose/reid.htm accessed 12 Oct 2014.
15 Mary Karr, 'An Interview with Craig Raine', *Ploughshares* 13:4 (1987): 138–48, at 140.
16 See Paul Davis, Rev. of *Public Property*, *Guardian* (28 Sep 2002): 25. See Robert Richman, Rev. of *Dangerous Play*, *The New Criterion* 4 (Jan 1986): 76.
17 Motion, 'Howard Hodgkin, "Emotional Situations"', in *Ways of Life*, p. 97.
18 Caesar, *Dividing Lines: Poetry Class and Ideology* (Manchester: Manchester University Press, 1991), p. 239.
19 Larkin, 'Statement', *Required Writing* (London: Faber, 1983), p. 79.
20 Alvarez, *The New Poetry* (Harmondsworth: Penguin, 1962), revised 1966.
21 As Corcoran points out, these narrative poems zealously declare their sources and allusions: Motion's source for 'Dangerous Play' was *White Mischief* by James Fox; Morrison's 'The Ballad of the Yorkshire Ripper' takes some of 'the dialect … from Richard Blakeborough's *Wit, Character, Folklore and Customs of the North Riding of Yorkshire* (2nd ed., Saltburn-by-the-Sea: W. Rapp and Sons, 1911), p. 247.
22 Fuller, *Collected Poems* (London: Chatto & Windus, 1996).

23 Byron, *Don Juan* II; Pound, 'Salutation the Second' and 'Salutation the Third'.
24 Childs, *The Twentieth Century in Poetry* (London: Routledge, 1999), p. 151.
25 Trotter, *The Making of the Reader: Language and Subjectivity in Modern American, English and Irish Poetry* (Basingstoke: Macmillan, 1984).
26 See Peter Barry and Robert Hampson, eds, *New British Poetries: The Scope of the Possible* (Manchester: Manchester University Press, 1993), p. 4.
27 Redmond, 'Lyric Adaptations', in *The Cambridge Companion to Twentieth-Century Poetry*, ed. Neil Corcoran (Cambridge: Cambridge University Press, 2007), pp. 245–58, at 246; see Ian Gregson on narrative poetry's advertising parodies, in *Contemporary Poetry and Postmodernism: Dialogue and Estrangement* (Basingstoke: Macmillan, 1996), pp. 120–22.
28 See the criteria for inclusion in 'The New Generation', in Peter Forbes, 'How We Made New Gen – the Faxes behind the Facts', *Poetry Review* 84:3 (1994): 52.
29 Smith, *Poetry and Displacement* (Liverpool: Liverpool University Press, 2007), p. 195.
30 Paterson, 'A Talking Book', *Landing Light* (London: Faber, 2003), p. 26.
31 Paterson, *God's Gift to Women* (London: Faber, 1997), p. 50.
32 Armitage, *Zoom!* (Newcastle-upon-Tyne: Bloodaxe, 1989), p. 69.
33 Graham, *New Selected Poems* (London: Faber, 2004), pp. 207, 178–79.
34 Shklovsky, 'Art as Device' (1917), *Theory of Prose* (1925; Elmwood Park, IL: Dalkey Archive Press, 1991), pp. 1–14.
35 Paterson, Armitage and Duffy are each poet-editors, and anthologisers. See Armitage and Robert Crawford's 1998 *The Penguin Anthology of Poetry from Britain and Ireland Since 1945*; Paterson and Charles Simic's argumentatively position-taking *New British Poetry* (St. Paul, MN: Graywolf Press, 2004), Duffy's more commercial *Answering Back: Living Poets Reply to the Poetry of the Past* (London: Picador, 2007).

8

SANDIE BYRNE

Poetry and Class

The phrase 'poetry and class' often seems to denote writing by working-class poets or poetry about the working class, which suggests that poetry about and/or by middle-class writers is the default. Few poems qualify as political interventions on behalf of marginalised middle-class ideals, traditions or dialects, which suggests that either such poems are not needed, or that they are not widely circulated. That certain poems not overtly political or interventionist, nor obviously written in dialect or sociolect, have been categorised as 'working-class', in line with the eighteenth-century genre of poems of the rural labouring class, indicates the existence of an ontological category whose salient feature is the social origin of the poet rather than the subject of the poem. 'Working-class poet' is a frequent appellation, even when the discussion is of a poem which has nothing to do with class.

This chapter will survey some poetry in English on the subject of social inequality; poetry which represents personal experience as exemplary of that of a social group. In many cases that poetry is written in a register marked for class. There is no attempt to define the social class of the poets, nor to look for an 'authentic' working-class voice. There is no reason to assume that middle- or upper-class poets won't write about social inequality, nor that working-class poets will write exclusively about the proletariat, or make public statements about exclusion, oppression or marginalisation. The fact is that some do. To pick out class from the nexus of nation, region, language, religion and class which construct identity in much poetry in English by poets from the Republic of Ireland or Northern Ireland or from poets of Irish descent, or from the nexus of ethnicity, colour, language and class would be futile, and to give justice to those complex relationships would require greater length than is available here.

Much poetry of the post-war period is the poetry of estrangement. The Butler Education Act (1944) gave many clever working-class children the opportunity to study beyond the age of fourteen and to take up free places at grammar schools (if their parents could find the money for uniforms, sports equipment and other things). This Scholarship Boy phenomenon documented so well by Richard Hoggart (the Scholarship Girl phenomenon is less well documented) displaced working-class schoolchildren from their familial and friendship networks and either assimilated them into middle-class culture or left them stranded, at home in neither, but often an observer of both. In particular, Scholarship Boys who became poets report an estrangement from the working-class father and the model of masculinity that he represents.

Blake Morrison finds in British poetry of the post-war period an obsession with fathers and masculinity, referring to the 'metrical muscularity' of Tony Harrison[1] and 'hard sophistication' of Paul Muldoon.[2] Neil Corcoran similarly argues that male poets of the time 'exhibit a common tendency that seems if anything a crisis of masculinity, as embourgeoised sons of farmers (Seamus Heaney), mushroom-gatherers (Muldoon), boxers (Craig Raine) and bakers (Harrison) come to terms with their estrangement from their working-class fathers'.[3] Whilst there is a common strand of guilt (about not engaging in physical labour) and fear (of being seen as sissy and posh), and a common representation of the father-figures as inarticulate or silent, in other respects those models of masculinity vary. Heaney's strong, reticent but benign father is poetry in motion: 'Digging', 'Follower', *Death of a Naturalist* (1966); Harrison's less enlightened and more harsh critic: 'A Good Read', 'Bookends' 1 and 2 (*from 'The School of Eloquence'*) is more often described as an older man worn out from the labour unsuited to his physique ('Marked with D'); Muldoon's is a more elusive but supportive figure: 'The Waking Father', *New Weather* (1973), 'Cherish the Ladies', and 'The Mirror', *Quoof* (1983), 'The Coney', *Meeting the British* (1987). Whereas the fathers in Heaney's and Muldoon's poems are farmers, strongly associated with rural ties and the past, those of Harrison and Raine are of the urban working class, and uninheritable occupations that leave no weight of guilt on the generations that choose not to take them up. Nonetheless, Harrison, like Heaney, makes an analogy between manual labour and writing: 'Facing North' 'Social Mobility'). Alan Brownjohn describes 'The School of Eloquence' sonnets as 'hammered into crude containers for heavy irony and his very own brand of chip-on-the-shoulder coarseness'.[4] The hammering metaphor is apt, given Harrison's representation of himself labouring, in competition with other men ('The Lords of Life'), or alone ('Cypress and Cedar') but the accusation of working-class-chip with its suggestion of a reduction of social ills to personal resentment seems crass.

An exception to the prevalent machismo of the 1960s to 1980s, according to Corcoran, is Douglas Dunn, whose anti-machismo stance is evident in poems such as 'The Sportsmen', 'Ratatouille', *Europa's Lover* (1982) and

Elegies (1985).[5] Feminist poetry of the period often engaged with mothers and motherhood, but tended to submerge class and sometimes racial distinctions in manifestos of female solidarity, or to focus on gender issues to the exclusion of others.

Children educated under the provisions of the 1944 Act in the late 1940s and 1950s were young adults, some at university, during the Labour governments of 1964–70 and 1974–76. They had benefitted from the Welfare State Acts: Family Allowances Act (1945); National Insurance Act (1945); National Insurance – Industrial Injuries Act (1946); and National Assistance Act (1948). They had seen the success of working-class dramatists and novelists, the Angry Young Men generation (few of whom wrote poetry on the subject of class), and of works such as Hoggart's *The Uses of Literacy* (1957). Working-class musicians were producing some of the most popular music of the time. There were outlets for their poetry in small literary magazines, alternative magazines, and underground magazines, all of which might take poems excluded from the London and Oxbridge-based prestige periodicals. Small presses were flourishing: Enitharmon was founded in 1967; Anvil Press in 1968; Carcanet in 1969; Peterloo Poets in 1972. Places such as Leeds and Hull as much as, if not more than, London, were hubs of poetry. That class would be on the agenda of poetry was perhaps over-determined.

No survey of British poetry and class or politics can overlook the importance of *Stand Magazine*. *Stand* was started by Jon Silkin on the proceeds of holiday pay in lieu of notice following his attempt to organise his fellow janitors to protest against being required to work overtime for basic pay. Its mission statement is to '"Stand" against injustice and oppression, and "Stand" for the role that the arts, poetry and fiction in particular, could and should play in that fight'. *Stand* has published work, in many cases early work, by poets including Michael Hamburger, Geoffrey Hill and George MacBeth, as well as fellow Leeds alumni Douglas Dunn, Tony Harrison, Ken Smith and Jeffrey Wainwright and Leeds tutor. Together with the university's *Poetry and Audience*, and Northern House, which was associated with *Stand* and published a number of these poets' early collections, this made Leeds an important fount of poetry.

In 1982 Morrison opened a review of Tony Harrison's *Continuous* (1981) by asserting that there were grounds for seeing Harrison as 'the first genuine working-class poet England has produced this century'.[6] Whilst other poets have a proletarian background, Morrison argues that they have not been interested in making poetry from it; yet others have painted the view from the factory floor, but themselves come from the haute bourgeoisie; Dunn is found guilty of being Scottish. Harrison claims a working-class background but like many other British and other poets by occupation, interests, income, even voice, can be seen to have migrated. This shibboleth of authenticity is at variance with Donald Davie's mistrust of poetic autobiography and 'sincerity'. Davie argues that whilst the 'story' of 'The School of Eloquence' Meredithian sonnets is interesting and touching, its interest is 'documentary, not intrinsic to its nature as poetry; and so we are bowled over on a first reading, but less so the next time, and the next.'[7] The human appeal of the poems, Davie asserts, guarantees popularity for the elegies, more so than for Harrison's 'unconfessional' pieces, which he finds deserve greater respect. Davie requires poets to prove their sincerity not by shouting at us or writing 'dishevelled', over-emotional, out-of-control poetry, but by control of form and tone and judicious fair-mindedness.[8]

Many of Harrison's poems on the relationship between language (spoken or written), high and low culture and social prestige, with notable exceptions, including the verse plays and several of the longer *Loiners* (1970) poems, are presented as autobiographical and discussed as such in interviews and prose writing, but they are also offered as episodes in a national class war, a record of repression and exclusion. The lyric poems might qualify as confessional, in Rosenthal's definition of a record of personal suffering, and a plea for sympathy, or in Davie's own definition 'merely the vehicle by which the poet acts out before his public the agony or discomfort ... of being a writer, or of being alive in the twentieth century'.[9] The extent to which affect, generated by our knowledge of 'authenticity' and sense of 'sincere feeling' will obfuscate the poetic effects as well as the political message, is debatable.

Harrison's 'Confessional Poetry', which precedes the sonnets in his *Selected Poems* (1987), seems to promise engagement with this argument, but turns instead on the question of autobiography and truth. Poems grouped in 'The School of Eloquence' such as 'Marked with D' and 'Bookends' are moving but also display control in the deployment of metre. The overall pattern of the first 'Bookends is iambic, but the extent of variation is considerable.

/ u / u / u u / /
Baked the day she suddenly dropped dead
u / u / u u / / u /
we chew it slowly that last apple pie
....

u / / u u / u / / u
You're like book ends, the pair of you, she'd say,
/ u / u / u / // ///
Hog that grate, say nothing, sit, sleep, stare

Antony Easthope suggests that iambic pentameter, rather than the natural concomitant of the English sentence, was the invention of Chaucer, yet that it has become, analogous to Western harmony in music and linear perspective in graphic art, an 'epochal form, one co-terminous with bourgeois culture from the Renaissance to now'.[10] Harrison's appropriation and disruption of the iamb may represent a characteristic appropriation and resistance to that epochal form and to the Received Pronunciation with which, Easthope argues, pentameter is particularly compatible.[11]

The iambic pentameter of *v.* (1985), in particular that of the dialogue, is so disrupted by variation in both line-length and stress that it may be more usefully read as having four strong stresses to the line. This would be appropriate for a poet much more attuned to consonance than to assonance.

> *So **what's** a cri-de-**coeur, cunt?** Can't you **speak***
> *the **language** that yer **mam spoke.** Think of **'er!***
>
> *Aspirations, **cunt!** Folk on t'**fucking dole***
> *[...]*
> *above the **shit** they're **dumped in, cunt,** as **coal***
> ***aspires** to be **chucked** on t'**fucking fire.***

Perhaps *v.*, as a more overtly political poem, in spite of its autobiographical narrative, would have escaped Davie's censure. The binary divisions of the poem are represented by the skinhead's sprayed words: United v, the opposing team. The shift from proper noun to adjective that makes the aggressive assertion of opposition the reverse: 'I wish on this skin's word deep aspirations,' and 'a call to Britain and to all the nations / made in the name of love for peace's sake'; and turns the historical and material (the miners' strike; unemployment) ahistorical and ideal; can seem rather softcore in comparison to the harder-edged work of more recent poets, particularly as the many divisions are ultimately resolved by union, sexual, romantic, of man and woman, as the narrator comes home to his wife. This is not, however, the retreat to the transcendent and metaphysical of which David Lloyd complains in an article on Heaney's work.[12] As always in Harrison's work, contradictions are acknowledged, overtly or tacitly or through image, in this case, coal. The worked-out pit on which Beeston Cemetery stands represents a lost industry and consequent unemployment, deprivation and discontent; the back-breaking labour of exploited workers, for which later workless generations might be grateful; the power that drove the Industrial Revolution, and made the British Empire, and made Leeds, for some, prosperous; and geological time, and memory. At the end of the poem it is burning among the cultural markers of a couple familiar with Alban Berg and the word strata. This, and the accusations of the narrator's skinhead-persona, acknowledge the futility yet necessity of poetic intervention and aspiration.[13]

Like Harrison, Ken Smith writes about his familial and geographical origins, but argues that his work is less particular and therefore more inclusive.

Whereas Harrison's poems of working-class childhood are urban in setting and concerned with the poet's dualistic view of his background (he is separated from the warm, loving continuities; he admires working-class reticences, strengths and autodidactism; he leaves a cultural desert in which poetry is unappreciated), Smith's childhood memories are rural in setting, their preoccupation poverty: the cold, harsh, bleak, comfortless country of East Yorkshire, and the hard life of the family of a silent, morose, itinerant labourer and shopkeeper. The poems of memory such as 'The Family Group', from *The Pity* (1967) represent a far from Arcadian pastoral; the man who works the land 'feels the weather in him'; 'angled' by work, he is 'crooked'. Whereas Harrison triumphantly acclaims that he writes in his own voice, Smith uses personae. Like the title of the collection of his poems to 2001, *Shed*, he can shed skins. In 'Wall Dreams' (2001) the narrator has a name 'somewhere about me' but is 'muddy with others'. Whereas for Harrison the personal and the political meet in the relationship between 'them' and 'uz' or '[ʌs] and ['uz'] as enacted in Leeds Grammar School, for Smith, in 'The Pity' (1967), they are represented by an act not personal to him but seminal in world history, the enforced witness by Mao Tse Tung of the execution by strangulation of his pregnant wife.

Later work, such as the long poem 'Fox Running' (originally published as a cyclostyled pamphlet in 1980), revised in *Poet Reclining* (1982) and the 'London Poems', *Terra* (1986), change terrain. Smith's fox is both displaced homeless human and outlaw-scavenger fox in a fusion which is not always successful. As an observer/inhabitant of inner-city poverty and decay, the Hughesian fox functions well, but its observations become infused with human social comment and judgement in the 'cool skinhead wind', in NF occupied country' and 'along 'Pakkibashers' Court'. The inner-city decay of Docklands during the Poll Tax riots and the 1980s visits of politicians broadcasting compassionate concern and plans for revitalisation are paralleled with the city of Henry Mayhew's *London Labour and the London Poor* (1864). If Smith's poems of childhood resist representing his labourer father as a helpless disenfranchised victim, then his later poems represent urban entropy and inner-city poverty as an inescapable, causeless phenomenon. Nonetheless, they assert the importance of recording. 'I'm the missing witness. And they never ask.'

Tom Pickard's work continues the theme of people and speech consigned to the scrap-heap. The title of his collected poems, *Hoyoot* (2014), connotes a number of kinds of throwing away: expelling people; the custom of throwing coins to children from a bridal car; the act of making redundant. An early poem, 'Birthplace Bronchitis' in *High on the Walls* (1968), a snapshot of the ruined health of northeastern labourers, is reminiscent of Harrison's view of his father coughing and spitting into the fire, and 'Unemployed' (1968) of a condensed speech from *v*. The episodes of sex, male and machismo sexual gratification of different kinds, which stud the earlier work, like the references to unemployment, might seem to echo Harrison, but the rhythms of the poems are not those of sex, heartbeat, and labour. Where Harrison occupies iambics and sonnets of lousy leasehold British canonical poetry, Pickard's work looks to imagism and modernism and the Beats in truncated free verse. Pickard has often acknowledged his debt to Basil Bunting, not least in Bunting's advice that he should make his own form. He has trenchantly rejected conventional forms, in a 2012 interview quoting from a recently written poem, 'To goad my frigging peers', beginning 'Fuck the sonnet, and announcing that he pisses upon those who use it as 'some talismanic indenture / an entrée to a toothless craft'.[14]

Pickard does express affectionate attachment to genres of popular and folk verse: children's play-rhymes, folk-songs and ballads. *The Ballad of Jamie Allan* (performed 2005; published 2007), about a piper, thief, scofflaw and folk-hero from the Northumbrian Scottish borders who died in Durham jail, abandoned by the aristocrats who had patronised him, came out of an opera libretto and uses a number of forms associated with ballads and folk tales, including the (roughly) eight, six *abab* quatrain, as well as the longer lines and closed couplets spoken by Allan's lover, Annie Bennett. That form is made lively by pairs and oppositions in Allan's 'Join the Army': 'Have you seen him? they axed. Could you say he's about? / He's slippy as eels and flash as a trout'. The work makes good use of the repetition, parallel syntax and *anaphora* of ballad and folk song, particularly in the lament of Jamie in his cell, 'The Ballad of Jamie Allan', which has an 'I was/I am' structure. Also employing *anaphora*, and a repeated question format, but in the more characteristic free verse, contemporary matter and confrontational tone is 'Who is the Whore of Armageddon?' in *Tiepin Eros/ Typing Errors: New and Selected Poems* (1994), which asks 'whose breath is bilious with unemployed bombs?' and 'Whose legs are knotted with varicose veins / from standing on the necks of health workers?'

Also intransigently northern, though born in London, by Holland Park in 1952, Sean O'Brien lived in Hull and became professor of creative writing at Newcastle University. 'A Corridor', published in the Huddersfield magazine *The North* 10 (1991), uses his trademark modified anapaests to chronicle lives that are envisaged as channelled and confined in bleak and shabby institutional corridors.

u / u u / u u / uu /
The shoulder-high tiles in municipal green,

u / u u / u u /uu /
The brown walls, the bare lavatorial floor

In the 1950s, when 'we were 'much smaller', and impressed by 'minor displays' of the state, which aims us all:

/ / u u /
From cradle to grave

In the title poem of *Cousin Coat* (2002), northernness is conceived as an invisible garment that has spent decades under the Aire Navigation Canal. It is history and identity, and means 'the North, the poor, and Troopers sent / To shoot down those who showed their discontent.' In O'Brien's north there is no comfort for 'comfy meliorists' who weep over photographs of Jarrow marchers; no comfort for the poor enlisted to fight and die for their country; no comfort for strikers who lose their jobs. 'Cousin Coat' is there to keep the poet honest when others 'cauterise the facts', to be memory, conscience, will and rage, and if he should stray into lies, to be at his throat. That will to stand witness and produce testimony is evident in 'On the Toon' (2011) which envisages the demise of public libraries in terms of the time (less than a life) that it takes to restore the ignorance that the library, a 'public mind' was designed to dispel. The poem comes in the threnodic *November*, which in addition to elegies for lost relatives and friends, laments such other, public losses. The encounter in a churchyard in *November*'s 'Sunk Island' (2011) might evoke echoes of Harrison's longer poem, *v.*, but the antagonist here is no skinhead projection from the psyche but a middle-class equestrian, and rather than a realist, linear narrative poem, 'Sunk Island' uses riddling incantatory symbolism. 'On the Toon' sets itself up as an *epyllion* with an invocation to the river-god Tyne before (in a somewhat overused device) becoming a Dantesque journey to the purgatory or hell, with Classical references, the guide a scantily-clad, WKD-drinking Lost Girl. Unlike the lyrical opening poem, 'Fireweed', which welcomes the silence and spaces of the post-train age, 'the strong neglect', 'On the Toon' represents as hellish all that is lost, neglected or unappreciated in northern working-class popular culture. The missing of the poem include not only people but elements assumed to be essential to a good life. O'Brien's poem for the 2013 austerity Budget, 'Oysterity' published in the *Guardian* (9 March 2013) playfully jumps between iambic trochaic trimeter and dimeter in a varying rhyme scheme to mock the anguished laments of the privileged over an oyster supper, lavish consumption, and its ironic return.

Born in 1963, Don Paterson missed much of the atmosphere of optimism about the Welfare State and burgeoning possibilities for poetry, and working-class writing and writers. Even in 1994 the Poetry Society's claim that poetry was the new rock 'n' roll seemed risible, in 1998 Oxford University Press stopped publishing contemporary poets,[15] and other consortia shaved their lists. As poetry editor of Picador, Paterson is well aware of the problems of finding a readership for new poetry, as well as that of making a living from poetry, though the many awards and prizes available help. His own writing has been published in a time when class has been declared a redundant concept (in Britain) and writing about it is no longer viable. Given that those fortunate enough to be *working* class are far from the bottom of the social pile today, the focus of the *working* working-class poet's speaking for the dispossessed has shifted slightly. As critical theory informed poetry criticism, the problematization of the existence of a sovereign self with free choice and agency, and of the validity of the voiced ventriloquizing the subaltern made some poems of the 1950s and 1970s concerned with class seem naïve or crude. Problematized also is the extent to which class can usefully be deployed as a dominant determinant of identity when individuals occupy multiple subject positions, constructed by, among other factors, gender, ethnicity, nationality, sexual orientation and regional affiliation. Nonetheless, inequalities and attitudes to perceived inequalities persist.

Far from all of Paterson's poems represent class-based attitudes or inequalities, and most of his best poems have other subjects. 'An Elliptical Stylus' from *Nil Nil* (1993), however, describes a painful encounter; a working-class father potentially humiliated in front of his son by a smirking shopkeeper. His narrator refuses the reader's expectation of any attempt to 'cauterize' the painful anecdote with 'something axiomatic' about articulacy and inheritance', since the father is quite capable of speaking for himself. If readers persist in looking for 'resonance', he will swing for us, and 'any other cunt' who is 'happy to let my father know his station', which, he concludes, probably includes 'yourself'.

Paterson forcibly distances himself from the kinds of inclusive poetry which invites pity or even empathy for the working-class character depicted with pathos as victim. He does not cite Harrison's depictions of Mr Harry and Mrs Florence Harrison as examples of the poetry he deplores, and indeed acknowledges Harrison as a major influence, but he does castigate 'sub-Harrison' types whose poetry ostensibly lends dignity to the working-class experience, but who are actually dealing with 'their own embarrassment with their social origins, and their awkwardness in using the language of their superiors'. To see 'the working classes patronise *themselves* in this way' is depressing.[16] Pickard brackets Dunn and O'Brien as writers of 'brilliant' poems which worry him, remarking that part of him thinks that in poems such as Dunn's 'The Come-on' and O'Brien's 'Cousin Coat' the poets are 'telling the bastards too much' of things that ought to be 'circulated between ourselves'.

If poems which employ words and phrases from the dialects and sociolects of Leeds, Manchester, or Newcastle reverse the working-class sense of exclusion from poems written in Standard English, then much writing from Scotland in the post-war era has taken this further, particularly the work of Tom Leonard and Liz Lochhead. Though he is best known for the collection set in Hull, *Terry Street* (1969) and the *Elegies* (1985) for his first wife, much of Douglas Dunn's poetry comes from his Renfrewshire roots, as well as from his travels in America, Australia, France and elsewhere. Unlike Leonard and Lochhead, Dunn does not write in Scots or Scottish-inflected English. 'The Come-on', from *The Barbarians* (1979) suggests that rather than writing in Scots, the barbarian will 'open the gate' through Standard English: 'they say we have no culture / We are of the wrong world' but that we will beat 'them' with 'decorum, with manners / As sly as language is'.

More aggressively adversarial, Dunn's 'Guerrillas' in *The Happier Life* (1972) are working-class schoolchildren who resent the presence in their schools of the sons and daughters of prosperous farmers and landowners, and take out that resentment by plundering the estates and farms. The trope of rural revenge is continued in 'Gardeners' from *Barbarians*, which invents for England a working-class revolution it didn't have, in an imaginary rural shire. Working men's 'coarser artistries' have built the designs of the more refined estate owner, whose stamp of ownership is on even the shire, which is named for him. In a section that makes much of inclusive and exclusive pronouns, the gardeners demand that he admit 'What likes of us did for the likes of you'. The gardeners who have raised the garden have now razed it, and the man who has been raised above them by virtue of his birth is now dangled by them, hanged in the shade of the garden.

Barbarians also includes a snapshot portrait of 'Glasgow Schoolboys Running Backwards' in high winds, going '[f]orwards in reverse, always holding their caps'. The *abab* iambic pentameter quatrain with variation is reminiscent of Harrison, as is the emblematic use of the cap – a schoolboy's which will become the adult flat cap also featured in Harrison's work. The partial and eye-rhyme, however, takes the place of Harrison's more frequent use of full rhyme or rhymes across audaciously broken words.

Terry Eagleton praises Dunn for being able to 'transcend the two major pitfalls of poetry concerned with working people – bourgeois voyeurism or sympathetic mythification'.[17] The representation of the defeated and disenfranchised people of Terry Street avoids mythification or idealisation, though the narrator figures as observer rather than participant. Similarly, 'Washing the Coins', *St Kilda's Parliament* (1981), records the lack of sympathy for one marginalised community by another. The division is between local labour and itinerant Irish workers employed to dig potatoes, the difference signified by the farmer's wife apologetically ruffling the speaker's hair, after mistaking him for an Irish boy.

'Green Breeks', from the same collection, dramatizes an episode from the autobiography of Sir Walter Scott.[18] Scott recollects the regular fist and stone-and-stick fights, 'bickers', between two sets of boys whom he distinguishes linguistically as he does socially: his group, the upper-class, 'reside' in a square, the lower-class 'inhabit' neighbouring areas. Of the upper he uses the register of the empire's military; they are a 'regiment' or 'company' (supported, Scott says, by elder brothers, domestic servants, and similar auxiliaries) who have been provided with 'colours' by a 'lady of distinction'. One has 'zeal for the honour of the regiment'. The other group are the 'lower rank', 'hardy loons', 'plebian'. The upper-class boys don't know the names of their 'enemies', but name one Green Breeks. When that lower-class boy dares to lay his hands on 'the patrician standard', one of the 'regiment' cuts him down with a knife glorified as a '*couteau de chasse*'. 'To save a flag, the honour of his class / He struck him on the head and cut him down'. The patrician boys throw away the knife and swear to secrecy, with the complicity of the watchman, who takes care not to see who inflicted the wound. After the injured boy is released from the infirmary, they do not meet him but through a go-between offer him a bribe, but he refuses, as he refuses to inform, finally accepting only some snuff for, Scott says, 'some old woman'. Dunn addresses Scott: 'Where was nobility? But Scott, you found / Your life's obsession on that cobbled ground'. Scott would write heroes in the mould of Green Breeks. Dunn demands that he give thanks, '[f]ace to face at last'.

Peter Porter gives Dunn a backhanded compliment in suggesting that his work is not, after all, like that of writers such as Tony Harrison, 'who jet into Kennedy with a little bag of their mam's sweets in their pocket or something'.[19] Porter cannot understand why 'if you've been educated in Latin, it makes you unable to speak to your daddy'. When he got to know Dunn, however, Porter realised that he was wrong about him, though he thinks that *Terry Street* is 'a little simple-minded in comparison with his later work'. Porter misremembers Harrison's 'Long Distance' and confuses the effect of a classical education on the educated with the effect assumed by those who haven't had that kind of education. Conversely, Edna Longley accuses Dunn of aiming at 'soft' targets which are already 'well-riddled'; his lyrical talent threatened by his 'ideological compulsions'.[20] Sean O'Brien, however, asserts that Dunn has done much 'to make apparent the unavoidable centrality of political subjects – class, power, history – in contemporary poetry'.[21]

Tom Leonard was far from the first poet to write in one of the dialects or sociolects of Scotland, but was at least one of the first who in doing so challenged the status of Scots and Gaelic, the traditionally literary and 'respectable' languages of Scotland. Leonard's collections include prose, posters, diagrams, cartoons and essays as well as poems, a number of which, whilst not suggesting a Glaswegian accent, do suggest a strong social awareness, for example 'Skills' (2004), and a strong sense of responsibility, 'Being a Human Being' (2006). In his prose 'The Proof of the Mince Pie', Leonard asserts that universities reify the notion that culture is synonymous with property, and that education and 'a good accent' are 'aspect[s] of the competitive, status-conscious class-structure of the society as a whole'. When 'beauty in language is recognised as the property of a particular class', he argues, then truth will be assumed also to be the property of that class. Anyone who doesn't '"speak right" is therefore categorised as an ignoramus'.[22]

In poems which do voice the accent of Glasgow, Leonard ignores conventional typographical representation of speech to give an impression closer to that of actual speech, breaking words and running others together. Like Harrison, Leonard sites the origin of the imposition of a dominant culture and a concomitant imposition of a sense of inferiority on the subordinate culture, in schools. 'Poetry', *Intimate Voices* (1984) narrates an experience of linguistic imperialism and sense of exclusion parallel to that of Harrison in Leeds Grammar School. An education which pronounced poetry 'poughit. rih' was 'nothing to do with me'.

Leonard unapologetically puts the Standard English/RP speaker in the position of outsider in 'Good Style', the last of the 'Six Glasgow Poems' (1969). It may be 'helluva hard tay read theez', but if we 'canny unnerston' we should 'get tay fuck ootma road'. His representations of working-class life are not nostalgic nor are his working-class characters idealised. Prejudice and bigotry that in Harrison's work come from the mouths of characters are expressed by Leonard's 'I's. He does not quote people speaking with a Glaswegian accent and invite his audience to find the characters funny, or quaint, or grittily real, or to otherwise patronise them; his poems speak in a Glaswegian accent, and they make the skinhead of *v.* look like a milksop. 'No Light' is narrated by someone who has knifed a man for correcting his English. The newsreader narrator of 'The Six O'clock News' from *Unrelated Incidents* (1976) contemptuously mimics Glaswegian speech to demonstrate why he reads the news in cut-glass RP. The reason he talks with a BBC accent 'iz coz yi / widni wahnt / mi ti talk / aboot thi / trooth' with a voice 'lik / wanna yoo / scruff'.

In the poetry of Liz Lochhead (b. 1947), the Scots of Glasgow and rural northwest Scotland is the marker of class as well as nationality: 'the way it had to be said / was as if you were posh, grown-up, male, English and dead'. 'Kidspoem/Bairnsang', *The Colour of Black and White* (2003). Unlike Harrison, Lochhead has accepted public positions which might seem to make her part of the Establishment. She was made Poet Laureate of Glasgow in 2005 and then followed Edwin Morgan as Scots Makar, though she writes that 'Poets need not' be garlanded; the head of a poet ought to be 'innocent' of leaves 'twisted. All honour goes to poetry' (*A Choosing*, 2011).

The transformation of working-class Glasgow into a City of Culture, its promotion as des res, is satirised by Lochhead in 'The Garden Festival, Glasgow 1988', from *Bagpipe Muzak* (1991), through the infiltration of the idiom and puff of English media and estate agents into Glaswegian Scots. Cutting hedges 'inty fancy shapes' and making an eighth wonder of 'plantin' oot the coat o' arms in floribunda' just make Scotland into 'A dream park, / A Disneyland where work disnae exist'. The title of the collection and of 'Bagpipe Muzac, Glasgow 1990', referencing Louis MacNeice's 'Bagpipe Music' (1937), juxtaposes the cultural symbol of Scottishness and sentiment with the ersatz and meretricious. It represents the spin of English politicians who by declaring Glasgow a City of Culture erase its homeless, its drug addicts and its unemployed: 'It's all go the PR campaign and a radical change of image'. It's 'Retro Time for Northern Soul and the whoop and the skirl o' the saxes' but 'All they'll score's more groundglass heroin and venison Filofaxes'.

One example from The New Generation Poets of 2004 and one from The New Generation 2014 illustrate that poetry on social divisions is no more dead than social division. Like Harrison in 'Rhubarbarians', Dunn describes a disparaged linguistic community as *Barbarians*. Similarly, Paul Farley uses the term 'Philistines' in *Tramp in Flames* (2006) to view working-class lives from the migrant's perspective, and in 'Brutalist' challenges the middle-class reader to envisage lives in tower blocks: 'cellarless, unatticked'. Helen Mort echoes *Continuous* in her *Divisions Street* (2013), though poems such as 'Scab' and 'Pit Closure as a Tarantino Short' consider the reconstruction of Sheffield in the 1980s as recorded history in film, and from Cambridge in the 2010s.

NOTES

1 Harrison associates the beat of iambs and trochees with the heartbeat 'with the sexual instinct, with all those physical rhythms'. John Haffenden, 'Interview with Tony Harrison', in Neil Astley, ed., *Bloodaxe Critical Anthologies 1: Tony Harrison* (Newcastle upon Tyne: Bloodaxe Books, 1991), p. 236.

2 Blake Morrison, 'The Filial Art: A Reading of Contemporary British Poetry', *YES* 17 (1987), 179–217, 211.

3 Neil Corcoran, *English Poetry since 1940*. Longman Literature in English Series. (Harlow: Longman, 1993), p. 154.
4 Alan Brownjohn, 'The Fascination of What's Difficult', *Encounter* 70: 3 (March 1979), 64.
5 Corcoran, *English Poetry*, p. 149.
6 Blake Morrison, 'Labouring', *London Review of Books* 4:6 (1 April 1982), 10–11, 10.
7 Donald Davie, *Under Briggflatts: A History of Poetry in Britain 1960–1988* (Manchester: Carcanet, 1989), p. 214.
8 Donald Davie, 'Sincerity and Poetry', *Michigan Quarterly Review* 5:1 (1966), pp. 7–8.
9 *Ibid.*, 4–5.
10 Antony Easthope, *Poetry as Discourse* (1983); rprt (London and New York: Routledge, 2003), pp. 53–54.
11 Easthope, *Poetry as Discourse*, p. 68.
12 David Lloyd, 'Pap for the Dispossessed: Seamus Heaney and the Politics of Identity' *Boundary* 2, 13: 2/3 (Winter-Spring 1985), 328–42.
13 As Derek Mahon does with self-challenging deprecation in 'Afterlives', *The Snow Party* (Oxford University Press, 1975).
14 'To Reach the Moon You Need a Rocket', Interview by Alex Niven, *3:AM Magazine* (2 November 2012) http://www.3ammagazine.com/3am/tom-pickard-interview/.
15 Carcanet saved fifty of them by establishing its 'Oxford Poets' in 1999.
16 Raymond Friel, 'Don Paterson Interviewed' in Robert Crawford, Henry Hart, David Kinloch and Richard Price, eds., *Talking Verse* (Williamsburg, VA: Verse, 1995), pp. 192–98, p. 193.
17 Terry Eagleton, 'New Poetry', *Stand* 11:2 (1970), 68–72, 70.
18 John Gibson Lockhart, *Memoirs of the Life of Sir Walter Scott* (Edinburgh: Robert Cadell, 1837–38), pp. 59–60.
19 Peter Porter on Douglas Dunn quoted by Nicholas Wroe, 'Speaking from Experience', *Guardian* (18 January 2003), p. 20. Porter may be thinking of the reference to Lifesavers bought for the father in Harrison's 'Long Distance'.
20 'Catching Up – Poetry I: The British', *Times Literary Supplement* 4008 (18 January 1980), 64–65.
21 Sean O'Brien, *The Deregulated Muse* (Newcastle-upon-Tyne: Bloodaxe Books), p. 66.
22 'The Proof of the Mince Pie', *Scottish International* (1973); rprt *Intimate Voices*, p. 65.

9

FRAN BREARTON

'In a between world': Northern Irish Poetry

'[B]e advised / My passport's green. / No glass of ours was ever raised / To toast *The Queen*'.[1] These are some of the most oft-quoted lines from Heaney's 'An Open Letter', even if they are among the least 'representative' of his *oeuvre*; and they were not uncontroversial at the time of their publication. As Marilynn Richtarik observes, whilst some commentators exempted Heaney from the criticism levelled at other Field Day pamphlets (of which 'An Open Letter' was the second in the 1983 series), others did not. Terence Brown argued that Heaney was 'complicating his awareness of Ulster's social and political dilemmas' in the poem, in positive ways; Eavan Boland, on the other hand, 'chided Heaney for his insistence upon something which she believed had very little to do with poetry: "Poetry is defined by its energies and its eloquence, not by the passport of the poet ..."'; others detected (and then variously defended or criticised) 'the old wood of green nationalism' visible under the 'new gloss' of the Field Day enterprise.[2] Since Heaney did (one presumes) toast '*The Queen*', or at least shook hands with her, when he attended her state dinner in Dublin in May 2011, almost thirty years after these lines were written, their popularity in the media (and they have had a considerable afterlife), whilst a useful shorthand for the affirmation of difference, also serves as a marker of changes in various political relations within the archipelago in recent decades. The lines provided the headline for Heaney's reported views on the flags protest in Northern Ireland in January 2013, where he observed 'There's never going to be a united Ireland. So why don't you let them [unionists] fly the flag?';[3] they were quoted in the debates leading up to the Scottish referendum in 2014;[4] they cropped up ubiquitously in the dozens of obituaries for the poet published across the world in 2013; and their fame accounts, presumably, for the otherwise unlikely presence of a Wikipedia 'stub' entry on Blake Morrison and Andrew Motion's 1982 *Penguin Book of Contemporary British Poetry* – which, so the story of the poem goes, and of which more anon, prompted them.

If these four lines (from a 198-line poem) have had a rather lively (political) history, the same goes for the 'green' passport itself. Both the Anglo-Irish Treaty of 1921 and the constitution of the newly established Free State (article 17) affirmed 'common citizenship', and, as Joseph O'Grady points out, 'in theory the citizens of the Irish Free State remained British subjects until 1935'. In practice, however, 'the change came much earlier, in April 1924, when the Irish government rejected the British demand that the description "British subject" be printed on each Irish passport'.[5] Not only fraught Anglo-Irish relations are evident in this debate, but also North-South relations, since it was noted at the time that the wording on the passport might compromise any possibility of reunification of the Free State with Northern Ireland. Although the decision was taken to issue Irish Free State passports in April 1924 (for 'citizens of the Irish Free State and the British Commonwealth of Nations'), these, excluding as they did the phrase 'British subject', were not recognised by British officials, and '[t]he problem finally was not cleared up – at least from the Irish point of view – until the passage of the Irish Nationality and Citizenship Act in 1935.'[6] (Only in 1939, the year of Heaney's birth, was reference to the British sovereign removed from the Irish passport – thenceforth issued simply to a 'citizen of Ireland'.) Heaney's entitlement to the Irish passport is affirmed in the same act, notwithstanding his birth and residence in Northern Ireland.[7]

If this, in microcosm, gives some hint as to the complex, highly emotive (on all sides), sometimes anomalous, and frequently contested questions of identity and belonging that characterise the history of 'these islands', it also intimates why those questions have been necessarily more urgent in Northern Ireland, caught as it is in an either/or (or both) constitutional relation to Ireland and Britain. Heaney's green passport in 'An Open Letter' (its aesthetic properties later to be subsumed, like those of the British 'blue', into a 'a limp vermilion mini-version'[8]) is an identity-marker, a declaration of allegiance which may be interpreted simply as 'Irish not British', in the way the lines are so often read on the global stage, but also more particularly, in the context of the North, as 'nationalist not unionist' – or, reductively but not wholly unreasonably, Catholic not Protestant. For whom 'An Open Letter' speaks, and to whom it is addressed (its claimed addressees, 'Blake and Andrew, Editors' of the opening line notwithstanding) are thus more complex questions than its most quoted lines might suggest, and to address those questions is to throw some light on the reception and preoccupations of 'Northern Irish Poetry' itself.

As Heaney himself acknowledges in 'An Open Letter', the inclusion of work by poets from Northern Ireland (Heaney among them) in 'British' anthologies was hardly unprecedented by the time of Morrison and Motion's own selection, and without generating public protest. Of his 'anxious muse', Heaney writes that 'Before this she was called "British" / And acquiesced ...'.[9] Heaney, along with Derek Mahon and Stewart Parker, is among the 'New Voices' of Edward Lucie-Smith's Penguin anthology, *British Poetry since 1945* (1970) – one of his earliest introductions to a wider audience, and in which he is described, misleadingly, as 'typical' of the group [of 'young poets centred on Belfast'] as a whole'.[10] (Heaney, Longley, Mahon, Muldoon, Paulin and McGuckian – Parker is dropped – then find their way into the second edition (1985) under the subheading 'Belfast'). Heaney, like Mahon and Longley, was one of Jeremy Robson's *Young British Poets* (1971), poets who 'have not been overwhelmed by American influences', who 'without being insular ... have continued to write within the English tradition'.[11] And Heaney was the eleventh of Michael Schmidt's *Eleven British Poets* from 1980 – and indeed the only Irish poet in that book.[12]

'But this time', 'An Open Letter' tells us, 'it's like the third wish, / The crucial test'. Given the timing (why, for instance, did Schmidt's anthology two years earlier not prompt the protest, where Heaney could have clearly spoken for himself alone?) there is more at play here than the muse's menopause (the adjective 'brings her out in a hot flush') or a poet's midlife crisis. Partly the response may be to do with the introduction to the book, and the increasing visibility of the Northern Irish poets on the world stage: 'So impressive is recent Northern Irish poetry', Morrison and Motion write, 'that it is not surprising to find discussions of English poetry so often having to take place in its shadow'.[13] 'Poetry', as Peter Lennon put it, is 'the other Northern Ireland ferment', and Heaney himself notes that 'we cannot be unaware ... of the link between the political glamour of the place (Ulster), the sex-appeal of violence, and the prominence accorded to the poets'.[14] Peter Porter opened a 1973 review of Michael Longley with 'Still they come from Ulster, the traditional virtuosi ...'. Longley is one of 'the honourable company of Northern Irish poets, alongside Seamus Heaney and Derek Mahon'.[15] A 1980 review of Mahon and Longley by Ian Hamilton is headlined 'The Ulster brigade'.[16] Heaney, 'the most important new poet of the last fifteen years, and the one we very deliberately put first in our anthology' is, for Morrison and Motion, a powerful weapon in their book's quarrel with Alvarez's influential *The New Poetry* (1962). Not so much the subaltern who speaks, Heaney is positioned – perhaps rather uncomfortably – as the major figure leading the cavalry charge, the force of his example a 'reason why British poetry has taken forms other than those promoted by Alvarez'.[17]

The 'prominence accorded to the poets' from Northern Ireland from the 1970s onwards is, of course, in one sense something from which they have benefitted. It is also the case that affirming to a distinctiveness to poetry from the North was a felt necessity in the Irish rather than British context too. The argument is made most forcefully by Derek Mahon (who later repudiates it) in his 1972 *Sphere Book of Modern Irish Poetry* where he argues that 'Northern poets' with 'an inherited duality of cultural reference' are 'a group apart', even as 'their very difference assimilates them to the complexity of the continuing Irish past'.[18] Belonging and not belonging is also the argument of his 1970 article 'Poetry in Northern Ireland', where he observes that 'Montague and Heaney, by reason of their Northernness, have avoided (Dublin literati please note) the narcissistic provincialism in which "Irish" literature is currently sinking'. They have 'something to say beyond the shores of Ireland'.[19] As a 'group apart', poets from the North are anthologised in Frank Ormsby's 1979 *Poets from the North of Ireland*, although his diplomatic title here gives some indication of the controversial nature of the enterprise. John Montague, in his 1974 *Faber Book of Irish Verse*, citing 'criticism in the Republic of the way Ulster writers tend to look to London as their literary capital', himself claims that 'the poems of Longley, Mahon, Heaney and Simmons share an epigrammatic neatness which shows the influence of a limited British mode';[20] Thomas Kinsella, on the other hand, in the 1986 *New Oxford Book of Irish Verse*, argues that what distinguishes Heaney or Mahon is their 'dual responsibility, toward the medium and toward the past' rather than what Mahon calls their 'Northernness': the 'Northern Ireland Renaissance', however 'strongly urged', is for Kinsella 'largely a journalistic entity'.[21] (Richard Kirkland traces the tensions and complexities of responses in Britain and Ireland to what was described as a 'cosy circle of Ulster poets' with its 'indulgent press', through the 1970s and after, noting both the assertion of 'cultural difference' and the 'co-option of Northern writers into an Irish literary tradition', both the denial and affirmation of a distinct 'northern aesthetic'.[22]) 'Northern' poetry, rather like that first ('southern') Irish passport has gone about the world both with and without 'official' recognition.

'An Open Letter' is addressed to recipients outside Ireland, and it may be said to have had one tangible effect on the UK publishing scene, in that the formula 'from Britain and Ireland' has now been adopted for most archipelagic offerings;[23] but it speaks more evidently to tensions within Ireland, and within Heaney himself. One is the pull between the different energies and ideals of the Field Day enterprise, for which this poem is written, and the creative synergy which emerged from the friendships between Heaney, Longley or Muldoon – between the different directions of 'Personal Helicon', dedicated to Michael Longley (a poem which affirms both closeness and aesthetic difference) or the Deane-Heaney (political) alliance of 'The Ministry of Fear'. Another is between Heaney's voice as individual or collective, the uneasy manoeuvring from 'I' to 'we' and back again: 'my passport's green'; 'no glass of ours' (and 'ours' means not the poets from Northern Ireland but Heaney's Catholic, nationalist community). Notably, Heaney describes himself in the poem as 'Footered, havered, spraughled, wrought / Like Shauneen Keogh, / Wondering should I write it out / Or let it go'. Shawn Keogh: the ineffective fiancé of Pegeen Mike in Synge's *Playboy of the Western World*; the only character, in a topsy-turvy world, who abides by the rules of civilised behaviour, but who is 'afeard' of the priest, less of a man than Christy Mahon. Far from being a forceful polemic, the poem as a whole manifests an uneasiness that renders it one more instance of the bigger questions facing Heaney – facing all the poets from Northern Ireland – writing under extreme pressure during the 'Troubles'.

In his 1975 study *Northern Voices: Poets from Ulster*, Terence Brown, without positing 'the existence of a distinctive Ulster poetic tradition' (he notes the degree to which London and Dublin predominate 'as the places of publication for poetry by writers from Ulster'), nevertheless identifies '[c]ertain thematic patterns' from Ferguson and Allingham in the nineteenth century, through to the 'new voices' emerging in the 1960s: 'The country and the city, the tension between parochialism and cosmopolitanism, aesthetic isolation in an unsympathetic *milieu*, the sense of landscape and of history'.[24] To these, one might add, as the 1970s progressed, a tension between imaginative freedom and social obligation, between the public and private voice. In *Wintering Out* Heaney asks the question 'What do I say if they wheel out their dead?', a question which presupposes the need to find what he elsewhere calls a response 'adequate to our predicament', and what Longley describes as the artist's duty 'to respond to tragic events in his own community', even if his 'first duty ... is to his imagination'.[25] In 'Exposure', Heaney sits 'weighing and weighing / My responsible *tristia*. / For what? For the ear? For the people?'[26] In 'Altera Cithera', Longley ponders 'A change of tune ... A new aesthetic, or / the same old songs / That are out of key...?'.[27] Mahon, caught in an unresolved tension between the 'cold dream / Of a place out of time' and the 'world of / Sirens, bin-lids / And bricked up windows' in 'The Last of the Fire Kings', asserts, later in the same collection, through the voice of 'Cavafy', that 'Reborn in the ideal society / I shall act and speak / With a freedom denied me / By the life we know'.[28] Longley too writes at the onset of the Troubles, 'I can't claim now, as I might have done a few years ago, that I myself have any longer a life which is my own entirely'. But, he insists, 'the imagination has a life of *its* own, a life that has to be saved'.[29]

In their particular consciousness of the tension between '[p]erfection of the life, or of the work',[30] as in the play of form habitually noted in critical responses to their work – positively, in Porter's 'traditional virtuosi', or negatively (in 'epigrammatic neatness') – the indebtedness of Northern Irish poets to W. B. Yeats is evident. The historical tensions and the virtuoso forms are related. In the context of the often challenging circumstances faced by Yeats as much as by his successors, we might heed what Peter McDonald notes of their work, in which 'form and performance are constantly moving, shifting modes that set the authorial will a fresh challenge each time a new poem has to be written. Poetic form is in that sense "living" rather than "dead", dynamic rather than static, for its kinds of order do not stand still ...'.[31] Edna Longley also points out that although 'Irish literary historigography has not yet fully worked out where "northern Irish poetry" came from', Larkin, Hughes and Hill – as influenced by Yeats – 'undoubtedly mattered as immediate precursors'. In that sense, 'Northern Irish poets ... brought Yeats back home, but in ways partly mediated by his impact elsewhere'. Part of her point is to set Yeats in an archipelagic context, and to do so, she argues, 'may also be to set northern Irish poetry there, to dissolve distracting arguments about national labels, to reveal peculiarly heightened cultural, and hence poetic, "interactivity". For good or ill, Northern Ireland is a cat's cradle of archipelagic history, language and traditions, with added local entanglements.'[32]

'For good or ill': if some debates about identity politics seem less than productive, the creative energies and formal varieties that emerge from the 'cat's cradle' following the establishment of 'Northern Ireland' in the 1920s tell their own story. ('An Open Letter' refers to Heaney's 'deep design / To be at home / In my own place'; it's worth noting, however, that one of the places he is at home is in the Burns stanza of this poem, as much as he is at home in variations on the 'English' or 'Italian' sonnet form.) Yeats's forms have their legacy not only in the 'incorrigible' plurality of MacNeice's *oeuvre*, he also informs the development of the first Northern 'revival', in the work of Hewitt, Rodgers, McFadden and Greacen during and immediately following World War II, as well as (in more or less 'mediated' ways) some of the poets of successive generations: Montague, Heaney, Longley and Mahon; McDonald, Ormsby, Muldoon, Carson and McGuckian; or more recently, Morrissey, Gillis or Flynn. In 'Meditations in Time of Civil War', Yeats forges a path for poetry away from other kinds of certainty – found in the 'affable Irregular' or the 'Lieutenant and his men' – and through resistance to other choices: namely, to have 'proved my worth / In something that all others understand or share'; to opt for pleasing the crowd rather than trusting, as he does in the end, the 'abstract joy, / The half-read wisdom of daemonic images' that will 'Suffice the ageing man as once the growing boy'.[33] The poem, 'a close encounter between form and history', which 'dramatis[es] a fractured psyche',[34] is a model for later Irish poets writing under pressure. ('For the ear? For the people?' asks similar questions. If it doesn't here answer them with the full assurance of Yeats's faith in 'abstract joy' at the close of 'Meditations', poetry is nevertheless, for Heaney, its own 'vindicating force'[35]). Michael Longley, in the mid 1970s, argued that '[t]he Irish psyche is being redefined in Ulster', that poems are born 'out of a lively tension between the Irish and English traditions', and that poets such as Larkin or Hughes 'encourage a fruitful schizophrenia in someone trying to write poetry in Ireland'.[36] Writing out of the 'cultural meetings that engendered the Irish Literary Revival',[37] Yeats is also an exemplary figure and precursor who poses, in 'Nineteen Hundred and Nineteen', the question relating to history which is also about form – form as something that both gives and resists, as 'living' and 'dynamic', to go back to McDonald, which 'does not stand still': Yeats's swan has 'wings half spread for flight, / The breast thrust out in pride / Whether to play, or to ride / Those winds that clamour of approaching night'.[38]

With the exception of MacNeice, the poets writing in the north of Ireland prior to the late 1960s 'renaissance' have received comparatively limited attention, and they scarcely feature in the Irish anthologies mentioned above – albeit more recent publications have offered some redress.[39] As Guy Woodward observes, Roy McFadden responded negatively to the suggestion in Jon Stallworthy's biography of Louis MacNeice that MacNeice's reputation was re-established by the 'next generation' of poets from the North. Woodward quotes McFadden's review in which that 'next generation' are themselves held partly accountable for a failure 'to point out [to Stallworthy] that the "next generation of Northern Irish poets" to that of MacNeice in fact consists of Craig, Greacen, McFadden, Fiacc and Montague'.[40] (Montague has also described himself as the 'missing link' in Ulster poetry.[41]) Partly McFadden is here asking for the influence of his generation to be more than it is: the period of 'obsessive coterie building, anthology compiling, and manifesto drafting' from 1940 onwards may have had what Greacen called an 'exhilarating tang' to it, but as Richard Kirkland goes on to observe, 'it failed to establish any significant legacy'. (He also notes that Greacen published no collection between 1948 and 1975, McFadden between 1947 and 1973; that 'after *No Rebel Word* of 1948, Hewitt would have no further major collection until the 1960s'; and that Rodgers 'was effectively finished as a poet' after his 1952 *Europa and the Bull*.[42]) Alongside other arguments made concerning those silences,[43] one might also risk the suggestion that it is the new 'energy' (as identified by Mahon) in the North from the 1960s onwards that reanimates the poets of an earlier period, rather than vice versa.

In that context, MacNeice *is* the exception: his poetry is not affected by the Northern 'renaissance', since he died (prematurely) in 1963; but that his poetry served to animate (even liberate) those who later paid tribute to his legacy is not in doubt. This is not to downplay John Hewitt's cultural importance, since Hewitt's candid articulation of his own sense of identity and belonging is one which serves later to open an important dialogue in Northern Irish poetry: in 'The Planter and the Gael' tour of 1970, poems such as Hewitt's 'Once Alien Here', in which he 'would seek a native mode to tell / our stubborn wisdom individual', or 'The Colony' ('We took the kindlier soils. It had been theirs ... We laboured hard and stubborn, draining, planting / till half the country took its shape from us'), were set alongside Montague's 'A Lost Tradition', with '[t]he whole landscape a manuscript / We had lost the skill to read, / A part of our past disinherited'.[44] But both on their own terms, and as poets who 'mediate' some of the more problematical aspects of Yeats, MacNeice (born 1907) and to a lesser extent Kavanagh (born 1904) – not a 'Northern Irish poet', but a poet from Ulster (Monaghan), whose 'black hills ... Eternally ... look north towards Armagh'[45] – are most often cited as the 'father figures' of the Northern Irish scene. They are the two poets Muldoon places first in his (controversial) *Faber Book of Contemporary Irish Poetry* (1986) before leap-frogging forwards to Kinsella (b. 1928 in Dublin) and Montague (b. 1929 in Brooklyn), poets whose reputations were established in the late 1950s and 1960s. Michael Allen argues that the '[y]oung Muldoon was only packing himself a poetic knapsack of "the best, the really excellent ..." (we still like Matthew Arnold up here) before setting out on his transatlantic journey'.[46] And the 'very best', however controversial a phrase, is also that which provides an example in the way Greacen, McFadden or even Hewitt, prior to the 1960s, did not. It is not, Richard Kirkland concludes, 'that the Belfast poets of the 1940s failed to identify the problems of aesthetics, culture, and politics that poetry in the North had to face during this period' – he quotes Greacen's acknowledgment in 1999 that '[w]e should have shared concerns about living in a divided community' – but 'it is in their ultimate failure to refashion these antinomies that their interest now resides'.[47]

In a recent essay on MacNeice, Paul Muldoon describes him as a poet whose 'systems of imagery' show 'a fascination with the relationship between the "journalism" of the day (*journée*) and the eternity of the poem ... with plurality and singularity, excess and exigency ... with systems of energy and entropy'.[48] The poet of antinomies, one might say, and part of whose debt to Yeats Muldoon identifies in the 'great bay-window' of 'Snow', pointing as he does to 'Yeats's frequent positioning in *The Winding Stair* of the speaker seated at a "window-ledge" … or looking through "great windows open to the south"'.[49] Yeats's 'Vacillation', also from *The Winding Stair* more explicitly articulates the point: 'Between extremities / Man runs his course; / A brand, or flaming breath, / Comes to destroy / All those antinomies / Of day and night …'.[50] That '[t]here is more than glass between the snow and the huge roses' at the close of 'Snow' encapsulates a poetics of paradox in MacNeice, where 'between', as Edna Longley has observed, both separates and joins.[51] The ambiguous positioning, not quite within or without; the moment, or poem, held [b]etween extremities' – or, as he puts it in 'Spring Sunshine', 'In a between world'[52] – are characteristic of his *oeuvre*. They are also characteristic of Northern Irish poetry more generally, given its uniquely 'troubled' context in which, as MacNeice writes elsewhere, 'one read black where the other read white, his hope / The other man's damnation'.[53] In 'Train to Dublin' eschewing 'idol or idea, creed or king', MacNeice gives us instead 'the disproportion between labour spent / And joy at random' in the knowledge of 'further syntheses to which … people at last attain'.[54] A later poem, 'The Window', though it tends to over-explain, takes the 'hour-glass' held vertically as a conceit for the contradictory forces at work on the poet – 'You feel like the tides the tug of a moon, never to be reached, / interfering always, / And always you suffer this two-way traffic, impulses outward and images inward / Distracting the heart'. Positioned horizontally however, with 'equilibrium' and 'without tremolo' it is possible to 'hold this moment / Where in this window two worlds meet'.[55] The poem's struggle to negotiate the 'mirrored maze – paradox and antinomy' in search of 'the core that answers' is, for later poets, the exemplary quest which finds its most profound expression in MacNeice's later poems: in 'All Over Again', 'each long then and there 'is 'suspended on this cliff / Shining and slicing edge that reflects the sun as if / This one Between were All …'; or in 'Coda', 'There are moments caught between heart-beats / When maybe we know each other better'.[56]

MacNeice, 'born in Belfast between the mountries and the gantries',[57] weaves patterns from the complicated threads of his west of Ireland ancestry, north of Ireland upbringing, and English education, bringing, among other things, the collision of tradition and modernity (in the form of the North's industrialised landscape) into the Irish poetry scene, and refashioning Yeats's embattled Civil War psyche for his own 'toppling hour'.[58] *Autumn Journal* (1939), the long poem poised on the cusp of momentous change, revisits, in section XVI, some of the dilemmas of Yeats's 'Meditations' and 'Nineteen Hundred and Nineteen': 'Nightmare leaves fatigue: / We envy men of action / Who sleep and wake, murder and intrigue / Without being doubtful …'.[59]

The poem, even structurally, both gives and resists in relation to history: as Glyn Maxwell has persuasively shown, its rhyming, like the Greek chorus with its *strophe* and *antistrophe*, 'I turn'/ 'I turn against' pattern that is an 'ever-changing, ever-constant principle', moves between 'closed' and 'open' form, in a play of 'day and night, Past and Present, private and public'.[60] As in 'Wolves', where 'The tide comes in and the tide goes out again', the poet also walks a line between 'flux and ... permanence'.[61] Jonathan Allison, quoting a 1926 letter from MacNeice to Anthony Blunt ('Only space is pure and isn't it dull, except from the edge. The shore of the sea is far jollier than the middle'), points out that although MacNeice 'would not have used the term "liminal" ... it seems clear that the shore is more attractive precisely because it is in-between the land and sea; it offers a zone of encounter where two elements meet. Dialogue is more interesting than monologue ...'.[62]

The 'between world' of MacNeice's poems – and the 'lively tension', to borrow Michael Longley's phrase, in evidence 'between English and Irish traditions' – is central to understanding his importance for other Northern Irish poets. For Derek Mahon, MacNeice was 'a familiar voice whispering in my ear',[63] and an enabler of his early work. At the start of Mahon's 'In Belfast', later retitled 'Spring in Belfast', the poet is 'Walking among my own this windy morning / In a tide of sunlight between shower and shower'. The immediate debt is to MacNeice's own 'Belfast', with its 'us who walk in the street so buoyantly and glib'[64]; more elusively, it is to MacNeice's 'Train to Dublin', with the 'idol living for a moment, not muscle-bound / But walking freely through the slanting rain'. The 'tide of sunlight' is evocative of recurrent MacNeicean images; the 'squinting heart' of 'In Belfast' obliquely rewrites Yeats's 'ambitious heart' at the close of 'Meditations', but more obviously, in the line's beginning and end ('Stone ... heart') alludes to the 'stone of the heart' in 'Easter 1916', with its rigidity of 'one purpose alone'.[65] The poem is elusive in its sense of 'belonging', slipping from first to third to first person, and who or what constitutes 'my own' is characteristically ambiguous: 'my own' as in the Belfast people; or simply the protestant community (that 'We could *all* be saved' implies they may be rather less 'saved' than others); or the inanimate 'wet / Stone' of the city itself. Since walking 'among' is also walking 'between', 'my own' might be comprised of the like-minded, sometimes lonely figures populating Mahon's early poetry – an artistic 'imagined' community, of whom MacNeice is one, and Larkin, whose 'streets, end-on to hills' in 'The Importance of Elsewhere' are echoed in 'the hill / At the top of every street', another.[66] '[S]eparate, not unworkable' is Larkin's position; workable *only* by separation, by a positioning 'between shower and shower', might be Mahon's. The poems articulate the felt pressure on the poet to belong – 'One part of my mind must learn to know its place' – but it is a pressure to which Mahon's response is always the restatement ('For the ear', in Heaney's phrase) of the problem, rather than a concession to 'the people'. In 'The Last of the Fire Kings', some of the pressures – 'improper expectations' as Edna Longley has termed them[67] – placed upon the Northern Irish poet, and to which Heaney's 'An Open Letter' may be seen to react, are evident. Opening with the desire to be 'Like the man who descends / At two milk churns ... and vanishes', he acknowledges that 'the fire-loving people / Will not countenance this', '[d]emanding' that he should 'die their creature and be thankful'. To 'countenance': 'to favour, patronize, sanction' (OED). The diction here projects onto the 'people' a sense of entitlement as regards the poet in their midst, but it does not, ultimately, bring the poet to rest in the 'world' the people demand he should 'inhabit'.[68] The poem is a window onto that world of 'Sirens, bin-lids / And bricked-up windows', and onto the 'place out of time, / A palace of porcelain', but it is situated in neither. (The shape poem, 'The Window', later discarded, also speaks to Mahon's affinity with MacNeice's 'more than glass between ...'.[69])

'In Belfast' and 'The Last of the Fire Kings' are characteristic of Mahon's earlier work, with their elusive self-positioning ('Nothing escapes him. He escapes us all',[70] as 'Grandfather' puts it), the manoeuvring between absolutes, and the play of light and dark. In the war 'between the fluidity of a possible life ... and the *rigor mortis* of archaic postures', Mahon tells us, poets contribute 'to the possibility of that possible life'. Poetry itself 'is a light to lighten the darkness; and we have had darkness enough, God knows, for a long time'.[71] The claims are tentatively phrased, but the central point – that 'a good poem is a paradigm of good politics' – is a conviction both learned from Mahon's precursors, and shared by his contemporaries. In the *Stepping Stones* interviews, Heaney comments that '[a]ll of us, Protestant poets, Catholic poets ... probably had some notion that a good poem was "a paradigm of good politics", a site of energy and tension and possibility, a truth-telling arena but not a killing field'.[72] He explicitly associates the phrase with the question of responsibility, and with the Yeatsian example, suggesting that 'what Mahon means, and what I would mean, is that we in Northern Ireland *qua* poets were subject to that larger call to "hold in a single thought reality and justice"'.[73] Balancing contrarieties is the poet's task learned, as in Heaney's 'Terminus', from the uniqueness of the context: 'When I hoked there', Heaney writes, 'I would find / An acorn and a rusted bolt. / ... a factory chimney / And a dormant mountain'. The allusion to MacNeice, already evident here, is all the more pronounced in Heaney's statement of his own origins in part III of the poem: 'I grew up in between'.[74]

In the 'Coda' to *Stepping Stones*, Heaney describes a 'sudden joy', experienced whilst driving from Dublin to Wicklow, in 'the sheer fact of the mountains to my right and the sea to my left', from the 'double sensation of here-and-nowness in the familiar place and far-and-awayness in something immense'.[75] That the embracing of the 'liminal', the 'betwixt and between' sensibility, the (sometimes paradoxical) balancing act performed, or an evocation of the joy (as well as 'itch'[76]) of contradiction, are characteristic elements in Northern Irish poetry is not, given the context, particularly surprising. In an early poem 'The Hebrides', Michael Longley deliberately positions himself 'at the edge of ... experience'; the poem is a 'fight ... for balance' that yet 'covet[s] the privilege / Of vertigo'.[77] As I have argued elsewhere, Longley's imaginative hinterland, with its origins found in the 'No Man's Land' of the First World War – No Man's Land being 'the very image', as Leed describes it, 'of the marginal, the liminal, the "betwixt-and-between" ... placed between the known and the unknown'[78] – is one that expands to become the 'site of ... tension and possibility'.[79] From the 'Blood on the kerbstones, and my mind / Dividing' in the early 1970s, and through 'The Echo Gate' where the poet is the 'skull between two ears that reconstructs / Broken voices, broken stone', the space 'between' is hard-won from a delicate balancing act, from the not-so-simple 'simple question / Of being in two places at the one time'.[80] Longley's worrying about 'responsibility', about his 'apology for poetry', is not manifest in these poems as the insistent self-questioning that characterises Heaney's work of the same period, but it is fully lived in the careful eschewal of reductive certainties, and in a language where beauty is allied with precision.[81] In *Gorse Fires*, the poet or his subjects are positioned 'Between now and one week ago'; 'Between hovers and not too far from the holt'; on 'the same train between the same embankments'; 'between two sleeping couples; 'between electrified fences'. In 'Meditations', Yeats wrests from his 'acre of stony ground' a place for the 'symbolic rose' to 'break in flower'; in Longley's 'Wind-Farmer', the 'small-holding' is the site where 'Between fields of hailstones and raindrops his frost-flowers grow'.[82]

A distinctiveness to 'Northern Irish poetry' may also be apparent in the tendency (as in this essay too) to talk of its poets not only in terms of coteries, but of 'generations'. To what extent the 'generational' thinking is critically engineered as well as poetically distinctive is a moot point. Nevertheless, in the 'boiling pot' of Northern Ireland (population 1.5 million) an extraordinary poetic energy that has had, in the last half century, an international visibility, may account for a more pronounced consciousness of inheritance on the part of the poets. A self-positioning in relation to that inheritance is evident too, of which perhaps the most obvious instance is the case of Paul Muldoon. Knowingly inscribing his first collection 'For My Fathers and Mothers' (and, in his first pamphlet, 'knowing [his] place' in all sorts of ways), Muldoon 'tell[s] new weather' in a manner sometimes reliant on the reader's knowledge of an earlier forecast, notably in the brilliantly allusive relationship to Heaney embedded in so many of the poems.[83] More broadly, the motifs discussed above may be seen as sufficiently recognisable to enable a parodic mode in Muldoon (one not without its political import) in which he affirms, as others have done before him, both affinity and difference in relation to his 'precursors'. Mahon's 'between shower and shower', or Heaney's 'The Other Side', have a fugitive afterlife in Muldoon's 'shower of rain' which 'stopped so cleanly across Golightly's lane ... He stood there, for ages, / To wonder which side, if any, he should be on'.[84] Longley's 'simple question' in 'Alibis' gets a second airing in Muldoon's 'Twice', with its '"Two places at once, was it, or one place twice?"'.[85] Muldoon, who shifts, like Brownlee's horses, 'from foot to / Foot ... gazing into the future',[86] has a 'betwixt-and-between' sensibility; but taken to the extreme it becomes, to borrow MacNeice's phrase, 'catdrop sleight-of-foot or simple vanishing act'.[87] Muldoon's precise and habitual imprecision ('I was three-ish'; 'we take four or five minutes to run down / the thirty-odd flights of steps'[88]) carries broader implications in the way it slips the nets of 'distracting arguments'. As with his own contemporaries – Ciaran Carson, caught so productively between two languages, or Medbh McGuckian, as 'not a woman's man' and 'beyond the reach of the mirror'[89] – his work also mediates earlier influences for a 'new' generation.

Miriam Gamble persuasively argues that 'the peace context renders identity in Northern Irish poetry more, rather than less, problematic', that 'the surface glitter of "normalisation" masks as well as embodies a malaise to which ... poets are attuned', and that 'fulfilling the role of conscience for a society which does not care to hear' is both essential and 'more difficult than speaking for and to a populace which audibly demands one's contribution'.[90] She is referring particularly to what might be termed a 'post-ceasefire' generation – Alan Gillis, Sinéad Morrissey, Leontia Flynn (the comments are applicable to her own work too) – of poets, and poet-critics, acutely aware of the history and reception of 'Northern Irish poetry'. The warnings of Alan Gillis's 'The Ulster Way' depend, rather like early Muldoon, for their ironic and mischievous effect on foreknowledge of an Ulster poetry way: 'There will be no gorse ... you will not be passing into farmland. / Nor will you be set upon by cattle ... There are other paths to follow'.[91] In Flynn's work, the in-between space, captured in the image from 'Two Crossings' of a woman 'carried back and forth by the boat's rocking / for the length of a corridor between two glass doors', sometimes contains the 'malaise' to which Gamble refers. In 'The Morning After Ruth's Going-Away Party', 'The needle snags on the record and then snags again'.[92] For Morrissey, the return 'home' in 'In Belfast' is to a place with 'history's dent and fracture // splitting the atmosphere'.[93] Her title carries an allusion to Mahon's own 'In Belfast' from *Night-Crossing*; but it is his 'Afterlives' which shadows Morrissey's return, the poem in which the problem of 'home' has a particular intensity: 'Perhaps if I'd stayed behind / And lived it bomb by bomb / I might have grown up at last / And learnt what is meant by home'.[94] If the context – Mahon's Belfast is a 'city ... changed / By five years of war'; Morrissey's a city 'making money' – has altered, Morrissey's sense of place, in Northern Ireland and in its literary traditions, still finds a characteristically ambiguous expression: 'I am / as much at home here as I will ever be'.

NOTES

1 Seamus Heaney, 'An Open Letter', Field Day Theatre Company Pamphlet no. 2 (September 1983), repr. in *Ireland's Field Day* (Notre Dame, IN: University of Notre Dame Press, 1986), p. 25.

2 See Marilynn J. Richtarik, *Acting between the Lines: The Field Day Theatre Company and Irish Cultural Politics 1980–1984* (Oxford: Clarendon Press, 1994), pp. 159–61.

3 'Seamus Heaney: I may not toast the Queen, but allow loyalists to fly Union flag if they want to', *Belfast Telegraph*, 30 January 2013.

4 Ian Jack, 'Would I Choose a British or Scottish Passport?', *Guardian*, 29 November 2013.

5 Joseph P. O'Grady, 'The Irish Free State Passport and the Question of Citizenship, 1921–4', *Irish Historical Studies* 26:104 (Nov. 1989): p. 397, http://www.jstor.org/stable/30008695, accessed 4 March 2015.

6 Ibid., p. 404.

7 See the 1935 Act at http://www.irishstatutebook.ie/1935/en/act/pub/0013/index.html and later, the 1956 Act, which stated that 'Pending the re-integration of the national territory, subsection (1) of section 6 [Every person born in Ireland is an Irish citizen from birth] shall not apply to a person ... born in Northern Ireland on or after the 6th December, 1922, unless, in the prescribed manner, that person, if of full age, declares himself to be an Irish citizen or, if he is not of full age, his parent or guardian declares him to be an Irish citizen. In any such case, the subsection shall be deemed to apply to him from birth'. http://www.irishstatutebook.ie/1956/en/act/pub/0026/index.html The 2004 Act amended this to 'every person born in the island of Ireland is entitled to be an Irish citizen'. The point is that an active *choice* as to Irish citizenship is made by those born in the North after 1922.

8 As a dissatisfied member of the House of Lords described the new European-style passport in 1988: http://hansard.millbanksystems.com/lords/1988/may/24/british-passport-new-format [Accessed 9/3/15].

9 'An Open Letter', p. 23.

10 Edward Lucie-Smith, ed., *British Poetry since 1945* (Harmondsworth: Penguin, 1970), p. 339.
11 Jeremy Robson, *The Young British Poets* (London: Chatto & Windus, 1971), p. 13.
12 Michael Schmidt, ed., *Eleven British Poets* (1980; London: Routledge, 1988).
13 Blake Morrison and Andrew Motion, 'Introduction', *The Penguin Book of Contemporary British Poetry* (Harmondsworth: Penguin, 1982), p. 16.
14 Peter Lennon, 'Poetry, the Other Northern Ireland Ferment', *The Times* (11 April 1985); Seamus Heaney, 'Calling the Tune', an interview with Tom Adair, *Linen Hall Review* 6:2 (Autumn 1989), 5.
15 Peter Porter, 'A Poet from Ulster', *Observer*, 5 August 1973.
16 *The Sunday Times*, 10 February 1980.
17 Morrison and Motion, 'Introduction', p. 13.
18 Derek Mahon, ed., 'Introduction', *The Sphere Book of Modern Irish Poetry* (London: Sphere Books, 1972), p. 14.
19 Derek Mahon, 'Poetry in Northern Ireland', *Twentieth Century Studies* 4 (November 1970): 89–93, 92.
20 John Montague, 'In the Irish Grain', *The Faber Book of Irish Verse* (London: Faber, 1974), p. 37.
21 Thomas Kinsella, 'Introduction', *The New Oxford Book of Irish Verse* (Oxford: Oxford University Press, 1986), p. xxx.
22 See Richard Kirkland, *Literature and Culture in Northern Ireland since 1965: Moments of Danger* (London: Longman, 1996), pp. 71–76.
23 A more recent anthology, *New British Poetry*, edited by Don Paterson and Charles Simic (Saint Paul, MN: Graywolf Press, 2004), which eschews this 'Britain and Ireland' approach, veers in the other direction from its 'British' anthology predecessors in deliberately *excluding* Northern Irish poets, even though Northern Ireland is 'under British rule', on the grounds that they 'tend to describe themselves as Irish not British'; but if inclusion can be controversial, exclusion must be so too. The choice may be read as both disadvantaging poets from the North and simplifying a fruitfully complex picture – as would also have been the case with their exclusion from this book.
24 Terence Brown, *Northern Voices: Poets from Ulster* (Totowa, NJ: Rowman and Littlefield, 1975), p. 2.
25 Seamus Heaney, 'A Northern Hoard', *Wintering Out* (London: Faber, 1972), p. 41; Seamus Heaney, 'Feeling into Words', *Preoccupations: Selected Prose 1968–1978* (London: Faber, 1980), p. 56; Michael Longley, letter to the *Irish Times*, 18 June 1974.
26 Seamus Heaney, *North* (London: Faber, 1975), p. 73.
27 Michael Longley, *An Exploded View* (London: Victor Gollancz, 1973), p. 56.
28 Derek Mahon, *The Snow Party* (London: Oxford University Press, 1975), pp. 10, 20.
29 Michael Longley, 'Strife and the Ulster Poet', *Hibernia*, 33:21 (7 November 1969), 11.
30 W. B. Yeats, 'The Choice', *Collected Poems* (London: Macmillan, 1950), p. 278.
31 Peter McDonald, 'Yeats, Form and Northern Irish Poetry', *Serious Poetry: Form and Authority from Yeats to Hill* (Oxford: Clarendon Press, 2002), p. 166.

32 Edna Longley, *Yeats and Modern Poetry* (New York: Cambridge University Press, 2013), pp. 192, 208.
33 Yeats, *Collected Poems*, pp. 229, 232.
34 Longley, *Yeats and Modern Poetry*, p. 211.
35 Seamus Heaney, *The Government of the Tongue* (London: Faber, 1988), p. 92.
36 Michael Longley, Untitled prose piece [c.1975], box 37 folder 21, Longley papers, Collection 744, Robert W. Woodruff Library, Emory University, Atlanta.
37 Edna Longley, *Yeats and Modern Poetry*, p. 209.
38 Yeats, *Collected Poems*, p. 235.
39 See Guy Woodward, chapter 2, *Culture, Northern Ireland, & the Second World War* (Oxford: Oxford University Press, 2015); Richard Kirkland, 'The Poetics of Partition: Poetry and Northern Ireland in the 1940s', in *The Oxford Handbook of Modern Irish Poetry* ed. Fran Brearton & Alan Gillis (Oxford: Oxford University Press, 2012).
40 See Woodward, *Culture, Northern Ireland*, p. 82.
41 John Montague, *The Figure in the Cave and Other Essays* (New York: Syracuse University Press, 1989), pp. 8–9.
42 Kirkland, 'The Poetics of Partition', pp. 211–12.
43 See Kirkland, 'The Poetics of Partition', p. 212, where he cites John Wilson Foster's argument that the pre-eminence of the Movement poets in the 1950s sent these 1940s Romantic poets into hiding, only surfacing again when it was 'safe' to do so.
44 *The Planter & the Gael: An Anthology of Poems by John Hewitt and John Montague* (Arts Council of Northern Ireland, 1970), n.p.
45 Patrick Kavanagh, 'Shancoduff', *Collected Poems*, ed. Antoinette Quinn (London: Allen Lane, 2004), p. 21.
46 Michael Allen, 'New Anthologies for Old', rev. of Derek Mahon and Peter Fallon, eds., *The Penguin Book of Contemporary Irish Poetry, Irish Review*, No. 9 (Autumn, 1990), p. 102.
47 Kirkland, 'The Poetics of Partition', p. 224.
48 Paul Muldoon, 'The Perning Birch: Yeats, Frost, MacNeice', *Incorrigibly Plural: Louis MacNeice and his Legacy*, ed. Fran Brearton and Edna Longley (Manchester: Carcanet, 2012), p. 141.
49 Muldoon, 'The Perning Birch', p. 145. See Louis MacNeice, *Collected Poems*, ed. Peter McDonald (London: Faber, 2007), p. 24.
50 Yeats, *Collected Poems*, p. 282.
51 See Edna Longley, *Louis MacNeice: A Study* (London: Faber, 1988), p. 127.
52 MacNeice, *Collected Poems*, p. 30.
53 MacNeice, *Autumn Journal* XVI, *Collected Poems*, p. 138.
54 MacNeice, *Collected Poems*, pp. 17–18.
55 MacNeice, *Collected Poems*, pp. 307–12.
56 MacNeice, *Collected Poems*, pp. 573, 610.
57 MacNeice, 'Carrickfergus', *Collected Poems*, p. 55.
58 'The Closing Album: I. Dublin', *Collected Poems*, p. 180. The poem revisits Yeats's 'Easter 1916' at the onset of World War II.
59 MacNeice, *Collected Poems*, p. 137.

60 See Glyn Maxwell, 'Turn and Turn Against: The Case of *Autumn Journal*', in *Incorrigibly Plural*, pp. 172–73, 186.
61 MacNeice, *Collected Poems*, p. 27.
62 Jonathan Allison, 'Pure Form, Impure Poetry, and Louis MacNeice's Letters', *Incorrigibly Plural*, p. 47. See also *Letters of Louis MacNeice*, ed. Jonathan Allison (London: Faber, 2010), p. 123.
63 Terence Brown, 'An Interview with Derek Mahon', *Poetry Ireland Review* 14 (Autumn 1985), 18.
64 MacNeice, *Collected Poems*, p. 25.
65 Mahon, *Night-Crossing* (London: Oxford University Press, 1968), p. 6; Yeats, *Collected Poems*, pp. 204, 232.
66 Philip Larkin, *Collected Poems*, ed. Anthony Thwaite (London: Faber and The Marvell Press, 2003), p. 105.
67 Edna Longley, *Poetry in the Wars* (Newcastle: Bloodaxe, 1986), p. 185.
68 Mahon, *The Snow Party*, pp. 9–10.
69 Mahon, *The Snow Party*, p. 25.
70 Mahon, *Night-Crossing*, p. 7.
71 Mahon, 'Poetry in Northern Ireland', p. 93.
72 Dennis O'Driscoll, *Stepping Stones: Interview with Seamus Heaney* (London: Faber, 2008), p. 123.
73 *Stepping Stones*, p.383. The phrase is from Yeats's preface to *A Vision* (1928).
74 Seamus Heaney, *The Haw Lantern* (London: Faber, 1987), pp. 4–5.
75 *Stepping Stones*, p. 475.
76 John Hewitt, 'What itch of contradiction bids me find / no prompting satisfactions for my mind / to make verse of …'. From 'Conacre', *The Collected Poems of John Hewitt*, ed. Frank Ormsby (Belfast: Blackstaff Press, 1991), p. 3.
77 Michael Longley, *No Continuing City* (London: Macmillan, 1969), pp. 28–9.
78 See Eric J. Leed, *No Man's Land: Combat and Identity in World War I* (Cambridge: Cambridge University Press, 1979), pp. 14–15.
79 See Fran Brearton, 'Michael Longley: Poet in No Man's Land', *The Great War in Irish Poetry* (Oxford: Oxford University Press, 2000), pp. 251–86.
80 See 'Letter to Three Irish Poets', *An Exploded View* (London: Victor Gollancz, 1973), p. 32; *The Echo Gate* (London: Secker & Warburg, 1979), p. 18; 'Alibis', *An Exploded View*, p. 59.
81 Longley is the only Northern Irish poet of those discussed so far in this essay who stayed in Northern Ireland.
82 Yeats, *Collected Poems*, p. 226; Longley, *The Ghost Orchid* (London: Jonathan Cape, 1995), p. 50.
83 Paul Muldoon, *New Weather* (London: Faber, 1973), p. 3.
84 Paul Muldoon, 'The Boundary Commission', *Why Brownlee Left* (London: Faber, 1980), p. 15.
85 Muldoon, *The Annals of Chile* (London: Faber, 1994), p. 12.
86 Muldoon, *Why Brownlee Left*, p. 22.
87 MacNeice, 'The Suicide', *Collected Poems*, p. 579.
88 See Muldoon, 'The Right Arm' and 'The Trifle', *Quoof* (London: Faber, 1983), pp. 11, 30.
89 See Medbh McGuckian, 'The Soil-Map' and 'Next Day Hill', *The Flower Master* (Oxford: Oxford University Press, 1982), pp. 29, 43.

90 Miriam Gamble, '"A potted peace / lily"? Northern Irish Poetry since the Ceasefires', *The Oxford Handbook of Modern Irish Poetry*, ed. Brearton & Gillis, p. 669.
91 Alan Gillis, *Somebody, Somewhere* (Oldcastle: Gallery Press, 2004), p. 9.
92 Leontia Flynn, *These Days* (London: Jonathan Cape, 2004), pp. 25, 38
93 Sinéad Morrissey, *Between Here and There* (Manchester: Carcanet, 2002), p. 13.
94 Mahon, *The Snow Party*, p. 2.

10

ALAN RIACH

Scottish Poetry, 1945–2010

After the Second World War, poetry in Scotland required regeneration. The Scottish Renaissance of the 1920s and 1930s had been a major force of revitalisation, led by Hugh MacDiarmid (C. M. Grieve, 1892–1978), aligning poetry, literature and all the arts in Scotland with renewed political ambition for an independent nation. After the war, MacDiarmid was still a major force among the new generation of poets, but the younger men and women would not follow his lead in any direct sense, and in any case, MacDiarmid had nothing but disdain for disciples.

The prevailing imperative among the major poets who began publishing in the late 1940s, 1950s and 1960s was not one of nationalism but of individual voice, language and, crucially, location. Each had his or her own favoured terrain in different parts of Scotland, a geography of the imagination that made singular use of co-ordinate points drawn from their places of birth or upbringing, their societies and languages. Most of them were men.

The generation of poets who began publishing in the 1970s and 1980s, many of the best of them women, brought another kind of regeneration, in terms of gendered identity. These poets demonstrated that their perspectives and experiences as women were as valid and valuable as those of the men of the previous generation, from whom they had learned much, and further, that regardless of gender experience, their enquiries and judgements were equally valid and vital. From the 1990s through to the twenty-first century, the increasing range of priorities and perspectives challenges any simplification of overall trend, but the general sense of multi-facetedness, plurality or diversity, within the changing dynamics of an increasingly self-aware, politicised nation, was repeatedly demonstrated by, and characteristic of, all the poets working in this era.

One book consolidates the immediate post-war situation: *Modern Scottish Poetry: An Anthology of the Scottish Renaissance 1920–1945* (1946), edited by Maurice Lindsay (1918–2009) and published by Faber after a meeting with T. S. Eliot to confirm the commission.[1] It included MacDiarmid and his contemporaries who had been publishing before the war, Pittendrigh McGillivray (1856–1938, who was also a significant sculptor), Violet Jacob (1863–1946), Marion Angus (1866–1946), Lewis Spence (1874–1955), Helen B. Cruickshank (1886–1975), Edwin Muir (1887–1959), William Jeffrey (1896–1946) and William Soutar (1898–1943), but crucially, the book also introduced a younger generation writing out of their experiences of the war, including George Bruce (1909–2002), Robert Garioch (1909–81), Norman MacCaig (1910–96), Sorley MacLean (1911–96), Douglas Young (1913–73), Ann Scott Moncrieff (1914–43), George Campbell Hay (1915–84), Sydney Goodsir Smith (1915–75), W. S. Graham (1918–86) and Lindsay himself.

It was revised in a number of editions, culminating in *The Edinburgh Book of Twentieth-Century Scottish Poetry* (2005), co-edited with Lesley Duncan, running to 420 pages containing 159 poets. Of the thirty-four poets from the first edition, twenty-eight remained. The number of women increased dramatically, while the range of geographical locations, languages and poetic forms was increasingly diverse.

The priorities represented in this anthology, in its various permutations from 1946 to 2005, arose from the vision of what Scottish poetry meant in MacDiarmid's *The Golden Treasury of Scottish Poetry* (1940). The key theme of variousness was evident in the languages in which Scottish poetry had been composed: not only Gaelic, Scots and English but also Latin and French. MacDiarmid's point was that Scottish poetry could not be defined (in Eliot's terms) as a single, organic entity, written in a long, unbroken tradition, in one language. Rather, it was one thing of many strands and characters, regenerated at particular moments in cultural history, and peculiarly responsive to the sometimes radical changes in national political identity.

The three decades following the Second World War, however, saw a marked emphasis upon matters of personal, individual, materialist reality, rather than the grand narratives of nationalism. These materialist and politico-social positions were to elaborate new strata of national understanding, deepening a sense of common humanity in the Cold War, post-Holocaust, post-nuclear world. The horrific truth of the radical egalitarianism enforced by the technology of arms underlies the poets' sense of humanity's potential, their faith in education, their sense of hope, and knowledge of the human propensity for self-destruction. Something of the character of the era comes through in the periodical *Poetry Scotland* (in the 1940s) and the annual anthologies *Scottish Poetry* (in the 1960s and 1970s) and *New Writing Scotland* (since 1983).

The presiding spirits of older, but less pessimistic, generations inform the anthology *Dream State: The New Scottish Poets* (1994; new edition 2002), edited by Donny O'Rourke: Edwin Morgan, Norman MacCaig and Iain Crichton Smith were still writing when the first edition appeared, and when, a quarter of a century after his death in 1978, MacDiarmid's rediscovered poems from sources mainly in the National Library of Scotland were published in *The Revolutionary Art of the Future* (2003), they caused front-page newspaper controversy.

Anthologies at the end of the twentieth and beginning of the twenty-first centuries take us further. The most revealing include: *The Faber Book of Modern Scottish Poetry* (1993) edited by Douglas Dunn; *Contraflow on the Superhighway: A Primer of Informationist Poetry* (1994) edited by Richard Price and W. N. Herbert; *The Poetry of Scotland: Gaelic, Scots and English* (1995) edited by Roderick Watson; *The New Penguin Book of Scottish Verse* (2001), edited by Robert Crawford and Mick Imlah; *Scotlands: Poets and the Nation* (2004) edited by Douglas Gifford and Alan Riach; *Modern Scottish Women Poets* (2005) edited by Dorothy McMillan and Michel Byrne; and *Scotia Nova: For the Early Days of a Better Nation* (2014), edited by Alistair Findlay and Tessa Ransford.

Of the poets returning from the Second World War whose moral, intellectual and poetic hopes had begun to form at the start of the Spanish Civil War in 1936, anti-fascism was a driving motive. Edwin Muir (1887–1959) continued to publish in the Cold War era, and some of his most important poems represent it. *The Voyage* (1946), *The Labyrinth* (1949), *Collected Poems, 1921–1951* (1952), the influential *An Autobiography* (1954), *One Foot in Eden* (1956) and posthumously, *Collected Poems* (1965) extended and deepened his perceptions and pathos. With restraint and depth, 'The Good Town' (1949) notes how once, when goodness prevailed, people took on its 'hue' but now 'the bad are up' and 'we, poor ordinary neutral stuff' will helplessly assume that character too. More famously, 'The Horses' (1956) delivers a pastoral image of regeneration after war, but 'Scotland's Winter' (1956) offers no relief. People are consigned to 'frozen life and shallow banishment.'[2] Written mainly in the late 1930s but not published until 1957, MacDiarmid's book-length anti-fascist poem *The Battle Continues* damned the South African poet Roy Campbell and praised the Spanish republican Federico Garcia Lorca. During the Second World War, MacCaig was a conscientious objector. Most of the others had been in North Africa: Edwin Morgan, G. S. Fraser, George Campbell Hay and Robert Garioch until his capture (he became a prisoner-of-war in Italy). Pre-eminent among them as war poets were Sorley MacLean and Hamish Henderson (1919–2002). The work of these last two exemplifies the range of address Scottish poets were committed to.

MacLean, writing in Gaelic and translating his own poems, knew how limited his readership would be. Coming from a long line of singers and tradition-bearers, his was a new departure into writing modern and contemporary poetry directly engaging with politics, warfare and lost love. Henderson's practice and legacy were different. He wrote an extended sequence of war poems, carefully crafted, poised and passionate: *Elegies for the Dead in Cyrenaica* (1948). This is from the First Elegy: 'There were our own, there were the others. / Their deaths were like their lives, human and animal. / There were no gods and precious few heroes'.[3]

At the same time, Henderson wrote popular ballads for the soldiers. As a nilitary intelligence officer, he liaised with the Italian partisans and read and translated Gramsci. Understanding the value of folk song and popular culture, he collected such material during the war and later recorded material in Scotland, working for the School of Scottish Studies at Edinburgh University. He also contributed his own written songs to this anonymous tradition, for everyday use. 'The Ballad of the D-Day Dodgers' was a response to the comment ascribed to the aristocrat Lady Astor that troops on the Mediterranean front were having a fine time. The soldierly irony and bitter black humour comes through when sung to the tune of 'Lili Marlene': 'We're the D-Day Dodgers, out in Italy – / Always on the vino, always on the spree.'[4] Other songs, such as 'The 51st Highland Division's Farewell to Sicily', 'The John MacLean March' and 'Freedom Come All Ye' are among the most famous, each long-lasting in popular currency. Folk song and balladry on contemporary topics extended throughout the period, including satiric anti-polaris and republican ballads by Andrew Tannahill (1900–86), comic renditions of Shakespeare ('Oor Hamlet') and conditions of skyscraper living ('The Jeelie Piece Song') by Adam McNaughton (b. 1939), and other songs by Matt McGinn (1928–77), Hamish Imlach (1940–96) and Dick Gaughan (b. 1948). The border between songs to be sung and poetry written to be read and considered is always permeable. Edwin Morgan wrote (and performed) the lyrics of 'in remote part / scottish fiction' for the band Idlewild, and when their album was released in 2002, he reached an entirely new audience of listeners and readers as a result.

In the immediate post-war ethos of hope and intention, to build a better future, the nationalist priority of the 1920s was merged with ideals of education and democracy. In Scotland, the value of juxtaposition – the grinning gargoyle beside the saint in the Gothic art of great cathedrals – was a poetic imperative, and every one of the pre-eminent poets of the second half of the twentieth century were engaged professionally in education, whether as teachers or university lecturers, journalists, cultural revivalists, editors or in other capacities. Many were founders of such organisations as the Saltire Society (founded 1936) or the Association for Scottish Literary Studies (founded 1970), or the first Department of Scottish Literature (at Glasgow

University), founded 1971 with poet Alexander Scott as its Head, or the Scottish Poetry Library, founded by poet Tessa Ransford in 1984. These developments are the long-term fruits of the 1920s, and more closely, of the cultural regeneration energised since 1945.

This was not simply self-aggrandisement. Arguably, the major works of the 1950s were focused on the capacities, nature and limits of language generally. In 1955, MacDiarmid published *In Memoriam James Joyce*, a book-length work said to be only part of an ultimately unfinished poem on an epic scale, similar to Pound's *Cantos*. The central theme of the work is the endless variety of languages in the world, the diversity of poetic and artistic expressions of human creativity, from Shakespeare to Fred Astaire, and the limitations placed upon expressivity by political power and imperialism, and the need to balance energy and form. Its ideas were extended in *The Kind of Poetry I Want* (1961). Publication of MacDiarmid's *Collected Poems* (1962), first in America, showed the extent of his work for the first time. Even so, it was not until the posthumous *Complete Poems* (1978) that a full measure might be taken, as the *Collected* was effectively only an extended selection. The core of all his writing is a celebration of difference: 'The effort of culture is towards greater differentiation / Of perceptions and desires and values and ends' and all these are to be held 'from moment to moment / In a perpetually changing but stable equilibrium ...'[5] Post-war Scottish poetry is a rich demonstration of this diversity.

W. S. Graham (1918–86) made significant impact with *The Nightfishing* (1955) but it was not until his *Collected Poems 1942–1977* (1979) that his intensity of dedication was fully appreciated. He spent most of his adult life in Cornwall, his poems explorations of loneliness and searching, poignant appraisals of the use and uselessness of language. In 'The Nightfishing' itself, and 'What is the language using us for?' the delicacy of his ear and the sensitivity of his judgement is at its best, and 'Loch Thom' is a magnificent epiphany describing the 'lonely, freshwater loch' in the hollow of hills above his native town, industrial Greenock, southwest of Glasgow, to which he would walk as a child. As an adult, his return visit is chilly, restrained, heart-wrenching.[6]

Seven poets have become iconic in Scottish poetry from the 1950s to the 1990s, each of them earthed in, arising from, and looking freshly at their favoured places, the terrain of their local attachments. The breakthrough volume for Somhairle MacGill-Eain / Sorley MacLean (1911–96) was *Dàin do Eimhir* (1943), heralding the regeneration of Gaelic poetry, but it was not until *Spring Tide and Ebb Tide: Selected Poems* (1977) that the scale of his achievement was recognised widely. This was followed by *Caoir Gheal Leumraich / White Leaping Flame: Collected Poems* (2011), edited by Christopher Whyte and Emma Dymock. Of the love poems, 'Coin is Madaidhean-allaidh' / 'Dogs and Wolves' stays in the memory, an extreme evocation of self-persecution, linking love and poetry, violence and unfulfilled desires, both personal and political, in an evocation of 'a hunt without halt, without respite.' After his first book, MacLean was recognised as the major force in modern Gaelic poetry. He translated his own poems, first written in Gaelic, into unforgettable English. His major subjects were love and war, but the range of MacLean's poems include the lyric-sequence 'An Cuilithionn' / 'The Cuillin' (1939) in which the mountain range on the island of Skye stands as a living symbol of heroic opposition to those forces that would foreclose life's potential, from the Clearances of the eighteenth and nineteenth centuries, to twentieth-century fascism. The central poem of his career is 'Hallaig', a haunting elegy for a cleared township on his native island of Raasay, where the ruined homes of his ancestors can still be seen in a beautiful location redolent with its own tragedy. MacLean's poem is likened to a bullet that will kill the deer of time and preserve the memory of his people and his place forever: 'chunnacas na mairbh beo.' / 'the dead have been seen alive'.[7] His later elegy for his brother Calum and his passionate denunciation of the authority of nuclear weaponry in 'Screapadal' are also required reading.

A poet of the Orkney Islands off the north coast of Scotland, George Mackay Brown (1921–96) evoked native land and seascapes, their history and legends, celebrating the generations of his parents and grandparents. His central themes are of the essential rhythms of the everyday, the rites and rituals that help keep things sacred. The theme of sacrifice, and particularly the martyrdom of St Magnus, he returned to repeatedly. His poems follow liturgical patterns of repetition with patience and bright imagery. The themes were forming from the earliest work, in *The Year of the Whale* (1965) and *Fishermen with Ploughs* (1971). *Winterfold* (1976) includes portrait-poems of wry humour and characters – tinkers, seafarers, old and young populate his poems (and fiction): 'Ikey: His Will in Winter Written' gives an entire life in its poised, retrospective, hopeful but plaintive account; 'Hamnavoe' is a portrait of his father and his home town, Stromness. 'The Old Women' is a piercing depiction of grief after death at sea. 'Uranium' is one of the most powerful poems of the modern militarised era, poised tremblingly, after ages of stone and iron, farming and fishing, before 'the magnificent Door of Fire'.[8]

Iain Crichton Smith (1928–98) is closly associated with Lewis in the Outer Hebrides, where austere religion permeates social convention and forms a hard strata of judgement which ultimately he turned to his own advantage. From his first book, *The Long River* (1955), through *Thistles and Roses* (1961), *Deer on the High Hills* (1962), *The Law and the Grace*

(1965) and many others, he elaborates a vision of polar dissension, austerity and plenitude, meanness and generosity, inanity and sophistication, banality and subtlety. Themes of belonging and exile are strong, while *A Life* (1986) is a verse-autobiography. In 'Poem of Lewis' the 'fine graces of poetry' are seen as irrelevent to his people, unless they come naturally, like water from the deepest well. The 'Old Woman' is a recurring figure in his poems, often denying human potential for regeneration, asserting the inadequacy of all human effort. And yet, through depression and breakdown, Crichton Smith recovered a capacity for quizzical humour and affirmation, and 'Two Girls Singing' celebrates wonderfully what he calls 'the unpredicted voices of our kind' – it is not only that they are 'of our kind' but also that they are, and always will be, 'unpredicted'.[9]

Robert Garioch (1909–81), an unassertive, shy-seeming Edinburgh poet, depicting characters and encounters taking place there, went to school and university and became a schoolteacher in Edinburgh, then in London and Kent before retiring in 1964 and working as an assistant on the *Dictionary of the Older Scottish Tongue*, describing himself as a 'lexicographer's orra body'. He was writer-in-residence at Edinburgh University and on Radio Forth, composing poems on events of the day. His *Complete Poetical Works* (1983) collects poems from a number of slim, small-press publications, his first being a joint collection with Sorley MacLean from 1940, *17 Poems for 6d* (sixpence in old currency), hand-printed by his own press. Yet his achievement is substantial, both for the sharp perception and humour of the occasional poems, the seriousness and sober reasonableness of tragic enquiry into human destructiveness and waste in the war poems, 'The Muir' and 'The Wire', and for the impressive translations of the Roman poet Giuseppe Belli, whose sonnets of Rome Garioch transposed effectively to Edinburgh, nowhere more movingly than in 'The Puir Faimly', the unsentimental, heart-breaking monologue of a helpless mother attempting to comfort her starving children. Garioch's 'Edinburgh Sonnets' are another masterly sequence full of elemental sympathy and civil grace.[10] He is poet of vernacular wit, compassion and insightful urban humour.

Sydney Goodsir Smith (1915–75), a flamboyant, lavish verbal profligate, was a New Zealander who adopted Edinburgh and the Scots language to produce vivid evocations of the old city and its raucous, sensitive, loving and drinking inhabitants in his poems and plays. If Garioch's urban Edinburgh Scots is authentically vernacular, Goodsir Smith's is rhetorically charged and gestural. While he is a fine lyric love poet he also developed a fluent, conversational Scots-language idiom in long-lined free verse, portraying characters and situations, in poems such as 'The Grace of God and the Meth-Drinker' and his masterpiece, the fabulous book-length sequence of love poems,

Under the Eildon Tree (1948). This gathers the stories of the great lovers of world literature into a Rabelaisian company where he finds himself in an affinity of comic and tragic realisation. Deirdre and Naoise and Helen and Paris are here, but alongside them equal in importance and as pungently present is the 'bonny cou' (a prostitute) from the Black Bull o' Norroway, an Edinburgh pub, and the dark bars and dingy alleyways and wynds of the historical old town are as populous with lusty lovers as the realms of fiction and myth. Grandiose gestures and declarations of love rub shoulders with massively reductive and deflating gutter-low perspectives. Elation is there, but so is the pox.[11]

Norman MacCaig (1910–96) began with two books, *Far Cry* (1943) and *The Inward Eye* (1946), avalanches of language at the furthest remove from the lucid, understated, eloquent, razory poems that came later. It took ten years before the short poems of *Riding Lights* (1956) signalled the new, verbally succinct, MacCaig. The tight but conversational regular stanza structures gave way in the 1960s to free verse, but equally restrained, minimal and nuanced. Ultimately, the collected poems are a thesaurus of similes and metaphors: a thorn bush is 'an encyclopedia of angles', a sheepdog rushes through a fence 'like a piece of black wind' and a hen 'stares at nothing, then picks it up'. Overtly descriptive of animals, birds, specific places in the north of Scotland around Lochinver and in Edinburgh, where he was a primary school teacher, and of particular people, his poems probe questions of the inadequacy, unreliability and limits of language itself, the borders of what language permits us to understand (his words, he says, are sometimes spoken not by him but by 'A man in my position'). In this he is close to W. S. Graham. Yet he is one of the funniest poets, with an extraordinarily dry, ironic humour and a shrewd sense of value. Precise annotation of trivia in 'Five minutes at the window' delivers a profound message about what political idealism always neglects at its peril. We are invited to note that a 'seagull tries over and over again / to pick up something on the road' while 'a white cat sits halfway up a tree.' Each observation invites the questions, 'Why?' and 'What are trivia?' And the answers come through silence, implication: 'My shelves of books say nothing / but I know what they mean.' He is suddenly 'back in the world again / and am happy' even though he acknowledges 'its disasters, its horrors, its griefs.' A master of tone, humour, irony, MacCaig is a great love poet of the natural world and a great elegist in the sequence 'Poems for Angus'.[12]

The title of Edwin Morgan's first book, *The Vision of Cathkin Braes* (1952), announces two key co-ordinates: a specific local reference to a hillside overlooking Glasgow, and an idea that a 'vision' is required to arise from that locality, to see it new but move out from it, to go further.

Morgan was gay man returned from war, working as a lecturer at Glasgow University, in a country where disclosure of his sexuality would have meant immediate dismissal; the 1950s were a difficult decade for him. It was not until *The Second Life* (1968) that the breakthrough came, a breathtaking step into the new generation, heralding a long career. Festive poems like 'Trio' (a snapshot of three people with a chihuahua walking at night in Glasgow 'under the Christmas lights') rubbed shoulders with lyrical, autobiographical poems like 'In the snack-bar' (about helping a disabled man to a public toilet) and concrete or sound poems, like 'The Loch Ness Monster's Song' which ends with the monster descending back into the loch: 'Gombl mbl bl – / blm plm, / blm plm, / blm plm, / blp.' The poems in this book – depictions of Glasgow, lyrically autobiographical, coded narratives of homosexual encounter, experimental concrete poems, poems addressed to other key figures of the time, both nationally (Joan Eardley, Ian Hamilton Finlay) and in contemporary popular culture (Marilyn Monroe, Edith Piaf) – written over a number of years, comprised a major intervention in what poetry in Scotland could do. Morgan was the most voluminous and varied of all Scottish poets since MacDiarmid. A professor of English at Glasgow University, he drew on the American poets of the 1950s and 1960s, especially the Beats and Black Mountain poets, and on poets from the Eastern Bloc countries, translating work from there, including Soviet Russia's Mayakovsky, to balance the emergence of his own vast florilegium of voices. Further experimentation continued in *Glasgow Sonnets* (1972), again, focusing closely on the city in a process of urban regeneration, and *Instamatic Poems* (1972), local and international snapshots of news images, momentary catches of events such as the funeral of Stravinsky observed by Ezra Pound in Venice, or a young couple being pushed through a plate glass window in Glasgow; *From Glasgow to Saturn* (1973), as wide-ranging as its title suggests, *The New Divan* (1977), which includes the long, meditative title poem drawing on his experience in North Africa in the Second World War, and *Star Gate* (1979), juxtaposing science fiction poems with personal elegies and playful, comic gestures. The achievement was confirmed in *Poems of Thirty Years* (1982) but then a different Morgan began to emerge. He had been thought of as predominantly an academic poet, gamesome ('The Computer's First Christmas Card'), ventriloquist ('The Apple's Song', 'Hyena'), curious and optimistic. Now came *Sonnets from Scotland* (1984), a key volume of the era, where national identity took first importance. This was not to be a self-glorifying parade, but rather an enquiry into possibilities, of how the past might be read anew, how the future might be made differently, what the implications of present urgencies might provoke. Like other major works of its time, in literary and cultural criticism and history as well as poetry, it was published in the context of national self-reappraisal in the aftermath of the disallowed devolution referendum and the election of the Conservative government in 1979. Morgan's initiative was not to take an explicitly politicised stance but to reimagine Scotland from prehistory ('There is no beginning') to unknown futurity. His *Collected Poems* (1990) was republished with his *Collected Translations* (1996), confirming his stature while demonstrably engaging international poetic conversations across a multitude of languages and cultures. *Hold Hands among the Atoms* (1991) addressed the end of the Communist era in cautionary terms while *Virtual and Other Realities* (1997) embraced the possibilities opening up with new technology. At the turn of the millennium, Morgan wrote three works of startling contrast, beginning with *Demon* (1999), an extended credo for the outlaw status all poetry demands. When tranquillity and serenity threaten to become complacency, in comes the Demon. *A.D. A Trilogy of Plays on the Life of Jesus Christ* (2000), a provocative, historical account, was followed by *The Play of Gligamesh* (2005), a version of the oldest story in Western literature (from c. 1700 BC). Largely written in verse, the plays should be considered as part of his poetic *ouevre*. He continued with *Cathures* (2002), a book of poems focused on Glasgow, of which he had been appointed Poet Laureate (1999–2005), and *A Book of Lives* (2007), collecting his late, more openly personal poems in the sequence 'Love and a Life'. He was appointed Scots Makar, or National Poet of Scotland, on 16 April 2004, a post he held till his death in 2010.[13]

With Morgan's example and encouragement a new generation of Scottish poets began publishing in the 1970s, pre-eminently Liz Lochhead (b. 1947), who was appointed to the position of National Poet of Scotland on 19 January 2011, succeeding Morgan. From the 1970s on, Lochhead opened the way for a number of Scottish women poets to be more widely appreciated, beginning with poems exploring her own experience as a young woman in Lanarkshire in the 1960s and 1970s and developing her skills in creating personae and characters through writing dramatic monologues, original plays and translations of classic drama, including *Medea* (2001). This is clear from her first, best-selling book, *Memo for Spring* (1972), her poetic encounter with the Hebrides, *Islands* (1978), her excursus into myth and folk-tale revised for contemporary bearings in *The Grimm Sisters* (1981) and *Dreaming Frankenstein & Collected Poems* (1984). Her attention to relationships, domestic situations, emotions in local or intimate contexts, is not an evasion of serious questions but a different approach to them. Her contemporary, Veronica Forrest-Thomson (1947–75), in *Collected Poems and Translations* (1990), brought together fierce intellectual passion with refreshingly clinical engagement in the sharpest of focal concentrations on the purpose, dynamics and artifice of language. The forensic intellectualism in her work is complementary to Lochhead's warmth and sympathy.

Meg Bateman (b. 1957), writing in Gaelic and translating her poems into English, published some of the most essential representations of feminine experience in *Aotromachd agus dàin eile / Lightness and other poems* (1997), *Soirbheas / Fair Wind* (2007), and *Transparencies* (2013). As editor and translator of anthologies of early Gaelic poetry, Bateman also provided both new versions of ancient texts and new ways of contextualising new writing.

From her first book, *The Adoption Papers*, Jackie Kay (b. 1961) used different voices to depict her own experience of growing up in Glasgow, a black child adopted by committed socialist parents. She later would go further into the autobiography, exploring themes of belonging, family, local, national and ancestral identity and questions of sexual disposition and social prejudice. Sensational as this seems, the subtlety of her versification is as impressive as her continuous good humour, humanistic sympathy and sheer eloquence. For Carol Ann Duffy (b. 1955), appointed British Poet Laureate in 2009, otherness is present in various poems: born in Scotland, she moved to England as a child, recollecting not only places and people from childhood but much more intimately a language, idiom and music foreign to the environment which her mature choices and adulthood had grown into.

Kay, Duffy, Lochhead and others, men as well as women, have written poems specifically on the theme of linguistic dislocation, and this extends questions of previous generations into a newly politicised context. The women who published increasingly from the 1970s made use of the achievements of their predecessors in the development of their own distinctive work. Meg Bateman learned from, respected, honoured and made creative use of the example of MacLean, as Liz Lochhead made of Morgan, or any younger poet made of that generation of men, much as they did of MacDiarmid. But none of them emulated anyone.

Characteristic of the generational change that took place in the 1970s and 1980s is Liz Lochhead's 'Mirror's Song', which begins with the command to the reader and the poet's persona and the mirror of the poem's title: 'Smash me looking-glass glass …' and ends with the line, 'a woman giving birth to herself'.[14] It is as if in such an act of self-generation, and regeneration, the exemplary struggle enacted in the poem takes its place along with the work of all the poets named in the process of a nation giving birth to itself. The sustained strength of character of Lochhead, the clever turns and challenges of Carol Ann Duffy, the self-assurance and poise of Jackie Kay, the balance of self-centredness and vulnerability of Meg Bateman, the personal, historical and universal themes of Janet Paisley, the gingery decisions and tentative annotations of experience of Kathleen Jamie, constitute a range of poetic voices and techniques and approaches to experience. One of the most accomplished poets of this generation, Elizabeth Burns (1957–2015), from her first collection *Ophelia* (1991), and most effectively in *Held* (2010), has quietly but with immense assurance established an inimitable tone and timbre.

A poetics of linguistic juxtaposition in modern Scottish poetry by many of these women is characteristic: in their different spellings, sounds, vocabulary, forms of address and structures of composition, they prompt active interpretation of how language operates in terms not only of the subjective lyrical voice but the power structures of society. This was emphatically the provenance of the first little book, *Six Glasgow Poems* (1969) by Tom Leonard (b. 1944), whose collections *Intimate Voices* (1984) and *Outside the Narrative* (2009) insist upon the validity of working-class experience and language, and demonstrate that validity with untiring moral ferocity and sometimes wild humour.

The continuities across the entire period, as much as the diversities of theme, language and range of individual sensibilities, outline the terrain most clearly. Gaelic poets contemporary with Sorley MacLean warrant full recognition in themselves: George Campbell Hay (1915–84), fluent in Gaelic, Scots and English, a songwriter and intellectual whose extended sequence *Mochtàr is Dùghall* (1982) explores an encounter between a Highlander and a North African soldier in the Second World War; Derick Thomson (1921–2012), not only a major Gaelic poet but professor of Celtic at Glasgow University and editor of the Gaelic literary magazine *Gairm* from 1953, tireless proponent of the language and all its capabilities. Pre-eminent poets of the 1960s include Tom Buchan (1931–95) and Alan Jackson (b. 1938), whose books, respectively, *Dolphins at Cochin* and *The Grim Wayfarer* (both 1969) remain among the iconic *livres de cachet* of that era. Ian Hamilton Finlay (1925–2006), whose English and Scots poems and concrete poetry, most extensively realised in the garden of Little Sparta at Stonypath, his home in the Lanarkshire hills, remains to be visited and explored every summer. The poetry-reading scene, since the Heretics group of the 1970s, includes festivals and regular events all over Scotland, such as St Mungo's Mirrorball in Glasgow. So many individuals have their own growing ouevres: Ron Butlin (b. 1949), Edinburgh Makar, 2008–14; Stewart Conn (b. 1936), whose *Stolen Light: Selected Poems* combines a true craftsman's care for structure and poise with a countryman's understanding of the hard realities of the farming world; Kenneth White (b. 1936), beginning with *The Cold Wind of Dawn* (1966), whose collected longer poems appeared in *The Bird Path* (1989); and collected shorter poems 1960–90 in *Handbook for the Diamond Country* (1990); Douglas Dunn (b. 1942), whose account in *Northlight* (1988) of his own transition back into Scotland from previous residence in England remains seminal, while earlier collections speculate on the nature of loss, regret and survival, and whose *Elegies* (1985) demonstrates how self-constraint holds depths of sorrow and a fundamental sense of human decency; John Purser (b. 1942), writing with incomparable immediacy of life as a crofter on Skye, and out of extensive knowledge of Scotland's composers and music; Aonghas MacNeacail (b. 1942), born on Skye but long resident in the Scottish Borders, committed to free verse, influenced by the American Black Mountain poets, therefore distinct from more traditional Gaelic forms, whose politics come through most forcefully in personal application: 'when i was young / it wasn't history but memory'.[15] Andrew Greig (b. 1951) established his reputation as an iconoclastic yet highly sensitised poet with *Men On Ice* (1977), consolidating it in *This Life, This Life: Selected Poems 1970–2006* (2006). John Burnside (b. 1955) began with *The Hoop* (1988), and his most memorable collections include *Common Knowledge* (1991) and *Black Cat Bone* (2011).

Since the 1990s online technology has changed the conditions of poets and people generally, in terms of composition, publication, acquisition of information and stimulation of the imagination. The conditions of Scotland's history, geography and politics have their own impositions, through and beyond new technologies, and every poet publishing in the first decade of the twenty-first century shows them at work. The early poems of Peter McCarey (b. 1956) are in *Collected Contraptions* (2011), and his vast project *The Syllabary* (online at: http://www.thesyllabary.com/) has generated an epic for the age of information techology. W. N. Herbert (b. 1961) begins his poem, 'Dingle Dell' with the line: 'There is no passport to this country, / it exists as a quality of the language.' The singularity of that last word belies its indicating not one but a plurality of languages, voices and forms of articulation.

This plurality is evident in the range of poets working in the early twenty-first century: David Kinloch, meditating on the relation between poetry and painting, travel and language; Thomas A. Clark, emphasising the values of taking one's time and walking in landscapes experienced not as possessions but visceral quotidian realities; Robert Allan Jamieson and Jen Hadfield in similar address but more focused on their chosen place, the Shetland archipelago; Ian Stephen in relation to Lewis and the wild places around it; Angus Peter Campbell and Rody Gorman, carrying forward Gaelic priorities; Don Paterson, turning domesticity into zircon-hard realisations of tenderness and relativity; Jim Carruth, appointed poet laureate of Glasgow in 2014; Richard Price, keeping the tentative nature of all such domestic relations in suspense, both in address to his subjects and his choice of forms and tones; Gerda Stevenson, also prioritising domesticity but equally in a fully politicised world; Graham Fulton, bristlingly satiric in social contexts, often based in Paisley; Rab Wilson, serious or flamboyant in Ayrshire Scots; Gerrie Fellows, exploring senses of displacement and belonging from her own experience, both as a New Zealander adopting Scotland and as a mother writing about in vitro fertilisation and the virtues of family, art and medicine; Robert Crawford, poet and professor, and Robin Robertson, poet and publisher; multiple-prizewinning Roddy Lumsden; Mick Imlah (1956–2009), poet and editor, whose last book, *The Lost Leader* (2008), carried strength and poignancy in equal measure; Kathrine Sowerby, who, in these lines from 'Coastline Disturbance', might be writing for generations yet unborn: 'We emerge after midnight filling the darkness with living. / Disappointments seem further across the ice'.[16]

If MacDiarmid proposed a multifaceted national identity, and the 'seven poets' generation created their work from the geographical places each one distinctively favoured, then the gendered, class-conscious, increasingly politicised world of the following generations has made the national identity an even more complex home to different diversities, accommodating – not always easily – nature and domesticity, chaos and order, cynicism and wonder, states and movements, self and others, internationality and self-determined nationality.

NOTES

1 Maurice Lindsay, ed., *Modern Scottish Poetry: An Anthology of the Scottish Renaissance 1920–1945* (London: Faber and Faber, 1946).
2 Edwin Muir, *The Complete Poems*, ed. Peter Butter (Aberdeen: Association for Scottish Literary Studies, 1991), p. 214.
3 Hamish Henderson, *Collected Poems and Songs*, ed. Raymond Ross (Edinburgh: Curly Snake Publishing, 2000), p. 52.
4 Ibid., p. 94.
5 Hugh MacDiarmid, *Complete Poems*, ed. W. R. Aitken and Michael Grieve (2 vols.), Volume 2 (Manchester: Carcanet, 1994), p. 1138.
6 W. S. Graham, *New Collected Poems*, ed. Matthew Francis (London: Faber and Faber, 2005), pp. 220–21.
7 Somhairle MacGill-Eain / Sorley MacLean, *Gheal Leumraich / White Leaping Flame: Collected Poems*, ed. Christopher Whyte and Emma Dymock (Edinburgh: Polygon, 2011), pp. 230–34.
8 George Mackay Brown, *Collected Poems*, ed. Archie Bevan and Brian Murray (London: John Murray, 2006). The quotation from 'Uranium' comes from *Seven Poets*, ed. Christopher Carrel (Glasgow: Third Eye Centre, 1981), p. 58.
9 Iain Crichton Smith, *New Collected Poems*, ed. Mathew McGuire (Manchester: Carcanet, 2011), p. 53.

10 Robert Garioch, *Complete Poetical Works*, ed. Robin Fulton (Edinburgh: Macdonald, 1983), pp. 81–91.
11 Sydney Goodsir Smith, *Collected Poems 1941–1975* (London: John Calder, 1975), pp. 147–87.
12 Norman MacCaig, *The Poems*, ed. Ewen McCaig (Edinburgh: Polygon, 2005), pp. 332–38.
13 Edwin Morgan, *Collected Poems* (Manchester: Carcanet, 1996).
14 Liz Lochhead, *A Choosing: Selected Poems* (Edinburgh: Polygon, 2011).
15 Aonghas MacNeacail, *A Proper Schooling* (Edinburgh: Polygon, 1997), p.13.
16 Kathrine Sowerby, 'Coastline Disturbance', accessed online 28/2/2015 at: http://glasgowreviewofbooks.com/2015/02/06/new-poetry-by-kathrine-sowerby/

11

KATIE GRAMICH

Welsh Poetry since 1945

The 1930s and 1940s was the period known as the 'First Flowering' of Anglophone Welsh poetry. Certainly there had been 'Anglo-Welsh' poets long before this period, as the very title of Raymond Garlick and Roland Mathias's anthology, *Anglo-Welsh Poetry 1480–1990*, indicates.[1] Notably, there had been a clutch of prominent early modern Anglo-Welsh poets such as Thomas and Henry Vaughan and Edward and George Herbert, who continue to exert an influence on some of their twentieth-century Welsh heirs. Nevertheless, the enormous social and demographic shifts of the late nineteenth and early twentieth century meant that, by the 1930s, the number of Welsh speakers in Wales dropped below 50 percent for the first time, and in many areas of South Wales, English was becoming the first language of a majority of the people.[2] The poets who came to prominence in the 'first flowering' of the 1930s and '40s, then, were of this talented generation of writers who were the first in their own families to have English as their mother tongue. As one of this generation, Glyn Jones, in his seminal critical memoir, *The Dragon Has Two Tongues* (1968) bore witness to the way in which he and his peers approached English with the relish and brío of explorers discovering a new-found continent.[3]

Glyn Jones was a contemporary of Dylan Thomas, Vernon Watkins and the prose writers Gwyn Thomas and Rhys Davies. All were from South Wales and had English as their first language, though their parents were native Welsh speakers and they retained a strong knowledge of Welsh-language forms and traditions, including folk and chapel culture, and, to some extent, strict metre poetry.[4] These poets inhabited a linguistic borderland, therefore, and their work is energised and defamiliarised by the tensions between two languages and two cultures.

Both Glyn Jones and Dylan Thomas sought recognition for their work in London in the 1930s. In another memoir entitled *Setting Out*, Glyn Jones states: 'All Dylan's aspirations were London oriented and so were mine; and so were those of all the young Anglo-Welsh writers whose work began to appear in the Thirties. Considering the condition of South Wales, its poverty and complete lack of artistic stimulus or interest, it's not surprising that should have been so.'[5] Most of the poets of the First Flowering seemed to defy the appalling poverty and deprivation of 1930s South Wales through the exuberance and extravagance of their linguistic experiments. This holds true also of a number of the prose writers, such as the aforementioned Gwyn Thomas and Rhys Davies, whose short stories, particularly, contain the kinds of figurative flights of fancy more often associated with poetic utterance. It is also important to note that Dylan Thomas and Glyn Jones, from an early stage in their careers, considered themselves to be both poets and short story writers, and there was a daring fluidity in their approach to these genres. Thomas's third publication, *The Map of Love* (1939) was a mixture of poetry and prose and contains short stories such as 'The Lemon', 'The Tree' and 'The Map of Love' which might be seen as prose poetry, and are at least as Delphic as the early poetry of *18 Poems* (1934) and *Twenty-Five Poems* (1936). Similarly, Glyn Jones's early prose has a surreal, poetic quality in puzzling but haunting stories such as 'Porth-y-Rhyd' from *The Blue Bed* (1937) and 'The Apple Tree' from *The Water Music* (1944).

Yet perhaps the phrase 'figurative flights of fancy' I have used to describe these writers' work is an Anglocentric label for a literary characteristic that had been prominent in Welsh-language poetry for many centuries. The work of the medieval Welsh poet, Dafydd ap Gwilym, known to both Thomas and Jones, is perhaps the best example of the dexterity and *joie-de-vivre* of a poetic tradition which prized craft, ingenuity and wit. The piled-up similes and analogies which adorn a poem such as ap Gwilym's 'Y Gwynt' (The Wind) reappear in works such as 'The Force that through the Green Fuse' (1933) and 'In the White Giant's Thigh' (1949), by Dylan Thomas, and 'Merthyr' (1954), by Glyn Jones.[6] The latter, moreover, translated Welsh poetry into English and borrowed extensively from its techniques and forms in his own writing.[7] That Dafydd ap Gwilym is still a potent force in Welsh poetry today is indicated by the fact that the contemporary poet Gwyneth Lewis has recently published a stylish translation of 'Y Gwynt'.[8]

The Welsh poetic tradition still exerted a strong influence on the practice of the poets of the 'First Flowering', then, even if, in their determination to be accepted and lauded by a metropolitan audience, they occasionally and disingenuously denied it. Even if the Anglophone Welsh poets of the period had wanted to 'make it new' and cut themselves off from the Welsh-language poetic tradition, it would have been difficult for them to do so, given that the tradition was not an archaic or residual echo but a vibrant, contemporary reality. In the face of the increasingly catastrophic decline of the Welsh language, ironically enough, the early twentieth century saw an astonishing renaissance in Welsh literature. Thus, Dylan Thomas and Glyn Jones were contemporaries not only of Louis MacNeice, Hugh MacDiarmid and W. H. Auden, but also of Welsh-language poets such as T. H. Parry-Williams, Saunders Lewis, Gwenallt, and Waldo Williams, nowadays considered to be among the greatest Welsh poets of the century. Moreover, these Welsh-language poets were often writing about the same people, locations and experiences as their Anglophone Welsh peers.[9]

Welsh poets of the '30s and '40s, writing in both languages, were aware of, and often in touch with, artistic movements beyond Wales, both in the British Isles and North America, as well as on the Continent. In the '30s, for instance, Glyn Jones wrote an essay in Welsh on French Surrealism for the avant-garde magazine, *Tir Newydd* (New Territory), edited by the Welsh-language experimental poet, Alun Llywelyn-Williams.[10] There were also links with Scottish Modernist writers such as Hugh MacDiarmid who, notoriously and unabashedly, stole a passage of prose by Glyn Jones and turned it into a 'found poem' of his own, entitled 'Perfect'.[11] Vernon Watkins who, along with R. S. Thomas, Roland Mathias, and Rowan Williams, can be seen as the heir of the Anglo-Welsh devotional poets of the early modern period, even spent the last years of his life teaching in America, where his distinctive mystical poetry, drawing both on Welsh folklore and customs and his extensive knowledge of European, especially German, poetry was appreciated perhaps more than it was at home. A poem such as Watkins's haunting 'Ballad of the Mari Lwyd' (1941) also shows the poet's awareness of Welsh metrics, its seven- and eight-syllable lines echoing both the form of the traditional English and Scottish ballad and the characteristic line-length of the Welsh *cywydd*.[12]

Dylan Thomas and Vernon Watkins both died prematurely (in 1953 and 1967, respectively) but in the '40s they, along with Glyn Jones and the war poet Alun Lewis, were the best-known Welsh poetic voices internationally. But another voice began to make itself heard soon after the war: the very different voice of R. S. Thomas. In fact, for a short period in the 1940s and early '50s Dylan Thomas and R. S. Thomas published their work at the same time and, occasionally, in the same place. Jeremy Hooker draws attention to Dylan's 'Poem in October' appearing in Keidrych Rhys's anthology *Modern Welsh Poetry* (1944) alongside R. S. Thomas's 'A Peasant', a strange juxtaposition if ever there was one. Hooker argues that 'Poem in October', for all its boastful celebration, its 'tower of words', is actually 'the expression of a predicament' for 'English words [are] imposed on the Welsh landscape, subjugating the native language.' R. S.'s more modest approach, focusing on the 'bald Welsh hills', appears to offer 'an escape from the tower' and to 'clear the ground for the poems he will construct upon it.'[13] In 1944, Dylan was at the height of his fame and had already published six volumes of work with major English and American publishers (Dent and New Directions), whereas R. S. had yet to publish a first volume. Both R. S.'s first two volumes (*The Stones of the Field*, 1946, and *An Acre of Land*, 1952) were published in small numbers by obscure Welsh companies; it would take the championship of John Betjeman to secure a London publisher (Rupert Hart-Davis) for his third volume, *Song at the Year's Turning* (1955). Dylan achieved international renown very quickly and at an early age, whereas R. S. struggled for recognition but outlived his contemporary by almost half a century, a period during which his home and international stature grew slowly but strongly. By the 1970s, younger Welsh poets felt themselves to be attempting to write in the shadow of two forbidding giants, who were facing in opposite directions.

Yet I contend that these two faces are two sides of the same poetic coin. One of the strongest elements in the Welsh poetic tradition was, and remains, praise poetry; Dylan positioned himself confidently in this tradition, as he demonstrates for example in the 1952 verse 'Prologue' to his *Collected Poems*, where he writes 'I, a spinning man / Glory also this star', going on imperiously to demand that the reader heed his bardic ecstasy: 'Hark: I trumpet the place, / From fish to jumping hill!'[14] In many ways, this feverish praise may be seen as a reaction to the depredations of war, which Thomas had witnessed first-hand both in the bombing of London and in the devastation of his hometown, Swansea, bombed flat in 1941, the latter memorably elegised in the radio broadcast 'Return Journey' (1947). In the wake of these losses, Thomas took on the role of praise poet with an urgency absent from his earlier, more introspective and 'difficult' verse. In poems like 'Fern Hill' (1945) and 'Over Sir John's Hill' (1949) Thomas's rhapsodic and formally intricate evocation of rural west Wales suggests a poet in search of a lost home, a place to dwell. By the post-war period, thanks to the largesse of his patron, Margaret Taylor, he was actually living in the boathouse in Laugharne, Carmarthenshire. And yet the celebratory 'Prologue' acknowledges the difficulty of finding a secure dwelling in the land, for it dramatizes the building not of a house but of an ark which, by the end of the poem, has set sail, 'rid[ing] out alone … Under the stars of Wales.' For Thomas, then, it is the building of poetry itself which enables some kind of hope and security in a blighted post-war world.

The other side of praise is satire and lamentation, and R. S. Thomas from the first excelled in this mode which has also been prominent in Welsh-language culture. In the same year that Dylan was writing his celebratory 'Prologue', R. S. was publishing uncompromisingly bleak poems such as 'The Welsh Hill Country', which remarks sardonically that 'The sheep are grazing at Bwlch-y-Fedwen, / Arranged romantically in the usual manner' but that beneath that picturesque scene '[t]he fluke and the foot-rot and the fat maggot' are '[g]nawing the skin from the small bones'. All this occurs, accusingly, '[t]oo far for you to see.[15] The three sestets of the poem, which appear at first disarmingly lyrical, build to a devastating indictment of the depopulation of the Welsh hill country and the death of a language and culture, uncompromisingly figured as a disease-raddled farmer whose 'embryo music [is] dead in his throat'.[16]

Both Thomases are drawing on, developing and experimenting with their Welsh poetic inheritance, not only in the modes they employ (praise/satire) but also in language, syntax and poetic technique (such as *cynghanedd*-like alliteration, evident in the above quotations).[17] Both also focus on the particularities of places in Wales, such as Dylan's Fern Hill, Sir John's Hill and Milk Wood or R. S.'s Welsh hill country, Abersoch, or Nant Gwrtheyrn. In this they are not dissimilar to other Welsh contemporaries, including Idris Davies and Lynette Roberts, both championed by T. S. Eliot at Faber in the 1930s and '40s, and both poets who, in their very different ways, reflected their locations in Wales through the refracting Modernist lens of their poetry.

Idris Davies's background as a collier in the Rhymney Valley is strongly reflected in his major works, *Gwalia Deserta* (1938), *The Angry Summer* (1943) and *Tonypandy and Other Poems* (1945). Predictably, Davies was patronised as a working-class poet by some London critics, including Geoffrey Grigson, who referred to *Gwalia Deserta*, a book-length poem about the Depression in South Wales, as the 'naïve' product of 'a simple and superficial mind,' concluding that it was '[n]othing to bother about'.[18] Davies was affronted by this judgement and emphasized that his work was meant to be as simple and accessible as he could make it because he sought to express the experience of the thousands of working people in the valleys who, he felt, had been rendered voiceless. Davies's idiom is unmistakeable – often awkward and seeking an adequate register, and yet redolent of the Welsh condition – then and now. Other London magazines were more welcoming to Davies's distinctive voice; *The Left Review* published his 'Mineowner', for example, a poem which demonstrates the simplicity and directness of Davies's language as well as its satirical edge: 'He knows the names of all unprofitable strata, / ... And the seat of his trousers shines.[19]

If Davies sought simplicity, Lynette Roberts seemed to go out of her way, like the early Dylan Thomas, to be sibylline. A rare female voice among the First Flowering, Roberts had settled in Llanybri, Carmarthenshire with her husband Keidrych Rhys, also a poet and editor of the important little magazine, *Wales* (1937–49; 1958–60). She published her first collection, *Poems*, in 1944 and her 'heroic poem', *Gods with Stainless Ears*, in 1951, both with Faber. Argentine-born, of Welsh ancestry, Roberts adopted a Welsh identity and set much of her poetry in a recognisable Carmarthenshire milieu (Dylan Thomas's Fern Hill is just a few miles up the road). Her poetry is a unique mixture of the domestic and the folkloric with the extravagantly Modernist. *Gods with Stainless Ears* fully lives up to its strange title, conjuring up her own difficult life as a poor young mother in a Welsh village at a time of war in terms which are at times surreal, at times devastatingly down to earth. Sadly, it cannot be said that she exerted an influence on later generations of Welsh poets since she abruptly stopped writing in the mid-1950s. By 1995 when she died, her work was largely forgotten, but recently she has been rediscovered, championed and brought back into the public domain by Patrick McGuinness's excellent editions of her work.[20] Her poem 'Lamentations' describes a wartime air raid on the village which kills her neighbour's livestock, mixed with painful recollections of her own recent miscarriage: 'Five hills rocked and four homes fell / The day I remember the raid so well ...'; the description of the carnage in the fields then modulates into a more personal grief: 'The emptiness of crib / And big stare of night ...'[21]

Roberts's best-known and most accessible poem remains 'Poem from Llanybri', written to the Welsh poet Alun Lewis, a fellow war-poet.[22] Roberts was experimental, Lewis more lyrical and traditional but both wrote powerfully elegiac poems with an emphasis on a community's suffering. Lewis's blank-verse 'All Day It Has Rained', with its poignant tribute to the First World War Anglo-Welsh poet Edward Thomas, is an excellent example of Lewis's craftsmanship, cruelly curtailed when he died in the war.[23]

Both Roberts and Lewis were strongly inspired by places: Argentina and West Wales for Roberts, Wales, India and Burma for Lewis. For Welsh poets who stayed at home, too, place and belonging have been major concerns throughout the century, and it is a national theme which persists in different guises in contemporary poetry. Arguably, this thematic focus may be taken as one response to linguistic loss: in the absence of a cohesive national language and a singular, unbroken cultural tradition, Anglophone Welsh poets turn from history to geography for their consolation and their desire to belong. 'Despite our speech we are not English' says the Welshman in R. S. Thomas's 1958 poem, 'Border Blues', and much Anglophone Welsh poetry of the second half of the twentieth century attempts to demonstrate that difference, often by reference to place and landscape.[24]

Another response to linguistic loss is to attempt to reclaim or save the threatened language. In 1962 the prominent Welsh-language poet Saunders Lewis (who had also co-founded Plaid Cymru, the Welsh Nationalist Party) broadcast an influential talk entitled 'Tynged yr Iaith' (The Fate of the Language) on BBC Radio Wales. In this talk Lewis asserted provocatively that:

> Welsh will end as a living language, should the present trend continue, about the beginning of the twenty-first century ... The Welsh language can be saved ... Let us set about it in seriousness and without hesitation ... It will be nothing less than a revolution to restore the Welsh language in Wales. Success is only possible through revolutionary methods.[25]

The response to Lewis's call in Wales was immediate and took the form of the founding of Cymdeithas yr Iaith Gymraeg (The Welsh Language Society); throughout the following decades the Society mounted public, law-breaking and often successful campaigns to defend and uphold the Welsh language. But what effect did this resurgence have on the Anglophone poets of Wales? Lewis's revolutionary call was the background to the founding of the periodical *Poetry Wales* in 1965, with an overt nationalist agenda explicitly supportive of the Welsh language. In an early editorial, Meic Stephens lays out his cards:

> I am not suggesting that all Anglo-Welsh poets should feel obliged to write about Welsh nationhood, but I am convinced that before a poet writing in English can fully justify his position as Anglo-Welsh he needs either to write about Welsh scenes, Welsh people, the Welsh past, life in contemporary Wales, or ... else attempt to demonstrate in his verse those more elusive characteristics of style and feeling which are generally regarded as belonging to Welsh poetry.[26]

This editorial credo is strikingly different from the timorous hopes of the First Flowering poets, as expressed by Glyn Jones, to make their mark in literary London. The new-found nationalism of the '60s gave rise to a 'Second Flowering' in poetry which Tony Conran, himself an important member of this generation of Welsh poets, has suggested 'played its part in establishing Anglophone Wales as a cultural centre of gravity again, after the Depression and two world wars. No one had to move to London now!'[27] Indeed, several of the poets of the Second Flowering were actually writers who *returned* to Wales from London or elsewhere, perhaps recognizing new cultural stirrings in their homeland. Prominent amongst these were John Tripp, Raymond Garlick and Sally Roberts Jones, though others such as Harri Webb had stayed in Wales all along.

Both Tripp and Garlick have urbane voices, the former somewhat louche and gloomy, the latter more positive and sophisticated. Garlick was also much more interested in, and influenced by, the Welsh-language tradition, as is evidenced by the intricate craftsmanship of his verse. He maintained a long and fascinating correspondence with R. S. Thomas about the craft of poetry, recently published, but it is Tripp who sounds insistently more R. S. Thomas-ish.[28] In a poem such as 'Diesel to Yesterday' Tripp's gloomy speaker laments the rain-blurred passage into Wales and the decay of his country but ends in a self-accusation not unlike the last six lines of R. S. Thomas's 'A Peasant': 'The bad smell at my nostril / Is some odour from myself …'[29]

Despite the insistent male pronouns of Meic Stephens's editorial in *Poetry Wales*, the late '60s and 1970s saw the first publications of several important women poets in Wales, including Sally Roberts Jones, Ruth Bidgood, Alison Bielski and Gillian Clarke. Brenda Chamberlain, a prodigiously talented visual artist and writer from North Wales, had already begun publishing, her first volume of verse, *The Green Heart*, appearing in 1958. Sally Roberts Jones published *Turning Away* (1969) and *The Forgotten Country* (1977) during these years and brought an unassuming, sensitive vision to bear on the contemporary scene in Wales. She celebrates the continuing rituals of a close-knit Welsh 'Community' (her adopted home, Port Talbot) in a free-verse poem of that name, while in 'Ann Griffiths' she pays tribute to her Welsh-language forebear, the hymnwriter, by adopting an intricately rhymed form. In so doing, she also stakes her claim to be one of Ann's poetic heirs.[30] A younger poet, Catherine Fisher, adopts a similar approach in her poem 'Gwern-y-Cleppa' where her poet-persona has an imagined encounter with Dafydd ap Gwilym in a wood near Newport that had once housed the renowned hall of Dafydd's patron, Ifor Hael.[31] In these ways, modern women poets from Wales avoid the shadow of Dylan and R. S. and at the same time assert their belonging to a Welsh poetic tradition.

Alison Bielski is a more experimental poet than Sally Roberts Jones; neither has to date received the critical attention their work deserves. Bielski started publishing with *Twentieth-Century Flood* (1964) and *Across the Burning Sand* (1970) and her work draws on both place and mythology, as evidenced in poems such as 'wild leek, Flatholm Island' and 'hunting the wren', but perhaps her most impressive work is her experimental sequence, 'sacramental sonnets'.[32]

The neglect of Bielski notwithstanding, some Welsh women poets who began publishing in this period did go on to achieve due recognition, notably Gillian Clarke, currently the National Poet of Wales. Clarke's work was published in *Poetry Wales* in 1970 and she went on to publish a pamphlet, *Snow on the Mountain*, and a first volume, *The Sundial*, in the 1970s. Her voice was new in this period: gentle, delicate, with a sensitive regard for the natural world, it was also unmistakably feminine, and the poetic voice adopted was frequently that of a mother. That this was new and discomfiting work is shown by the reception she received in some quarters; as she herself has said 'Reviews of my first collection ... spoke somewhat patronizingly of my concern with domestic issues and the natural world, and I and those who shared my concern were regarded as writing about marginal matters, away from the centre.'[33] Undeterred, Clarke undertook ambitious works of feminist recuperation in influential works such as 'Letter from a Far Country','Cofiant' and 'The King of Britain's Daughter' but she was never a poet of confrontation like R. S.;[34] her poetic instincts have ever been toward celebration and reconciliation.

Clarke has frequently collaborated with the Welsh-language poet Menna Elfyn, who has published her poetry in parallel text volumes, with the English translations written by a range of Anglophone poets including R. S. Thomas himself, Gillian Clarke, Tony Conran, Robert Minhinnick and Nigel Jenkins.[35] Elfyn has performed a role in the Welsh-language tradition similar to that of Gillian Clarke in English: she has transformed and discomfited it, insisting upon the importance and centrality of women's experiences, even hitherto 'unmentionable' ones. Yet in recent years, Elfyn's vision has certainly become more all-encompassing and international; she has overcome the 'problem' of writing in a minority language by embracing translation without alienating her Welsh readers.

Language continues to be a thematic preoccupation in contemporary poetry in Wales, unsurprisingly perhaps in a recently devolved country which has become more self-aware about its cultural and linguistic heritage. Concern about the fate of Welsh has not gone away; poets still worry, like R. S. Thomas, that we are 'elbowing our language/Into the grave that we have dug for it'.[36] But bilingual contemporary poets such as Gwyneth Lewis approach the matter in a more playful manner, although there is no doubting the sincerity of her concern for her mother tongue. In the preface to her 2003 collection entitled *Keeping Mum*, she writes:

> I live a double life. I was brought up speaking a language which predates the Roman invasion of Britain. When I'm frightened I swear in Brythonic idioms. Yet I'm a city dweller, and surf the net using the language of the Saxons who pushed the Welsh into the hills of western Britain in the sixth century. I write in both languages ...
>
> In 1999 I wrote a book-length detective story investigating the murder of my mother tongue, calling it *Y Llofrudd Iaith*, 'The Language Murderer'... The first section of *Keeping Mum* represents as much of *The Language Murderer* as I was able to translate in a fairly direct fashion.... Revisiting the subject stimulated entirely new poems in English, and I allowed these to take shape. These are translations without an original text – perhaps a useful definition of poetry.[37]

Keeping Mum itself is a grimly playful pun, characteristic of Lewis's work. To 'keep mum' is to be silent, but the poems are about trying to 'keep mum', the mother tongue, alive. However, the attempt is unsuccessful – mum dies, horribly, leaving us forever silenced, forever keeping mum. The major irony in the whodunit form of *Y Llofrudd Iaith* and *Keeping Mum* is that the murderer is finally unmasked as the poet herself. In other words, if the language dies, it is the poet's fault for not keeping her alive – because that is surely the poet's task.

Poems such as Gwyneth Lewis's 'What's in a Name?' and 'Her End' in *Keeping Mum* could be described as macaronics, since they constitute a deliberate linguistic mixture, employing both the Welsh and English languages. Macaronic poetry generally is comic or satirical and there is certainly an element of that in Lewis's lively writing, but there is also a strong undertow of seriousness and a sober attempt to address and explore what it means to live bilingually. Several Welsh-language poets have undertaken similar macaronic experiments, such as Grahame Davies in his self-mocking 'Pontcanna Blues': 'Mi alwodd rhywun '*yuppie*' ar fy ôl i, / Wrth ddod yn ôl o'r *deli* gyda'r gwin ...' and continues with the tongue-in-cheek refrain, 'Mae *blues* Pontcanna yn diflasu 'myd.'[38] [Translation below]

The poem is humorous but also a serious reflection of the linguistic realities of contemporary Wales, where the greatest increase in the number of Welsh speakers has been amongst young people in the capital city, Cardiff, which was in the past quite Anglicised. These new Welsh speakers of the capital are generally middle-class professionals, like the self-regarding speaker in Davies's poem, who is gently mocked.

At the opposite end of the social scale from Davies's Pontcanna yuppie are the characters who inhabit the work of Mike Jenkins and other poets associated with the 'Red Poets' movement.[39] Jenkins uses a version of the Merthyr dialect in both poems and short fiction, such as *Red Landscapes: New and Selected Poems* (1999) and *Barkin'* (2014). In the politically-engaged tradition of Idris Davies, Jenkins is more playful than his forerunner but equally seeks to give voice to a people and a class who have often been silenced. He draws movingly on his many decades as a schoolteacher in Merthyr and Cardiff to create vignettes of Merthyr characters and their predicament, as in his poem 'Mouthy' and his tender tribute to the Dowlais-born historian, 'Gwyn Alf'.[40] Other poets who came to prominence in the '90s also sometimes use Welsh dialect, such as Stephen Knight in 'The Heart of Saturday Night', a heartbreaking villanelle in Swansea demotic.[41]

These contemporary examples indicate that yet another aspect of a long Welsh poetic tradition is still alive, namely the idea of the poet as a public figure, a voice of the people. This is arguably the true 'bardic' voice, and it is overt in the work of poets such as Jenkins and Clarke but still discernible in the work of poets who might be regarded as more recondite, such as Lynette Roberts and Dylan Thomas, were it not for the fact that they responded to the communal crisis of war with a truly public, elegiac voice. Alongside this communal role goes the fact that poetry in Wales remains popular in a way which, arguably, is not the case elsewhere in the British Isles. One of the most popular Welsh radio programmes is 'Talwrn y Beirdd', a poetry competition in which opposing teams compose poems on set subjects in set forms within a limited time. Moreover, the team members, like policemen, become ever younger. A parallel development in Anglophone Welsh poetry is the rise of new performance poets like Rhian Edwards and Mab Jones, whose entertaining and often comic poetry has concealed depth and poignance.

Much recent poetry from Wales has had an ecological focus, in common with work by poets elsewhere in the British Isles. However, this concern with the world of nature is not a new one, though recent poems on the theme have an understandable edge of urgency in the face of anxieties about climate change and pollution. Poets like Ruth Bidgood, whose first volume was published in the 1970s, have been writing quasi-sacramental poems about the interrelation of people and place for decades. Most of Bidgood's quiet but resonant verse gives a concern for the land 'a local habitation and a name', in her case very specifically mid-Wales. More overtly political and international is the verse of Robert Minhinnick and of John Barnie. Minhinnick's ability to see the big picture by focusing on a tiny detail is electrifyingly exemplified in 'The Orchids of Cwm-y-Gaer', which sees the effects of the Chernobyl disaster in a woodland near Bridgend.[42] John Barnie's poems draw inspiration both from the fragile Welsh landscape and from North American vistas and forms, as in the wonderfully supple 'About the Usk' where the river is made to speak and chide its human onlookers.[43] But perhaps the most plangent and unmistakeable of the voices concerned about humans' abuse or neglect of nature is that of R. S. Thomas. In a collection such as *Experimenting with an Amen* (1986) he combines the vocabulary of science with that of religion and philosophy to create an increasingly epigrammatic and thought-provoking meditation on the human condition. This impassioned engagement with modern science is characteristic of the later Thomas, endowing his work with richer layers of meaning and resonance. There is an enrichment of subject along with the stark expression of an old man's rage in volumes such as *No Truce with the Furies* (1995).

R. S. Thomas was with us for a long time. Like his speaker in 'A Thicket in Lleyn', he 'was still', surrounded by the birds he loved, (they netted me in their shadows, / brushed me with sound'), left on the tip of the Lleyn peninsula to meditate on the pre-Cambrian rocks and the sea. Just occasionally, his first-person speaker is joyful; he advises us to rejoice in the 'spray from the fountain / Of the imagination, endlessly / Replenishing itself out of its own waters.[44] More often, though, he sees the error of our ways, the roads not taken, as in his vision of 'Adam's other / Kingdom', 'Afallon' (the original Welsh of Avalon): 'what he might have / Inherited had he / Refused the apple …' But even in an elegiac old man's poem such as this, there are traces and echoes of grace – 'Rhiannon's birds', the 'lichened manuscripts / of stone' and, above all, 'the brook of our language'.[45]

R. S. Thomas's work itself has become part of the 'lichened manuscripts' which contemporary Welsh poets writing in both languages must read. Many have initiated a dialogue with R. S., sometimes challenging the great poetic father, sometimes imitating or mocking him. The contemporary poet Peter Finch, Cardiff-born like R. S. himself, writes and performs self-consciously modernist poetry which is nevertheless highly aware of the Welsh poetic tradition, including the work of R. S. Thomas. Finch's poem 'Hills' is both a pastiche of the verse of R. S. and at the same time suggests something of the endlessly replenishing fountain of the poetic imagination. It riffs on R. S.'s poem, 'A Peasant', which begins 'Just an ordinary man of the bald Welsh hills', turning the opening line around, repeating, transforming and playing with it, in a manner which is both a tribute and cheeky riposte: 'Just a bald man of the ordinary hills, / Welsh sheep gaps, docking pens, cloud shrouds' and the poem goes on until it becomes mere ludic sound 'Just grass gap, bald gap, garp grap, / gap shot, sheep slate, gap grap …'[46]

Welsh poetry since 1945 has, paradoxically, both travelled a long way and stayed in the same poetic territory. Like the poets of the 'First Flowering' who were excited by the newness and endless possibilities of the English language, contemporary poets from Wales still express that liveliness and willingness to experiment with a language which they now emphatically call their own. Nevertheless, the Welsh language is still, miraculously, alive, I would argue largely thanks to the inspirational passion of poets like Saunders Lewis and R. S. Thomas. That 'other' ancestral Welsh tradition is still a ghostly presence in the work of many modern poets, while some boldly try to render the bilingual reality of contemporary Wales with macaronic experiments. Praise and satire, elegy and tirade, pastiche and whodunit: the current state of Anglophone Welsh poetry is vital and various, constantly replenished out of its own waters, as R. S. Thomas would have it.

NOTES

1 Raymond Garlick and Roland Mathias, *Anglo-Welsh Poetry 1480–1990*, 2nd edn., (Bridgend: Seren, 1993).

2 For statistics relating to the decline and revival of the Welsh language, see: Hywel M. Jones, 'A Statistical Overview of the Welsh Language', available at: http://www.comisiynyddygymraeg.org/English/Publications%20List/A%20statistical%20overview%20of%20the%20Welsh%20language.pdf.

3 Glyn Jones, *The Dragon Has Two Tongues: Essays on Anglo-Welsh Writers and Writing* (London: Dent, 1968).

4 For an explanation of the Welsh strict metre poetic tradition, including 'cynghanedd', see Tony Conran, Introduction, *Welsh Verse* (Bridgend: Poetry Wales Press, 1986) and/or Gwyn Williams, *An Introduction to Welsh Poetry: From the Beginnings to the Sixteenth Century* (London: Faber, 1953).

5 Glyn Jones, *Setting Out: A Memoir of Literary Life in Wales* (Cardiff: Cardiff University College, 1982), p. 12.

6 Dylan Thomas, 'The Force that through the Green Fuse' and 'In the White Giant's Thigh' in *Selected Poems* ed. Walford Davies (London: Dent Everyman, 1993), p. 17 and pp. 76–78; Glyn Jones 'Merthyr' in *Selected Poems* (Llandysul: Gomer Press, 1975), pp. 30–33.

7 See, for example, Glyn Jones 'The Seagull', a version of Dafydd ap Gwilym's 'Yr wylan' and Jones's poems 'Swifts', 'Henffych, Ddafydd'(Hail, Dafydd) and 'Wind – Seagull's llatai' (llatai = love messenger) where he emulates the Welsh *cywydd* form, as practised by ap Gwilym, in *Selected Poems*, p. 44, pp. 85–89. Dylan Thomas's debt to strict metre poetry has been much discussed, e.g. by the contemporary Welsh poet Alan Llwyd in his 'Cynghanedd and English Poetry', *Poetry Wales*, 14, No. 1 (Summer 1978).

8 Gwyneth Lewis, 'The Wind', shortlisted for the Stephen Spender Prize for Poetry in Translation 2014, and available at: http://www.stephen-spender.org/2014_prize/2014_open_2nd_GL.html.

9 See Katie Gramich, '"Still Linked to Those Others: Landscape and Language in Post-War Welsh Poetry', in *Poetry and Geography: Space and Place in Post-War Poetry* eds. Neal Alexander and David Cooper (Liverpool: Liverpool University Press, 2013), pp. 61–74.

10 For an English account of Alun Llywelyn-Williams and a comparison with Alun Lewis, see M. Wynn Thomas, 'The Two Aluns', in his *Internal Difference: Literature in Twentieth-Century Wales* (Cardiff: University of Wales Press, 1992), pp. 49–67.

11 See Meic Stephens, 'Sad Case of a "Perfect" Welsh Skull in a Scottish Cupboard', *New Welsh Review*, 23 (Winter, 1993–94): 37–42 and Hugh Manson 'Hugh MacDiarmid and Keidrych Rhys: The Arrow from Wales' in *Almanac: The Yearbook of Welsh Writing in English*, vol. 14 (2009–10): 208–13.

12 Vernon Watkins, 'The Ballad of the Mari Lwyd' in *The Collected Poems of Vernon Watkins* (Ipswich: Golgonooza Press, 1986), pp. 41–56.

13 Jeremy Hooker, 'Poets, Language and Land: Reflections on English-Language Welsh Poetry since the Second World War' in *Welsh Writing in English: A Yearbook of Critical Essays*, vol. 8 (2003): 142.

14 Dylan Thomas, 'Prologue', *Selected Poems*, ed. Walford Davies (London: Dent Everyman, 1993), p. 2, lines 39–43. The poem dates from 1952 and was written especially for the *Collected Poems* of that year.

15 R. S. Thomas, 'The Welsh Hill Country' in *Song at the Year's Turning: Poems 1942–1954* (London: Rupert Hart-Davis, 1955), p. 46, lines 1–5. First published in *An Acre of Land* (1952).

16 Ibid., line 18.

17 R. S. Thomas's borrowing from Welsh-language literature has been analysed by Jason Walford Davies in his essay '"Thick Ambush of Shadows": Allusions to Welsh Literature in the Work of R. S. Thomas' in *Welsh Writing in English: A Yearbook of Critical Essays*, Volume 1 (1995): 75–127; available at: http://www.google.co.uk/url?url=http://rsthomas.bangor.ac.uk/documents/wwe1_75-127.doc&rct=j&frm=1&q=&esrc=s&sa=U&ei=JEiIVKKYEMn2UtiCgZAJ&ved=0CCwQFjAC&usg=AFQjCNEDj1wHlRwO1emUoTaoa1PBOnQxyA.

18 Geoffrey Grigson, Review of *Gwalia Deserta*, *New Verse* 31/32 (1938): 26. Idris Davies's letter in response was published in the following issue (No. 1, 1939, 30–31). In it he suggests that *New Verse* had become the magazine of a clique: 'The same names appear and reappear in its pages. Auden, Allott, MacNeice, and Spender ... When these people, and perhaps yourself, were learning their Latin verbs in cushy places, I had to do my job in the coal-mine. Since then, however, I have done a little Latin myself ...'

19 Idris Davies, lines 1 and 4 of 'Mineowner' in *The Complete Poems of Idris Davies* ed. Dafydd Johnston (Cardiff: University of Wales Press, 1994), p. 120. *The Left Review* was not the only London magazine receptive to Welsh material; *Life and Letters To-day* under the editorship of Robert Herring was notably pro-Welsh – see Meic Stephens, 'The Third Man: Robert Herring and *Life and Letters To-day*' in *Welsh Writing in English: A Yearbook of Critical Essays* vol. 3 (1997): 157–69.

20 Lynette Roberts, *Collected Poems*, ed. Patrick McGuinness (Manchester: Carcanet, 2005) and Lynette Roberts, *Diaries, Letters and Recollections*, ed. Patrick McGuinness (Manchester: Carcanet, 2008).

21 Lynette Roberts, 'Lamentations', *Collected Poems*, pp. 8–9.

22 See Lynette Roberts, 'Poem from Llanybri', *Collected Poems*, p. 3.

23 Alun Lewis, 'All Day It Has Rained' in *Poetry 1900–2000: One Hundred Poets from Wales*, ed. Meic Stephens (Cardigan: Parthian Books, 2007), pp. 175–76. For further discussion of Alun Lewis's life and work, see John Pikoulis's admirable *Alun Lewis: A Life* (Bridgend: Poetry Wales Press, 1983).

24 R. S. Thomas, 'Border Blues' in *Collected Poems* (London: Dent, 1993), p. 69.

25 Saunders Lewis, 'The Fate of the Language', translated from the Welsh original, 'Tynged yr Iaith' (1962) by G. Aled Williams in *Presenting Saunders Lewis* ed. Alun R. Jones and Gwyn Thomas (Cardiff: University of Wales Press, 1973), pp. 127–41.

26 Meic Stephens, 'The Second Flowering', *Poetry Wales* 3.3 (Winter, 1967–68): 7.

27 Tony Conran, 'Poetry Wales and the Second Flowering' in *Welsh Writing in English*, ed. M. Wynn Thomas (Cardiff: University of Wales Press, 2003), p. 253.

28 See Jason Walford Davies, ed., *R. S. Thomas: Letters to Raymond Garlick 1951–1999* (Llandysul: Gomer Press, 2009).

29 John Tripp, 'Diesel to Yesterday' in *Anglo-Welsh Poetry 1480–1990*, ed. Raymond Garlick and Roland Mathias, pp. 262–63 [263]. Cf. R. S. Thomas, 'A Peasant', op. cit., pp. 177–78.

30 Sally Roberts Jones, 'Community' and 'Ann Griffiths' in *Anglo-Welsh Poetry 1480–1990* ed. Raymond Garlick and Roland Mathias, pp. 283–84, p. 285.

31 Catherine Fisher, 'Gwern-y-Cleppa' in *The Unexplored Ocean* (Bridgend: Seren, 1994).

32 Alison Bielski, 'Wild Leek, Flatholm Island', 'Hunting the Wren' and 'Walking with Angels' in *Welsh Women's Poetry 1460–2001: An Anthology*, ed. Katie Gramich and Catherine Brennan (Dinas Powys: Honno Press, 2003) p. 197, pp. 197–202, p. 204.

33 Gillian Clarke, 'Beginning with Bendigeidfran', in *At the Source: A Writer's Year* (Manchester: Carcanet, 2008), p. 14.

34 Gillian Clarke, 'Letter from a Far Country', 'Cofiant', 'The King of Britain's Daughter' in *Collected Poems* (Manchester: Carcanet, 1997), pp. 45–56, pp. 121–36, pp. 170–83.

35 See, for example, Menna Elfyn, *Perfect Blemish/Perffaith Nam: New and Selected Poems 1995–2007* (Tarset: Bloodaxe, 2007).

36 R. S. Thomas, 'Reservoirs', *Selected Poems* (London: Penguin, 2003), p. 74.

37 Gwyneth Lewis, 'Preface', *Chaotic Angels: Poems in English* (Tarset: Bloodaxe, 2005), pp. 143–44.

38 Graham Davies, 'Pontcanna Blues' in *Blodeugerdd Barddas o Farddoniaeth Gyfoes* (Barddas Anthology of Contemporary Poetry), ed. Tony Bianchi (Llandybïe: Barddas, 2005), p. 285. A rough translation would be: Someone called me a yuppie behind my back / As I came home from the deli with the wine; / Now I can't find the guacamole bowl / And I'm worried that my friends will be annoyed / ... The Pontcanna blues are getting to me. (Pontcanna is a trendy and expensive area of Cardiff).

39 See: http://www.redpoets.org/.

40 Mike Jenkins, 'Mouthy' and 'Gwyn Alf' in *Poetry 1900–2000*, ed. Meic Stephens (Cardigan: Parthian Books, 2007), p. 735, pp. 737–39.

41 Stephen Knight, 'The Heart of Saturday Night' in *Poetry 1900–2000*, pp. 804–5.

42 Robert Minhinnick, 'The Orchids of Cwm-y-Gaer', in *Poetry 1900–2000*, pp. 720–21.

43 John Barnie, 'About the Usk', in *Poetry 1900–2000*, pp. 505–7.

44 R. S. Thomas, 'A Thicket in Lleyn', in *Selected Poems* (London: Penguin, 2003), p. 181.

45 R. S. Thomas, 'Afallon', in *No Truce with the Furies* (Newcastle upon Tyne: Bloodaxe, 1995), p. 25.

46 Peter Finch, 'Hills', available at: http://www.peterfinch.co.uk/hills.htm.

12

SARAH LAWSON WELSH

Black British Poetry

'Mekin Histri': Black British Poetry from the Windrush to the Twenty-First Century

The arrival in 1948 of the SS Windrush, a ship carrying more than 280 Jamaicans to Britain marks a foundational, if also a fetishized[1] place in any understanding of post-1945 Black British poetry. Whilst Windrush was not strictly the 'beginning' of black migration to Britain, the 1948 British Nationality Act did enable New Commonwealth and Pakistani citizens to enter and settle in Britain with greater freedom than ever before, and Windrush has become a convenient label for this first post-1945 generation of black migrant writers in Britain. This generation's 'arrival', the accelerating endgame of empire, the rise of anti-colonial independence movements and the cultural activity and confidence which accompanied them, created the conditions for an extraordinary period of literary creativity in Britain, as black and Asian writers came to England to work, to study and to be published. Mainstream presses showed unprecedented interest in publishing black migrant writers and the beginnings of organized association between writers from different territories in Britain can be also traced to this time. An early forum was the BBC radio programme, *Caribbean Voices*, conceived by Una Marson in 1943 and subsequently edited by Henry Swanzy (and later V. S. Naipaul) between 1946 and 1958. *Caribbean Voices* broadcast weekly, live from London to the Caribbean and enabled regular cultural exchanges between Britain and the Caribbean, as well as forging a sense of common West Indian literary endeavour in Britain.

The next generation of writers (of the late 1960s and 1970s)[2] had different experiences, affiliations and concerns. The term 'Black British' was first used in this era within intersecting public debates about race and immigration, education, unemployment and crime, nationalism, citizenship and the multicultural policies of the period; from the start 'Black British' was a volatile and much contested term. Much Black British writing from this time reflects the wider cultural, social and political debates of the time and frequently needs to be read in terms of specific events, such as the race-related disturbances in parts of British cities in 1981 and 1985. It was often grassroots or activist in nature, located outside of the canonical, the institutional and the academic.[3] Groundbreaking collections such as Linton Kwesi Johnson's *Dread Beat and Blood* (1976) can thus be usefully read as 'textual uprisings'[4]: deeply imbricated within the often racist politics and policies of the time regarding multiculturalism, policing, nationalism and citizenship but ultimately never purely determined or defined by them.

Indeed, Black British poetry has never been purely and simply about 'Black British' issues, despite criticism which sometimes seems to suggest otherwise. As John McLeod usefully points out: 'Black writers do not speak for black Britain, of course; but neither do they write necessarily for black Britain first and foremost ... contemporary writers talk of 'discrimination and stuff' but not exclusively so; there are 'other things' to speak of too, which are inseparable from Britain's ongoing racial predicaments but not confined to them, and in which all are involved.'[5] It's especially important to recognize this, given that the prevalent public stereotype of Black British poetry since the 1970s has been that it is limited to political themes and weakened by its primarily performative mode. Famously, in an entry in *The Oxford Companion to Twentieth Century Poetry*, edited by Ian Hamilton, Mario Relich defined dub poetry as 'over-compensation for deprivation.'[6]

If 'Black British' had originally been used as a marker of alliance between different minority ethnic groups and their own experiences of, and struggles against, a racist and often-exclusionary mainstream society in 1960s and 1970s Britain, in the 1980s the term began to be adopted to signify a new generation of writers, born or based in Britain.[7] The 1980s saw the publication of some groundbreaking anthologies of Black British writing, further experimentation with new poetic forms and with creole or 'Nation language'[8] and a greater visibility for Black British women's writing in particular. In the 1990s multicultural policies, new funding streams[9] and the opening up of spaces for black and minority ethnic artists proved particularly conducive to the wider publication of Black British writing. It also saw the development of what Lauri Ramey (2004) and Sarah Broom (2006) have termed new 'tribes' of poetry,[10] often with a strong performance aesthetic, and continued literary experimentation with dub, rap, hip-hop and other primarily black musical forms. By the millennium, Black British writing was altogether more established, with a lively performance scene, new national and regional initiatives starting to support new Black British writers and visible signs of public recognition of this as a rich and diverse body of writing.

'Black British' or 'British'?

'Here comes a black Englishman with a brolly
To forget either would indeed be folly.'[11]

By the early 2000s, the term 'Black British' was also being used in a much more confident, nuanced and historicized sense to refer to an identifiable body of literature,[12] a Black British aesthetic[13] and even a Black British canon[14] although not always in an unqualified or unproblematic way. Whilst some have distanced themselves from the term as reductive[15] or in favour of a more transnational approach to Black British writing,[16] others have sought to 'privilege "black"', not as a biological or racial category (although it signifies on both these levels) but as a political signifier which first became valent in Britain in the late 1960s and 1970s'[17] and which continues to be relevant.

Indeed, the very commissioning of this chapter in a Cambridge Companion to post-1945 British poetry may suggest a greater acceptance of the term and a recognition that the poetry itself has grown in confidence, diversity and sophistication, as well as visibility. In her introduction to *Write Black Write British* (2005), poet, critic and editor Kadija Sesay argues for a move away from the use of the more generic 'postcolonial' to describe Black British writers, in line with the specificity of their experiences and the 'shift away from this canon to a development of a new one ... for many emerging writers'.[18] Sesay's formulation constitutes a kind of 'benign model of black British influence and tradition'[19] and she, like others, makes a claim for generationalism as a way of navigating Black British poetry in the post-1945 period but what is striking here is the idea of a separate tradition or canon of writing.

Sesay's words here and in her introduction to *IC3: The Penguin Book of New Black Writing in Britain* (2000), are good examples of this impetus towards confident specificity (or perhaps a new separatism) in the development of a 'new' Black British 'canon'. However, a powerful counter impulse has been to simply see such poetry as 'British'. This is a major tension or fault line in the landscape of contemporary Black British poetry. Certainly, for every poet, anthologist or editor who prefers to speak of 'British poetry' as an inclusive, perhaps even post-racial, category which transcends the dangers of ghettoization[20] and the hierarchies of value implicit in 'Black British poetry', or the problematic 'lumping together' of African, Caribbean, Black British and British Asian writers under the one term,[21] or which seeks to frame Black British writing in terms of all those transnational forces, influences and cultural exchanges which have made it what it is,[22] there is another who argues for the continued need for the category of 'Black British poetry'.

One such is poet, novelist and anthologist, Bernadine Evaristo, in her preface to the recent *Ten New Poets Spread the Word* anthology, co-edited with Daljit Nagra (2010). Quite legitimately Evaristo points to the continued marginalisation of black and Asian poets in Britain in terms of their under-representation within the lists of major British poetry publishers (Nagra is only the second black poet to be published by Faber in its eighty-year publishing history), their selective inclusion in poetry anthologies and the recurrent problem of asymmetric representation and tokenism experienced by Black British and British Asian poets in relation to the Poetry Society's 'Generations' or the receipt of major literary prizes. Reflecting on the findings of a 2005 Arts Council Report[23] (which she helped to initiate), Evaristo argues that the use of the terms 'Black' and 'Asian' poet are still necessary, important and politically urgent.[24] Likewise, Kwame Dawes argues, that the term is valuable precisely because it historicises 'a black British presence in Britain [which younger writers often forget or disavow] and [because it reminds us of] the more complicated connectedness between what we call British writing (read white) and colonial/postcolonial writing' as one which is not one-sided.'[25]

The continued use of 'Black British' then, captures a profound 'historical forgetfulness' of specific black histories in Britain, what British-Jamaican cultural critic Stuart Hall famously called 'a kind of historical amnesia [in] the British people that has only increased over the postwar period.'[26] The publication of deeply affecting collections such as Dorothea Smartt's *Ship Shape* (2008), which recover Black Atlantic histories and historicise the black presence in Britain as one which, importantly, pre-dates the migrant arrivals of the mid twentieth century, goes some way to addressing this amnesia[27] but there is still a general lack of awareness of Black British writing beyond a few stellar and canonically acceptable figures. A few poets, such as Zephaniah and Kay, are relatively well known, but for most poetry readers (as opposed to those who attend community events, poetry slams and other live performance events, especially in the regions), Black British poetry is still very much a hidden, marginalised affair. Moreover, the current 'poster boys and girls' for Black British writing – Salman Rushdie, Andrea Levy, Monica Ali, Zadie Smith – are almost exclusively novelists rather than poets. As Dawes argued in 2005: 'the publishing world [still] does not reflect the kind of activity that is going on in poetry among Black British writers.[28]

To divide the last seventy years of Black British poetry into three main 'generations': Windrush, second generation, millennial, is to oversimplify what is undoubtedly a cultural history of 'partial discontinuity'.[29] However, such a structure allows one to trace the main contours of the poetry in terms of political and aesthetic differences between the different generations of

Black British poets, different configurations of ethnic identity and identifications with or against the nation, and different notions of the relationship between Black British and British poetry.

Generation One: Windrush: 'But Let Me Tell You How This Business Begin'

For the first 'Windrush' generation of writers, identification to the nation was primarily to the countries from which they had migrated rather than the 'motherland' itself.[30] They saw themselves first and foremost as exiles and only gradually as West Indian or Caribbean, a collective identity which was largely engendered in Britain.[31] Nor did they generally use the term 'Black writer' in any coherent or nuanced way at this stage. This generation, often posited as the starting point of a Black British canon, were mostly Caribbean, overwhelmingly male and publishing mainly prose fiction rather than poetry. The very visibility of a small number of mainly male Caribbean writers tended to overshadow other black writing of the period and the contribution of women and poets in particular. Later generations of Black British writers such as Nichols and Evaristo have spoken of the lack of formative influence from these male 'Windrush writers'.

Una Marson: Literary Foremother

Jamaican poet and activist Una Marson was a key figure of the time whose cultural and political contribution to this period has only been recovered and reappraised in the last twenty years.[32] Marson is fascinating in terms of her transnational networks in this early period (for example, she met Abyssinian Emperor Haile Selassie in London shortly after the Italian invasion of Abyssinia, and, as his personal secretary, accompanied him to Geneva in 1936) but the significance of her creative and artistic contribution has often been overlooked, as it was in her own time. Her poems explore the intersecting politics of race and gender in a colonial context but also offer a fascinating response to the English poetic canon in the form of some wonderfully subversive, rather than purely imitative, experiments with European poetic forms such as the sonnet.[33] Thus in her earlier poem, 'If', she writes with an intertextual nod to Kipling's famous poem of the same name: 'If you can love and not make love your master / If you can serve yet do not be his slave. / If you can hear bright tales and quit them faster; / And, for your peace of mind, think him no knave'.[34]

However, Marson's 'If' explores the 'master' and 'slave' dynamic of the heterosexual love relationship in a new and unsettling context of colonial histories and gender roles.[35] In this way, terms which are assured and relatively unproblematic within a canonical tradition of English love poetry, become freighted with new and complex meanings and reroute our reading of Kipling's original whilst illuminating both poems. Marson's aesthetic is subtly subversive rather than radically oppositional but she is nonetheless an important figure who, in this and in her use of Nation language voice portraits, deserves to be seen as a poetic foremother.

James Berry: Pioneer Poet

James Berry arrived in Britain in the 'Windrush' year of 1948. Although he did not become a full-time writer until 1977, he was to be foundational to the story of Black British poetry as a poet, a mentor and an editor. Early Berry poems such as 'On an Afternoon Train from Purley to Victoria, 1955'[36] perfectly capture the cultural confusions of the host society in encountering the new black settlers in Britain: 'Where are you from? She said. / Jamaica I said. / What part of Africa is Jamaica?' she said. / Where Ireland is near Lapland I said. Hard to see why you leave / Such sunny country she said. / Snow falls elsewhere I said. / So sincere she was beautiful / As people sat down around us.'[37] Berry's first collections[38] reflect upon the differences and tensions between a Jamaican boyhood, a West Indian migrant's experience of Britain, the encounter with Africa, firstly as a mythic and colonially disavowed place and then as key to the poet's growing sense of global connection in a world where race remains a major fault line. Some of Berry's earliest poems from the 1950s were collected in two ground-breaking anthologies he edited in the late 1970s and early 1980s.[39] Berry's early poetic experimentation with Nation language and with forms such the haiku, the oral proverb, the love lyric and particularly the 'letter home' creole voice portrait created poems which challenged stereotypical notions that early Black British poetry was overwhelmingly public rather than personal, a voice of protest and rage rather than of reflective lyricism.

New Beacons: Radical Politics and Small Black Presses

Berry was also one of the first poets to benefit from the establishment of small independent black presses in Britain in the mid-1960s and 1970s. A shift towards a more radical ideology and aesthetics in Black British poetry during this period can be directly traced to a number of global and transnational movements. Firstly, the growth of nationalist movements in the lead-up to independence in certain African and Caribbean countries during this period provided very visible models for confident and intensified cultural activity amongst black writers in Britain. Secondly the civil rights movement in America in the 1960s provided another model of resistance politics. Specific to a Caribbean context also was the cultural nationalism associated with the short-lived political union of the West Indian Federation (1958–62). Amongst those influenced were Kamau Brathwaite, a young Barbadian poet and postgraduate student at Cambridge University, and Trinidadian journalist, poet and cultural activist John La Rose who, after a period in Venezuela, had settled in Britain in 1961. Four years later in London, La Rose established New Beacon Books, with the aim of publishing and distributing radical works by pan-African, Caribbean and black diasporic writers.[40] In London the year after (1966), La Rose and Brathwaite founded CAM, the *Caribbean Artist's Movement*. CAM would provide a vital, if short-lived, forum of critical and cultural exchange for black writers and artists in Britain much as *Caribbean Voices* had done for writers in the 1950s. CAM folded in 1971 and Brathwaite returned to Jamaica. Indeed, many of the black writers in Britain in this period still saw themselves as Caribbean rather than British.[41] The possibility of return 'home' made them 'sojourners' rather than 'settlers', figures who in the long term did little to sustain black literary creativity in Britain.[42]

Second Generation

'It Dread Inna Inglan': The Poetry of Linton Kwesi Johnson

The radical ideologies of Pan-Africanism, Black Power and a growing interest in Third World politics, writing and resistance, all influenced the development of Black British poetry in the late 1960s and 1970s.[43] The International Book Fair of Radical Black and Third World Books, the alternative face of writing and publishing at the time, provided a much needed network for transnational association and exchange between black writers. Johnson, the singular black British poetic voice of the 1970s, emerged through this grassroots activist route, his earliest work developing out of poetry workshops which he and others organised within the Black Panther movement. He was also closely affiliated with the Race Today Collective, established in 1972, which published his early collections and those of other Black British poets, such as Jean Binta Breeze's *Riddym Ravings and Other Poems* (London, 1988).

As Johnson's early poetry charts, the 1970s were a difficult decade for many young black Britons, with growing unemployment, racist attacks and discriminatory policies such as the notorious SUS law which allowed the police to stop and search any youth (in practice overwhelmingly any black youth) under suspicion of unlawful possession or activity. This is the world of *Dread Beat and Blood* (1975) and *Inglan is a Bitch* (1981), with 'Sonny's Lettah' arguably the most important poem of this decade.[44] Johnson's is a reggae aesthetic: his poetry often references reggae artists and is set within sound system culture but it is also, more importantly, 'under sprung' with reggae rhythms and uses reggae techniques.[45] Johnson coined the term 'dub poetry' to define this new, primarily voice-based form which originated in Jamaica but which, like reggae, became a global phenomenon.

The subjects of Johnson's highly politicised poetry, his striking use of Nation language and his unique performance style quickly ensured him a high profile in Britain. Not only did Johnson's poetry present a coruscating challenge to the manifold exclusions and racisms of British society but his vision for Britain's black and working class populations was a thoroughly radicalising one, grounded in demotic language, solidarity and community action.

Johnson's 'incendiary poetics'[46] are often read as primarily oppositional in their critique of Britain and Britishness, vis-à-vis the racism, oppressive policing and Thatcherite politics of the era; indeed, his name is synonymous with the 'development of a distinctly black political consciousness in the 1970s'.[47] However, he has always identified himself as a Black British poet first and foremost, and this marked an important shift from the Windrush generation. Johnson's legacy has been immense, as both a poetic forerunner and mentor figure. His influence can be clearly seen in the early poems of Merle Collins, Valerie Bloom and Grace Nichols, and although there were predecessors, in both a Caribbean and Black British context, Johnson has been a crucial Nation language pioneer.

Anthologizing Black British Writing: Bluefoot Traveller

The activity and process of anthologisation, both specialist and mainstream, provides one means to trace the early construction of poetic agendas and 'manifestos' for Black British poetry, as part of a more concerted effort to define a Black British literary aesthetic. Indeed, the paratextual frames of key anthologies of the period can tell us much about the ideological, political and aesthetic concerns of this generation of writers. In his 1976 introduction to *Bluefoot Traveller*, Berry compared 'Westindians' in Britain with their African-American counterparts: 'Westindians here are a long way away from the dynamic cultural activities of American blacks or their fellow Westindians at home. They are grossly underexplored, underexpressed, underproduced and undercontributing'.[48] Indeed, SuAndi and Nichols have since spoken about looking to African-American poets such as Leroi Jones, Amiri Baraka, Nikki Giovanni, Sonia Sanchez or Ntozake Shange as their only available models in the absence of accessible or visible Black British ones.[49] More optimistically, a 1974 *Savacou* special issue (9/10), edited by La Rose and Salkey 'cite[d] a wealth of cultural activity among people of Caribbean descent in Britain, mostly London, at this time'. However, crucially, it 'represent[ed] the cultural identity of these people as explicitly and unproblematically expatriate, "away from home"'.[50] 'Home' in Fred D'Aguiar's phrase, was 'always elsewhere'.[51] By 1981 and the second, revised edition of *Bluefoot Traveller* Berry was slightly more optimistic: 'Since the first *Bluefoot Traveller* ... new developments have called for a fresh selection of poems. Britain's Caribbean community ... involves itself much more intensely in expressing its cultural background. It has become more active in writing and publishing and in the opening of local bookshops'.[52] He also noted that although 'Suitable work from women writers had not been submitted or found ... in the original anthology ... That situation has changed here'.[53]

'The Power to Be What I Am': Black British Poetry and Feminism

Many of the key Black British poets of the 1980s were women.[54] The increased publication and visibility of a range of Black British women's writing owed much to two factors: new national and local funding streams for 'ethnic minority arts' and growing networks of black feminist association.[55] These were to nurture a number of new writers and facilitate some of the most promising publications by black women in Britain in the early 1980s[56] as well as the beginnings of a critical tradition of Black British women's writing.[57] Bernadine Evaristo has recently referred to this time as 'a sisterhood, warts and all ... which allowed us to produce literature on our own terms. It has rarely been so since'.[58]

Amongst the women poets who benefited from feminist publishing in this period were Grace Nichols and Maud Sulter. Nichols's remarkable first poem cycle, *I Is a Long Memoried Woman* (1983) was published by a small black press (Karnak), but her next four collections were all, significantly, published in London by the foremost feminist press of the decade: Virago.[59] What links the disparate poems in these collections is a central focus on the black woman's body and voice, the links between female sexuality and creativity, an interest in recovering and reworking black histories and in revisiting European and gender myths in some highly or inventive ways.[60] Nichols is particularly interested in the intersecting racial and gender politics of representations of the black female body (in both historical and contemporary contexts) and latterly, has written a series of poems inspired by or addressed to well-known paintings.[61] Although she has always eschewed the term 'feminist' her poetry is unashamedly woman-centred and empowering: 'From dih pout / Of mih mouth / From dih/ Treacherous / Calm of mih / Smile / You can tell / I is a long memoried woman.[62]

In comparison, Sulter's *As a Black Woman* (1985) now reads as perhaps impossibly remote in its poems of radical black feminist separatism, but it was extremely important in and of its time. The poem 'Thirteen Stanzas' stands out in the collection in its form and linguistic experimentation and is an important reminder that Black British women writers can also be Scots, an identity (and disruption of Britishness) Jackie Kay has also explored in her poetry.[63]

Anthologising Black British Poetry in the 1980s and 1990s

The 1980s saw a shift toward the more inclusive, if rather flawed, ideology of multiculturalism, and the encouragement of 'ethnic minority' arts. Many anthologies from this period reflect this new agenda of representing diversity. The most important of these was the influential *News for Babylon: The Chatto Book of Westindian-British Poetry*, edited by Berry (1984). Not only did it raise the profile of Black British poetry but it launched the careers of a number of younger poets. Four years later the much touted and reviewed *The New British Poetry* appeared, edited by Gillian Allnutt, D'Aguiar, Ken Edwards and Eric Mottram. In it, Black British and women poets were each allocated a separate editor and section of their own, a controversial move which was seen by some as reductive and unhelpfully divisive. The title of E. A. Markham's influential *Hinterland: Caribbean Poetry from the West Indies and Britain* (1989), is completely in keeping with this period when the dominant ideology of multiculturalism seems to have encouraged the emphasis on cultural difference and diversity rather than 'Britishness'. The categorising (and marketing) of black writers in Britain clearly continued to exercise and unsettle a number of critics and anthologists and the admission of Black British poets to mainstream collections was slow.[64] It wasn't until the 1990s that Black British poets were admitted to these more generic collections, initially often along gender lines.[65]

Nineties Poets: Revisiting Windrush, Rewriting the Nation

Some really provocative collections from this period[66] are notable for their problematising of black poets' identification with the nation (whether home or elsewhere) and their rewriting of the map of Britishness from a new perspective. As these poets critiqued notions of a singular, monocultural

Britishness they reminded us that Britain and its 'elsewheres' are as much imagined places, or 'imaginary homelands', as a physical spaces or geopolitical entities. As suggested by the title poem of Pakistan-born Moniza Alvi's first collection, *The Country at My Shoulder* (1993), Black British and British Asian writers often have 'a country at their shoulder … one which is fit to burst'; their versions of 'Britishness' are multiple, whether contingent or counter to dominant versions of the 'nation'. This sense of 'Britishness remapped' and the shift away from 'roots' to 'routes' as an organising principle for the anthology is particularly well captured in *Out of Bounds: British Black and Asian Poets* with its organisation of poems by the regions within the British Isles to which they refer, rather than ethnic or cultural origins of the writer.[67]

In Jackie Kay's first collection, *The Adoption Papers* (1991) such tensions between multiple belongings are explored within the context of transnational adoption. In her long poem sequence, Kay uses different typefaces to signify the intercutting, antiphonal and sometime overlapping voices of daughter, adoptive mother and birth mother as they come to terms with their individual and collective histories, in a moving and powerful exploration of the politics and experiences of transracial adoption: 'After mammy telt me she wisnae my real mammy / I was scared to death she was gonnie melt / or something or mibbe disappear in the dead / of night …'[68]

By 1998, Kay was obviously a well-established enough 'name' for poet-anthologist Lemn Sissay to declare: 'the obvious names of Black poetry in Britain are not here. There is no Zephaniah, no Agard and no Nichols. With the exception of … Johnson and … Kay, I want to bring you something else. I want to bring to you the new generation of poets who are knocking on the doors of the houses … who are putting their words to music … the raw, the fresh Black and British poets'.[69]

Indeed, the 1990s were notable for the emergence, in print and performance, of a range of new poetic voices, many of which were included in Sissay's collection, *The Fire People*, as well as the creation of a range of new, small but significant, independent presses publishing Black British writing, such as Bloodaxe, Mango Publishing (1995–), SAKS (1996–) Hansib, Aark Arts (late 1990s–) and Peepal Tree Press (1986–).

The fiftieth anniversary of Windrush in 1998 generated much visibility for contemporary Black British writing, with, for example, John Agard as poet in residence at the BBC. Roy Sommer argues that the late 1990s were 'accompanied by a historical turn in black British literary studies [which] not only helped to turn the anniversary into a media event, but also initiated a process of canon formation …'[70] However, arguably such short-term media interest in the anniversary continued to mask a longer-term neglect and lack of a critical tradition for Black British writers. As Caryl Phillips has reflected: 'in the 1970s there was not what we might term a black British critical tradition.'[71] Similarly, Johnson observed as late as 1996: 'In terms of my own work, I could have benefited from a critical tradition. We didn't have one at that time and we're only beginning to scratch at one in this country now'.[72] Nasta has called for 'an attempt to move beyond what I call 'apprenticeship criticism' in terms of black women's writing in this country, pieces which celebrate the new voices of black writers, their startling experimentation with language and so on and [the need to] attempt to consolidate and excavate more fully'.[73] Crucially, this means historicising Black British writing and developing a Black British critical tradition, a call which was to some extent answered by the wider lens and substantial scholarship of a range of critical texts at the end of the century.

Millennial Poets

In 2014 there are many signs that Black British poetry is thriving. Daljit Nagra's, *Look We Have Coming to Dover* (2007), is an extraordinary first collection in which Punjabi family histories, migrant dreams and the language and political ideologies surrounding UK immigration are mapped onto a British poetic landscape which is both familiar and startlingly defamiliarised. One of the striking features of this collection is its complex dialogue with English poets such as Matthew Arnold, as well as Nagra's forging of a highly original poetic voice and a 'jazzed hybrid language'. In the title poem of the collection, Nagra returns to Arnold's most famous poem 'Dover Beach', registering both the town's iconic place in British cultural nationalism ('The White Cliffs of Dover') and its centrality as a site of border-crossing for more recent migrant histories: 'Swarms of us, grafting in ... / banking on the miracle of sun- / ... passport us to life. Only then / can it be human to hoick ourselves, bare-faced for the clear. / Imagine my love and I, / our sundry others, Blair'd in the cash / of our beeswax'd cars, our crash clothes, free, / we raise our charged glasses over unparasol'd tables / East, babbling our lingoes, flecked by the chalk of Britannia!'[74]

Nagra's 'Kabba Questions the Ontology of Representation, the Catch 22 for 'Black' Writers'[75] is a kind of 'meta-poem' which examines the politics of representation and reception for Black British and British Asian poets, the role of colonial education and the continuing power of the English canon and canonical processes with particular reference to the category 'Poets from Other Cultures' in the UK National Curriculum for English. A Punjabi father asks, in exasperated and crowded demotic, on behalf of his school-aged son: 'Vy giv my boy / dis freebie of silky blue / GCSE antology with its three poets / from three parts of Briten – yor HBC / of Eaney, Blak / Clarke, showing us how / to tink and feel? For Part 2, us / as a bunch of Gunga Dins ju group, 'Poems / *from Udder Cultures / and Traditions.*' '*Udder*' is all / vee are to yoo, to dis cuntry- / '*Udde*r'? To my son's kabbadi posseee, all / Yor poets are '*Udder*'!'[76]

Agbabi's *Telling Tales* (2014) takes on a similar dialogue with a canonical tradition of English poets but to very different ends, as Chaucer's *The Canterbury Tales* is turned upside down and voiced by a gleeful cast of modern-day Black British poets and would-be poets, fully imagined speakers who satirically capture the zeitgeist of the contemporary British poetry scene. Indeed, the inclusion of short fictionalised biographies at the end of the text can make them seem even more convincing than Chaucer's originals and in this way, Agbabi encourages us to read both texts in dialogue in new and provocative ways. Thus Harry Bailey, the host of Chaucer's original poem becomes Harry 'Bells' Bailey who 'worked as a bouncer when studying at London Guildhall Uni. Ended up managing pub. Now owns five gastropubs, including the legendary Tabard Inn in Southwark. There hosts monthly storytelling night, *Plain Speaking*, which mixes live performance with Skype'. (*Telling Tales*, p. 115).

His is the Prologue, as is appropriate, and it is breathtaking: a contemporary mix or 'mashup' of Chaucer's most famous lines and Eliot's reworking in the opening to 'The Waste Land' (1922) with a nod to other canonical poets such as Percy Shelley[77]:

> When my April showers me with kisses
> I could make her my missus or my mistress
> But I'm happily hitched – sorry home girls –
> Said my vows to the sound of Bow Bells
> Yet her breath is as fresh as the west wind,
> When I breathe her, I know we're predestined
> To make music; my muse, she inspires me,
> Though my mind's overtaxed, April fires me,
> How she pierces my heart to the fond root
> Till I bleed sweet cherry blossom en route
> To our bliss trip ...'[78]

Two current collections which show the richness and diversity of contemporary Black British poetry are Dean Atta's 2013 collection *I Am Nobody's Nigger* and Karen McCarthy-Woolf's *An Aviary of Small Birds* (2014). Atta's collection combines both angry and reflective poems which deal with race, queer sexuality and life in London. The title poem is a coruscating attack on the use of 'nigger' in a post-racial, popular cultural context and reminds of the contexts of power and specific histories of oppression which this racist term still evokes. By way of contrast, McCarthy-Woolf's collection pieces together the aftermath of a much-wanted first child dying during childbirth, in poems freighted with the unbearable and minute details of living with this loss but which also reaffirm the redemptive power of poetry and of the natural world.

McCarthy-Woolf is one of the poets to have benefited from national initiatives such as the 'The Complete Works' poet-mentoring project, which led to a number of new first collections as well as high-profile anthologies such as *Ten Poets Spread the Word* (2010) and its sequel, *Ten: the New Wave* (2014) which she edited.[79] Formal and informal association (such as the writing groups Malika's Kitchen [2000–] and Kwame Dawes's Afro-Poets school) and regional initiatives (such as Yorkshire's 'Inscribe', directed by Smartt and Sesay, 'Commonword Cultureword', 'TangleRoots' on mixed race narratives and 'Identity on Tyne' in the northeast) have also supported the emergence of other new Black British poetic voices. In 2015 Black British poets' affiliations to the nation are mainly British but importantly, they *work* internationally, borrowing from other cultures and literary traditions not just British ones. Similarly, their subjects are global, such as the important work and poetry on trauma and torture of Sri Lankan-born Sene Senetrivatne.

Red, Kwame Dawes's 2010 anthology of contemporary Black British poetry includes more than eighty poets, established and new, a far cry from Berry's situation in the 1970s. Perhaps, as Dawes suggests, we should be optimistic about the 'exciting future' for Black British poetry, 'given the remarkable number of gifted poets emerging in the UK today, and given the work being done by many articulate and proactive advocates for Black British writing in general and poetry in particular'.[80] And yet, as Evaristo points out, Black British poetry collections still comprise only 1 percent of all those published in Britain. Her ''Why it Matters' is nothing less than a manifesto and a provocation, not just to poetry readers but to the UK publishing industry as a whole:

> What if poetry publishers, nearly all of whom are white and male, used their position of power and privilege to be more proactive in actively seeking out new voices away from the usual networks? It might mean publishing beyond personal taste. It might mean nurturing talent when it's found, rather than dismissing it as not good enough – yet. It might mean being open to poetry that comes out of unfamiliar cultures and traditions. It might mean being aware that including more diverse voices on a poetry list can only enrich and strengthen it.... Editors are the ones with the power to make a difference. The ball is in their court.[81]

In 2014 at least, the public face of Black British poetry is very different from its first-generation beginnings, having successfully 'breached' the gates of some major institutions, including the literary 'establishment' and academia. Poetry by Agard, Nichols, Imtiaz Dharker and Alvi has long been integrated into the National Curriculum for English (albeit often under the guise of 'Poems from Other Cultures and Traditions', as Alvi and Nagra have noted) and these poets are some of the most sought-after participants in workshops for British secondary school pupils. Black British writing is recognised as an important area of study on a growing number of university curricula in the UK (as well as in the States and parts of Europe) and in 2012, an international conference at Cambridge University was devoted to the teaching of Caribbean and Black British poetry. Anthologies of Black British poetry abound, weighty volumes of Black British poets' *Selected Poems* are published by mainstream publishers such as Bloodaxe and the even more peerlessly canonical Penguin, although specialist independent presses such as Peepal Tree or Flipped Eye are still a lifeline for most new Black British poets. Black British poets such as Kay, Kei Miller, D'Aguiar and Dawes are professors of creative writing at British or American universities, others have residencies at major institutions such as the Tate Gallery, the South Bank Centre, the BBC and the Royal Shakespeare Company and Black British poets win prestigious prizes such as the Forward Prize for Poetry and Somerset Maugham Prize. Since the Poetry Society launched its 'New Generation Poets' list in 1994, at least five Black British poets have been included. The controversial shortlisting of Benjamin Zephaniah for a chair in poetry at Cambridge University in 1991 is still widely remembered and he, Agard and Nichols are all well-respected writers for children as well as adults. There has also been, for the first time, a black British Children's Laureate: Malorie Blackman. Johnson, arguably the most significant Black British poet of the last forty years, is regarded affectionately as a kind of 'national treasure' alongside others such as Zephaniah and Kay, and his *Selected Poems* was published in no less than the Penguin Classic series in 2002, the first black poet and only the second living poet to be included in the series. Poetry in both printed and performed form is more visible than ever and Black British poets are at the very heart of this renaissance.

Acknowledgements

My thanks go to Drs Alberto Fernandez Carbajal and Sheree Mack for their careful reading and insightful comments on this chapter.

NOTES

1 The quote 'Mekin Histri' has been taken from Linton Kwesi Johnson, 'Mekin Histri', in *Selected Poems* (Harmondsworth: Penguin, 2002), pp. 64–66. This process of fetishization reached its apotheosis when a giant model of the Windrush ship and its Caribbean passengers was featured in the national pageant which was the opening ceremony of the 2012 London Olympics.

2 In *IC3: the Penguin Book of New Black Writing in Britain* (Harmondsworth, Penguin: 2000), editors Courtia Newland and Kadija Sesay divide their contributors into three phases or generations: the settlers, the explorers and the crusaders. I add to these the millennial generation.

3 Susheila Nasta, 'Beyond the Millennium: Black Women's Writing', *Women: A Cultural Review* 11:1/2 (2000): 72–73.

4 Ibid., p.73.

5 'Extra Dimensions, New Routines', *Wasafiri* 25:4 (2010): 51.

6 Ian Hamilton, ed., *The Oxford Companion to Twentieth Century Poetry* (Oxford and New York: Oxford University Press, 1996), p. 258.

7 Courtland and Sesay call these 'Explorers'.

8 See Kamau Brathwaite, *History of the Voice* (London: New Beacon, 1984) for a more detailed study of the history and use of this linguistic term.

9 Such as MAAS, the Minority Arts Advisory Service, originally set up in 1976 as a result of an Arts Council report designed to survey and to encourage ethnic minority arts in Britain.

10 For example, Ramey discusses 'urban griots' and 'trickster figures' in R. Victoria Arana and Lauri Ramey, eds., *Black British Writing* (Basingstoke: Macmillan, 2004), p. 110. See also Sarah Broom, *Contemporary British and Irish Poetry* (Basingstoke: Palgrave Macmillan, 2006), pp. 251–57.

11 John Agard, 'True Grit', in *We Brits* (Newcastle: Bloodaxe, 2006), p. 10.

12 See Alison Donnell, ed., *Companion to Black British Culture* (London: Routledge, 2002), James Procter, ed., *Writing Black Britain: 1948–1998* (Manchester: Manchester University Press, 2000), Arana and Ramey, eds., *Black British Writing* (New York: Palgrave Macmillan, 2004).

13 See Arana, ed., *'Black' British Aesthetics Today* (Newcastle: Cambridge Scholars Publishing, 2009).

14 See Gail Low and Marion Wynne Davies, eds., *A Black British Canon?* (Basingstoke: Palgrave Macmillan, 2006), John McLeod, 'Some Problems with "British" in a "Black British Canon"', *Wasafiri* 17:36 (2002): 56–59.

15 See Fred D'Aguiar 'Against Black British Literature' [1988] in Maggie Butcher ed., *Tibisiri* (Dangaroo Press: 1989), pp. 106–114.

16 See McLeod 2002.

17 Procter, *Writing Black Britain*, p. 5.

18 *Write Black Write British: From Post Colonial to Black British Literature* (Hertford: Hansib, 2005), p. 5.

19 McLeod, 2002, p. 57.

20 See for example, D'Aguiar, 1988.

21 For example, Low and Wynne Davies, eds., 2006. The subsuming of 'British Asian' or more recently, 'British Muslim' into 'Black British' is especially

problematic, and a number of writers have remarked on this. However, for the purpose of this chapter, I use the term 'Black British' to refer to poets and poetry by Black *and* Asian poets, born or based in Britain.

22 See Caryl Phillips, 'Following On: the Legacy of Lamming and Selvon', in *A New World Order: Selected Essays* (London: Secker & Warburg, 2001), pp. 232–38 and McLeod, 2010.

23 'The Spread the Word Writer Development Agency was commissioned to look into why so few black and Asian poets were being published … the final report, *Free Verse* (2005) … revealed that less than 1% of poetry books published in Britain are by black and Asian poets', 'Why it Matters', *Ten Poets Spread the Word* (Newcastle: Bloodaxe, 2010), p. 11.

24 Ibid., p. 11.

25 Kwame Dawes, 'Negotiating the Ship on the Head: Black British Fiction', in *Write Black Write British*, 2005, p. 280.

26 Stuart Hall [1976], 'Racism and Reaction', in *Five Views of Multi-Cultural Britain* (London: Commission for Racial Equality, 1978), p. 11.

27 Dorothea Smartt, *Ship Shape* (Leeds: Peepal Tree Press, 2008). See also Moniza Alvi's 'Arrival 1946' or Agard's 'The Ship', Grace Nichols', *I Is a Long Memoried Woman* (London: Karnak, 1983) and *Startling the Flying Fish* (London: Virago, 2005), Sheree Mack's *Family Album* (Newcastle: Flambard Press, 2011) and Sesay's *Irki* (Newcastle: Bloodaxe, 2013).

28 Dawes, 2005, p. 290.

29 McLeod, 2010, p. 46.

30 The quote 'But Let Me Tell You How This Business Begin' taken from Derek Walcott, 'The Schooner Flight', in Edward Baugh, ed., *Selected Poems* (New York: Farrar, Straus & Giroux, 2007), p. 129.

31 Trinidadian writer Sam Selvon acknowledged this in his seminal essay 'Finding West Indian Identity in Britain', *Kunapipi* IX:3 (1987): 34–38.

32 See Delia Jarrett-Macaulay, *The Life of Una Marson: 1905–65* (Manchester and New York: Manchester University Press, 1998) and Una Marson, *Selected Poems*, ed. Alison Donnell (Leeds: Peepal Tree Press, 2011).

33 See also Patience Agbabi's experimentation with the sonnet form in 'Problem Pages' (2008) which stages the imagined literary and other 'problems' of English and American writers and, most recently in her reworking of *The Canterbury Tales, Telling Tales* (Edinburgh: Canongate, 2014).

34 Una Marson, 'If', in Donnell and Lawson Welsh, eds. (1996), p. 129.

35 See Donnell's introduction to Marson, *Selected Poems* (2011) for more detailed discussion of this.

36 In Berry, ed., *News for Babylon* (London: Chatto & Windus, 1984), p. 190.

37 Ibid.

38 *Fractured Circles* (London: New Beacon Books, 1979) and *Lucy's Letters and Loving* (London: New Beacon Books, 1982).

39 Berry, ed., *Bluefoot Traveller* (London: Limehouse Publications, 1976, and London: Nelson Educational, 1981) and *News for Babylon* (1984).

40 See Ruth Bush's recent study of New Beacon as 'the first independent publisher for Caribbean and Black interest [writing] in the UK'. (http://www.georgepadmore-institute.org/launch-online-publication-new-beacon-books-pioneering-years, accessed 15 December, 2014).

41 For example in his preface to *Breaklight: An Anthology of Caribbean Poetry* (London: Hamish Hamilton, 1971), p. xv, Jamaican writer Andrew Salkey referred to 'a mere handful living in voluntary exile in London.'

42 Bernadine Evaristo, 'Black British Women's Writing', Keynote address to First International Conference on Black British Women Writers, Brighton University, July 2014.

43 The quote 'It Dread Inna Inglan' taken from Linton Kwesi Johnson, 'It Dread Inna Inglan', in *Inglan is a Bitch* (London: Race Today, 1980), pp. 19–20.

44 'Sonny's Lettah', often known as the anti-SUS law poem, takes the form of a moving letter from a son to his mother whilst he is Brixton jail.

45 See Kwame Dawes, *Natural Mysticism: Towards a New Reggae Aesthetic in Caribbean Writing* (Leeds: Peepal Tree Press, 1999) for a more detailed examination of this.

46 Henghameh Saroukhani, 'Penguinizing Dub: Paratextual Frames for Transnational Protest in Linton Kwesi Johnson's Mi Revalueshanary Fren', *Journal of Postcolonial Writing*, 2014: 1.

47 Ibid., p. 1.

48 Introduction to *Bluefoot Traveller*, p. 9.

49 See Arana and Ramey, eds. (2004), p. 116.

50 Alison Donnell, 'Nation and Contestation: Black British Literature', *Wasafiri* 17:36 (2002): 13.

51 Fred D'Aguiar, 'Home', in *British Subjects* (Newcastle: Bloodaxe, 1993), pp. 14–15.

52 Berry, Introduction to *Bluefoot Traveller*, p. 6.

53 Ibid., p. 6.

54 The quote 'The Power to Be What I Am' taken from Grace Nichols, 'Holding my Beads' in *I Is a Long Memoried Woman* (London: Karnak, 1983), p. 86.

55 For example, groups such as the Brixton Black Women's Group (BBWG) and the Organisation of Women of Asian and African Descent (OWAAD) were founded in 1973 and 1978, and the Asian Women Writers' Collective in 1984. Nasta (2000) and Evaristo (2014) both acknowledge that much black British women's writing has 'traditionally existed outside the academy … in the world of community writing workshops, performance arts and organized groups such as the Asian Woman writers' alliance …' (Nasta 2000, p. 72).

56 See Barbara Burford's, *A Dangerous Knowing: Four Black Women Poets* (London: Sheba Feminist Press, 1984), *Watchers and Seekers: Creative Writing by Black Women in Britain* (London: The Women's Press, 1987), ed. Rhonda Cobham and Merle Collins and the international collection, *Charting the Journey: Writings by Black and Third World Women* (London: Sheba Feminist Press, 1988), ed. S. Grewal, Jackie Kay, Liliane Landor, Gail Lewis and Pratibha Parma.

57 See Beverley Bryan, Stella Dadzie and Suzanne Scafe's seminal essay collection: *The Heart of the Race* (London: Virago, 1985) and Lauretta Ngcobo's *Let It Be Told: Black Women in Britain*, (London: Virago, 1987), which included both autobiographical essays and poems.

58 Evaristo Keynote (Brighton, 2014).

59 See *The Fat Black Woman's Poems* (1984), *Lazy Thoughts of a Lazy Woman* (1989), *Sunris* (1996) and *Startling the Flying Fish* (2005).

60 See 'Eve' in *Lazy Thoughts* (1989), p. 14, and 'Icons' in *Sunris* (1996), pp. 29–30.

61 See *Picasso, I Want my Face Back* (Newcastle: Bloodaxe, 2009) and *Paint Me a Poem: New Poems Inspired by Art in the Tate* (London: A & C Black, 2004).
62 *I Is a Long Memoried Woman* (London: Karnak, 1983), p. 3.
63 See 'In My Country' in *Out of Bounds* (Newcastle: Bloodaxe, 2012), p. 71.
64 Having been excluded from *The Penguin Book of Contemporary British Poetry*, edited by Blake Morrison and Andrew Motion in 1982, Black British poets gradually found themselves admitted to the pages of a range of more mainstream anthologies in the 1980s, from a single poem (by Johnson) in Tom Paulin's *The Faber Book of Political Verse* (London: Faber and Faber, 1986) to the rather more generous selection in Sylvia Paskin et al., *Angels of Fire – An Anthology of Radical Poetry in the '80s* (London: Random House, 1986).
65 See Judith Kinsman's, *Six Woman Poets* (1992), Linda France's *Sixty Woman Poets* (Newcastle: Bloodaxe, 1993), Margaret Busby's international collection, *Daughters of Africa* (London: Vintage, 1992) and most significantly *Bittersweet* (Newcastle: Bloodaxe, 1998), edited by Karen McCarthy-Woolf. In 1996 a volume dedicated to Kay, Nichols and Merle Collins appeared in the Penguin Modern Poets Series. Black British poetry also featured in more generic collections such as Michael Horowitz's *Grandchildren of Albion: Voices and Visions of Younger Poets in Britain* (Stroud, Gloucestershire: New Departures, 1992) as well as arts and poetry magazines such as *Poetry Review* and *Artrage* (1992–95), the magazine outlet of MAAS.
66 For example, D'Aguiar's *British Subjects* (Newcastle: Bloodaxe, 1993), Alvi's *The Country at My Shoulder* (Oxford: Oxford University Press, 1993) and Agard's *Half-Caste* (London: Hodder, 2004) and *We Brits* (Newcastle: Bloodaxe, 2006).
67 Jackie Kay, James Procter and Gemma Robinson, eds., *Out of Bounds: British Black and Asian Poets* (Newcastle: Bloodaxe, 2012). See also Sarah Lawson Welsh, '(Un)belonging Citizens, Unmapped Territory: Black Immigration and British Identity in the Post-1945 Period', in Stuart Murray, ed., *Not on Any Map: Essays on Postcoloniality and Cultural Nationalism* (Exeter: Exeter University Press, 1997), pp. 43–66.
68 Jackie Kay, *Darling* (Newcastle: Bloodaxe, 2007), p. 27.
69 Introduction to *The Fire People*, (Edinburgh: Payback Press, 1998), p. 8.
70 "Black' British Literary Studies and the Emergence of a New Canon', *Orbis Litterarum* 66:3 (2011): 246.
71 Phillips, 2001, p. 233.
72 Interview: LKJ Talks to Burt Caesar, *Critical Quarterly*, 38:4 (1996): 72.
73 Nasta, 2000, p. 78.
74 *Look We Have Coming to Dover* (London: Faber and Faber, 2007), pp. 32–33.
75 Ibid., pp. 42–43.
76 Ibid., p. 42.
77 See also Ramey, 'Black British Poetry', in Arana and Ramey (2004), pp. 130–31.
78 Agbabi, *Telling Tales*, p. 1.
79 Lesser known but important anthologies include: Debjani Chatterjee, ed., *The Redbeck Anthology of British Asian Writing* (Bradford: Redbeck, 2000) and Asher Hoyles and Martin Hoyles, eds., *Moving Voices: Black Performance Poetry* (Hertford: Hansib, 2002).
80 Introduction to *Red* (Leeds: Peepal Tree Press, 2010), p. 20.
81 Evaristo, *Ten New Poets*, p. 14.

13

JAN MONTEFIORE

Poetry, Feminism, Gender and Women's Experience

Since the term 'gender' applies to all sexes, in a world of gender equality this chapter would not be needed. A separate chapter on women's poetry might seem open to Vicki Bertram's pointed observation in *Gendering Poetry* that 'most studies of contemporary poetry ignore the work of women poets until their final chapter, when they bundle the women together and offer a cursory overview, with no clear rationale for so doing beyond a vague expectation that those poets will have something in common.'[1] Yet the story of the contribution of women to British poetry from 1970 cannot be told without addressing the question of feminism, and more particularly the post-1969 'women's movement' as we called it at the time, now better known as 'second-wave feminism'.

The visibility of women's poetry since the mid-1970s is evident in the wave of anthologies appearing in the late twentieth century (many from Bloodaxe Press, by far the most woman-friendly poetry publisher in the UK) with introductions arguing the rationale for the editors' choice of women's poetry and how it should be read, and in recent critical accounts of women's poetry, notably Jane Dowson and Alice Entwistle 's magisterial *History of Twentieth Century British Women's Poetry* (2005) and Deryn Rees-Jones' innovative critical study *Consorting with Angels* (2005).[2] Lilian Mohin's groundbreaking 1979 feminist anthology *One Foot on the Mountain: An Anthology of British Feminist Poetry, 1969–1979* was followed by Diana Scott's *Bread and Roses: Women's Poetry of the Nineteenth and Twentieth Century* (1982), and Jeni Couzyn's *Bloodaxe Book of Contemporary Women Poets* (1985) which offered a more generous selection from fewer poets. The more 'mainstream' anthologies *Making for the Open: The Chatto Book of Post-Feminist Poetry* edited by Carol Rumens (1985) and *The Faber Book of 20th Century Women Poets* edited by Fleur Adcock (1987) are both a continuation of this feminist work of making women poets visible and a reaction against it. The much more inclusive *Sixty Women Poets* edited by Linda France (1993) and Deryn Rees-Jones' *Modern Women Poets* (2005) both include substantial selections of mid-twentieth-century poets as well as established and younger names.[3] Like Dowson and Entwistle's *History*, these anthologies seek to establish and to make available the tradition(s) of women's poetry since 1940.

Women poets have long felt the absence of women forebears, which 'both results from and conspires in women's uncertain relation to English poetic tradition.'[4] Louise Bernikow pointed out in the introduction to her pioneering anthology *The World Split Open: Women Poets 1552–1950* (1974) that the absence of women from the canon is not an objective fact but a constructed absence. 'What is commonly called literary history is actually a record of choices. Which writers have survived their time and which have not depends on who noticed them and chose to record the notice', the power to select the canon having 'always belonged to white men' whose taste has excluded women.[5] That the absence from Bernikow's anthology of Sylvia Townsend Warner, Stevie Smith, E. J. Scovell and Lynette Roberts, not to mention a great many pre-1850 poets, now looks surprising, is a tribute to the labours of scholars, editors, critics and publishers since 1974. And now that Carol Ann Duffy is Poet Laureate it would clearly be untrue to write, as I did in *Feminism and Poetry* (1987) that 'people feel … the woman poet is a slight and freakish phenomenon compared with her substantial sister the novelist, let alone her massive and weighty poetic grandfathers'.[6] Yet it remains true that a woman writing poetry is rarely thought of simply as a poet, and that women's relationship to the great works of the past is not straightforward. As Jo Shapcott has remarked, 'there aren't enough models of women writing poetry, so that when we encounter the tradition we have to find a way to completely engage with what's gone before, a way to possess it.'[7] That said, the confidence of Shapcott's ambition 'to engage, to possess' is noticeable and heartening, suggesting how finding themselves – or positioning themselves – at an angle to tradition(s) can be a powerful stimulus to women's poetry.

Feminism and Poetry

An account of women's poetry since 1980 must begin with feminism, which has been an immensely energising and fertile influence on women poets, both directly in the poetry that was inspired by the Women's Liberation Movement, and more obliquely in poetry by women whose consciousness of themselves was affected by feminist thinking, whether or not they choose to define themselves and the work they endorsed as feminist. British feminist poetry of the 1970s,[8] sometimes described as 'the poetry of consciousness-raising',[9] is best approached through Lilian Mohin's classic anthology *One Foot on the Mountain*, presenting fifty-five poets in alphabetical order of first name, from Alison Fell to Zoe Fairbairns:

> The poems here are never resigned. Nothing is assumed to be inevitable or seen as 'natural'. Feminists have to be more conscious than anyone else. We must continuously see and say that what the world/ men has declared invisible or invalid is real and important.... The work in this book comes out of the efforts we are making, a collective sense of effort and of discovery. We intend to tell each other everything we can, every secret, because we know this intimate, difficult exchange makes a difference, is the process of change.[10]

This extract from the anthology's blurb, announcing 'a collective effort and discovery', testifies that this was not a poetry of individual vision but of shared conversation. As Claire Buck and others have insisted,[11] the poetry of feminist activism was a group endeavour, drawing on and extending the common ground of consciousness shared by women. Most feminist poetry of this era appeared not in individually authored poetry collections but in feminist magazines, notably *Spare Rib*, *Red Rag*, *Writing Women* and *Distaff*, or in group-authored pamphlets like *Licking the Bed Clean* (1978) and its successor *Smile Smile Smile Smile* (1980), *Cutlasses and Earrings* (1977), *Hens in the Hay* (1980), and the lesbian feminist anthology *Beautiful Barbarians* (1980).[12] This is not only because few of the poets were then established names, but because this poetry not only drew on but was written as contributions to the collective activity of consciousness-raising. In this mode of informal but lively activism, widespread among 'second-wave' feminists during the 1970s and, less intensely, the 1980s, a group of women would meet – usually weekly, in a member's house – to put questions to themselves which each would answer from personal experience. The group would then collectively use these personal testimonies to draw conclusions about the political root of women's so-called 'personal' problems.[13] What differentiated C-R from what would now be called 'support groups' for women is that personal experience was not simply shared as an end in itself, but was informed by and contributed to a highly political critique. This practice deeply marked the feminist 'poetry of consciousness-raising' in *One Foot*, whose characteristics are well defined by Claire Buck as 'a clear fidelity to ... political ideals translated into a poetics concerned with cultural critique, an accessible language and form, and the expression of women's experience.'[14]

Readers might expect this emphasis on women's experience to produce a lot of directly personal 'confessional' poetry. This certainly exists in *One Foot*, notably in Caroline Halliday's 'Confession' about the childhood experience of being sexually abused by a priest ('The steering wheel was pressing into my back. / So I sat there, he's an uncle really. / It was the kind of hard, slimey feeling of his tongue. The taste, and prickly too') and Judith Kazantzis on her ambivalence about motherhood in 'Towards an Abortion' and her pleasure in her own menstruating body in 'The Bath': 'the lost fronds of a cradle unwound / a gentle loss / my finger winds a tiny curl of my leaving / – soft head / – birthing myself in the bathwater.'[15] And a few poems in *One Foot* re-write myths and fairy tales: Judith Kazantzis's 'Mrs Noah' and 'Medea', anticipating Carol Ann Duffy, and Gillian Allnutt's resonant epigram 'The Talking Princess', who wakes and asks 'my adoring prince' to turn her dream into reality: 'I woke / and have not slept since'.[16] But subjects are more often 'prosaic', with many poems about women's rights: Diana Scott's 'Six Poems for Hospital Workers', Gill Hague's 'For a Housewife', Katharyn Rosa Gabriella's 'An Item of BBC News', Janet Dubé's 'It'll Take a Long Time' and 'I Shall Get Stopped'. But these poems are not straightforward polemics. In Alison Fell's 'For Maria Burke, Who Knocked At My Door While I Was Writing About The Alienation Of Life In The Cities Under Capitalism', the poet measures herself and her own politics against the stark need of Maria, a homeless mental patient who is presumably an early victim of 'care in the community', turning up barelegged in plimsolls to what she hopes is a squat where she knows 'some man':

> 'No, not a squat,' I snapped,
> 'And who was the man?'
>
> The powerful deeply suspect
> the powerless
> of manipulations and lying...
>
> I showed her the spare room
> she thanked me several times
> stripped to her bra while
> I was still there.
> Only those who have homes are entitled
> to modesty.[17]

There is an obvious, conscious irony in the title's dedication to a person who is never likely to read it. Although the poem is experiential in the sense of deriving from personal witness, it sets the victim's raw suffering at one remove. The reader is asked to share the poet's disturbance at being confronted with a person experiencing in the 'hairless' flesh what she has been trying to analyse in abstract terms. This confrontation and disturbance give depth and clarity to the angry, compassionate feminist critique of the way damaged outsiders are deprived of dignity. The attack on patriarchal society as represented by the authority and privilege of Maria's male consultant whose wife's body 'belongs to him only' unlike Maria's which 'belongs to anybody', avoids self-righteous rant because of the poet's self-scrutiny as another of the 'powerful' (at least in relation to Maria) who suspect the 'powerless' of manipulation. If Fell's poem attempts to live out the challenge of the *Redstocking Manifesto* 'We regard our personal experiences, and our feelings about that experience, as the basis for an analysis of our common situation.... We identify with all women',[18] it also testifies to the difficulty of rising to that challenge.

Yet the idea of basing a poetics on women's experience is problematic – and not only because of the divisions and differences between women, whose emergence famously disrupted the aspiration of feminists to 'identify with all women'. As I argued in *Feminism and Poetry*, the poetry of experience was itself shaped by the inheritance of Romanticism, which underlies the 'belief that poetry gives us access to the [woman] poet's experience, and that poetry is a form of transcendence'. Wordsworth's famous definition of the poet as 'a man speaking to men' becomes 'women speaking to each other' – but this can become another false universal.[19] Nor is the language of poetry transparent; there is, for instance, a recognisably feminist rhetoric of bodily 'experience' in several poems in *One Foot*, such as Judith Kazantzis' 'Bath', which is visible in its explicitly transgressive feminist themes of menstruation, masturbation ('my finger winds a tiny curl'), its triumphant conclusion of 'birthing myself', and in its marine imagery of anemones, fronds and tidal currents. Fleur Adcock's well-known complaint that such poetry is '"primal scream" writing: slabs of raw experience untransformed by any attempt at ordering and selection',[20] is, however, misconceived; as Claire Buck has usefully written, 'it is not that the poems reflect experience that lies outside of or prior to its expression in the poem. Rather ..., experience is written in terms of available conventions or its representation'. Thus in 'Girl's Gifts', Alison Fell uses flowers to represent female sexuality and creativity: 'I mould petals, weave stems, with love / my little finger inches in the folds: / it is done, red and gold'. But the flowers are not innocently 'there', devoid of the symbolism which determines their possible meanings within a specifically feminist discourse about women's culture and creativity represented by a flower basket which is made by a child for her grandmother while her mother watches, 'a shadow in the window'). As Buck has pointed out,

> The poem also creates a current of unease, to do with a temporality that interweaves adult sexuality with infantile eroticism. On the one hand, the poem memorializes a moment of childhood, which for poet and reader is past. On the other, it mixes in the present continuous tense of fantasy – 'I am making a tiny secret basket' – with the conditional tense: 'I would lick the green leaf, taste the bronze / and yellow silk of my snapdragon' ... The assertion that the gift is 'secret' combines with self-consciousness to introduce an element

> of sexual transgression into the positive female sensuality and creativity celebrated by the poem.[21]

Post-1990 poetry by women has taken the exploration of fantasy and sexuality further, in ways that I discuss in this chapter.

The aspirations of feminist poetry provoked a reaction amongst some poets who rejected its claims in favour of the humanist ideal of writing without gender considerations. The best known exponent of this view is Anne Stevenson in her essay 'Writing as a Woman' which refuses the title of 'feminist poet':

> For better or worse, women and men writers in the West, in the later twentieth century, share a common consciousness. Their language is a reflection, or a definition, of that consciousness. If anything we want *more* understanding, more communication between the sexes ... If there is to be a new creative consciousness, – one that is not based on the phallic values of conquest, power, ambition, greed, murder and so on – then this consciousness must have room for both male and female – a consciousness that the greatest literature has, in fact, been defining for some time now.[22]

The intellectual strength of Anne Stevenson's insistence that art transcends lies in her refusal to be, as she sees it, ghettoised. Her weakness, as with other proponents of this argument, lies in idealising the humanist tradition which she endorses, failing to see the exclusions and injustices which underpin the canon of 'great literature' including (as Bernikow had pointed out) its exclusion of women poets. Similar positions are taken by Carol Rumens and Fleur Adcock in their introductions to, respectively, *Making for the Open: The Chatto Book of Post-Feminist Poetry* (1985) and the *Faber Book of 20th Century Women Poets*. Both editors distance themselves from feminist poetry and its 'experiential' rhetoric, and their anthologies include few poems which could be called feminist. For Carol Rumens, 'the political orientation of much women's publishing ... has sometimes, particularly in the case of poetry, led to the elevation of the message at the expense of the medium. Those writers concerned with "the stern art of poetry" as an end in itself have tended to be swamped by the noisy amateurs proclaiming that women, too, have a voice'. Instead, she endorses 'post-feminism: 'a psychological, rather than a political condition ... [which] implies a mental freedom which a few women in any age have achieved'.[23] Fleur Adcock is similarly dismissive of the notion of a tradition of women's poetry: 'If I have a theory about the tradition informing poetry it is that there is no particular tradition: there have been poets, and they have been individuals, and a few of them have influenced a few others ... [If] women's poetry were a special genre, a minor and recognizably different offshoot from the main process, it might make sense to see it as a unity, but as things are, women have been involved in the currents and movements as little or as much as men, and have been as various'. Both Rumens and Adcock have been attacked for eating their feminist cake while pretending to refuse it, since their anthologies took advantage of a feminist-generated marked for women's poetry while stereotyping feminists as 'noisy amateurs' and 'primal scream[ers]'.[24] This, however, is not entirely fair to books which, whatever their editorial caveats, did help to put a wide variety of women's poetry into circulation.

A different take on gender and women's experience can be seen in Jeni Couzyn's *Contemporary Women's Poetry* (1985), whose selections from the work of eleven poets in order of age, each prefaced by the poet's own statement of what poetry means and the role poetry has played in her own life, sought to establish a tradition of visionary poetry by women in the mid-twentieth century. Despite the title, two of the chosen poets – Stevie Smith and Sylvia Plath – were already dead, while the others were all 'seniors', Couzyn herself being the only one born after 1940. The book contained many poems musing on – and questioning – marriage and motherhood, and a few of protest against male chauvinism, notably Plath's 'The Zookeeper's Wife', Denise Levertov's 'The Mutes' (though not her 'Hypocrite Women') and Fleur Adcock's 'Instructions to a Vampire'. But the principal emphasis is on transcendence and spirituality (religion, not always orthodox, is a key theme), either directly as in the visionary poems of Kathleen Raine, or indirectly in the re-telling of myths, as in Levertov's 'A Tree Telling of Orpheus' or Jenny Jones's 'Persephone'.

Such retelling is characteristic of Stevie Smith, who opens this collection, and whose poetry is preceded by Couzyn's only critical introduction.[25] Smith who was, not coincidentally, a storyteller as well as a poet, has become an exemplary figure for women poets, almost in the way that Virginia Woolf has become *the* exemplary woman writer. Linda France's *Sixty Women Poets*, which begins with poems published since 1971, the year of Smith's death, 'honour[s] her influence and importance';[26] and together with Plath and Sexton, she is accorded a whole chapter in Deryn Rees-Jones's study *Consorting with Angels*. Stevie Smith is an inspirational figure because of her preoccupation with such 'major' questions of the meaning of human destiny as the nature of courage and the dialectic between natural vitality and the death drive ('Mary laughed: "I love Life, / I would fight to the death for it"'[27]), her re-writings of myth and fairy tale in her own highly original terms, her verbal and pictorial inventiveness, her quirky wit, her sheer productiveness (her *Collected Poems* runs to 571 pages) and the sketches with which she 'illustrated' her poems which often complicate her texts more than they clarify, as with the well-known figure of the long-haired women accompanying the 'dead man [who] lay moaning' in 'Not Waving But Drowning').[28] Equally important is Smith's genre-bending love of doggerel or nonsense ('Our Bog is Dood', 'Hih yih, yippity-yap'), her performances, including her public chanting of her own poems, her punning ('Do take Muriel out'), and her often disrespectful allusions to and parodies of traditional English poetry. Later poets look back with admiration and affection to 'this poet [who] / discovered / Marvels: a cat that sings, a corpse that comes in / Out of the rain'.[29] Knowledgeable in yet sceptical of religious and poetic traditions, Stevie Smith was her own woman. Unlike Plath, who notoriously worried about her own status as a woman poet,[30] she wrote without gender anxiety, following her own thoughts into fantasy and truth in ways that upset conventional paradigms.

The notion of poetry informing these earlier anthologies, as women speaking of their own lives, was criticised by the poets Denise Riley and Wendy Mulford, poets often identified with the 'Cambridge School' (though neither has lived in Cambridge for many years), both widely respected though never popular. Mulford, who has published Riley and other like-minded poets in her 'Reality Street Editions', has consistently queried the idea of authenticity of the self. In her early 'Notes on Writing: a Marxist/ Feminist Viewpoint, she asks: 'Who was this "I" speaking? Who was speaking me? ... How could the lie of culture be broken up if the lie of the self made by that culture remained intact?'[31] In a later essay, Mulford celebrates a poetry in which 'there is no unified lyric voice – its claims are exploded, its modes of expression done to death. In its place, we, the readers, follow the text in all its provisionality, its multiple meanings, its erasures, silences, chora'.[32] This is a poetics and a politics of language, not experience; Mulford's own poems live up to her own manifestos for an impersonal play of language, characteristically setting fragmentary phrases against each other. Denise Riley is more ambivalent about the concept of the lyric 'I', which her poetry attacks yet can't leave alone. Her critique of the self can be seen in her well-known early poem 'A Note on Sex and the "Reclaiming of Language"':

> The Savage is flying back home from the New Country
> in native-style dress with a baggage of sensibility
> to gaze on the ancestral plains with the myths thought up
> and dreamed in her kitchens as guides

The ironies of this poem are pointed against the search for an authentic female self: its portrayal of the sophisticated yet naive 'Savage', aspiring to primitivism in her 'native-style dress', satirises the fantasy of authenticity involved in any quest for the truly female. Having announced that 'she will be discovered' as the object of meaning, the poem interrupts itself:

> the work is
> e.g. to write 'she' and for that to be
> a word only and not a strong image
> of everything which is not-you, which sees you

'The work' of the poem undoes feminist mythmaking around the self which, unconsciously indebted to colonial presuppositions, has made 'She' represent both the primordial land and the woman looking for it – for 'ancestral plains' signify primordial authenticity to the traveller, just as she represents the Irrational (as opposed to civilised man) to her own culture which defines her as its Savage. Because she cannot go outside the world defined by language, when she seeks for her true identity by exploring her 'homeland' she finds herself already defined – and defined as a commodified cliché at that: 'The Savage weeps as landing at the airport / she is asked to buy small carvings, which represent herself.' By writing 'she' differently – or rather, by musing on how this might be done – the poem shows up what Mulford calls 'the lie of culture' underpinning the contradictory fantasy of self-discovery. Later poems by Riley deconstruct the lyric 'I' in a play of self-fragmenting, self-exploring language which 'resists fixity, positioning, even utterance'[33] via throw-away quotations, often taken from popular songs. Yet for all their sharp critiques of feminist self-expression, these poets do not distance themselves from feminism and its aspirations; rather, they seek to turn the energies of poetry towards deconstructing 'the lie of culture'.

Contemporary Women Poets

From the 1990s onwards, a much wider range of poets and of themes were introduced by the anthologies *New Women Poets* (1990), edited by Carol Rumens, *Sixty Women Poets*, edited by Linda France (1993), *Making for Planet Alice*, edited by Maura Dooley (1990), and *Modern Women Poets*, edited by Deryn Rees-Jones (2005) – not forgetting the *New British Poetry 1968–1988* (1989), edited by Gillian Allnutt, and a wave of collections by new poets including Carol Ann Duffy, U. A. Fanthorpe, Jackie Kay, Mimi Khalvati, Medbh McGuckian, Jo Shapcott and many others. British poets who have come to prominence since 1985 include Anna Adams, Fleur Adcock, Patience Agbabi, Gillian Allnutt, Moniza Alvi, Sujata Bhatt, Alison Brackenbury, Jean 'Binta' Breeze, Kate Clanchy, Gillian Clarke, Merle Collins, Elsa Corbluth, Wendy Cope, Jeni Couzyn, Maura Dooley, Mary Dorcey, Carol Ann Duffy, Helen Dunmore, U. A. Fanthorpe, Vicki Feaver, Elaine Feinstein, Alison Fell, Lavinia Greenlaw, Sophie Hannah, Maggie

Harris, Selima Hill, Frances Horovitz, Kathleen Jamie, Jenny Jones, Sylvia Kantaris, Jackie Kay, Mimi Khalvati, Lotte Kramer, Liz Lochhead, Medbh McGuckian, Elma Mitchell, Sinéad Morrissey, Wendy Mulford, Suniti Namjoshi, Grace Nichols, the late Dorothy Nimmo, Ruth Padel, Shena Pugh, Denise Riley, Michele Roberts, Carol Rumens, Fiona Sampson, Carole Satyamurti, Jo Shapcott, Anne Stevenson, Michelene Wandor and Susan Wicks. Although, as Vicki Bertram has forcefully pointed out,[34] women rarely if ever hold positions of authority as commissioning editors of poetry in British publishing houses, Fiona Sampson edited the leading British poetry journal *Poetry Review* between 2005 and 2012, and Colette Bryce currently (2015) edits *Poetry London*, while in 2009, Carol Ann Duffy became our first female Poet Laureate. In *Feminism and Poetry* (1987) I attempted to theorise a 'tradition of women's poetry'; but it is now possible – indeed necessary – to go beyond this and think in terms of plural, intertwining traditions – some of whose strands of course go back well before the 1980s (a point made implicitly by Rees-Jones's editorial decision to begin her anthology *Modern Women Poets* with fourteen poets, including Charlotte Mew [b. 1869], Mina Loy [b. 1882] and Edith Sitwell [b. 1887], who were born in the nineteenth century).

If 'post-feminist' had not now come to be commonly understood as 'shrugging off feminism as irrelevant', it would be a useful term to describe this wave of influential, increasingly eminent women poets. It is not only social changes in gender rules since the 1970s but the work of their feminist predecessors that has enabled them to write freely of sensuality and the body, to experiment with fantasy, with language and with imagery. That does not, of course, mean that the poets necessarily saw themselves as either part of the poetry of women's movement, or as following its lead. In 1988, Carol Ann Duffy distanced herself emphatically from the kind of experiential rhetoric and feminist symbolism associated with *One Foot* or *Bread and Roses*: 'we've been allowed ... children, what bastards men are, looms ... I haven't got any children and I don't define myself entirely as a woman; I'm not interested in weaving'.[35] Yet Duffy's own bravado and inventiveness have inspired and liberated other women poets. Kate Clanchy has written that 'My road to Damascus was reading Carol Ann Duffy's *The Other Country* ... I transformed my thinking – here was a woman writing about desire, anger, loss, and not in disguise, through the mirrors and refractions that I had been taught to look for, but directly, in full colour, with music, with smells. I thought – perhaps I can do that'.[36] And one can see continuities between the themes of 'desire, anger, loss' in the poems in *One Foot* and the directly personal quality of later autobiographical poems by women, especially clear when poets write of the construction of femininity. Michelene

Wandor's 'Pin Money' anticipates Gillian Allnutt's 'Convent' where 'girls are expected / to wear gloves ... each finger stitched / to the palm'.[37] On tensions between mothers and daughters, compare Michèle Roberts' angry 'I have been wanting to mourn': ('I want a funeral first / where I can mourn / mothering, and mourn / me, losing and lost') with the grimly comic repetitions of Wendy Cope's 2012 pantoum 'You're Not Allowed ('You're not allowed to wonder if it's true. / She loves you very much. She's told you so'), printed on the page opposite 'Daily Help', Cope's tender elegy for the family's cleaner Mrs Arnold, to whom the child turned for mothering.[38] Likewise, Carol Gilfillan recalling her mother's rebuke for 'the brilliant / red clot that remained and / flowered with transparent petals' in the toilet anticipates Vicki Feaver's 'Women's Blood': 'Burn the soiled ones in the boiler, / my mother told me, showing me how to hook / the loops of gauze-covered wadding pads / on to an elastic belt, remembering / how my grandmother had given her / strips of rag she'd had to wash out'.[39] It is likewise easy to trace a link between Kazantsis's outrageous (in 1979) celebration of her own sensuality in 'Bath' and Helen Dunmore's 'Wild Strawberries': 'I lipped at your palm – / The little salt edge there / The tang of money you'd handled' and the boldness of Grace Nichols's 'Fat Black Woman': 'Come up and see me some time / My breasts are huge exciting / amnions of watermelon / your hands can't cup ... there's a purple cherry / below the blues / of my black seabelly'.[40] Jo Shapcott later transformed the idea of the woman in 'In the Bath' into a meditation on prehistory and geography, her body cells 'spread thin and making the surface of the world / sparkle'. As Deryn Rees-Jones remarks, 'seeing the body in terms of its component cells and the molecules of water that cover it offers a kind of transcendence from the reductiveness of "writing just about what you see"'.[41] The musing woman in her bath might say like John Donne 'I am a little world', or at least the image of one: 'She loved the water trails over her body curves / ... making graph patterns which she thought might follow / the activity in her brain – all she wanted / was to be a good atlas, a bright school map / to shine up the world for everyone to see'.[42]

Many late twentieth-century poets, including Shapcott, have used the dramatic monologue, which is perhaps attractive to women because as Rees-Jones has suggested, 'it emphasises an artificiality that women already sense in the construction of their own subjectivity'.[43] Some poets have exploited it for directly feminist ends, notably U. A. Fanthorpe sending up the roles of damsel in distress, dragon and rescuing knight in 'Not My Best Side', or in 'Only Here For the Bier' turning minor female characters from Shakespeare's plays into middle-class Englishwomen, blinkered and a bit pathetic, like the naive 'Waiting Gentlewoman' who regards Lady Macbeth as 'a super person' who should be referred to a professional therapist ('All this about *blood*, and *washing*. Definitely Freudian'), but herself would, like the Doctor, prefer to get away from Dunsinane: 'I hope Daddy comes for me soon'.[44] Because monologues open a gap between the poet and the voice of the poem, they tend towards irony while giving the poet freedom to range far beyond herself into diverse experiences. This combination can be seen with great clarity in the work of Carol Ann Duffy; hence the uncertainty of her 'Standing Female Nude' in which the artist's model muses sceptically ('They tell me he's a genius') on the 'Little man' at work on objectifying her image, contemplating his achievement with postmodernist irony: 'In the tea-leaves / I can see the Queen of England gazing / on my shape. Magnificent, she murmurs / and moves on. It makes me laugh'.[45] Duffy's most famous early poem 'Psychopath', which powerfully imagines someone twisted by his painful childhood and under pressure to behave like a real man, gets its verbal 'punch' from a collage of registers, all ironised: 'My reflection sucks a sour Woodbine and buys me a drink. Here's / looking at you. Deep down I'm talented. She found out. Don't mess / with me, angel, I'm no nutter'.[46] Her best-selling sequence of monologues *The World's Wife*, in which some of the poems are spoken by mythical women like 'Thetis', 'Circe' or 'Salome' and some by wives of legendary figures, 'use the stories in tangent with autobiographical narratives, so that myth and fairytale … offer a personal and collective fantasy of avenging through violence male power and its prohibitions'.[47] The strategy of these poems is a relentless cutting-down-to-size of male heroes – literally so in 'Queen Kong' which turns the roles of conventional male besotted with feminine delicacy and vulnerability upside down: 'I'd gently pick / at his shirt and his trews, peel him, put / the tip of my tongue to the grape of his flesh … Next day, I shopped. Clothes for my man, mainly'.[48] 'Frau Freud' is 'sick up to here / with the beef bayonet, the pork sword' and all phallic symbols; 'Mrs Aesop' is equally sick of her husband's voice ('By Christ, he could bore for purgatory'); 'Pygmalion's Bride' is repelled by her creator's desire ('His nails were claws'), 'Eurydice' resents Orpheus's pretensions: 'even the mute, sullen stones at his feet / wept wee silver tears. / Bollocks. (I'd done all the typing myself, / I should know.)', and Circe not only turns male chauvinist pigs into their proper form, she gives instructions on how to cook them: 'Look at that simmering lug, at that ear, / did it listen, ever, to you, to your prayers and rhymes, / to the chimes of your voice, singing and clear? Mash / the potatoes, nymph, open the beer'.[49] Despite being so obviously anti-male, these poems invite not questioning but recognition and assent (as Deryn Rees-Jones says, they prompt reader 'to exclaim: *Men!*')[50]; they would clearly lend themselves to performance, and have indeed been a great success at public readings and literary festivals. Unlike earlier feminist retellings of myth like Judith Kazantsis's 'Clytemnestra' or Vicki Feaver's 'Judith', 'The World's Wife' is not primarily about women's experiences and their unwritten stories; however angry, its poems exist a long way from feminist activism. The point of their ironies is the woman poet's power of turning myths into grist to her postmodernist mill, to be ground into cruelly comic fantasies.

If Duffy's trademark monologue is the demotic and/or disillusioned voice, Jo Shapcott's shape-shifting monologues explore and play with different aspects of identity. She may speak as an animal in 'Goat', as a neglected lettuce at the bottom of the fridge in 'Vegetable Love' or as a speck of dust in 'Her Lover's Ear'; yet although the *personae* are so far-fetched, one remains aware of the poet behind them – explicitly so in 'Goat' where the poet who hates being in a crowd is surprised to find herself loving 'the push of goat muscle and goat bone, the smell of goat fur, goat breath and goat sex'. These are poems of appetite; the goat 'could have eaten the world', the passionate lettuce is enchanted with the 'thought … of being ingested with the rest / into his body cells where I'll learn / by osmosis another lovely version / of curl, then shrivel, then open again to desire'. The title 'Vegetable Love' echoes Andrew Marvell's 'To His Coy Mistress' ('My vegetable love should grow / Vaster than empires and more slow'), while 'Her Lover's Ear' recalls John Donne exploring his mistress's body, and perhaps Gerard Manley Hopkins: 'the air pushed me round the helix / I leaned outwards on the bend like a biker'[51] sounds like the hawk swerving 'as a skate's heel sweeps smooth on a bow-bend' in 'The Windhover'. Besides intertextual playfulness, Shapcott often engages with science, as in the erotic trope of osmosis quoted above. The poet's own intelligence is visible in her lightly worn learning, but differently from her male predecessors: instead of making her lover the objectified spectacle, she slides in and out of her imagined identities. As Vicki Bertram has pointed out, 'the focus on visuals is replaced with an emphasis on touch and motion, because it is the speaker's version of events that predominates, and she is preoccupied with the feel, not the look of things.'[52] Identities in the poems thus become fluidly permeable, especially in *Tender Taxes*. Her 'translations' from Rilke invoke the figure of the Rilkean angel who passes from one side to another, as in Luce Irigaray's idea of an unimagined sexuality beyond the phallic. Rees-Jones argues convincingly that Shapcott's 'desire to create a permeable "I" places her in the forefront of women poets in her attempt to destabilise the relation between self and other in the lyric and to radically rethink the relationship of the woman poet to both body and text'.[53]

The voices of Grace Nichols and Jackie Kay represent different angles on tradition and experience, writing both directly and indirectly from their own otherness as black or mixed-race women. In her award-winning sequence *i is a long memoried woman* (1983) and her 'Fat Black Woman' who 'symbolises a certain largeness of spirit that is lacking in the West,'[54] Nichols alternates between Standard English and creole, often in the same poems, making a confident, humorous critique of Western culture. The 'Fat Black Woman' poems alternate between third person and dramatic monologue, occasionally combining both, as in 'Shopping', when she finds 'Nothing soft and bright and billowing / to flow like breezy' and 'curses in Swahili / Yoruba / and nation language under her breath', concluding that 'when it come to fashion the choice is lean / Nothing much beyond size 14'. Other poems directly contest the power of dominant discourses – 'O how I long to place my foot / on the head of anthropology', followed by the splendid refrain 'Steatopygous sky / Steatopygous sea / Steatopygous waves / Steatopygous me',[55] which transforms the word (pronounced 'stay-at-o-pig-us') which classified and denigrated African women into a celebration of the generous amplitude of the ocean, the waves and the fat black woman herself. Good-tempered, the poem nonetheless packs a powerful critical punch.

Jackie Kay likewise speaks both inside and outside conventional English society thanks to her mixed-race origin as the child of a Nigerian father and a white Scottish mother, adopted as a very young baby by a white working-class communist couple. Her celebrated debut, *The Adoption Papers* (1991), autobiographical yet fictional in its handling of the birth mother's and the daughter's anxieties and desires, explores the creative tensions of difference and alterity. The three voices of the biological mother, the child and the strong, lovable adoptive mother, each speak of dislocation, pain and anxiety. The birth mother grieves, forever keeping her child's baby photograph secretly 'in my bottom drawer'. The adoptive mother who felt adoption was 'scandalous ... telling the world your secret failure' has to face telling her daughter that she is adopted, and later on must cope with the teenager's wish to get in touch with her lost mother, touching off a nightmare about the other woman coming back to steal her baby. (The sequence is as full of fantasy and dream as of testimony). The lively, sensitive daughter is frightened when 'After mammy telt me she wisnae my real mammy / I was scared to death she was gonnie melt / or something and mibbe disappear in the dead / of night' – though this countered by her mother's loving integrity: 'I always believed in the telling ... I told my daughter – / I bet your mother's never missed your birthday, / how could she?' She must also cope with the racism of classmates (fighting back is of limited use, but her mother always backs her: 'You tell your little girl to stop calling / my little girl names and I'll tell my little girl / to stop giving your little girl a doing') and, even worse, of teachers, and experiences alienation from her skin colour: 'sometimes when I look in the mirror / I give myself a bit of a shock / and say *Do you really look like that*?'[56] Yet for all its pain and tension (in the last lines, the daughter is still vainly dreaming of letters from her birth mother), the narrative of *The Adoption Papers*, aptly described as 'a loving deconstruction of … female displacement'[57] is exhilarating. Like the other poems by women surveyed in this chapter, it queries received wisdom, opens up new possibilities and imagines new identities.

NOTES

1 Vicki Bertram, *Gendering Poetry: Contemporary Women Poets and Men Poets* (London, Pandora Press, 2005), p. 157.

2 Vicki Bertram, ed., *Kicking Daffodils: Twentieth Century Women Poets* (Edinburgh, Edinburgh University Press, 1997); Alison Mark and Deryn Rees-Jones, eds., *Contemporary Women's Poetry: Reading/ Writing/ Practice* (Basingstoke, Palgrave Macmillan, 2000); Jane Dowson and Alice Entwistle, *A History of Twentieth Century British Women's Poetry* (Cambridge: Cambridge University Press, 2005); Deryn Rees-Jones, *Consorting With Angels: Essays on Modern Women Poets* (Newcastle, Bloodaxe, 2005); Jane Dowson, ed., *Cambridge Companion to Twentieth Century British and Irish Women's Poetry* (Cambridge: Cambridge University Press, 2011).

3 Lilian Mohin, ed., *One Foot on the Mountain: An Anthology of British Feminist Poetry, 1969–1979* (London: OnlyWomen Press, 1979); Diana Scott, ed., *Bread and Roses: Women's Poetry of the Nineteenth and Twentieth Century* (London: Virago 1982); Jeni Couzyn, *Bloodaxe Book of Contemporary Women Poets* (Newcastle upon Tyne: Bloodaxe, 1985); Carol Rumens, ed., *Making for the Open: The Chatto Book of Post-Feminist Poetry* (London: Chatto, 1985); Fleur Adcock, ed., *Faber Book of 20th Century Women Poets* (London: Faber and Faber, 1987); Linda France, *Sixty Women Poets* (Newcastle: Bloodaxe, 1993),Deryn Rees-Jones, *Modern Women Poets*, complementing her feminist study *Consorting with Angels: Essays on Modern Women Poets* (both Newcastle: Bloodaxe, 2005).

4 Quoted from Jane Dowson and Alice Entwistle, *History of 20th Century British Women's Poetry*, p. 1.

5 Louise Bernikow, *The World Split Open: Women Poets 1552–1990* (New York, 1974; London: Women's Press, 1979), pp. 3–4.

6 Jan Montefiore, *Feminism and Poetry: Language, Experience, Identity in Women's Writing* (London: Pandora Press, 1987), p. 2.

7 Epigraph to Jane Dowson and Alice Entwistle, *A History of 20th Century British Women's Poetry*, p. 1, quoted from Jo Shapcott's interview in *Poetry London* 36 (Summer 2001).

8 Claire Buck, 'Poetry and the Women's Movement in Post-War Britain', in James Acheson and Romana Huk, eds., *Contemporary British Poetry: Essays in Theory and Criticism* (New York: State University of New York Press, 1996, pp. 81–111); Dowson and Entwistle, *History of 20th Century British Women's Poetry*, pp. 139–52.

9 Dowson and Entwistle, title of chapter 7 of *History of 20th Century British Women's Poetry*, pp. 139–52.
10 Lilian Mohin, *One Foot on the Mountain*, Editorial Introduction, pp. 3–4.
11 Claire Buck, 'Poetry and the Women's Movement, p. 88–91; Deryn Rees-Jones, *Consorting with Angels*, pp. 146–47; Dowson and Entwistle, *History of 20th Century British Women's Poetry*, pp. 140, 146–47.
12 Alison Fell et al., *Licking the Bed Clean: Five Feminist Poets* (London, Teeth Imprints, 1978), *Smile Smile Smile Smile* (London: Sheba Feminist Press, 1980), Michelene Wandor and Michèle Roberts, *Cutlasses and Earrings* (London: Playbook, 1977); Chris Cherry et al., *Hens in the Hay* (Edinburgh: Stramullion Co-Operative Ltd, 1980); Lilian Mohin, ed., *Beautiful Barbarians: Poetry by Lesbian Feminists* (London: Only Women Press, 1980).
13 See Website of www.womensliberation.org (accessed 28 November 2014) and Lilian Mohin, ed., *Beautiful Barbarians: Poetry by Lesbian Feminists* (London: Only Women Press, 1980).
14 Claire Buck, 'Poetry and the Women's Movement', p. 87.
15 Caroline Halliday, 'Confession', Judith Kazantzis, 'The Bath', in *One Foot*, pp. 54, 119.
16 Gillian Allnutt, 'The Talking Princess', in *One Foot*, p. 88.
17 Alison Fell, 'To Maria', in *One Foot*, pp. 15–16.
18 The (New York) Redstockings Manifesto, quoted in Anna Coote and Bea Campbell, *Sweet Freedom: The Struggle for Women's Liberation* (London: Picador, 1982), p. 15.
19 Jan Montefiore, *Feminism and Poetry*, pp. 11–13.
20 Fleur Adcock, ed., *The Faber Book of 20th Century Women's Poetry*, p. 13.
21 Buck, 'Poetry and the Women's Movement in postwar Britain' in James Acheson and Romana Huk, eds, *Contemporary British Poetry: Essays in Theory and Criticism* (Albany: SUNY Press, 1996), pp. 98–99; Alison Fell, 'Girl's Gifts', in *One Foot*, pp. 11–12; Montefiore, *Feminism and Poetry*, pp. 18–19.
22 Anne Stevenson, 'Writing as a Women', in Mary Jacobus, ed., *Women Writing and Writing About Women* (London: Croom Helm, 1979), pp. 174–75.
23 Carol Rumens, ed., *Making for the Open*, pp. xv–xvi.
24 See Vicki Bertram 'Post-Feminist Poetry? "One More Word for Balls"', Huk and Acheson, eds., *Contemporary British Poetry*, pp. 269–92.
25 Couzyn, *Contemporary Women Poets*, pp. 34–40. The introduction to Plath (pp. 145–48) is biographical, not critical.
26 Linda France, *Sixty Women Poets*, editorial introduction, p. 14.
27 Stevie Smith, 'A Dream of Comparison', in *Collected Poems* (London: Allen Lane, 1975), pp. 231–34.
28 Rees-Jones, *Consorting with Angels*, pp. 86–88.
29 Patricia Beer, 'In Memory of Stevie Smith', in *Collected Poems*, 1988.
30 See particularly Rees-Jones, *Consorting with Angels*, pp. 94–97.
31 Wendy Mulford, 'Notes on Writing: A Marxist/ Feminist Viewpoint,' *Red Letters* 9 (1979), reprinted in M. Wandor, *On Gender and Writing* (London: Pandora Press 12983), pp. 31–41.
32 Wendy Mulford, 'Curved ... Odd ... Irregular: A Vision of Contemporary Women's Poetry', *Women: A Cultural Revew* 1:3 (Winter 1990), p. 263.

33 Quotations from Dowson and Entwistle, *History of 20th Century British Women's Poetry*, pp. 168, 165. See also Buck 'Poetry and the Women's Movement', pp. 95–97.
34 Bertram, *Gendering Poetry*, pp. 38–39.
35 Carol Ann Duffy, 1988, quoted in Bertram, *Gendering Poetry*, p. 86.
36 Kate Clanchy, 1996, quoted in Dowson and Entwistle, *History of 20th C British Women's Poetry*, p. 175.
37 Michelene Wandor, 'Pin Money', in *One Foot*; Gillian Allnutt, 'Convent', in France, ed., *Sixty Women Poets*, p. 28.
38 Michèle Roberts, 'I Have Been Wanting to Mourn', *One Foot*, p. 194; Wendy Cope, 'You're Not Allowed' and 'Daily Help', in *Family Values* (London: Faber, 2012), pp. 10–13.
39 Carol Gilfillan, 'Blood We Are Taught to Hate', in *One Foot*, p. 46; Feaver, 'Women's Blood', in Rees-Jones, ed., *Modern Women Poets*, p. 217.
40 Grace Nichols, 'Invitation', in *The Fat Black Woman's Poems* (London: Virago 1984), p. 13; Helen Dunmore, 'Wild Strawberries', in France, ed., *Sixty Women Poets*, pp. 120–21.
41 Rees-Jones, *Consorting with Angels* p. 224, quoting Shapcott's interview with Janet Philips, *Poetry Review* 91 (Spring 2001).
42 Andrew Marvell, 'To His Coy Mistress', in Alastair Fowler, ed., *The New Oxford Book of Seventeenth Century Verse* (Oxford: Oxford University Press, 1991), p. 591; Jo Shapcott, 'Vegetable Love', 'In the Bath', in *Phrase Book* (Oxford: Oxford University Press, 1992) pp. 15, 28; W. H. Gardner, ed., *Poems of Gerard Manley Hopkins* (London: Oxford University Press, 1963), p. 73.
43 Rees-Jones, *Consorting with Angels*, p. 158.
44 U. A. Fanthorpe, 'Waiting Gentlewoman', in *Collected Poems 1978–2003* (Calstock: Cornwall, 2005), p. 98.
45 Carol Ann Duffy, 'Standing Female Nude', in *Selected Poems* (London: Penguin 1994), p. 20.
46 Carol Ann Duffy, 'Psychopath', in *Selected Poems*, p. 46.
47 Rees-Jones, *Consorting with Angels*, p. 158.
48 Carol Ann Duffy, 'Queen Kong', in *The World's Wife* (London: Picador, 1999), pp. 31–32.
49 Carol Ann Duffy, 'Frau Freud', 'Mrs Aesop', 'Pygmalion's Bride', 'Eurydice', 'Circe', in *The World's Wife*, pp. 55, 19, 52, 59, 47.
50 Rees-Jones, *Consorting with Angels*, p. 163.
51 Jo Shapcott 'Goat', 'Vegetable Love', 'Her Lover's Ear', in *Phrase Book* (Oxford: Oxford University Press, 1992), pp. 11, 15, 18.
52 Bertram, *Gendering Poetry*, p. 103.
53 Rees-Jones, *Consorting with Angels*, pp. 224–27.
54 Bertram, *Gendering Poetry*, p. 121.
55 Grace Nichols, 'The Fat Black Woman Goes Shopping', 'Thoughts Drifting through the Fat Black Woman's Head while Having a Full Bubble Bath', *The Fat Black Woman's Poems*, pp. 11, 15.
56 Jackie Kay, *The Adoption Papers* (Newcastle on Tyne: Bloodaxe Books, 1991), epigraph (untitled) p. 10; 'Chapter 5: The Tweed Hat Dream', p. 19; 'Chapter 6: The Telling', p. 22; 'Chapter 7: Black Bottom' pp. 25, 27.
57 Dowson and Entwistle, *History of 20th Century British Women's Poetry*, p. 199.

14

FIONA BECKET

Ecopoetics and Poetry

This essay follows a particular trajectory through examples of writing since 1945, spanning the post-war period and culminating in the present, to consider to what extent specific political, social and economic contexts have shaped, produced and inflected 'nature poetry'. The alternative to proceeding by means of reference to the polarised, oppositional values of 'nature' and 'culture' is often to project a continuum, although such a structure is inevitably implicitly also informed by the dominant binary. Ecopoetics sounds as though it is taking 'nature poetry' to be the principal category for discussion, but *oikos* is global, local, regional, animal, vegetable, mineral. When urban culture produces urban poetry, there is the critical tendency for a weighting towards metropolitan creativity (and often by implication 'the modern') to kick in, or the continuum reappears in the spirit of mapping the urban as constituting an alternative nature to, say, the pastoral or the post-pastoral. In this spirit, much post-war British poetry could be said to inhabit the provincial/city dichotomy in which questions of place significantly inflect questions of subjectivity. Other conceptual dichotomies with significant theoretical agency persist, such as the explicitly anthropocentric 'human-non-human'. Conceived within the emergent field of the environmental humanities, an ecopoetics destabilises the power of these binaries, and informs the ways in which poetic language and poetic creativity hold hardwired dualistic structures of thought and apprehension to account. This process, which is critical and dynamic, is separable from *ecopoesis* which might be more aptly understood as the making of a home ground in language in ways which, we might have to accept, are not bound by the narrow association of *oikos* with an *a priori* 'nature'. In this context it is important not to see 'environment' as a cuckoo-value, steadily pushing other values out of the nest in the scramble to raise *ecopoesis* above other creative and thoughtful, and equally political, trajectories in post-war British poetry. As Jon Silkin asserts in his 'Note on "Flower" Poems', printed as an afterword in *Nature with Man* (1965), 'To remove nature, to isolate it from human nature and then write about it, is an extremity as unproductive as the one which sees all nature as a (symbolic) version of man'.[1] In Silkin we get a clear sense of a poet who, in insisting on contiguity between 'nature' and 'man', produces a body of work in which nature poetry is nothing if not connected to reflections on the political, economic and social contexts that informed, in different degrees, post-war British writing: the aftermath of atrocity manifested in death camps, and the nuclear bomb; the divisions of the Cold War and the power of the state; reformulations of the human subject, and the animal other, in the phases of late capitalism. It is in relation to these contexts, it could be argued, that 'nature' poetry is framed, and extended, in the period after 1945, with a significant conceptual shift occurring at the point of the emergence of the grand narrative of anthropogenic climate change and the consequent re-scaling of the relationships between local environments and planetary ones.

If ecocriticism is something of a late arrival, ecopoetics is not so, and what follows is a far from exhaustive account of some of the ways in which British poetry in the period under discussion fashions, responds to, and produces *oikos*. For some, the balance in the present work will appear misguided – there is arguably a disproportionate emphasis on the generally critically underexamined Jon Silkin compared with the towering presence of Ted Hughes in the period, for instance, whose work is barely touched on in this essay; but Ian Hamilton Finlay is treated as central, a major figure in the exploration of the intersections of place, space and word. More recent poets, writing in contexts that are informed by the emergence of environmentalism and the maturation of green politics, include John Burnside, Kathleen Jamie and Alice Oswald. Because the field is international, there is something of a distortion introduced in the confinement of a discussion around ecopoetics to British writing. Nevertheless, it is hoped that the contexts invoked usefully suggest a conversation about a trajectory in British poetry since 1945 that could be said to produce an ecopoetics. If the discussion is inflected by the familiar binaries of human–non-human, nature-culture, it is also characterised by a consciousness that one of the tasks of ecopoetics is to scrutinise those distinctions in ways which throw into relief the multiple intersections of ethics and poetry.

Ian Hamilton Finlay's work is characterised by extraordinary diversity. The garden space, in Finlay's work, is a space in which to encounter poems that are 'environmental' by virtue of the combination of language or semic elements, materials and location. At Little Sparta, Finlay's garden near Dunsyre, pathways ensure the participation of the visitor/reader and lead to built and inscribed environments: fallen pillars redolent of temples, bee hives, aphorisms and poems removed from the page and relocated to unexpected materials and forms (portals, bridges); the unexpected juxtaposition of boats' names and classifications, and toy-sized aircraft carriers. Poem-objects to be placed outdoors demand a degree of reflection on materials (stone, glass, wood) as well as processes (letter-carving, engraving). Finlay argued for poems 'as natural as the inscription on a stone of a memorial'.[2] One can hold in one's hand a flimsy home-made object which appears to minimise language, such as 'Kamikaze Butterflies',[3] but one can also stand on a graven stone and look from it over a landscape that is uniquely informed by the participant, the one who looks. Finlay's work (not only the constructions-in-space) could be said to constitute the terms of an ecopoetics because it is interested in, and engaged in creating, connections between human culture (of which language is one index), the human subject and the environment. The poem-objects supplement, augment, define and even oppose the environments within which they address meaning. Such objects of poetry also appeal to the temporality of materials, different from human temporality: they cannot remain pristine in the weathered environments and micro-climates of Little Sparta, but must inevitably have change inscribed on them by the elements and the local conditions – not regionality so much as bioregionality. There is no unequivocal or direct reference in Finlay's work that could retrospectively constitute a manifesto or 'pilot plan' to justify the environmental integrity of his work. Nevertheless, some of the most effective work (such as 'Wave/Rock' [1968]) brilliantly strips away the 'I' which, retained, recreates the distance between the participant-viewer and nature that ecopoetics might seek to close.[4] In a letter to fellow visual poet and originator of the 'typestract', Dom Sylvester Houédard, Finlay states, 'The new poetry will be a poetry without the word "I". It will be silent, & will be a sign of peace & sanity.... I think self poetry is bad, now'.[5]

Finlay's preoccupation with the interconnections to be developed between place, a regional culture (such as an island culture as in the Orkney poems) and a global sense – as we see in 'Net/Planet' (*Selections*, 148) – as well as the connections to be made visible between language, materials and place constitutes an aesthetic that is not separable from a consciousness of environment that contains and implicates the human. Dom Sylvester Houédard astutely observed that Finlay's

> love of humour (& trouble), of trout strong tea & rain – his sense of tradition – make 'this strange place, the world, a home': his awareness of this strangeness of the place, of the need for poets, poetoypography, to make it unstrange, is his opening to the nonsemantic.[6]

The concentration on making the world 'unstrange' as a condition of human dwelling is important if we are to understand the shaping of eco-consciousness in relation to Finlay's work. As always, the terminology is crucial. In Finlay's 'Detached Sentences on Gardening' lurks an aphorism that begs, in our moment, to be examined in the full glare of contemporary green critique: 'Ecology is Nature-Philosophy *secularised*' (*Selections*, 179). In this pithy sentiment is embedded Finlay's distaste for an impersonal culture of knowledge. There is a suspicion here of an attitude to environment that overlooks mind. Something of the subjective remains, constructively for Finlay, in the casting of knowledge (and experience) as 'Nature-Philosophy' to which 'Ecology', as an expression of circumscribed knowledge, seems an impoverished antidote – the response merely of an anti-Nature epoch (the present) to place or, perhaps, to places. Finlay goes on to assert that 'Classical gardens elevate nature. That for the present age is their crime' (*Selections*, 185). So to argue for the development of an ecopoetics in Finlay's work is not to assume an unproblematic or uncritical intellectual engagement with either the doctrines or the discourse of environmental politics. On the contrary, it is to attend to Finlay's *sui generis* approach to the categories of 'garden' and 'nature', even to 'writer', informed by the ways in which a highly personal sense of classicism, secularism and barbarism inflect his creativity. Finlay's garden, to take the example of the 'book' of Little Sparta, is a manifestation and expression of a highly individual nature-philosophy the forms of which implicate tranquillity and violence, wit and word-play, reflections on conflict, revolution and utopias. It is not an ecological project. If Finlay's dedication to the pastoral, reformulated in his own terms, and the idyllic space of the garden, was tested in later years – producing the garden republic and reflecting the oppositional stance the poet adopted in the context of external pressures – the return ultimately was to the contemplation and refashioning of space that first inspired him. Finlay's achievement was not to bring out innate features of the actual space, say, of Little Sparta, but to create new, surprising and connected spaces/narratives within the environs of his home.

Finlay inhabits and creates environments and meta-environments, and examines and exploits the shifting boundaries between nature and culture. Charles Tomlinson has been called an 'ecological' poet, described by Timothy Clark as interested in 'modes of habitation, with the frontier or space of negotiation between human and non-human', best exemplified in *A Peopled Landscape* (1963).[7] Finlay's landscapes are inscribed and perhaps 'voiced' rather than peopled, but Tomlinson requires individuals and communities (the farmer's wife, the land labourer, the night shift at the steel foundry) to be established in a certain relation to the spaces they inhabit. That these spaces have a material presence to which poetry should in some sense be true is a perception that is tied to notions of creative responsibility: 'Distrust / that poet who must symbolize / your stair into / an analogue / of what was never there' (*New Collected Poems*, 77). In this spirit the 'purple tide' of Charles Tomlinson's bluebells (NCP, 473) with its appeal to the sense modalities of sight and smell, appeals also to language as indicative of the limitations of human understanding and, paradoxically, a principal field of creativity. 'If they are blue', the poem reflects, 'It is only our words so call and colour them' (474). The bluebells retain a significance and 'presence' (474) apart from the poet as *aisthetes*. It is this figure that stimulates the meditation in 'The Tree' on the image, in a poem which is characterised by its uncompromising analysis of appearances. Tomlinson's materialist tendency reveals in the object a self-sufficiency so that the felled tree and sawn timber is properly an iteration of the living tree rather than a diminution of it. The poem stages the effects of eyes being opened onto the otherness of the tree, resistant and irreducible to a category as instrumental as resource, or as an object that has been set aside. Its resource value here is more aesthetic than it is economic. What is exposed by the tree-feller's saw is 'a map of grains and stains', framed by the 'rind' (98) and revived by the wash of recent rain which has 'flushed the colour through' (99) while the cut sections of the trunk form a sculptural unity in the place where the living tree grew. The aestheticisation of the tree is not secondary to its original integrity, nor is it a means of the self-aggrandisement of the one who perceives as the poet fashions the encounter with non-human things for the consumption of others (readers of poetry). Rather, the poem reveals in the encounter with the object a process of self-effacement in which the poet's agency is crucially secondary to that of the tree ('I / between its Janus faces, / was compelled to echo it' [99]). Ultimately, this is an ethical stance which displaces the relationship of human mastery over non-human nature into something more reciprocal – doubly effective in a poem in which the tree has been brought down.

Of course it is a risk to extract from a single poem, or poems from a single volume, a general principle, but there are links between Tomlinson's work and Silkin's insistence on revealing, or abiding by, the connection between man and nature. The challenge to the reader might then be to understand how such contiguity fashions the creative endeavour to produce the 'materialist poetry' most accomplished in, for instance, *Nature with Man*.[8] In the 'Note on "Flower" Poems' Silkin is concerned with the 'proximity' of human and non-human nature: intelligence rather than consciousness stimulates man's separation from a capitalised 'Nature' but such a separation is always already partial and itself contingent. 'Proximity' is a more positive and arguably a more powerful concept than the 'estrangement' between man and non-human nature that Merle E. Brown identifies in the 'Afterword' to Silkin's *The Peaceable Kingdom*, first published in 1954, although estrangement carries with it the unavoidable possibility of connection: distance only qualifies the nearness implied by 'proximity'.[9] In, and transcending, *The Peaceable Kingdom*, connection is possible only through an unsentimental and selfless love, whether love of the 'unnecessary beasts' in 'Caring for Animals' ('Attend to the unnecessary beasts' is the poem's injunction [PK, 30]) or that shown by the stooping woman who feeds the birds and is not separable from them in her craving for the hand that 'bears the profound gift of love' (PK, 31). The myths and parables, history and natural histories of *The Peaceable Kingdom* combine with memory and connection to produce poems whose ethical power is not divorced from the careful acts of attention paid to the damaged fly, hopping birds, running foxes and human subjects. In the Epilogue to *The Peaceable Kingdom* is an assertion: 'All the people in my poems walk into the dark' (PK, 39). This is one detail in the highly conscious pattern of variations on the language of *The Peaceable Kingdom*'s Prologue. The pairing of Prologue and Epilogue as very particular 'bookends' or, better, the twin cardinals of the volume, is a pairing which permits the poet to make himself visible as the custodian of the society therein. Human and non-human animals alike who are subject to violence, grief, pain and loss are also assured of the poet's ethical guardianship – a position of moral authority which emerges out of acts of creation: for instance, of the tiny fly that dies, 'His speck of body accused me there.... So I must give his life a meaning' (PK, 17). By the time of Silkin's final volume, the kingdom, subject to the poet's paternal care, is transformed into a republic in which poets are 'bitter-seeking animals' who must 'make conscience' (*Making a Republic* [MR], 36).

Perhaps Silkin's most accomplished volume in terms of *ecopoesis* is *Nature with Man*. This is a claim made not with reference to its content – although the Flower poems are perhaps central to our understanding of Silkin's shaping of the terms of difference that define the human–non-human continuum – but in relation to its careful consideration of the social, the human, often *in extremis*, in ways that implicate forms of wildness. In Silkin's poetry, nuclear weaponry is a continuation of, and distortion of, nature and emerges as a dominant signifier of the capacity of human kind to engineer the reversion of culture to nature. By the force of negation, in its power to lay waste indiscriminately, the bomb-technology is the Cold War's major contribution to environmental consciousness along with intensive agro-business, and industrial-scale pollution of macro as well as micro-environments. The first section of 'Defence', an anti-war poem dismissive of authority and contemptuous of ruling-class paternalism, is almost discursive and stages the attempts of an official, a woman, to inform the citizenry about personal safety in the event of nuclear attack. This is a redefinition of what was the home front, as the incapacity of simple domestic things to protect the body from radiation is underlined – even after Hiroshima and Nagasaki, government advice cynically upholds the efficacy of brown paper and urine-soaked sheets. The nuclear bomb itself is unnameable. It is 'the thing' which is of nature and re-forms nature. The blast will 'infect' water, a verb that, unlike its alternative, 'contaminate', suggests disease rather than fallout, a linguistic clue to suggest the estrangement from the phenomenon experienced by the minor civil servant as she imparts her wisdom. The tone of mockery is suspended in the poem's second section at the heart of which are the syntactically counterintuitive lines, 'The whole of nature / Is a preying upon' (NM, 19). These lines divide scenes of bodies – the unborn, and insects – liquefying and fusing in the intense heat of nuclear explosion, from reflections on the moral capacity of mankind as the highest kind of animal, 'whose mind is large' that he might 'Legislate for / All passionate things, / All sensate things' (19). The poem institutes a willed degeneration of the differences between animal and vegetable in its evocation of 'the sensuous / Grass, whose speech is all / In its sharp, bending blade' (19). These are wonderful, oblique references to mankind's moral authority, thrown into relief by the genuine capacity of scientific advances to re-scale the human. The environment of the front room as the locale projected to protect the individual caught in the zone of the bomb blast has also become the global environment. The final section of the poem represents the official as dwarfed by the sphere, the globe (a manufactured pearl) on which she appears to rest, turning it, like some rudimentary yet familiar creature, with her feet, as if all other mobility is denied her.

The first poem in *Nature with Man* shares its title and begins the book boldly by figuring the human as a catastrophic reaching out, an extension of nature that turns on itself, biting through its own neck in a figuration of embodiment which is redolent of raw and meaty forms and which hints, in the naming of 'Scale, sinew' (9), at evolutionary phases. Nature's human head, once severed, has rolled into the bullrushes that fringe the bruised earth, and in doing so 'Has soured the earth, whose body / Decays and perishes' (NM, 9). On one level the poem is a mournful lamentation ('O pity, pity, pity' [10]) for a nature that can be figured only in terms of dehiscence, pain and decay. The rhetorical shift from the second to the final section fashions a movement from the interrogative 'But are the humans here?' (9) to a denunciation of nature's 'most developed / And treacherous creature, man' (10) whose principal manifestation of agency is to redirect towards himself the plenitude of nature which has, true to the poem's language of embodiment, become a:

Monstrous and huge eye:
The entire process

> Of nature perverted
> Into the search for him. (NM 10)

In this way the poem that launches the collection aggressively interrogates the even-handedness of the connective 'with' in the poem's title (and in the volume's). Nevertheless, to interpret the poem as a singular rejection of the human is to overlook the clear sense that it offers of fundamental connectivity – even if such connectivity is impossible to control or predict, and uneven. The dominant strain of metaphor in 'Nature with Man' is muscular – the earth is bruised, the soul is 'weedy' (weak as stalks of grass) forced apart from, and, as a singularity, unable to connect with, the 'membered flesh'. Corporeality, however, is othered and bettered by the force of ideas emanating from minds (plural) which conceptually inhabit the severed head. Equally conceptually, ideas are figured as reticulated. Minds give out:

> Great reticulations
> Of ideas, nets wilful and sharp (10).

The fundamental form or model that drives the poem, then, is ecological; a form that in its most raw state is without the tempering power of ethical consideration – 'In pride and thought that cut / The smiling face of pleasure' (10). It is a poem, too, that, as we have seen, insists on soul, diminishing but not absent from a text that fast enacts its private genesis or creation myth triangulating bloody body, shrinking soul and dynamic mind.

No other poem could better begin this collection which, in a reticulated mode, prints poems that connect the social and the personal, the spiritual and the aesthetic, with the focus often on death, loss and pain. In the translations of Ungaretti, Silkin is clearly attracted by the ways in which place passes through human consciousness, often resulting in the abdication of ego so that powerful subjectivity gives way to a vision of integration – 'I / Most see myself / In the universe / A compliant / Thread' (26) – or where human being is most effectively figured with reference to the non-human as in 'The Child's Life'. The volume pivots on the 'child' poems near its centre but passes beyond the figure of the child and the questions stimulated by the nature of child-being, towards the flower poems that, while not formally separated or isolated from the rest, would appear to constitute the dominant grouping of poems in the volume – a collection which is concluded in the 1965 Chatto edition by Silkin's 'Note on "Flower" Poems' already alluded to in the present essay. 'The Child', 'The Continuance' and 'Something Has Been Teased from Me' are poems that engage with ideas of split-subjectivity in ways that consistently make an appeal to a world of non-human forms. This is particularly noticeable in 'Something Has Been Teased from Me' which develops a language of a reticulated network of stems, roots and soil, and of the fruiting body of the maternal form which, like the human form of the child, is barely present. Every human subject, in this poem, is communicable as root, reed, fibre, fruiting: the child ('it is grass I think this bone and blood / Is like' [37]) will 'grow like grass, wastefully' (38). Brilliant, however, is the subtle connectivity between maternal breast milk that 'trickles through the tubules' at the end of 'Something Has Been Teased from Me' and the first two lines of the next poem, 'Dandelion' (the first of the Flower poems in this edition):

> Slugs nestle where the stem
> Broken, bleeds milk. (38)

In such examples of reticulation, underpinned by a poetics that extends human subjectivity into the non-human world of forms and processes, is developed a literary ecology but one that is acutely sensitive to the personal and extra-personal experiences that inform the poetry.

To jump ahead, Kathleen Jamie's 'Daisies' (*The Tree House*, 32) offers an interesting parallel to Silkin's 'A Daisy'. Both poems begin with reference to the plants' undifferentiated number and common value. In Silkin's account of the daisy poem in the 'Note on "Flower" Poems' the concentration is on a quality of innocence 'got through experience' and, therefore, distinguished from naivety: the poet reaches for 'the uncompromising simplicity of the Daisy's appearance' (NM, 55). Silkin's daisy is not separable from the thought that underpins the collectivity of flower poems, and derives in part from the consideration given by the poet to the creative tensions between what is 'wild' and endures, and what is cultivated – the dual nature of flowers that informs the Note, in which questions of human experience are posed in botanical contexts, just as in *The Peaceable Kingdom* human 'types and situations' are approached through an engagement with non-human animal life (NM, 54). Whether or not this is a compromising anthropocentric manoeuvre is not the interesting question in relation to Silkin, and nor is it in relation to Jamie, whose daisy poem comes without a discursive framework or 'explanation'. In Silkin, the daisy is a thing, an object of contemplation. In Jamie's poem, in contrast, the daisies are voiced, a mode of addressing the reader which, in this collection, characterises only one other poem, 'The Wishing Tree', in which the theme of resilience in the face of human intervention – the tree as a conduit for superstitious behaviour – is the principal tone struck. Implicitly, 'The Wishing Tree' poses a question about agency in relation to the non-human. Cast as the 'wishing' tree (an oddly generic description which avoids species identity) it has visibility and significance as a result of its refashioning in the context of emotions like belief and hope. However, in an eco-materialist context the tree's agency, or to put it another way, the agency of trees, was never in doubt. Human intervention re-directs agency towards human concerns – in this instance the wishing tree becomes the repository of human hope manifested by the rough insertion of coins into its boughs. The local effect is to poison the immediate area of damage but the tree voices its capacity not only to endure but to flourish, and in this way 'The Wishing Tree' stages a triumphant return – 'I am still alive – / in fact, in bud' (TH, 4). The action of pressing coins into the soft, or green, tissue of the tree enacts a human-centred appeal to nature manifested in the donation of precious objects in a gesture that is itself an echo of older, forgotten activity: in antiquity, offering to the body of the earth/water something valuable in a theatre of exchange in which the potential of reciprocity between the divine and the human is a given. This recasting, through ritual, of the landscape into spiritual homeland, and the affect produced by natural features, is the subject of 'Hoard' in the same collection. The poem asks of the human subject, 'What kind of figure did he cut' (TH, 36). In 'Hoard' the human figure is diminished, has less definition, than either the bog moss, sphagnum, with which his wound is crammed, or, indeed, the wishing tree and, unlike the tree, the warrior who seeks blessing or benediction, is voiceless.

Jamie's daisies are given to voice their ubiquity. They are marked out by their commonality and abundance, but ultimately the poem is elegiac in that the developed metaphor of the flower's 'eye' culminates in a reflection on what the flower's temporality causes it to miss – the contrasting longevity of the cosmos, manifest in the night sky. The second part of the poem offers a concentration on sleep and death also redolent of Silkin's 'A Daisy' which asks of daisies 'Why should not one bring these to a funeral?' (NM, 43). The innocence invoked in the opening lines of Jamie's poem is not that which Silkin reaches for through experience – here Jamie's poem asks for an uncomplicated engagement with the plant: commonality is 'our nature, / were we not so, we wouldn't be daisies ...' (TH, 32). As in Silkin's flower poem there is much concentrated play on the 'day's eye', but in Jamie the limit of the nominal metaphor signals the limit of the plant's cultural significance – there is no constructed meaning in relation to daisies on the scale of that invested in, for example, the unique form of the wishing tree. The multitude is productive of 'innocence'. Silkin equates the closed petals of the daisy at night with the untroubled sleep of children. It is because he seeks to accommodate humanity in his reticulated universe that consciousness is implicated at all. 'A Daisy' – singular, not plural, because the multitude is composed of integrated individuals – unscented, makes its appeal to the eye, and the poem ends on a note which prioritises sensational knowledge. The daisy stimulates mind: 'And its invisible organ, / That feeling thing' (NM, 43).

In Tomlinson's 'The Tree' we noticed a moment in which the agency of the tree propelled the poet into an act of reciprocity, sustaining the engagement with non-human natural forms, and their ecologies. In Jamie's *The Tree House* in which the titular image could be said to invoke the place where we are ('where we've knocked together ... a dwelling of sorts' [TH, 42–43]), several poems reproduce the trope of watching/looking in ways that inform the imperatives as well as the challenges of such engagement. In 'Basking Shark', for instance, the poem accentuates the helplessness of the watcher on the cliffs for whom distance confirms one insight, that the basking shark is not beached but in its physical alignment with its environment 'could come to sense the absolute / limits of its realm' (TH, 23). A not unrelated note is struck in John Burnside's poem 'Koi', but the direction of travel is very different, away from a lyrical theorisation of direct encounter with the non-human other that reveals (inevitably) difference, and more towards the power of poetry to accommodate and create difference:

> The trick is to create a world
> From nothing
>   – not the sound a blackbird makes
> In drifted leaves (*Selected Poems*, 82)

Burnside's koi 'hang in a realm of their invention / with nothing that feels like home' (84). In this they have exceeded all expectations and are invested with a degree of resilience produced by creativity, but the questions that the 'living fish' ultimately prompt lead back to human imagining: 'we will ask / how much they know of us' (84). While the specific creative contexts of Jamie, Burnside and others are vital to understanding the power and reach of their work, from the point of view of environmental poetry their work plays out preoccupations to be discerned also in the body of Ted Hughes's work around whether, and how, the non-human other inhabits environments, being in possession neither of language nor, it has been surmised, 'World'. Those connections, however, are for a longer study.

In Alice Oswald's *Dart* (2002), to pick up this question, the point of interest does not reside so much in the river's 'mutterings', to quote the poet's preamble, but in the fact that the poem's form aligns semiotic space and the river's ecology, which includes the fact of human habitation. In the brief preamble to the poem Oswald describes the work as 'a sound-map of the river', a formulation which disrupts assumptions of mapping as primarily a visual schematisation of human and physical geographies, and which redirects attention to the aural experience of the text. This redirection does not undermine but, rather, complements the visual elements of the text, in places that mimic a highly literary mode of self-consciousness – for instance in the blank space of a page which is headed 'silence' (D, 22) – and in the invocation of speaking subjects, indicated in a font smaller than that of the body of the text in the right-hand margins ('Naturalist', 'forester', 'swimmer', 'oyster gatherers', for example). These are not, in fact, individuated speakers but operate as elements in the way the river's singular voice, 'water's soliloquy' (D, 48), is scored. While it is a given to interpret this as a decentring of the human element, literally marginalised in the appearance of the poem, it is perhaps more productive to view the text as an attempt to integrate cultural and environmental forms in ways that throw familiar hierarchies into relief. The substance of the poem attends to human activity understood in relation to, and oriented towards, the very different temporality of the river, 'a whole millennium going by in the form of a wave' (D, 45). The form of *Dart* embodies the wave – the wave of language, of generation, of change: 'all these scrambled and screw-like currents / and knotty altercations of torrents' (D, 42).

Dart also identifies what some might call Oswald's bioregional consciousness although a recent commentator has argued for the evidence in *Dart* that Oswald can be seen has having a 'glocal' purview – a formulation that acknowledges the immediate concentration in the poem on the intimate histories of the river Dart and its tributaries in its southwest locale, but which also recognises in the poem a more global frame of reference.[10] The poem indeed acknowledges the wider world in ways that necessarily reveal economic and other forms of impact on the communities of the Dart, and not without a tragic inflection: the salmon stocks are depleted by rival fishing off Greenland, 'That's why we're cut-throats on weekdays' (D, 41); and the 'lad from Kevicks' on his blighted solo journey by catamaran to New Zealand to meet up with a girlfriend who did not wait (D, 35). The poem also negates an undifferentiated sense of the local – 'Dartmouth and Kingsweir – / two worlds' (D, 43). More pressing than the relation between the local and global in Oswald's thought, however, are the ways in which *Dart* relates the natural ecological processes of the river to disparate and often conflicting fields of human activity – that of the licensed angler and the poacher, and the bailiffs, for instance; the different experiences of the day trippers on the river compared to the difficult and dangerous existence of numerous river workers, or those whose industries depend, like the tin worker, on the extent to which water can be managed to give up its mineral resources.

That observable natural phenomena have to be seen in relation to human concerns is evident in *Dart* and produces the complex connectivity which we associate with Oswald's long poems. The poem aestheticises the river and is highly self-conscious about the process in its collage of metonymic (semiotic) reference. Cutting across the axis of historical accounts and individuated narratives is the recourse to myth and, on occasion, to its domestic echoes. There are shades of Ian Hamilton Finlay in the pleasure taken by Oswald in the names of boats:

> Oceanides Atlanta Proserpina Minerva
> yachts with their river-shaking engines
> Lizzie of Lymington Doris of Dit'sum (D 34).

Elsewhere in the poem the waternymph and the goddess, the 'King of the Oakwoods' and, ultimately, the Hellenic Proteus become figures for natural phenomena that reveal the power of symbolic meaning.

To conclude, this discussion has been selective in the examples highlighted and is acutely aware of the exclusions involved in the attempt to make the idea of ecopoetics meaningful and relevant. Considering many of the examples adduced above a key figure for consideration is the perceiver, the *aisthetes*, now removed from the ideological insistence on the 'aesthete' as an historical category, to be responsive primarily to abstractions of beauty: ecopoetics acknowledges the ironies produced by such a project. Ecocentrism is produced by the understanding that the world we inhabit is more non-human than human, and acknowledges that the false duality of 'nature and man' has produced enough unacceptable consequences to permit the interrogation of narratives of economic and social progress in the wake of environmental destruction. To feel towards an ecopoetics is to acknowledge what is at stake in the making of *oikos* and it is, therefore, implicated in narratives that interrogate inherited, 'naturalised' habits of thought that constitute nature as inferior. Ecopoetics extends the potential of language to explore and create the contiguity of non-human and human environments, and is sensitive to established hierarchies and, to invoke Silkin, reticulated models of connection. In this context, evidently, it embodies and enacts an ethical cognizance of non-human otherness and does so in contexts that acknowledge the ideological environments which produce us.

NOTES

1 Jon Silkin, 'Note on "Flower" Poems', in *Nature with Man* (London: Chatto and Windus, The Hogarth Press, 1965), pp. 54–56, p. 56. I take this opportunity to thank Jon Glover for his generosity and kindness in permitting, without a second thought, the extent of quoted material from Silkin's work in this essay.

2 Ian Hamilton Finlay, Letter to Henry Clyne, 1966, quoted in Alec Finlay, ed., *Selections: Ian Hamilton Finlay* (Berkeley, Los Angeles, London: University of California Press, 2012), p. 37.

3 Ian Hamilton Finlay, *Kamikaze Butterflies Cherry Blossom Splinters* (Dunsyre: Wild Hawthorn Press, 1973).

4 Ian Hamilton Finlay, 'Wave/Rock', *Selections*, p. 28. This poem was originally fashioned in glass in 1966.

5 Quoted in Dom Sylvester Houédard, 'Concrete Poetry & Ian Hamilton Finlay', in Nicola Simpson, ed., *Notes from the Cosmic Typewriter: The Life and Work of Dom Sylvester Houédard* (Occasional Papers, 2012), pp. 157–63, p. 162.

6 Houédard, 'Concrete Poetry & Ian Hamilton Finlay', in *Notes from the Cosmic Typewriter: The Life and Work of Dom Sylvester Houédard*, p. 162. 'Poetoypography' is a composite construction that acknowledges Finlay's skill in, and passion for, toy making as an adjunct to 'poetic' creativity. Of the toy Finlay said 'It is open in the right way' ('Concrete Poetry & Ian Hamilton Finlay', p. 162).

7 Timothy Clark, *Charles Tomlinson*, Writers and Their Work Series (Plymouth: Northcote House, 1999), p. 6.

8 Terry Eagleton describes the ways in which Silkin might be seen as a materialist poet, picking up on Silkin's use, articulated in the 'Note on "Flower" Poems', of 'complexity'. Eagleton identifies Silkin's sense of 'the disparate, contingent, unfusable features of the natural process, and of the oblique, precarious relations between that process and history', Terry Eagleton, 'Nature and Politics in Jon Silkin', *Poetry Review* 69:4 (June 1980), 8. I am much obliged to Emma Trott for drawing my attention to this essay.

9 Jon Silkin (1954), *The Peaceable Kingdom*, rev. by Jon Silkin, illustrated by Bruce Chandler (Hancock, ME: The Heron Press, 1975).

10 Rowan Middleton, 'Connection, Disconnection and the Self in Alice Oswald's *Dart*', *Green Letters: Studies in Ecocriticism* (2014), np.

15

PETER BARRY

Poetry and the City

It is impossible to represent something as vast and complex as a city within the 'little room' of a brief lyric poem. Writers who seek to portray cities use 'big forms' like the novel, often sequences of novels, like the twenty that make up Zola's Rougon-Macquart cycle on Paris. All a short poem can do is give glimpses of a city, but that has strong validity and appeal, as cities are experienced mainly in disjunctive snippets and glimpses, even when we live in them for many years. Here, for example, is the opening of the second of seven sonnet-length pieces which make up a short sequence called 'Fantasia on a Theme from IKEA – *seven descants on "ground"*' in Philip Gross's collection *The Water Table* (Bloodaxe, 2009), which won the T. S. Eliot poetry prize in that year: '*Dream On!* The girl in the car park snaps / her phone shut. End of story. She folds him away, / … slaps / him in her hipster pocket, snug / … / Behind her, billboards plead: Dream *this*'. (p. 19). The girl and the overheard fragment of conversation are a text without a context, a fragment randomly collaged against the urban 'ground' of billboards, and only retrospectively thematised, or recollected in tranquillity, by the poetic, motif of dreaming. When the phone is pocketed, he (the disappointed dreamer) 'may / be as close as he'll get (and yet not know) / to what he's dreamed of', while we (proxy reader-dreamers) can think 'So / much they need us, dreams. We are such stuff: / flesh, matter.' And he (the poet, or, anyway, the poem) asks 'Where else to found / their celestial cities but on grit and clay, / hormones and DNA?' It seems in our age incongruous that from biblical to post-medieval times, the countryside represented the tainted, post-lapsarian realm, in which a living might be scraped by sweated labour, while the city stood for the celestial hereafter, the easeful City of God. Yet this form of reversed pastoralism is a frequent subcurrent in urban poetry. By inserting the word 'celestial' before 'cities', the potential locale of Eden-like fulfilment is urbanised, so that the sense of closure proper to a sonnet can be neatly attached: 'Where else to ground / their being? The phone in her pocket chirrs, cheep / cheep. Poor lovebird. She puts it to sleep.'

So the disembodied glimpse, often with elements of reversed pastoral, is one way of representing the city in poetry, and the ultimate archetype of this trope is perhaps Pound's 'In a Station of the Metro'. Another way of doing cities in poems is to extend the glimpse, by taking a more prolonged look at a small part of a city, at 'Part of a Place', to borrow the first chapter title of David Kennedy's *Douglas Dunn* (Northcote House, 2008) which is about Dunn's debut collection *Terry Street* of 1969. This sequence of eighteen poems is about the terraced street in Hull where Dunn lodged as a student, and it takes up less than half of the book to which it gives its name. Dennis O'Driscoll writes that Larkin was responsible for 'arranging the manuscript, advocating *Terry Street* as the title (Dunn himself had fancied *Faces in the Street*)'.[1] Dunn's title would have been adequate if the Terry Street poems had been mixed in with the others, but the dominant mood would then have been a more familiar urban mode of male writing, where the male gaze is drawn to a glimpsed female face that becomes the focus of sustained romantic longing (as in the first poem of Part 2; 'But there's one face, seen only once, / A fragment of a crowd ... Those we secretly love, who never know of us'). This is familiar territory – an urban archetype with Petrarchan origins, and in a statement about *Terry Street* Dunn remarks that these poems are not 'slum-pastorals'. The first poem (perhaps the weakest in the sequence) gestures towards a cultural overview imbued with Raymond Williams and Richard Hoggart, contrasting student hipness ('being seen with a copy of *International Times*, // Or the Liverpool Poets') with working-class gaucherie ('Spanish Burgundy, or beer in rampant pubs' against a background of 'The litter of pop rhetoric'). The poems are at their best when they seem just to look and listen, without trying to be sociological, and the very best ('Men of Terry Street', 'The Terry Street Fusiliers', 'A Removal From Terry Street', 'On Roofs of Terry Street', 'Late Night Walk Down Terry Street') are mostly the shorter poems, which have 'Terry Street' in the title. The less successful ones try to suggest the inner lives of the people observed, usually women, as in 'The Silences', where we are told that 'Looking at worn clothes, they sense impermanence. / They have nothing to do with where they live, the silence tells them', which is perhaps too obviously a projection of what the poet himself feels. Inevitably, *Terry Street* re-visited seems changed, but its best poems in this older urban mode have never been bettered.

Another technique of urban poetics is to represent the city by its own absence, by where it conspicuously is not, using elements of the surreal, a formula which is increasingly common, and sometimes amounts to a form of magical urban-poetic realism. Thus, Jacob Polley's 'The North-South Divide', imagines that the south of England has disappeared under the flood plains of climate-change, so that 'a whale hangs a moment / singing in the vault/ of St Paul's' and 'hagfish haunt Leicester Square, / anglerfish twinkle / through Trafalgar's oyster beds'. It ends: 'the South you knew / … / from nursery rhymes and bad news / is gathering a storm … / … / to its … / heavy-breakered bosom'. (*Identity Parade*, ed. Roddy Lumsden, Bloodaxe, 2010, pp. 273–74). This poem – it has fewer than forty minimalist lines – is a vest-pocket epic that envisages a Britain where there is nothing south of Manchester but sea, and the metropolis has become, not a Poundian mosaic of crystallized memories, a 'city now in the mind indestructible', but randomly-drifting flotsam of Ozymandian detritus.

Paul Farley uses the same technique in 'Treacle' (from *The Boy from the Chemist Is Here to See You* (Picador, 1998), where a tin of Tate & Lyle treacle evokes the city that produced it: 'Feel the weight of this tin in your hand, / … / breathe its scent, something lost from our streets // like horse-shit or coalsmoke; its basenote / a building block as biblical as honey /the last dregs of an empire's dark sump.' Here the history of Liverpool hovers as an absence, its wealth founded on the slave trade, the sugar plantations, and (as I well recall) the pervasive smell of molasses around its docks. The poem is also something like a distillation of the sentimental side of the city's character, for that supply of sugar produced sweet factories (in Everton, for instance, home of the football team consequently known as 'The Toffees'), and the sweetness seems a correlative of the sometimes 'syrupy' harmonies of the Beatles, as Farley has implied in interview.

The moods and techniques of several of these urban-poetry modes – the 'glimpse', the use of 'absence', the more sustained look, the use of surreal elements, and the reversed pastoral – are seen in combination on a larger scale in Ciaran Carson's 'Schoolboys and Idlers of Pompeii' in *Belfast Confetti* (Bloodaxe, 1989, pp. 52–56). In this poem, the ultra-long line of his fraught and terse sonnet-like pieces – 'Gate', 'Last Orders', 'Barfly', 'Night Out', 'Belfast Confetti' (the last being the title poem, missing from the book itself, in a typically Carsonian touch) – follow their own logic of association, so that several such poems seem to have joined up into longer ones, as in 'Loaf', 'Ambition', 'Bedtime Story', and 'Jawbox', all pursuing a hypnotic argument which they unfold in their own time. The imagery is densely imbricated and impacted (as is often the case in urban poetry) and moulded into a way of telling that fixes the reader-listener like a filibuster in slow motion. 'Schoolboys and Idlers of Pompeii', then, is representative of a distinct Carsonian type, when the pages become typographically prose-like. The subject matter is the absent city, distant in both time and place, that has become its own ghost, a 'Poempeii' recreated brick-by-brick by expat ex-citizens in the Woolongong Bar in Adelaide. Here the Falls Road Club, whose members have never left home, meet every Thursday to carry on 'reconstructing a city on the other side of the world', 'detailing streets and shops and houses which for the most part only exist now in the memory'. When they reminisce it's often about things that happened before they were born, such as 'the policeman who was shot dead outside the National Bank at the corner of Balaklava Street in 1922'. But 'the story does not concern the policeman; rather, it is about the tin can which was heard that night rolling down Balaklava Street into Raglan Street, and which was heard again for years after, whenever there was trouble in the offing; thousands heard it, no one saw it'. The streets, of course, are long gone, which is nothing to do with the Troubles in particular, for every British provincial city had its terraced heart ripped out in the urban clearances and forced migrations of the 1960s. Then: 'they all start to remember more, their favourite hidey-holes in entries and alleyways / and back yards, till they are lost in the comforting dusk and smog and drizzle of the / Lower Falls, playing: games of imitation, games of chance, of luck, of initiation; the / agglomerate tag or tig called *chain-tig*'. The memory seems like an energy source that feeds endlessly on itself, defying entropy, so that nothing can definitively end or disappear, as the tin-can rolls on forever along Balaklava Street and Raglan Street. All this combines a hard, down-to-earth 'loco-specificity' – the habit of naming actual streets, routes, people, moments, and episodes – with elements of magical urban realism.

Carson's urban world always seems a predominantly masculine space. Some years ago I wrote that women seem to write differently about cities, but describing the difference with any precision is difficult. But the 'woman urban poet', if Boland's Dublin is the model, makes more frequent use of 'indicative plurality', as I will call it, than do male writers. Thus, in representing Dublin, we might contrast Boland's work with the Joycean 'epiphany' version of the same place, which is all singularity – a unique moment of perception as the sudden product of (say) a casual upward glance at the Custom House clock, a moment fixed and localised, like what in Greek was called a *hapax*, a unique occurrence of a word or phenomenon. Compare that kind of essential singularity of perception with the opening prose-poem of *A Poet's Dublin*, called 'City of Shadows': 'As dusk fell on the city, a conversational life intensified. Libraries filled up: the / green-cowled lamps went on and light pooled onto / open pages. The pubs were crowded. The cafés were full of / students and apprentice writers like myself, some of them / talking about / literature, a very few talking intensely about poetry'. The plurals evoke an urban crowd of 'our' kind of people – students, writers, academics and so on – and their typical activities, the library for the day, the pub or café when the library closes. The scene has no protagonist-figure for whom this place is merely 'ground' or setting, for the poet inserts herself anonymously into this urban crowd, and on no particular day. For Joyce in *Portrait*, by contrast, there are no 'apprentice writers like myself' – that's the whole point of the novel – and no anonymous body of 'students', just the named few who are the privileged auditors of the hero's peripatetic monologue. That local-specificity, and the illusion of a real-time, mimetic narrative, results in a tendency for most of the nouns to be singular, and for a lot of them to be proper names, all these attributes often being absent in Eavan Boland.

In 'The Harbour', the 'City of shadows and of gradual / capitulations' is seen from the viewpoint of its many invaders, and the speaker again self-dissolves, becomes less than a subject, less than a unique, foregrounded, Joycean protagonist, dissolving herself into the invading hoard: 'And by me. I am your citizen: composed of / your fictions, your compromise, I am / a part of your story and its outcome. / And ready to record its contradictions'. This ending stakes a large claim – the poet speaks for the city, even as the city, becoming its chronicler. She equates the city with its mist and rain, feminising it, and seeing these elements as a distillation of the urban essence, the aspect of cities that Jonathan Raban (in his book of that title) calls *Soft City*, the softness lying in the fact that 'Cities ... are plastic by nature. We mould them in our images'.[2]

Moulding the city into a transhistorical continuum sometimes seems the default trope of urban poetry writing. In some cases the technical virtuosity seems almost distractingly prominent, as is often the case with Patience Agbabi, whose sonnet 'The London Eye', (in *Bloodshot Monochrome*, Canongate, 2008) uses many of the characteristics so far discussed, compacted into very dense poetic matter indeed, producing a poem which has an air of metropolitan slickness and is capable of a number of (possibly cross-geared) readings. On the surface, much of this is easy to decode: a smart couple meet for a romantic date at the London Eye, navigating towards each other in the contemporary way, with texts and tweets, and staging their personal drama on social media as they perform it, conscious of being constantly observed, and observing: 'Through my gold-tinted Gucci sunglasses, / the sightseers. / ... / / Through somebody's zoom lens, me shouting/ to you, / ... / Big Ben strikes six. My SKIN.Beat™ blinks, replies / 18.02. We're moving anticlockwise'. The date doesn't work out – her style is at odds with his, and vice-versa, and it isn't going to lead anywhere. But another scenario is suffused with all this. I draw in what follows on the reading by Lee M. Jenkins in Jane Dowson's *The Cambridge Companion to Twentieth-Century British and Irish Women's Poetry*. The poem was commissioned for a volume commemorating Wordsworth's 1802 'Westminster Bridge' sonnet, and it images a cross-tempered, cross-temporal date between the two poets. Then as now,

Italian was in vogue – she has the Gucci sunglasses and he's on the bridge composing his own sonnet in the Italian (Petrarchan) form. She spots him there and calls him up on her mobile, but the signal across the centuries is breaking up. '*Hello … on … bridge … 'minster!*' she calls, but she's late – 200 years late, to be exact – as the time-date on the liquid display blinks 18.02, though as they're moving anticlockwise, like the Eye, perhaps their two time zones will eventually coincide. But their poetic styles won't, as her sonnet is in the English/Shakespearian form, ending with a rhyming couplet. Their respective sexual politics are mismatched too – Wordsworth expects women to turn up punctually for a date, and the reason he is crossing Westminster Bridge, is that he's on the Dover stagecoach en route to Dover (with his sister, Dorothy who, as often, is written out of the record) to catch the packet-boat to Calais in order to meet Annette Vallon. He will make a settlement of thirty pounds a year on their daughter, and then be free to marry Mary Hutchinson. The business done, he walks on the beach and writes another sonnet, 'It is a beauteous evening, calm and free'. The irony of that title would not have escaped the eye of Agbabi's persona on the Eye. In her poem, then, the city lives simultaneously in multiple epochs, so skilfully managed that it runs the risk of having its technique outshine everything else.

A similar encapsulation of several of the urban modes so far discussed is seen in the 'Chandler spin-off, / a spoof in style, but from the blonde's perspective' of Sinéad Morrissey's 'The High Window' (pp. 61–62 in her 2013 Carcanet collection *Parallax*, which won the T. S. Eliot prize for that year). A *Dublin Review of Books* critic rightly distinguishes her technique from a hegemonic male poetic mode that may seem superficially similar, writing that 'Morrissey's playfulness is not Ashberyesque … there is no whimsical nonsense in a Morrissey poem'.[3] Forty years of hard-selling the Ashbery brand have not succeeded in making it interesting, whereas Morrissey's poems always seem to have a rigorous line of wit that runs through a whole poem, being used once and then discarded. In 'The High Window' the scenario is rather like that of Woody Allen's *The Purple Rose of Cairo* (1985), in which the glamorous character steps out of a film ('let's say … the one about the coin / called a *Brasher Doubloon*, gone missing / from a Pasadena mansion') and into the real life of the female viewer: here the hard-boiled private eye has left the mean streets of 1930s L.A. to be seduced by the reclining poet: 'I've … unplugged the telephone, / set out two highballs, and before the children cry / upstairs, pulled you down beside me by your tie'. The virtuosity and fluency of tone and imagery, the savvy wit and rapidity of pace, and the easy criss-crossing of demarcations between 'highbrow' and 'lowbrow' cultures make these two poets seem a long way from Terry

Street. There is, perhaps, a 'gadgety' air to poems like these – they incorporate all these cross-time effects partly because they can, because poetic image-making allows any number of rapid switches and permutations, just as the proliferating gadgets of our screen-worlds allow us to create endless 'samples' and combinations of disparate and disjunctive spheres. But it does seem powerfully expressive of shifting modes of contemporary urban experience.

Another distinct style in which women poets write the city is that of the urban verse-novel, sometimes in the form of crime-fiction thrillers, as seen in Val Warner's *Tooting Idyll* (Carcanet, 1998), and Deryn Rees-Jones's *Quiver* (Seren, 2004). The form is old, arguably going back to Pushkin's *Onegin* in modern times, and perhaps even to the *Iliad* and the *Decameron* before that. The contemporary popularity of the verse-novel is partly due to the fact that it links the generic forms of poetry and the novel into mutually deconstructive interlock.[4] And, in turn, it is this generic 'softness' which gives the form its particular urban appropriateness. The above-mentioned examples use the conventions, atmosphere and content of the crime-fiction thriller, including the 'heightened' urban setting, and the cinematographic noir-ish atmosphere, as the protagonist is plunged into a situation that cannot be fully understood. All this is linked with aspects of the bizarre and the mythological, and with the idea of the double, using a linked and parallel character who seems to co-exist alongside the protagonist in a time-warped zone or a realm of chronotopic slippage, of the Agbabi kind discussed above. This may sound Carsonian too in some of its features, but it needs to be distinguished from Carson's practice because Carson only does this kind of thing in fully-worked narrative form in his novels (as, for instance, in *Shamrock Tea*, Granta, 2002). However, a case could also be made – quite easily – that books like *Shamrock Tea* are really verse-novels. More importantly, the Warner and Rees-Jones examples are also different from another male poetic form, namely the 1980s sub-genre of 'secret narrative', which were 'fractured' or 'tricksy' narrative fragments, quite often with a colonial setting, and typified by many of the pieces in Andrew Motion's collection *Secret Narratives* (1983). The differences are several – the women's examples are full-scale, fully-worked and resolved, and they challenge social norms rather than seeming to reinforce them. They differ from conventional screen thrillers, too, in that there is no Poirot-or-Morse-ex-machina waiting to explain all and restore normality at the end.

Val Warner's collection consists of two sequences, the first (like the book as a whole) called 'Tooting Idyll', and the second 'Mary Chay'. 'Tooting Idyll' has three reflective monologues, all centred on the same house in Tooting Bec, South London, but each being a different story. In the first, set in June

1939, the house is occupied by two male lovers, one about to become a soldier, the other a conscientious objector. In the second, set in June 1984, the same house is occupied by a man and a woman of left-wing convictions with an adopted child and another adoption in progress. In the third, the perspective is that of 'a cross-dressing female friend after the VE Day [Victory in Europe] fiftieth anniversary commemoration of 1995', as the jacket blurb describes it. In these, the doppelgänger motif is apparent, as is the device of a triple time span that superimposes a through-running, 'social-outsider' scenario on the house. The second part of the book is the sequence 'Mary Chay' (which, like the first, is about seventy pages long), also in three parts, but in this case the three are continuous sections of the same story. The story is described in the blurb as 'a murder in Victoria [London] in 1994, seen from many viewpoints and deploying a variety of forms'. The murder of Mary Chay is not a real event, in spite of its powerful *vérité* atmosphere, but amalgamates features of a number of actual murders widely reported in the tabloid press in the 1990s. One of the poems has a *Sun*-style headline characteristic of the era 'Lesbo thread in Hugh Street strangling', and the 'Mary Chay' of the sequence is a young woman, friendless and unattached, and visiting a house in Hugh Street, near Victoria Station, a street which does exist, and then consisted mainly of low-rate, discount hotels. These verse-novels, unlike the Boland poems just discussed, are usually loco-specified (actual street names, walks that can be followed on the map, specified bus routes and so on). The doppelgänger effect lies in the switches of focalization, firstly to the mind of the DI who is having trouble coping with the new, computerised forensic technologies, which can identify DNA from (say) a trace of saliva, and then to the young WPC who is dressed as the murder victim for the police re-enactment of the murder-victim's last walk. Mary Chay walked from Waterstones, where she bought a book (Carey's *Oscar and Lucinda* – nothing is just generic in this genre) down Charing Cross Road, till she is / was 'sucked underground down Leicester Square tube.' The WPC is just acting the role (she's 'on stage', she tells herself), proud of achieving such a good likeness ('I'm her to a T'), but the 'neutral eyes' gunning for her (the colleagues who scrutinise passers-by for signs of recognition) suggest the eyes that were probably already 'gunning for' Mary Chay at this stage in her walk. The WPC is aware that her pretence of professional detachment won't work, for 'She's under my skin' and is conscious of walking 'in dead sister's shoes'. I count *Tooting Idyll* as one of the most outstanding collections of poetry published in post-war Britain.

Rees-Jones's *Quiver* is set in Liverpool, but the focalisation has more of a 'mono-anchorage', since the perceiving persona throughout is Fay Thomas, a 'poet with writer's block', who becomes a murder suspect when, out running 'one morning in a local cemetery, she finds the body of Mara (her geneticist-husband's former lover)' who has been 'pierced with an arrow like a fallen bird'. Subsequently she is questioned by the police, sees Mara in the street and goes to a rendezvous with her, tracks the movements of her husband, and at the climax of events, as she and her husband dine in Chinatown as the start of the Year of the Horse is being celebrated, an attempt is made on their lives, just as the police had predicted, and the solution of the mystery is revealed. Fay and Mara are linked as figure and ground throughout the narrative, and another running motif (literally) is the myth of Actaeon, re-told in the title-poem 'Quiver', in which the partly-metamorphosed hunter, having seen Artemis/Diana bathing, is pursued and killed by his own hounds. The hallucinatory or fictive overlay is stronger in Rees-Jones's sequence than in Warner's, and again, the idea of performance is prominent here, with Chandleresque echoes, as in Morrissey, and Carsonian notions of performance as a repetition structure. The city of Liverpool is recognisably present, but in a hyped-up, self-consciously noir-ish way, so that it is not a place, really, but a representation of itself, a place-in-a-film, even when its streets are named, as in 'Liverpool Blues', where there seems to be a touch of tonal homage for the original Liverpool Poets (p. 27): 'The skyline in the moonlight, the river running thin, / my lover weeping lotus blossom for his next of kin. // In Berry Street, in Bold Street, in Princes Park and Princess Street / I've seen a girl I never knew and never thought to meet'. Rees-Jones's 'Pavillion Poetry' series of verse-novels from Liverpool University Press will include, in 2015, *And She Was* by Sarah Corbett (see note 4), in which two young lovers meet on the Heathrow Express, and, in 'A side street in an unknown city: Felix Morning wakes up with no memory'. Now that it has its own series imprint, the urban verse-novel genre, in which women have been the pioneering practitioners, looks set to thrive.

The final way to do the city in poetry is to work on a project that has epic or architectural proportions that seem to match the scale and complexity of the city itself. But even the prolonged gaze of these epic-length poems is usually upon a very specific aspect or district of a city, rather than a city as a whole. The major examples of this kind of enterprise look likely to remain unrivalled, partly because the poets who would undertake such a project will probably now have full-time university posts in creative writing, and will therefore be subject to all the pressures that now come with academic positions. Another reason why such writing now seems less frequent is the ubiquitous presence of the Internet, with its tendency to homogenise scholarship and mindset, so that (for example) anyone speaking of literature and the city is expected to stay firmly within the parameters of the insights of Lefebvre, Soja and Jameson. Anyway, whatever the causes, such epics now seem representative of the 1960s, '70s, and '80s. I will list some outstanding works of this type in the period of post-war British poetry: firstly, the Birmingham epic of Roy Fisher's *City*, originally published by Migrant Press in 1961, is a prose-and-verse sequence of some eighteen or nineteen pages, notionally centred on the perceiving subjectivity of its 'unwilling hero', rather than being a collage of documentary material, historical data and street-specific perambulations.[5] Re-reading it now, it is the relentless, through-drive of its idiosyncratic seeing-eye that strikes me, so that the tone sometimes seems more like that of Frank O'Hara's New York *flâneur* in his *Lunch Poems* (City Lights, 1964), whereas in the past I associated it mainly with Charles Olson, the library-bound, open-field polymath of the 1950s *Maximus Poems* (University of California Press, 1992).

Another major example of the contemporary urban epic is Allen Fisher's London *Place* sequence, focused on South London, originally published over a period of fifteen years, beginning with *Place Book One* in 1974, and now available between a single set of covers in a book of more than 400 pages.[6] Here, the Olsonian, open-field method is very much one of the models. The structure is complex, and the rich textual collage includes historical, personal, mythological, technological, scientific, municipal and other material, woven into intricate cross-connections, running themes and intermittent motifs. Reading *Place*, then, seems to reproduce something of the urban experience, as when, turning a city corner, it can't be predicted what kind of locale will be encountered. Likewise, when turning a page of *Place*, a running thread may be abruptly abandoned, only to be taken up again some twenty pages later, as explained in a structural overview that leaves the reader wondering whether they have quite grasped the meaning of the word 'structural'. So *Place* is multiple and pretty-well without a dominating, thematising consciousness, unlike *City*, so that it requires the reader to navigate a drift or *dérive* across its sections, picking up disparate accumulations of facts, data, and remarks, and breaking off, from time to time, to dip into some of the listed sources. In other words, as we read, we need to become the writer reading, rather than the writer (or persona) seeing.

Another of these older-style urban epics is Iain Sinclair's *Lud Heat*, subtitled 'A Book of the Dead Hamlets'. In its latest reprint (Skylight Press, 2012) it is (sensibly) separated from the related, but inferior, sequence *Suicide Bridge*. The 140 pages of *Lud Heat* centre on dark historical and mythological forces allegedly at work in East London and manifested in negative energies emanating from the seventeenth and eighteenth-century churches of the architect Nicholas Hawksmoor. This is a London which plays out a transhistorical psycho-drama, and yet is solidly rooted in the streets and locales of the near present-day. It combines the loco-specificity and documentary elements of Allen Fisher, with the through-running, heightened sense of idiosyncratic personal perception seen in Roy Fisher's *City*. It has been immensely influential.

Yet another visionary epic, this time centred on the King's Cross area of London, is Aidan Dun's *Vale Royal*, which appeared in 1996, as a late addition to this set of London poetic epics, and published by Goldmark Books, to great acclaim from eminent urbanists like Iain Sinclair, Peter Ackroyd and Derek Walcott. Vale Royal is the author's name for the valley of the Fleet River, and Dun sees St Pancras Old Church (behind the station) as the locus of mainly benign creative and Blakean energies. In his bardic persona as the 'Sun Child', Dun passes out of the present into 'a more fluid city', and where *Lud Heat* is obsessively dark, *Vale Royal* is mostly up-beat and lyrical. The book was published with two CDs containing Dun's complete reading of the text in his characteristic, high-energy, lilting performance style. His more recent work remains epic in scale and urban-based, but more sombre in tone, including the collection of shorter poems *The Uninhabitable City* (Goldmark, 2005).

How might such large-scale urban-centred poetry projects be continued by a university-embedded poet in the pressured present, one who is necessarily engaged in a wide range of project grants and collaborative work of various kinds? A possible answer might be seen in a work-in-progress by Zoë Skoulding, who is based in Bangor, North Wales. Her collection *Remains of a Future City* (Seren, 2008), includes the poems 'Forest with A-Z of Cardiff', 'Preselis with Brussels Street Map' and 'Llanddwyn Beach with directions from Copenhagen', which all use the idea (cognate with the psycho-geographical/situationist practices associated with Iain Sinclair, among many others) of exploring one place using the map of another, in each case a Welsh rural space with a European metropolis. Skoulding has been closely involved in collaborative poetry and translation projects which undertake such walks as a collaborative activity, in particular with European women poets, in a project called *Metropoetica*.[7]

One result of this approach is Skoulding's extended sequence called 'Teint', which is about the *Bièvre* (the Beaver), a tributary river now entirely buried within Paris, that flows into the Seine, and was much polluted, by tanning, and by the dye-manufactures of Les Gobelins, among others. A substantial extract from this large-scale work appeared in 2014.[8] The structure is similar to that of Roy Fisher's *City*, in that sections of verse are interspersed with prose quotations (given in French and English) from historical and other sources, sometimes very brief, like this one from Claude Lepetit's, *Rivière des Gobelins*, 1668: '*Est-ce de la boüe ou de l'eau? / Est-ce de la suye ou de l'encre?*' // Is it mud or water? / Is it sweat or ink? / The stanzas in the extract all have a similar format, all beginning with a 'not', and including references, sources and data in the manner of Allen Fisher in *Place*, which has major sections on the lost and buried rivers of London, and a running motif about their ongoing environmental presence in culture, and in memory, in the contours of streets and roads, and as an influence on the health and well-being (or otherwise) of citizens living in their vicinity. Skoulding's stanzas use lines with a caesura, following which the line drops down a level; I quote one complete stanza, indicating the caesura with angled bracket: 'Not a river but its > nymph already complaining / late 1500s in > Baif's lament for injured / water where your goblins > where your poisons tint / inhuman dyers taint > the mixing of our waters / her own name blotted out > by *Gobelins* she runs / in the glint of bare life > are you even listening / the city doesn't > count what lies underneath'. The mid-line fracture or caesura seems suggestive of the ebb and flow of a water source, and the sustained lilt of the lyric is reminiscent of Aidan Dun. The notion of a buried – but still living – collective urban subconscious, embodied in 'lost' rivers, superseded trades and historical texts, is very strong, and it is good to see continuation of this kind of urban writing. The whole poem (initiated at a residency in 2013 at the former *Récollets* convent in the 10th arrondissement of Paris, near the Gare de l'Est) is a unique eco-historicist transposition of the UK urban epic to a continental setting. It is an expansion of the author's practice of 'over-mapping' (reading one place in terms of another), but scaling it up culturally, and, I hope, signalling a possible re-birth of the urban-epic format of the 1960s to '80s in the twenty-first century phase of post-war British and Irish urban poetry.

NOTES

1 See: 'Crucial Collection: Douglas Dunn, "Terry Street"', *The Poetry Ireland Review* 86 (May 2006): 31–33, available at: http://www.jstor.org/stable/25580735?seq=1.
2 *Soft City* (London: Hamish Hamilton, 1974), p. 10.
3 See 'When Not To Listen', Gerard Smyth, *Dublin Review of Books* 63 (January 2015), available at: http://www.drb.ie/contributors-articles/when-not-to-listen#sthash.Djb2iaIP.dpuf.
4 For the verse-novel vogue in Britain, see Sarah Corbett, 'Is There a Contemporary Verse-Novel in the UK?', in *The Long Poem Magazine*, 7, 2012, 34–36.
5 *City* is in Fisher's *The Long and the Short of It: Poems 1955–2010* (Newcastle-upon-Tyne: Bloodaxe, 2nd rev. edn., 2012).
6 Allen Fisher, *Place* (Hastings: Reality Street Editions, 2005).
7 I am grateful to Bronwen Williams, holder of the 'Devolved Voices' Leverhulme Studentship, for bringing aspects of Skoulding's latest work to my attention.
8 In *The Fortnightly Review*, August 2014, available at: http://fortnightlyreview.co.uk/2014/08/bievre/.

16

JON GLOVER

Poetry's Outward Forms: Groups, Workshops, Readings, Publishers

Only twenty or twenty-five years ago poets were employed in universities but only rarely *because* they were poets or to teach writing. It could be contended that in the last few years there has been a massive shift of cultural capital – sharing financial and ideological interest in poetry, poets and associated social and educational structures. Today, perhaps poetry's hotspots have shifted to universities. Although other creative subjects (art, drama, music) have long been part of university degrees, creative writing has, after a long wait, become both welcome and controversial. Higher Education's Quality Assurance Agency[1] has to define 'Benchmarks' for study and assessment in all subjects, and its Benchmark on English includes important statements about writing. There is to be a QAA Benchmark on Creative Writing, and there is already one, widely used, drafted by the National Association of Writers in Education.[2] NAWE publishes substantial resources to support writers who work from primary school to PhD levels. There are additional debates on learning and teaching, with research material on creative writing in degrees located in the Higher Education English Subject Centre[3] run by the Council for College and University English. There are also many books on creative writing, some aimed at the general public and some for university students. Although some are of particular significance (for example, those by Hobsbaum and Wainwright) listed in Further Reading, it is not my intention to comment on them here though they might be thought of as a vital part of poetry's visible, outward structure.

It may seem odd to open an account of poetry's outward forms, its public and institutional infrastructures, with a list of agencies which promote standards, frameworks, guidelines and rules. So I start with more unofficial outward forms though they are probably better known to writers than the QAA Benchmarks.

Originally conceived in Devon by John Moat and John Fairfax, with early support from Ted Hughes, Arvon was a sort of democratisation of the Cambridge and London Group philosophy in which sharing poetry, and discussion of new manuscripts from an author who was sitting with the rest of the group, was thought the most creative, and personally engaging, method of passing on both motivation and skill:

> Arvon was founded in 1968 by two poets, John Moat and John Fairfax.... John Moat wrote that they were inspired to create Arvon 'as a place where individuals, and in particular young committed writers, could be given a sanctuary away from ... the creative deprivation imposed by the system of standard education – and there offered ... the guidance of writers'.[4]

Week-long residential courses, with different visiting poet-tutors and guest readers, are offered to the public on a non-competitive basis for a fee which may be subsidised by the Arts Council or Charities. Seen initially as a new opportunity for an aspiring writer to gain the sort of contact and encouragement that was normally, if haphazardly, provided by the ethos of Cambridge, Oxford, Leeds, Glasgow, Belfast or Manchester, some people now attend repeatedly from the UK and abroad. Arvon tutors themselves often work as creative writing tutors in universities; the symbiosis has evolved in a new way.

The historic isolation of Arvon centres (a version of England's 'poet-in-nature', from Wordsworth through Hughes?) offers one of poetry's outward 'support' forms. Poetry 'slams' and organisations such as 'Write Out Loud' (founded in Bolton, but now working nationally), offer another. In public, and usually urban settings, they organise readings and performance-poetry events, for which some speakers may be specifically invited but others read, or perform, with open mic, or from open floor:

> Sharing poetry with others gives us more of a buzz than being published. We are not knocking publication; just saying that performance poetry offers different opportunities for poets. It's live, acoustic and encourages people to talk and listen to each other: face-to-face![5]

Poets are voted on for prizes and status: the 'slam'. As so often, it is contact, reading aloud, and the development of self-esteem which count. Is this so different from meetings of young writers, that I am going to examine below, in post-war London or Oxford clubs, pubs and flats that set a number of currently famous writers on their roads to prominence?

For many current aspiring poets there may seem to be a new career path. A master of arts degree in creative writing seems now to be one stepping stone. A pamphlet, possibly resulting from a competition run by a company associated with a university or publishing house, is another stage. Inclusion in a university anthology is expected by writers and readers. Many graduates from the master's programs at the universities, such as East Anglia, will help to edit their annual anthology and be delighted to see their names in print[6]; with luck, London agents and publishers' editors on campus visits will also be glad to see marketable work.

Such anthologies are revealing about outward forms. In 2014 the *Poetry Business*, in collaboration with the University of Sheffield, produced *CAST*, with forty young poets, each contributing about five poems. Of these, about fifteen poets had just completed a creative writing MA. Thirty five had published a pamphlet, and some, such as Helen Mort and Liz Berry, had already had a successful book out before *CAST* appeared. Indeed, Helen Mort had been shortlisted for the T. S. Eliot Prize, and Liz Berry won the Forward Best First Collection Prize. Simon Armitage's 'Foreword' reveals something of the present outward form and defends it against accusations of 'normalisation':

> The fact that the styles and approaches on display here are so varied also says a great deal about how individual voices can develop through such learning and practice, giving the lie to the idea of a 'workshop' poet or poem.[7]

The importance of 'region' is identified along with workshops, MAs, and experience of publication. My suspicion is that there are similar proud prefaces to anthologies from Bath Spa, Glasgow, Manchester and Kent. This is from the *UEA 2012 Poetry Anthology*:

> A course begins as strangers, moves towards a kind of community then spreads out again though the networking world that is now our given may, for some, confirm and perpetuate that sense of community.[8]

But a conventional academic career path is not inevitable. Kate Tempest, according to articles in the *Guardian*, became uninterested in study at school because she was so interested in other things, including poetry, music and art. She has by now written plays, performed rap, self-published poems:

> Eventually she self-published *Everything Speaks in Its Own Way*, that included audio and visual elements. After seeing the launch event [Don] Paterson approached her about writing a book for Picador, and her growing reputation as a performer also led to a commission from Paines Plough theatre company to write a play.[9]

She has studied to a high level though not through a conventional school-to-university route. At age twenty-eight, she has been chosen as one of the 'Next Generation' of poets.[10]

There are many interesting facets to her work, her career and the ways in which she is described and assessed. She has been most committed to writing, performing and social/community relationships as the given; not as a follow-on to scholarship and qualifications. Apparently, she heard Ancient

Greek plays and *The Odyssey* spoken as a child at home. Blake, Joyce or Shakespeare were heard as part of life.

Jon Silkin was twenty-eight when, without a degree, he became a Gregory Fellow in poetry at the University of Leeds in 1958. I am interested in the ways in which for Silkin, in 1950, writing poetry was a necessity, and the necessary skills were 'acquired' (or fulfilled) by him without formal study and without paper qualifications. For Kate Tempest, the 'given' included Sophocles and Blake, for Silkin it included the Bible and Milton.

It is instructive to compare and contrast outward forms of poetry in 1950 as they were used (or found) by Geoffrey Hill, born 1932, and Jon Silkin, born 1930. Geoffrey Hill started his BA at Keble College, Oxford, in October 1950. During his three years as an undergraduate he met student poets and helped to edit *New Poems*[11] and *Oxford Poetry*.[12] He had his own Fantasy Press Pamphlet.[13] Donald Hall has recalled those days:

> Because I expressed my irritation with Oxford poetry, people feared me and I found myself deferred to. I was appointed literary editor of the *Isis*, and secretary of OUPS, which meant I would preside over the Poetry Society the following term. I would invite poets from the larger world to read us their poems, which they did for expenses only. I entertained Louis MacNeice, Vernon Watkins, Kathleen Raine, W. R. Rogers, C. Day-Lewis, Dylan Thomas.[14]

The contacts and emerging friendships seem endless. And usually they were associated with some sort of action leading to more writing and publication:

> My closest friend was Geoffrey Hill, whom I met at the end of my first year. He had published a poem in *Isis* that I admired.... I invited him to submit poems for the Fantasy Poets pamphlet series.... That summer, when I was back briefly in New Hampshire, Hill mailed me his manuscript. I read 'Genesis' and other extraordinary poems written by a twenty-year-old from a Worcestershire village. I woke in the middle of the night to turn on the light and read the poems again, they were so shockingly good. The next year at Oxford I saw Hill almost every day.[15]

'Genesis', written as an undergraduate, is still often the first poem in one of Hill's readings, sixty-five years on. At Oxford there were no creative writing classes. But the opportunity to liaise with other student-poets, to exercise choice as an editor, and to be responsible for the publication process might have been important for Hall, Hill and others, even if they were part of a self-sustaining parallel culture rather than because their work arose from the curriculum.

Silkin was in the army until late 1950 when he was just twenty. He had been writing poems from his early teens, and one written while he was sixteen was kept and printed in his first pamphlet, *The Portrait*, for which the other poems were written during National Service. The starting points were the Bible and Milton together with an irrepressible curiosity. He recalled meetings at home of the League of Nations and a flow of refugees from Europe calling in at this 'safe house'. As far as I can see from his archives he had not, by 1950, met any notable poets and neither had he wandered the countryside alone with an anthology of English poetry as had Geoffrey Hill with his edition by Charles Williams.[16] Both were only children. Geoffrey Hill was exempted from National Service because of deafness in one ear. Silkin's 'academy' was developed after National Service, through years of manual labour, including grave-digging, and working as a bricklayer's mate. Both were acutely aware of the war – they saw its results from the bombs that fell nearby.

Who were gatekeepers in post–Second World War literary England? Publishers and the BBC were often controlled by graduates from Oxford and Cambridge; they gave contracts to poets who themselves had studied, usually Classics or English literature, at those universities. By 1954, without university study, and without a middle-class job (and little money), Silkin was reading his poems on the BBC, appearing in journals all over the UK, and even in *Poetry* (Chicago). He read in London poetry societies and groups, including the ICA,[17] and occasionally with Hobsbaum's 'The Group'.[18] He knew the important poet and editor C Day Lewis,[19] who worked at Chatto and Windus, and other poetry journal editors including Dannie Abse, famous for the journal *Poetry and Poverty*, and Howard Sergeant, Editor of *Outposts*. Sergeant, with Abse, edited the anthology *Mavericks*.[20] It is paradoxical, perhaps, that, on the one hand Silkin was a 'drop out', an 'angry young man'. On the other hand, he was familiar with, and could enjoy or manipulate the poetry 'establishment'. He did not meet poets in Oxford but in another 'clubby' environment, Soho and Fitzrovia, where he also met Dylan Thomas (and other poets). Donald Hall met them through a University, Silkin in the pub. By 1952 he had founded his own magazine, *Stand*.

It is tempting to see creating *Stand* as a unique case of a special socio-political-poetic 'action'. At the time, several poet-editors, like Silkin, left school early with few qualifications. After National Service he worked as a cleaner in London, was dismissed for trying to found a union branch, and with £5 redundancy money, went into the office and bought enough paper on which to print the first issue of the magazine. It seems that, as with Dannie Abse and W. Price Turner, for Silkin to offer to *Stand's* readers work by new poets was an absolute priority. There was not an overriding ambition to 'cleanse the dialect of the tribe'[21] or, as Abse put it, to spend time through 'style and structure' to create a new poetry, nor to 'save the corpse of *The New Apocalypse*, or indeed even attempt to keep it breathing with an iron lung ...'.[22]

Another version of generating cultural capital and passing it on is in the history of The Group. Founded in Cambridge in the early 1950s by Philip Hobsbaum, and linked to other young poets, Ted Hughes and Peter Redgrove, it grew into one of the most important catalysts for writing poetry in the second half of the twentieth century. In his forward to the 1963 *A Group Anthology* Edward Lucie-Smith uses the now common 'workshop' word for discussion of pre-circulated 'cyclostyled' poems.:

> When he [Philip Hobsbaum] was an undergraduate at Cambridge he was a prominent member of a group which was founded as a workshop for verse writers, but which later developed into a forum for writers of verse. This Cambridge group was closely linked with the undergraduate magazine *Delta*.[23]

As at Oxford, these activities were not part of any curriculum although they had begun in a competitive university environment. Discussion, especially for those such as Hobsbaum who studied with Leavis, had become almost a commodity, and founding, editing and passing on a magazine was integral to the process. There was a vital commitment to starting with the text, to reading aloud, and to agreement that 'the process by which words work in poetry is something open to rational examination'.[24] Poems were often performable as dramatic monologues and were seen as part of a relationship between author and audience: 'poetry is regarded as a function of speech'.[25] As part of a group experience, poetry had acquired a capital value.

Hobsbaum saw this 'means of production' of poetry as something with its own mission. He seems to have been assumed that there were forces, or 'pressures', working against poetry. His epilogue concluded thus:

> And I do not see why the approach adopted here should not work, with suitable amendments, in other places and times. The pressures against anyone writing at his best are very strong. The writer needs a community to keep him in touch with his audience; at the same time, the worst thing for any writer would be a clique.[26]

Poetry at work as part of the enterprise economy (or the creative or cultural economies) might gladden any contemporary university vice chancellor's heart, although for Hobsbaum, poetry and university might have been seen as oppositional. Some of Hobsbaum's talk is not dissimilar from Sheila Rowbotham's commitment to writing, discussion, networking and political action experienced at the same time in the 1960s and described so well in her book *Promise of a Dream*.[27] By the time she toured the country selling *Black Dwarf*, she had met Ken Smith and other *Stand* people in Leeds; such a political-personal-cultural association may look fanciful now, but in the 1960s, it was natural.[28] Silkin himself also knew Shiela Rowbotham's close friend, the social historian E. P. Thompson.

Of course, by the time Hobsbaum wrote in 1963 about the possibility of poetry discussion groups spreading through the universities he had already been a research student at the University of Sheffield, working with William Empson from 1959 to 1962. In 1960 he wrote from Sheffield to Jon Silkin, then an undergraduate reading English at Leeds, *after* having been Gregory Fellow in Poetry there from 1958 to 1960, inviting him to read in Sheffield. Following Silkin's reading, which went well, Hobsbaum wrote again:

> I'm making it part of my job here [in Sheffield] to encourage a tradition of intelligent discussion and creative writing too – in practice, I have found the two much associated....[29]

He went on to say that he wanted to start something like 'Leeds's excellent *Poetry and Audience*' (letter to Jon Silkin, 29 Oct 1960 Special Collections, Brotherton Library, University of Leeds). Although not published in *A Group Anthology*, Silkin had attended some of the London Group meetings, and Hobsbaum had been included in one of the earliest copies of *Stand* (No. 11, 1956), an issue which also published work by another future professor, Bernard Bergonzi. In an essay on the poetry of A. C. Jacobs, Hobsbaum mentions that some of the London Group members were Jews and that evenings were specified for discussing their work. It is a theme to which he returned in an interview published in *The Dark Horse* in 2002, and it leads to an interesting difference between perceived personal aims in 'teaching' criticism, and aims in 'teaching' writing:

> [Philip Hobsbaum] George MacBeth said to me critically once, 'All your geese are swans.' I said, 'Well, it's just the reverse of reviewing and criticism: when it comes to books, treat the book as no good, until it proves itself otherwise. With students, assume they're good: let them prove they aren't.' [Interviewer] *Have the people you've acted as advocate for been outsiders, like yourself?* It's writers are outsiders. When you're perfectly integrated, and happy with your life, you won't write. I'm a Freudian: writing is the grain of sand in the oyster.[30]

The first 'Writers in Residence' in the UK were the Gregory Fellowships at the University of Leeds. In the early 1940s, the Bradford printer and art enthusiast Eric Gregory met in London with then professor of English at Leeds Bonamy Dobrée. They agreed to initiate something quite radical for the arts after the war. Gregory set aside a sum of money to fund what we would now call 'artists in residence', in poetry, painting and sculpture, at the University of Leeds. They would not be attached to particular academic departments, and fellows would not have routine teaching. The aims were:

> (i) to bring our younger artists into closer touch with the youth of the country so that they may influence it; and (ii) at the same time to keep artists in close touch with the needs of the community. At present there is too great a gap between art and society, and it is hoped that this scheme would constitute a small step towards closing it.[31]

By 1949, Dobrée and Gregory had involved close friends in supporting the project and became members of an informal senate committee, chaired by the vice chancellor, which met to consider appointments for the first time on 15 July. The friends who joined Gregory and Dobrée were Dr. T. S. Eliot and Dr. Henry Moore. Art theorist and historian Herbert Read, also a prominent poet, soon also joined the 'Advisory Committee'. Eliot and Dobrée had been friends and colleague since the 1920s and, from 1943, had been discussing the future of university education. In a letter to Dobrée (10 March 1943) Eliot compared Leeds University, in 'the midst of a large industrial town',[32] with Exeter – there was a different sort of challenge here for the future of the arts. When the university agreed in 1943 to the challenge, the fellowships would be implemented in a way incredible today: there were no 'job specs', no application forms, no advertisements and no interviews, although there were sometimes dinners with Dobrée and his friends to assess the quality of a potential candidate.

By 2010, about one-third (forty-one) of the universities in the UK had established MA programmes in creative writing. Nearly half of those were in older universities (e.g., Queen's University Belfast, Glasgow, Manchester, Newcastle, Oxford, Birkbeck), and the others were split between the post-1962 group (e.g., Sussex, Lancaster, UEA, Warwick), and the ex-polytechnics and institutes (e.g., Manchester Metropolitan, Liverpool John Moores,[33] Sheffield Hallam, Bolton). The first MA programme was founded in 1970 by Malcolm Bradbury and Angus Wilson at UEA, followed by the first creative writing PhD programme in 1987. The first UEA graduates were novelists, but poetry was soon added there and elsewhere. For many writers, students and applicants, such degree courses have become a well-established norm.

It is worth comparing this with post-war literary London and the new world seen in 1975 by poet David Wright:

> If you knew where to go, and sooner or later you found out, there was almost no person of interest or achievement, past or potential, whom you did not meet ... Since the fifties I have not seen anything like it except on a very minor scale in one or two provincial centres like Leeds and Newcastle-upon-Tyne, and even there it is being killed, as happened long ago in London, by the

> power-shovels of redevelopment and property speculation. The new universities – Keele, Lancaster, York and so on, isolated communities shut in glasscrete compounds often miles from the life of the cities to which they are attached – make a poor swap.[34]

Wright was a Gregory Fellow at the University of Leeds from 1965 to 1967, so he had some first-hand experience of that city. He had followed James Kirkup, John Heath-Stubbs, Thomas Blackburn,[35] Jon Silkin, W. Price Turner and Peter Redgrove who ran Group-style meetings for students.[36] The university did not move in the 1970s to incorporate creative writing into its degree programmes, and eventually funding dried up. Individual creative writing modules were, and are, offered but not dedicated awards.

However, Newcastle-upon-Tyne developed its own symbiosis between poets, publishers, the Arts Council and the universities. It was the birthplace of the great modernist poet Basil Bunting (1900–85). Bunting was working at the regional newspaper, *The Evening Chronicle*, where he met the much younger poet, Tom Pickard, in 1963, leading to Bunting returning to poetry and his writing *Briggflatts* (1966). Pickard, and his wife, Connie, founded the Morden Tower poetry centre, or book room, in 1964 where many of the world's greatest poets have read their work. They also founded a bookshop, Ultima Thule, which specialised in poetry, alternative culture and politics, from 1969 to 1973. Northern Arts, the northeast 'branch' of the Arts Council, offered funding to Jon Silkin's journal *Stand*, and Silkin moved to Newcastle-upon-Tyne. Tony Harrison left Leeds in 1962 to work in Nigeria until 1966. After a year at Charles University in Prague, he was given a Northern Arts Fellowship at the Universities of Newcastle and Durham. He has lived in Newcastle almost continuously ever since. *Stand* and *Northern House* (the pamphlet publisher founded in Leeds) were then based in Newcastle until Silkin's death in 1997.

Several people, after helping to edit and produce *Stand*, moved on to set up their own presses, notably Neil Astley, who worked for *Stand* from 1975 to 1978, and then founded *Bloodaxe*, now one of the most important publishers of poetry in the UK. How far was the publication machinery of *Bloodaxe*,[37] *Stand*, *Northern House*, and later, *Writing Women* and *Mslexia*,[38] something rooted in Newcastle tradition, and how far was it an outward form imported? Some critics, such as W. E. Parkinson, have found the Newcastle Renaissance, with its modernist orientation and U.S. influence, divorced from local culture, and thus stultifying:

> The work of Tom Pickard, Barry MacSweeney and Basil Bunting lacks a distinctive regional voice, but paradoxically it is in the work of immigrants like Jon Silkin and Tony Harrison that a regional voice is heard.[39]

Others have examined more accurately and sympathetically the reality of influences between Bunting and younger writers.[40] In 1966, Rodney Pybus, who worked in northeast journalism and television, published in *Stand* on 'Writing: the North East':

> Earlier this year *Stand* invited contributions from people living in the North East, partly in the hope of finding some new regional talent, partly to provide material for a survey of contemporary writing in the area. In terms of quantity the response was moderately encouraging; but in terms of quality it was hugely disappointing.[41]

One might almost hear the cold accountant's breath from 'North East Arts' behind Pybus's tone, and the unusual, for *Stand*, project of a survey – Pybus counted and assessed the contributions; so what was the regional Arts Council paying for? These themes re-emerged in one of Bloodaxe's earliest books, an anthology of *Ten North-East Poets*.[42] Neil Astley quoted Pybus on the quality of local writing being 'worse than third rate', with the exceptions of Pickard, MacSweeney and dialect poet Fred Reed, and his Preface remains an important examination of endemic problems for writers, readers and arts-funders. The issues were taken up again for a national readership in reviews of Astley's anthology by Michael Schmidt in the *New Statesman* ('... the Muse seems to bestow her attentions exclusively on men up on Tyneside'); Douglas Dunn in the *TLS* ('It *does* seem self-consciously regional ... but ... far healthier than the phenomenon that used to be described by that ailing pejorative *provincial* ...'); and Peter Porter in the *Observer* ('Some of their poetry reads like [Hoggart's] *The Uses of Literacy*').[43]

Whatever the successes, and however real the connections, it seems to emerge that the culture of poetry's outward forms in Newcastle was very different from that which had functioned in Leeds, and was different again from the personal, and informal, publishing-editorial-university links as obtained in Oxford, Cambridge and London. That said, Harrison has always been a national and international figure, as playwright and poet, whilst maintaining his base in Newcastle. Silkin's recently published *Complete Poems*[44] makes it possible for the first time to see his mix of an international with non-southern, non-London identity in his northern poetry.

The Universities of Newcastle-upon-Tyne, Northumbria and Durham, have all by now set up their own creative writing degree programmes with important poets and novelists on the staff.[45] But it is notable that the processes of 'handing on' poetry and its publication have continued in the northeast as essentially independent operations; most small magazines and publishers are not 'owned' by higher education.

How far have women poets been affected by poetry's outward forms? In the 1966 London conference on 'Patriarchy' Cora Kaplan said

> A very high proportion of women's poems are about the right to speak and write. The desire to write imaginative poetry and prose was and is a demand for access to and parity within the law and myth-making groups in society.... To be a woman and a poet presents many women poets with such a profound split between their social, sexual identity (their 'human' identity) and their artistic practice that the split becomes the insistent subject, sometimes overt, often hidden or displaced, of much women's poetry.[46]

The appointment of Carol Ann Duffy in 2009 as Poet Laureate may indeed have been founded on new belief that 'The decision to storm the walls and occupy the forbidden place is a recognition of the value and importance of high language ...'[47] as Kaplan put it in 1976. But one suspects that Duffy's appointment has not risen from a single dramatic rebellion, but from wider and more general consciousness-raising since the second feminist movement in the 1970s. How interesting it is that the Poets Laureate, or Makars, of Wales, Scotland and Belfast are all women (at the time of writing). That said, there has perhaps been as much a recoding and re-forming of language as taking 'high language' over from men. On the one hand, *Writing Women* and *Mslexia* have staked their own territory. On the other hand it could be claimed that, with or without the help of creative writing courses, women are now writing wonderful poetry and that it is being recognised by awards, appointments, and publication by editors of books and journals once thought of as male-orientated. It could also be claimed that Kaplan's assumption that historic male experience (leadership, war, ruling by ruling language) which had been generalised into poetry's universals is now seen in a new way. It could be claimed that Plath, Sexton and Rich did not take over male speech and poetic forms but made their own, and this might be claimed too for new generations: Medbh McGuckian, Sinéad Morrissey, Helen Mort, Rebecca Goss, Julia Copus, Lucy Burnett, Karen McCarthy Woolf, Eavan Boland.

The annual rota of national competitions might be thought of as a de facto outward form. And, as with all anthologies which seem to be 'there' to make a mark, *Salt and Bitter and Good*,[48] *Making for the Open*,[49] *Bread and Roses*[50] and *The Penguin Book of Women Poets*[51] have announced the presence of women poets with an unquestionable power. Interestingly, two Penguin anthologies of war literature, *The Penguin Book of First World War Poetry*, edited by Jon Silkin, and *The Penguin Book of First World War Prose*, edited by Jon Glover and Jon Silkin, may have helped to promote feminist thinking on poetry of war and women's poetry in general. Absence (or perceived absence) from a book's list of contents is always a stimulus. Catherine Reilly's anthology of women's war poetry, *Scars Upon My Heart*, was set on many university reading lists against Jon Silkin's book.[52] In effect, it helped to raise many issues 'about' women's and men's poetry, past and present; not just 'one-to-one' engagement with accepted subject matter (battle, violence, the body, childbirth, death), but the inheritance and creation of differing forms and traditions.

There have been important poets coming from Cambridge in the 1960s after Hughes, Elaine Feinstein and the Group. In the early 1960s Terry Eagleton (before he moved to Oxford), John Barrell and Anthony Rudolf were prominent poets and editors. John Barrell was named in *Stand* as its Cambridge rep., a post which Eagleton later held in Oxford. Barrell published his poems in a *Stand*-University of Leeds-Northern House pamphlet. Anthony Rudolf was later a *Stand* rep. and founded the Menard Press. They all studied and thought of poetry as part of social action. They also offered practical support to poetry as one of its outward forms wherever they went on to live. J. H. Prynne is a Cambridge poet, and his work has been influential. However, I am puzzled as to whether and how it has been sustained through poetry's outer forms. It is more an example of poetry's informal but robust networking.[53]

So many who help poetry contribute to vital networking. John Lucas has continued to write and edit in Nottingham, and some of his work promotes a broad regional identity. For example, his edition of *Poetry: The Nottingham Collection* includes Tom Paulin and Peter Porter (they taught at Nottingham and Nottingham Trent). Ian Gregson and Carol Rumens have both been important promoters of creative writing in cities and universities, especially Bangor but also Hull.[54] David Morley is professor of poetry at the University of Warwick. He is a Carcanet poet, and after his first degree in science, he entered grass-roots creative work in community arts in the North. The University of Warwick encourages creative writing at all degree levels and has its own creative and critical journal, *The Warwick Review*, edited by Michael Hulse. Susan Bassnett has been a guiding force there as poet, theorist and translator.

Another group of poetry's movements, from Cambridge to other cities and universities, involves Philip Hobsbaum. After Sheffield, he had a post from 1962 at Queen's University, Belfast. He found himself in an environment already fostering new poetry. How far the endemic energy and talent of Seamus Heaney and Edna and Michael Longley, would have grown anyway without Hobsbaum's presence might be challenged and debated. But the presence of someone who had developed the Group technique with Hughes, Redgrove, Lucie-Smith, MacBeth, Mitchell and Porter, as well as liaising with Jon Silkin on the importance of students' writing being linked with publication (the link with Silkin in Leeds and Sheffield), was an important new ingredient. It was not part of a degree programme though it had an intense academic aura. Hobsbaum was the 'chairman':

> Edna Longley, who came from Dublin to Belfast in the early 1960s and joined his creative writing group there, says: 'It was very intimidating, run like a seminar in an autocratic way, which created a sense of occasion – and a sense of controversy'. The rules in Belfast and Glasgow were as they had been earlier in Cambridge and London.[55]

Members of the Belfast Group included James Simmons, Ciaran Carson and Paul Muldoon. Meetings continued after Hobsbaum left Belfast.

There are important records of meetings, and the poems discussed, available from the Emory University:

> Hobsbaum reports that the first half of the Group meetings was always devoted to the work of a single writer, and that those present would discuss each piece immediately after it was read.... At the close of the reading and discussion, there would be a brief break for coffee and biscuits, before reconvening for an open session where anyone could read work they wished to share. Philip Hobsbaum recalls Arthur Terry reading Robert Lowell in the second half of a Group meeting, and Michael Allen remembers Marie Devlin (later Heaney) reading her own poems.
>
> ***
>
> As Seamus Heaney has put it, 'What happened Monday night after Monday night in the Hobsbaum's flat in Fitzwilliam Street somehow ratified the activity of writing for all of us who shared it.'[3] (Seamus Heaney, 'The Belfast Group: A Symposium', p. 62.)[56]

Belfast, in spite of the Troubles (or because of them?), maintained its sense of the importance of writing. The university sponsors the Seamus Heaney Poetry Centre which is both a location, a resource centre, including digital archives of poets reading, produces a poetry journal called *The Yellow Nib*, and is the focus for creative writing learning and teaching to PhD level.[57] T. S. Eliot Prize winner Sinead Morrissey teaches creative writing there and is the first Belfast Poet Laureate. Interestingly, she is also a Carcanet poet. As with the Manchester University Centre for New Writing, the Seamus Heaney Centre attracts community interest and offers diverse contacts for those not going through conventional degree studies; in the best sense, a hub.

It seems that Hobsbaum found converting his methods into the formality of course design, with outcomes and assessment, unattractive. Nevertheless, eventually it worked in Glasgow:

> But Hobsbaum was then persuaded to start a University Extra-Mural class in creative writing, which opened in 1969 with no fewer than 75 students, and

> he was able to take from it the members for 'Glasgow Group Mark II', which ran from 1972 to 1975. James Kelman, Liz Lochhead and Jeff Torrington were recruited in that way; writers who taught the extra-mural class also joined, including the American poet Anne Stevenson, who was to be Hobsbaum's partner for several years. Aonghas MacNeacail came, writing in English and Gaelic, and Alasdair Gray read to the group early drafts of his novel Lanark.[58]

Glasgow attempted to mix formal study and contact with brilliant writers who may have found being systematised difficult.

Creative writing has also been important at St Andrews with Douglas Dunn, and now Don Paterson as leaders. Paterson left school at sixteen, worked as a musician and was 'captivated by poetry upon encountering poet Tony Harrison'.[59] Paterson still edits the poetry list for Picador-Macmillan, so is part of the vital trend in creative writing in being someone who helps to set the trends through his editorial choices, as well as contributing to them himself. There is another successful programme at Stirling, where Kathleen Jamie is poet and professor, and programmes at Aberdeen, Strathclyde and Dundee.

Michael Schmidt arrived in Glagow in 2006 charged with developing MLitt and PhD elements both for resident and distance learning (online) students. This has been highly successful, and marks another example of symbiosis between poet, publisher, critic and academic. Michael Schmidt as Course Leader has an important combination of the Oxford-Leeds model of sharing writing with the now more conventional 'programme-design' model. The Oxford-Leeds model does not involve teaching as such. It works on a subversion-cum-symbiosis principle in which a university plants a poet on campus (or nearby) to act as a practitioner who will attract those who want to learn informally. This was the Dobrée and Eliot ethos as built in to the Gregory Fellowships at Leeds, and which the university has re-started in 2014 with the appointment of Helen Mort, not to a department, but through its Academy of Cultural Fellows, to offer creative writing workshops to any and all.[60]

Michael Schmidt first moved from Oxford, where he had studied and in 1969 had re-launched the Carcanet title, to Manchester in 1971 at the invitation of Professor Brian Cox. Schmidt developed Carcanet, founded *PN Review* in 1972 (as *Poetry Nation*), and carried out much English literature teaching. He did not teach creative writing formally until 1993, when with Dr Richard Francis, he started teaching creative writing at undergraduate level, and then set up a master's programme, and creative PhDs, which continue to thrive.[61] He then joined the nearby Manchester Metropolitan University where he led their MA and creative PhD programmes. Poet and Northern House Editor Jeffrey Wainwright was already there, and the

Department of English and Creative Writing was soon joined by Simon Armitage and Carol Ann Duffy (who was to become Poet Laureate in 2009). The older Manchester University further developed its own poetry and prose fiction courses led by John McAuliffe, Ian McGuire, M. J. Hyland and Vona Groarke, with Professors Martin Amis, Colm Tobin and Janette Winterson. Throughout the country, historic suspicion of traditional English studies departments towards teaching creative writing, especially those recently dominated by cultural theory, has been rather undermined by the appearance on their corridors of so many of the writers listed on their syllabuses, and about whom they theorise.

Schmidt has worked through many of the issues which preoccupied creative writing course designers embedded in English Departments. Thus, in both the programmes that he led at Manchester Metropolitan and Glasgow Universities, he wanted to make sure that all of the MA and MLit students, whatever their backgrounds and previous degree reading, would have a common familiarity with the greatest books. Indeed, he discouraged the students' own writing until they had all read Homer, Horace and Sappho. He led an assessed module on 'Transmission' in which students learned from the practical business of designing and implementing their own forms of publication. Perhaps this was a way of formalising part of the Oxford model – ensuring that everyone had a sophisticated and common grounding in the main texts of Western literature so that the students' own decisions to set sail were based on their knowledge of the history of poetry's geography and navigation. Students also had to put their own writing into action – so often the crucial element of becoming a poet within, and without, the academy.

So, what are the outer forms of poetry at the time of writing? Universities have created a new context and a new ethos. In effect, poets and poetry are now massively helped and financially supported by universities. Does this mean that poets and poetry are now created by, and their identities dictated to by, universities? So far, this seems not the case. I have tried to show that the intense moral and structural individualism of poetry ensured that in post-Second World War England new poetry was written, published, and its processes 'handed on', without state subsidy or creative writing degrees. To some extent, the big publishers, established journals and the BBC, gave a lead by their very presence. But reading, writing and formation of new journals and small presses went on, as it were, without permission. Rather than universities forming committees to re-define poetry from the top down, Schools of English have realised that they would have to import existing practitioners. In effect, what has been created is rather like the laboratory in science, technology and medicine. What is learned is re-learned and renewed and changed by 'doing', and 'visibly sharing what you do'. The creative writing 'workshop' is not only a good educational method, but it has already stimulated great writing. Obviously, great poets themselves have been exemplary guides. And how interesting it is that the present outward creative ladders and scaffolding have been enabled and positioned by those who so loved to promote writing through discussion, publishing, practice, and example – T. S. Eliot, Bonamy Dobrée and F. R. Leavis.

NOTES

1 http://www.qaa.ac.uk/en.
2 http://www.nawe.co.uk/.
3 http://www.english.heacademy.ac.uk/.
4 http://www.arvon.org/about-us/history-arvon/.
5 http://www.writeoutloud.net/public/background.php.
6 Recently through Eggbox Publishing, Norwich.
7 Simon Armitage; 'Forward', *CAST* (Sheffield: Smith | Doorstop, 2014), p. 10; Armitage is professor of poetry at the University of Sheffield.
8 Moniza Alvi, Lavinia Greenlaw, George Szirtes, 'Introduction', *UEA 17 Poets 2012* (Norwich: Eggbox, 2012), p. ii.
9 Nicholas Wroe, 'The Poet, Musician and Playwright on Her Rise to Fame', *The Guardian* Review, 4 October 2014, p. 12; also see Laura Barton, 'Poet, Performer, Novelist: the Rise of the Uncategorisable Kate Tempest', *The Guardian*, 13 September 2014, p. 15; Dorian Lynskey, 'Original Poetry Material', *The Guardian*, 24 October 2014, *G2* p. 6.
10 The Poetry Book Society chooses, with appropriate publicity, a number of 'New Generation' poets every ten years.
11 Jonathan Price and Geoffrey Hill, eds., *New Poems* Vol. 2 No. 2 (Eynsham, Oxford: Fantasy Press, 1952[?]).
12 Donald Hall and Geoffrey Hill, *Oxford Poetry 1953* (Eynsham: Fantasy Press, 1953). This included contemporary Oxford student poets A. Alvarez, Alan Brownjohn, Don Collis, Alistair Elliot, Donald Hall, Geoffrey Hill, Jenny Joseph, J. E. M. Lucie-Smith, George MacBeth, John Mallet, Adrian Mitchell, Jonathan Price, John Reed, E. Margaret Strahan, Anthony Thwaite. Pamphlets from the Fantasy Press and from Reading University School of Art and the Marvell Press were mentioned as examples of publications by good young poets in Robert Conquest's Introduction to *New Lines*, (London: 1957), p. xiii.
13 Geoffrey Hill, *Geoffrey Hill* [eponymous title] (Eynsham, Oxford: 1952).
14 Donald Hall, *Unpacking the Boxes* (New York: Houghton Mifflin, 2008), p. 103.
15 Ibid., p. 105.
16 Charles Williams, *New Book of English Verse* (London: Gollancz, 1935).
17 The Institute of Contemporary Arts. See Dannie Abse's memoir, *Goodbye, Twentieth Century* (London: Pimlico, 2001), pp. 113–16 for an account of Emanuel Litvinoff's reading of his poem 'To T S Eliot' with Eliot in the audience.

18 See *A Group Anthology* (London: Oxford University Press, 1963), and Philip Hobsbaum's interview by Gerry Cambridge published in *The Dark Horse 14* (Bothwell, South Lanarkshire, summer 2002), 30–50.

19 Cecil Day Lewis (1904–72). Poet famous in the 1930s with Auden, Spender and MacNeice, director and senior editor of Chatto and Windus. Poet Laureate 1968–72. Silkin stayed with him and drove him around London house-hunting.

20 Dannie Abse, ed. *Poetry and Poverty* 1–7 (London: Villiers Publications, 1949–54); Dannie Abse and Howard Sergeant, eds., *Mavericks* (London: Editions Poetry and Poverty, 1957).

21 T. S. Eliot, *Little Gidding* (London: Faber and Faber, 1942).

22 Dannie Abse, *Poetry and Poverty* 4, p. 4. (Perhaps the image came from Abse's day job as a doctor specialising in chest complaints.)

23 Edward Lucie-Smith, *A Group Anthology* (London: Oxford University Press, 1962), p. v.

24 Edward Lucie-Smith, 'Forward', *A Group Anthology* (London: Oxford University Press, 1962), p. vii.

25 Ibid., p. viii.

26 Philip Hobsbaum, 'Epilogue', *A Group Anthology* (London: Oxford University Press, 1962), p. 123.

27 Sheila Rowbotham, *Promise of a Dream: Remembering the Sixties* (London: Allen Lane Press, 2000 and London: Penguin, 2001). Her account of selling the first *Black Dwarf* reads like a *Stand* sales journey: '163 *Dwarfs* sold so far ... *Dwarfs* have penetrated Leeds Gas Board, Burn Bridge Bourgeoisie, tramps at St. George's Crypt [Leeds], Ripon Grammar School, a Welsh College, Tony Jackson and "Utima Thule", Leeds CND, Tyne Tees Television, the people in the Pack Horse [pub] in Leeds.... We have been rejected by Hebden Bridge library because we aren't local, by a Communist because we weren't the *Morning Star*, and by a man on the dole in Newcastle because there was nothing for him in the paper' (p. 183).

28 Shiela Rowbotham, *Promise of a Dream* (London: Penguin, 2001), p. 56.

29 Philip Hobsbaum, letter to Jon Silkin, Leeds University Library, Special Collections BC MS Silkin.

30 Philip Hobsbaum, 'Interview', in *The Dark Horse* (summer 2002), p. 46.

31 Leeds University senate paper, 'Committee on Gregory Fellowships in Art', 2 June 1943, University of Leeds, University Archives.

32 T. S. Eliot, letter to Bonamy Dobrée, 10 March 1943, University of Leeds, University Archives.

33 In spite of the popularity of the Mersey Poets with the publication of *Penguin Modern Poets 10: The Mersey Sound* (1967) it seems that Liverpool did not become a major site for handing on poetry through 'outward forms' until initiatives from John Moores University. But also see Phil Bowen, *A Gallery to Play to: The Story of the Mersey Poets*, (Exeter: Stride Publications, 1999).

34 David Wright, 'Another Part of the Wood', *Poetry Nation* 4 (1975), pp. 121–28.

35 For an important insight into how the Gregory Fellows, including Thomas Blackburn, got on together see Julia Blackburn's memoir *The Three of Us* (London: Vintage, 2009). Thomas Blackburn wrote a small creative writing

handbook for the Milk Marketing Board [sic] called *Write Your Own Poetry* (The Project Club, Project Book 107, [London?] Wolfe Publishing: 1970), a strange example of poetry's outward support.

36 For more on 'passing on' poetry in Leeds, see Jeffrey Wainwright, '"Space available": A Poet's Decisions', in *The Oxford Handbook of Contemporary British and Irish Poetry*, ed. Peter Robinson (Oxford: Oxford University Press: 2013).

37 One of the very first Bloodaxe publications was, significantly for this Chapter, a pamphlet, *Tristan Crazy*, by Ken Smith. Smith had been a co-editor of *Stand* in Leeds and after and was a Leeds graduate. The pamphlet appeared in 1978, and the address of *Bloodaxe* on the editorial page was 19 Haldane Terrace, Newcastle-upon-Tyne – the home address of Jon Silkin and *Stand*. *Bloodaxe* was Smith's publisher until his death in 2003. Astley's next pamphlets, from another address, were by John Cassidy, *The Fountain* and *Changes of Light*, both 1979. Cassidy, from Bolton, had previously been published by Hutchinson under Dannie Abse's editorship.

38 *Writing Women* 1:1 (Oct. 1981–88, Newcastle-upon-Tyne), *Mslexia* (March 1999, Newcastle-upon-Tyne). Both supported by Northern Arts.

39 W. E. Parkinson, 'Poetry in the North East', in *British Poetry Since 1960*, Michael Schmidt and Grevel Lindop, eds. (South Hinksey, Oxford: Carcanet, 1972), p. 111.

40 Rebecca A. Smith, 'Barry MacSweeney and the Bunting Influence', *Jacket Magazine* 35, Early 2008, http://jacketmagazine.com/35/smith-macsweeney.shtml.

41 Rodney Pybus, 'Writing: North-East', *Stand* 8:2 (Newcastle-upon-Tyne, 1966), 11.

42 Neil Astley, ed., *Ten North-East Poets* (Newcastle-upon-Tyne: Bloodaxe, 1980).

43 Michael Schmidt, 'Sweet Voices', *New Statesman* (London, 6 March 1981), 21; Douglas Dunn, 'The Newcastle Nexus', *TLS* (London, 9 Jan. 1981), 39; Peter Porter, 'The Muse in the North East', *Observer* (London, 15 March 1981), 33.

44 Jon Silkin, *Complete Poems*, Jon Glover and Kathryn Jenner, eds. (Manchester: Northern House, Carcanet, 2015).

45 Including Bill Herbert and Desmond Graham, the latter is a poet, editor, critic and biographer in the Leeds tradition.

46 Cora Kaplan, 'Language and Gender', in *Papers on Patriarchy Conference London 1976* (Lewes, Sussex: Women's Publishing Collective, 1976), p. 22.

47 Ibid., p. 22.

48 Cora Kaplan, ed., *Salt and Bitter and Good: Three Centuries of English and American Women Poets* (New York and London: Paddington Press, 1975).

49 Carol Rumens, ed., *Making for the Open* (London: Chatto and Windus, 1985).

50 Diana Scott, ed., *Bread and Roses* (Harmondsworth: Penguin) 1982.

51 Carol Cosman, Joan Keefe and Kathleen Weaver, eds., *The Penguin Book of Women Poets* (Harmondsworth: Penguin, 1983).

52 Jon Silkin, *The Penguin Book of First World War Poetry* (Harmondworth: Penguin, 1978), Jon Glover and Jon Silkin, *The Penguin Book of First World War Prose*, (London: Penguin, 1990); Catherine Reilly, *Scars Upon My Heart*, (London: Virago, 1981). There are interesting reflections on Silkin's and Glover's moral and gendered aesthetics in Agnes Cardinal, Dorothy Goldman, Judith Hattaway, eds., *Women's Writing of the First World War* (Oxford: Oxford University Press, 1999).

53 See, e.g., Edward Larrissy, 'Poets of a Various Art', in *Contemporary British Poetry: Essays in Theory and Criticism*, James Acheson and Roman Huk, eds. (Albany, NY: SUNY Press, 1996).

54 Ian Gregson and Carol Rumens, eds., *Old City, New Rumours* (Nottingham: Five Leaves, 2010).

55 Neal Ascherson, 'Books: The Great Brain Spotter: The List of Past Members of Philip Hobsbaum's Writing Classes Reads Like a Who's Who of Modern Literature. How Has He Managed It?', in *The Independent* (28 February 1993), http://www.independent.co.uk/arts-entertainment/books--great-brain-spotter-the-list-of-past-members-of-philip-hobsbaums-writing-classes-reads-like-a-whos-who-of-modern-literature-how-has-he-managed-it-1475910.html, accessed 18 July 2015.

56 http://beck.library.emory.edu/BelfastGroup/web/html/overview.html.

57 For further information see: http://www.qub.ac.uk/schools/SeamusHeaneyCentreforPoetry/.

58 Neal Ascherson, 'Books: The Great Brain Spotter: The List of Past Members of Philip Hobsbaum's Writing Classes Reads Like a Who's Who Of Modern Literature. How Has He Managed It?' *The Independent* (28 February 1993).

59 http://www.poetryfoundation.org/bio/don-paterson.

60 'A gift from alumnus Douglas Caster (Electronic and Electrical Engineering 1975) will now allow Helen to develop her writing as a Cultural Fellow in Poetry, working in the school of English and with a mission to bring poetry to the community. The Academy revives the tradition of the Gregory Fellowships, which saw a string of talented creative take up residence here in the post-war years.' http://campaign.leeds.ac.uk/news/helen-joins-academy/.

61 Graduates from the programme at Manchester (Victoria) University while Schmidt was there include poet and novelist Sophie Hannah and poets Ian Pople and Steven Blythe.

FURTHER READING

General Works

Acheson, James, and Romana Huk, eds., *Contemporary British Poetry: Essays in Theory and Criticism* (Albany: State University of New York Press, 1996).

Alderman, Nigel, and Michael Thurston, *Reading Postwar British and Irish Poetry* (Chichester, West Sussex: Wiley-Blackwell, 2014).

Alvarez, A., ed., *The New Poetry* (Harmondsworth: Penguin, 1962; 2nd edn. 1966).

Bedient, Calvin, *Eight Contemporary Poets* (London: Oxford University Press, 1974).

Bergonzi, Bernard, *Wartime and Aftermath: English Literature and Its Background 1939–1960* (Oxford: Oxford University Press, 1993).

Booth, Martin, *British Poetry 1964 to 1984: Driving through the Barricades* (London: Routledge and Kegan Paul, 1985).

Brinton, Ian, *Contemporary Poetry: Poets and Poetry since 1990 (Cambridge Contexts in Literature)* (Cambridge: Cambridge University Press, 2009).

Broom, Sarah, *Contemporary British and Irish Poetry: An Introduction* (Basingstoke: Palgrave Macmillan, 2005).

Bunting, Basil, *Briggflatts* (London: Fulcrum Press, 1966).

Childs, Peter, *The Twentieth Century in Poetry: A Critical Survey* (London: Routledge, 1999).

Corcoran, Neil, *English Poetry Since 1940* (Harlow: Longman, 1993).

ed., *The Cambridge Companion to Twentieth-Century English Poetry* (Cambridge: Cambridge University Press, 2007).

Crozier, Andrew, 'Thrills and Frills: Poetry as Figures of Empirical Lyricism', in *Society and Literature 1945–1979*, ed. Alan Sinfield (London: Methuen, 1983), pp. 199–233.

Davie, Donald, *Under Briggflatts: A History of Poetry in Great Britain, 1960–1988* (Chicago: University of Chicago Press, 1989).

Gregson, Ian, *Contemporary Poetry and Postmodernism: Dialogue and Estrangement* (Basingstoke: Macmillan, 1996).

Hamilton, Ian and Jeremy Noel-Tod, eds., *The Oxford Companion to Modern Poetry*, 2nd edn. (Oxford: Oxford University Press, 2013).

Hulse, Michael, David Kennedy, and David Morley, eds., *The New Poetry* (Newcastle: Bloodaxe, 1993).

Kennedy, David, *New Relations: The Refashioning of British Poetry, 1980–1994* (Bridgend: Seren, 1996).
Larrissy, Edward, *Reading Twentieth Century Poetry: The Language of Gender and Objects* (Oxford: Blackwell, 1990).
Motion, Andrew, and Blake Morrison, eds., *The Penguin Book of Contemporary British Poetry* (Harmondsworth: Penguin, 1982).
Nuttall, Jeff, *Bomb Culture* (New York: Delacorte Press, 1968).
O'Brien, Sean, *The Deregulated Muse: Essays on Contemporary British and Irish Poetry* (Newcastle: Bloodaxe, 1997).
Paterson, Don, and Charles Simic, eds., *New British Poetry* (Saint Paul, MN: Graywolf Press, 2004).
Press, John, *Rule and Energy: Trends in British Poetry since the Second World War* (London: Oxford University Press, 1963).
Raban, Jonathan, *The Society of the Poem* (London: Harrap, 1971).
Roberts, Neil, ed., *A Companion to Twentieth-Century Poetry* (Oxford: Blackwell, 2001).
Sheppard, Robert, *The Poetry of Saying: British Poetry and Its Discontents 1950–2000* (Liverpool: Liverpool University Press, 2005).
Robinson, Alan, *Instabilities in Contemporary British Poetry* (Basingstoke: Macmillan, 1988).
Robinson, Peter, ed., *The Oxford Handbook of Contemporary British and Irish Poetry* (Oxford: Oxford University Press, 2013).
Schmidt, Michael, and Peter Jones, eds., *British Poetry Since 1970: A Critical Survey* (Manchester: Carcanet Press, 1980).
Trotter, David, *The Making of the Reader: Language and Subjectivity in Modern American, English and Irish Poetry* (Basingstoke: Macmillan, 1984).
Tuma, Keith, *Fishing by Obstinate Isles: Modern and Postmodern British Poetry and American Readers* (Evanston, IL: Northwestern University Press, 1998).
Waugh, Patricia, *Harvest of the Sixties: English Literature and Its Background 1960 to 1990* (Oxford: Oxford University Press, 1995).
Wheatley, David, *Contemporary British Poetry (Readers' Guides to Essential Criticism)* (London: Palgrave Macmillan, 2014).
Williams, Nerys, *Contemporary Poetry (Edinburgh Critical Guides)* (Edinburgh: Edinburgh University Press, 2011).

Poets of the Forties and Early Fifties: The Last Romantics?

1. Anthologies

British Poetry since 1945, ed. Edward Lucie-Smith (Harmondsworth: Penguin, 1970).
Images of Tomorrow: An Anthology of Recent Poetry, ed. John Heath-Stubbs (London: SCM Press, 1953).
The New Apocalypse: An Anthology of Criticism, Poems and Stories (London: Fortune Press, 1940).
A New Romantic Anthology, ed. Stefan Schimanski and Henry Treece (London: Grey Walls Press, 1949).
The White Horseman: Prose and Verse of the New Apocalypse, ed. J. F. Hendry and Henry Treece (London: Routledge, 1941).

2. *Criticism*

Duncan, Andrew, *Origins of the Underground: British Poetry between Apocryphon and Incident Light, 1933–79* (Cambridge: Salt, 2008).

Goodby, John, *The Poetry of Dylan Thomas: Under the Spelling Wall* (Liverpool: Liverpool University Press, 2013).

Kendall, Tim, *Modern English War Poetry* (Oxford: Oxford University Press, 2006).

Lopez, Tony, *The Poetry of W. S. Graham* (Edinburgh: Edinburgh University Press, 1989).

Mellor, David, ed., *A Paradise Lost: The Neo-Romantic Imagination in Britain, 1935–55* (London: Lund Humphries in association with the Barbican Art Gallery, 1987).

Nicholls, Peter, 'Surrealism in England', in *The Cambridge History of Twentieth-Century English Literature* (Cambridge: Cambridge University Press, 2004), pp. 396–416.

Perkins, David, 'The English Romantic Revival, 1934–1945',. in *A History of Modern Poetry: Modernism and After* (Cambridge, MA: The Belknap Press, 1987), pp. 170–203.

Sinclair, Andrew, *War Like a Wasp: The Lost Decade of the Forties* (London: Hamish Hamilton, 1989).

The Movement

Acheson, James and Romana Huk, eds., *Contemporary British Poetry: Essays in Theory and Criticism* (Albany, NY: State University of New York Press, 1996).

Appleyard, Bryan, *The Pleasures of Peace: Art and Imagination in Post-War Britain* (London: Faber, 1989).

Bloom, Clive, and Gary Day, *Literature and Culture in Modern Britain, Volume Three: 1956–1999* (London: Longman, 2000).

Corcoran, Neil, *English Poetry since 1940* (London: Longman, 1993).

Davie, Donald, *Under Briggflatts: A History of Poetry in Great Britain 1960–1988* (Chicago: University of Chicago Press, 1989).

Day, Gary. *Literature and Culture in Modern Britain, Volume Two: 1930–1955* (London: Longman, 1997).

Day, Gary and Brian Docherty, *British Poetry 1900–1950: Aspects of Tradition* (London: Macmillan, 1995).

Ford, Boris, ed., *Modern Britain: The Cambridge Cultural History* (Cambridge: Cambridge University Press, 1992).

Hewison, Robert, *Culture and Consensus: England, Art and Politics since 1945* (London: Methuen, 1995).

Hoggart, Richard, *The Uses of Literacy: Aspects of Working-Class Life with Special Reference to Publications and Entertainments* (London: Chatto and Windus, 1957).

Homberger, Eric, *The Art of the Real: Poetry in England and America since 1939* (London: Dent, 1977).

Kynaston, David, *Family Britain 1951–57* (London: Bloomsbury, 2009).

Modernity Britain: A Shake of the Dice 1959–62 (London: Bloomsbury, 2014).

Larkin, Philip, *The Oxford Book of Twentieth-Century English Verse* (Oxford: Oxford University Press, 1973).
Leader, Zachary, *The Movement Reconsidered: Essays on Larkin, Amis, Gunn, Davie and Their Contemporaries* (Oxford: Oxford University Press, 2009).
Morrison, Blake, *The Movement: English Poetry and Fiction of the 1950s* (London: Methuen, 1980).
Paterson, Don and Charles Simic, eds., *New British Poetry* (Toronto: Anansi, 2004).
Wilson, A. N., *Our Times: The Age of Elizabeth II* (London: Hutchinson, 2008).

Beyond All This Fiddle

Alderman, Nigel and C. D. Blanton, eds., *A Concise Companion to Postwar British and Irish Poetry* (Malden, MA: Wiley-Blackwell, 2009).
Alderman, Nigel and Michael Thurston, *Reading Postwar British and Irish Poetry* (Chichester, West Sussex: Wiley-Blackwell, 2014).
Davie, Donald, *Thomas Hardy and British Poetry* (Oxford: Oxford University Press, 1972).
Under Briggflatts: A History of Poetry in Great Britain, 1960–1988 (Manchester: Carcanet, 1989).
Duncan, Andrew, *The Failure of Conservatism in Modern British Poetry*, (Cambridge: Salt Publishing, 2003).
Center and Periphery in Modern British Poetry (Liverpool: Liverpool University Press, 2005).
The Long 1950s: Morality and Fantasy as Stakes in the Poetic Game (Bristol: Shearsman Books, 2012).
Gifford, Terry, ed., *The Cambridge Companion to Ted Hughes* (Cambridge: Cambridge University Press, 2011).
Gregson, Ian, *Contemporary Poetry and Postmodernism: Dialogue and Estrangment* (Basingstoke: Macmillan, 1996).
Homberger, Eric, *The Art of the Real: Poetry in England and America since 1939* (London: Dent, and Totowa, NJ: Rowman and Littlefield, 1977).
Kerrigan, John and Peter Robinson, eds., *The Thing About Roy Fisher: Critical Studies* (Liverpool: Liverpool University Press, 2000).
Kirkham, Michael, *Passionate Intellect: The Poetry of Charles Tomlinson* (Liverpool: Liverpool University Press, 1999).
McDonald, Peter, *Serious Poetry: Form and Authority, from Yeats to Hill* (Oxford: Clarendon Press and New York: Oxford University Press, 2002).
Picot, Edward, *Outcasts from Eden: Ideas of Landscape in British Poetry since 1945* (Liverpool: Liverpool University Press, 1997).
Sherry, Vincent, *The Uncommon Tongue: The Poetry and Criticism of Geoffrey Hill* (Ann Arbor: University of Michigan Press, 1987).
Swigg, Richard, *Charles Tomlinson and the Objective Tradition* (Lewisburg, PA: Bucknell University Press, 1994).
Wootten, William, *The Alvarez Generation: Thom Gunn, Geoffrey Hill, Ted Hughes, Sylvia Plath and Peter Porter* (Liverpool: Liverpool University Press, 2015).

Poetry and Performance: The Mersey Poets, the International Poetry Incarnation and Performance Poetry

Barry, Peter, *Contemporary British Poetry and the City* (Manchester and New York: Manchester University Press, 2000).

Bernstein, Charles, ed., *Close Listening: Poetry and the Performed Word* (Oxford: Oxford University Press, 1998).

Breeze, Jean 'Binta', ed., 'Word – Sound – Power', special issue *Critical Quarterly*, 38:4 (Winter 1996).

Buck, Claire, 'Poetry and the Women's Movement in Britain', James Acheson and Romana Huk, eds., *Contemporary British Poetry: Essays in Theory and Criticism* (Albany, NY: State University of New York Press, 1996).

Craig, David, *The Real Foundations: Literature and Social Change* (London: Chatto & Windus, 1973).

Foley, John Miles, *How to Read an Oral Poem* (Urbana, IL and Chicago: University of Illinois Press, 2002).

Gräbner, Cornelia and Arturo Casas, eds., *Performing Poetry: Body, Place and Rhythm in the Poetry Performance* (Amsterdam and Atlanta, GA: Rodopi, 2011).

Henri, Adrian, *Environments and Happenings* (London: Thames and Hudson, 1974).

Henri, Adrian, Roger McGough and Brian Patten, *The Mersey Sound* (Harmondsworth: Penguin, 1967).

Horovitz, Michael, *Children of Albion: Poetry of the 'Underground' in Britain* (Harmondsworth: Penguin, 1969).

Kane, Daniel, Mark Donnelly, David Sterritt, Peter Whitehead, and Raymound Durgnat, 'Dossier: *Wholly Communion*', *Framework: The Journal of Cinema and Media*, 52:1 (2011).

Kinnahan, Linda, 'Feminism's Experimental "Work at the Language-Face"', in *The Cambridge Companion to Twentieth-Century British and Irish Women's Poetry*, Jane Dowson, ed. (Cambridge: Cambridge University Press, 2011), 154–78.

Klawitter, Uwe and Claus-Ulrich Viol, eds., *Contemporary Poetry in Britain and Ireland* (Heidelberg: Universitätsverlag Winter, 2013).

Lucie-Smith, Edward, ed., *The Liverpool Scene: Recorded Live along the Mersey Beat* (London: Donald Carroll, 1967).

Middleton, Peter, *Distant Reading: Performance, Readership, and Consumption in Contemporary Poetry* (Tuscaloosa, AL: University of Alabama Press, 2005).

Murphy, Michael and Deryn Rees-Jones, eds., *Writing Liverpool* (Liverpool: Liverpool University Press, 2007).

Nagy, Gregory, *Poetry as Performance: Homer and Beyond* (Cambridge: Cambridge University Press, 1996).

Novak, Julia, *Live Poetry: An Integrated Approach to Poetry in Performance* (Amsterdam and Atlanta, GA: Rodopi, 2011).

Ong, Walter J., *Orality and Literacy: The Technologizing of the Word* (London and New York: Routledge, 1982).

Wade, Stephen, *Gladsongs and Gatherings: Poetry and Its Social Context in Liverpool since the 1960s* (Liverpool: Liverpool University Press, 2001).

Wandor, Michelene, ed., *On Gender and Writing* (London: Pandora Press, 1983), pp. 42–50.

Warner, Simon, 'Raising the Consciousness? Re-visiting Allen Ginsberg's Liverpool Trip in 1965', in Christoph Grunenberg and Robert Knifton, eds., *Centre of the Creative Universe: Liverpool & the Avant-Garde* (Liverpool: Liverpool University Press, 2007), pp. 95–108.

Wilson, Andrew, 'A Poetics of Dissent: Notes on a Developing Counterculture in London in the Early Sixties', in Chris Stephens and Katharine Stout, eds., *Art & The 60s: This Was Tomorrow* (London: Tate Publishing, 2004), pp. 93–111.

High Late-Modernists or Postmodernists?

Barry, Peter, *Poetry Wars: British Poetry of the 1970s and the Battle of Earls Court* (Cambridge: Salt, 2006).

Barry, Peter, and Hampson Robert, eds, *New British Poetries: the Scope of the Possible* (Manchester: Manchester University Press, 1993).

Caddel, Ric, and Peter Quartermain, eds., *Other: British and Irish Poetry since 1970* (Hanover, NH: University Press of New England, 1999).

Clarke, Adrian, and Robert Sheppard, eds., *Floating Capital: New Poets from London* (Elmwood, CT: Potes and Poets Press 21, 1991).

Crozier, Andrew, and Tim Longville, eds., *A Various Art* (Manchester: Carcanet, 1987).

Duncan, Andrew, *The Failure of Conservatism in Modern British Poetry* (Great Wilbraham: Salt, 2003).

The Council of Heresy: a Primer of Poetry in a Balkanised Terrain (Exeter: Shearsman, 2009).

Etter, Carrie, ed., *Infinite Difference: Other Poetries by U.K. Women Poets* (Exeter: Shearsman, 2010).

Kennedy, David, and Christine Kennedy, *Women's Experimental Poetry in Britain 1970–2010: Body, Time and Locale* (Liverpool: Liverpool University Press, 2013).

Ladkin, Sam, and Robin Purves, eds., *Complicities: British Poetry 1945–2007* (Prague: Literaria Pragensia, 2007).

Chicago Review, British Poetry Issue, 53:1 (2007).

Milne, Drew, 'Neo-Modernism and Avant-Garde Orientations', in Alderman, Nigel, and C. D. Blanton, eds., *A Concise Companion to Postwar British and Irish Poetry* (Chichester: Wiley-Blackwell, 2009), pp. 155–75.

Mengham, Rod, and John Kinsella, eds., *Vanishing Points: New Modernist Poems* (Cambridge: Salt, 2004).

Monk, Geraldine, ed., *Cusp: Recollections of Poetry in Transition* (Exeter: Shearsman, 2012).

Pattison, Neil, Reitha Pattison and Luke Roberts, eds., *Certain Prose of the English Intelligencer* (Cambridge: Mountain, 2012; 2nd rev. edn 2014).

Riley, Denise, ed., *Poets on Writing: Britain, 1970–1991* (Basingstoke: Macmillan, 1992).

Sheppard, Robert, *When Bad Times Made for Good Poetry: Episodes in the History of the Poetics of Innovation* (Exeter: Shearsman, 2011).

Thurston, Scott, ed., *Talking Poetics: Dialogues in Innovative Poetry* (Bristol: Shearsman, 2011).

Tuma, Keith, ed., *Anthology of Twentieth-Century British and Irish Poetry* (Oxford: Oxford University Press, 2001).

Stretching the Lyric: The Anthology Wars, Martianism and After

Barry, Peter, and Robert Hampson, eds., *New British Poetries: The Scope of the Possible* (Manchester: Manchester University Press, 1993).
Bayley, John, 'Contemporary British Poetry: a Romantic Persistence', *Poetry*, 146:4 (July 1985): 227–36.
Caesar, Adrian, *Dividing Lines: Poetry Class and Ideology* (Manchester: Manchester University Press, 1991).
Childs, Peter, *The Twentieth Century in Poetry: A Critical Survey* (London: Routledge, 1999).
Davis, Paul, Rev. of *Public Property*, *Guardian* (28 September 2002), p. 25.
Fenton, James, 'A Martian School of Two or More', *LRB* 1:4 (December 1979): 16.
Forbes, Peter, 'How We Made New Gen – the Faxes behind the Facts', *Poetry Review* 84:3 (1994): 52.
Frost, Elisabeth, 'Found in Translation: an Interview with Christopher Reid', *Electronic Poetry Review* 6 (Spring 2003). www.epoetry.org/issues/issue6/text/prose/reid.htm accessed 12 October 2014.
Gregson, Ian, *Contemporary Poetry and Postmodernism: Dialogue and Estrangement* (Basingstoke: Macmillan, 1996).
Karr, Mary, 'An Interview with Craig Raine' *Ploughshares* 13:4 (1987): 138–48.
Larkin, Philip, *Required Writing* (London: Faber, 1983).
Motion, Andrew, Review of *John Donne: The Reformed Soul*, by John Stubbs. *Ways of Life: On Places, Painters and Poets* (London: Faber, 2008).
'Howard Hodgkin, "Emotional Situations"', in *Ways of Life: On Places, Painters and Poets* (London: Faber, 2008).
Redmond, John, 'Ringmaster', Rev. of *Expanded Universes* by Christopher Reid, *LRB* 18:23 (November 1996): 25–26.
'Lyric Adaptations'. *The Cambridge Companion to Twentieth-Century Poetry*, ed. Neil Corcoran (Cambridge: Cambridge University Press, 2007), pp. 245–58.
Richman, Robert, Rev. of *Dangerous Play* by Andrew Motion. *The New Criterion* 4 (January 1986): 76.
Shklovsky, Viktor, 'Art as Device', 1917, *Theory of Prose*. Elmwood Park, IL: Dalkey Archive Press, 1991: 1–14.
Smith, Stan, *Poetry and Displacement* (Liverpool: Liverpool University Press, 2007).
Trotter, David, *The Making of the Reader: Language and Subjectivity in Modern American, English and Irish Poetry* (Basingstoke: Macmillan, 1984).

Poetry and Class

Astley, Neil, ed., *Poetry with an Edge* (Newcastle: Bloodaxe, 1997).
New Blood. (Newcastle: Bloodaxe, 1997).
Barry, Peter, *Contemporary British Poetry and the City* (Manchester: Manchester University Press, 2000).

Corcoran, Neil, *English Poetry since 1940* (Harlow: Longman, 1993).
Herbert, W. N. and Hollis, Matthew, eds., *Strong Words: Modern Poets on Modern Poetry* (Newcastle: Bloodaxe, 2000).
Hoggart, Richard, *The Uses of Literacy: Aspects of Working-Class Life* (1957); rprt, (Harmondsworth: Penguin, 2009).
Larrissy, Edward, *Reading Twentieth-Century Poetry* (Oxford: Blackwell, 1990).
O'Brien, Sean, *The Deregulated Muse: Essays on Contemporary British and Irish Poetry* (Newcastle: Bloodaxe, 1998).
Robinson, Peter, *Twentieth-Century Poetry: Selves and Situations* (Oxford: Oxford University Press, 2005).
Warner, Ahren, and Roddy Lumsden, *The Best British Poetry of 2013* (Cromer, Norfolk: Salt, 2013).
Wheatley, David, *Contemporary British Poetry (Readers' Guides to Essential Criticism)* (Basingstoke: Palgrave Macmillan, 2014).

'In a between World': Northern Irish Poetry

Alcobia-Murphy, Shane, *Sympathetic Ink: Intertextual Relations in Northern Irish Poetry* (Liverpool: Liverpool University Press, 2006).
Andrews, Elmer, ed., *Contemporary Irish Poetry: A Collection of Critical Essays* (Basingstoke: Macmillan, 1992).
Brearton, Fran, *Reading Michael Longley* (Tarset: Bloodaxe, 2006).
Brearton, Fran, and Alan Gillis, eds., *The Oxford Handbook of Modern Irish Poetry* (Oxford: Oxford University Press, 2012).
Brearton, Fran and Edna Longley, eds., *Incorrigibly Plural: Louis MacNeice and His Legacy* (Manchester: Carcanet, 2012).
Campbell, Matthew, ed., *The Cambridge Companion to Contemporary Irish Poetry* (Cambridge: Cambridge University Press, 2003).
Clark, Heather, *The Ulster Renaissance: Poetry in Belfast 1962–1972* (Oxford: Oxford University Press, 2006).
Corcoran, Neil, ed., *The Chosen Ground: Essays on the Contemporary Poetry of Northern Ireland* (Bridgend: Seren Books, 1992).
The Poetry of Seamus Heaney: A Critical Study (London: Faber, 1998).
Goodby, John, *Irish Poetry since 1950: From Stillness into History* (Manchester: Manchester University Press, 2000).
Haughton, Hugh, *The Poetry of Derek Mahon* (Oxford: Oxford University Press, 2007).
Kirkland, Richard, *Literature and Culture in Northern Ireland since 1965: Moments of Danger* (London and New York: Longman, 1996).
Longley, Edna, *The Living Stream: Literature and Revisionism in Ireland* (Newcastle: Bloodaxe, 1994).
McDonald, Peter, *Mistaken Identities: Poetry and Northern Ireland* (Oxford: Clarendon Press, 1997).
Wills, Clair, *Improprieties: Politics and Sexuality in Northern Irish Poetry* (Oxford: Oxford University Press, 1993).
Reading Paul Muldoon (Newcastle: Bloodaxe, 1998).

Scottish Poetry 1945–2010

Brown, Ian and Alan Riach, eds., *The Edinburgh Companion to Twentieth-Century Scottish Literature* (Edinburgh: Edinburgh University Press, 2009), see John Corbett, 'Language, MacDiarmid and W.S. Graham', pp. 112–22; Robyn Marsack, 'The Seven Poets Generation', pp. 156–66; Michelle Macleod, 'Language and Identity in Modern Gaelic Verse', pp. 167–80; and Donny O'Rourke, 'Poetry in the Age of Morgan', pp. 204–13.

Carrell, Christopher, ed., *Seven Poets* (Glasgow: Third Eye Centre, 1981).

Falconer, Rachel, ed., *Kathleen Jamie: Essays and Poems on Her Work* (Edinburgh: Edinburgh University Press, 2015).

Fergusson, Maggie, *George Mackay Brown: The Life* (London: John Murray, 2006).

Gifford, Douglas, Sarah Dunnigan and Alan MacGillivray, eds., *Scottish Literature in English and Scots* (Edinburgh: Edinburgh University Press, 2002), see 'Decline and Revival', pp. 721–36, 'Scottish Poetry after 1945', pp. 737–93.

Gish, Nancy, 'Complexities of Subjectivity: Scottish Poets and Multiplicity' [on Liz Lochhead, Jackie Kay and Kathleen Jamie], in *Assembling Alternatives: Reading Postmodern Poetries Transnationally*, ed. Romana Huk (Middletown, CT: Wesleyan University Press, 2003), pp. 259–74.

Hay, George Campbell, *Collected Poems and Songs*, ed. Michel Byrne (Edinburgh: Edinburgh University Press for The Lorimer Trust, 2 vols., 2000).

Hendry, Joy and Raymond J. Ross, *Norman MacCaig: Critical Essays* (Edinburgh: Edinburgh University Press, 1990).

McGonigal, James, *Beyond the Last Dragon: A Life of Edwin Morgan* (Dingwall: Sandstone Press, 2010).

McGuire, Matt and Colin Nicolson, eds., *The Edinburgh Companion to Contemporary Scottish Poetry* (Edinburgh: Edinburgh University Press, 2009).

Moffat, Alexander and Alan Riach, *Arts of Resistance: Poets, Portraits and Landscapes of Modern Scotland* (Edinburgh: Luath Press, 2008).

Riach, Alan, ed., *The International Companion to Edwin Morgan* (Glasgow: Association for Scottish Literary Studies, 2015).

Hugh MacDiarmid's Epic Poetry (Edinburgh: Edinburgh University Press, 1991).

Ross, Raymond J. and Joy Hendry, eds., *Sorley MacLean: Critical Essays* (Edinburgh: Scottish Academic Press, 1986).

Sassi, Carla, ed., *The International Companion to Scottish Poetry* (Glasgow: Association for Scottish Literary Studies, 2015).

Varty, Anne, ed., *The Edinburgh Companion to Liz Lochhead* (Edinburgh: Edinburgh University Press, 2013).

Walker, Marshall, 'Poets of the Scottish Renaissance from Hugh MacDiarmid to Edwin Morgan', in *Scottish Literature Since 1707* (Harlow: Longmans, 1996), pp. 277–317.

Whyte, Christopher, *Modern Scottish Poetry* (Edinburgh: Edinburgh University Press, 2004).

Welsh Poetry since 1945

Conran, Anthony, *The Cost of Strangeness: Essays on the English Poets of Wales* (Llandysul: Gomer, 1982).

Conran, Tony, *Frontiers in Anglo-Welsh Poetry* (Cardiff: University of Wales Press, 1997).
Davies, Damian Walford, ed., *Echoes to the Amen: Essays after R. S. Thomas*, (Cardiff: University of Wales Press, 2003).
Goodby, John and Chris Wigginton, eds., *Dylan Thomas (New Casebook Series)* (Basingstoke: Palgrave Macmillan, 2001).
Gregson, Ian, *The New Poetry in Wales* (Cardiff: University of Wales Press, 2007).
Hardy, Barbara, *Dylan Thomas: An Original Language* (Athens: University of Georgia Press, 2000).
Hooker, Jeremy, 'Poets, Language and Land: Reflections on English-Language Welsh Poetry since the Second World War', *Yearbook of Welsh Writing in English* 8 (2003): 141–56.
Jarvis, Matthew, *Welsh Environments in Contemporary Poetry* (Cardiff: University of Wales Press, 2008).
Jones, Glyn, *The Dragon Has Two Tongues*, (London: Dent, 1968; reprint Cardiff: University of Wales Press, 2001).
Minhinnick, Robert, ed., *Poetry Wales: Forty Years* (Bridgend: Seren, 2005).
Williams, Daniel, ed., *Slanderous Tongues: Essays on Welsh Poetry in English 1970–2005* (Bridgend: Seren, 2010).

'Mekin Histri': Black British Poetry from the Windrush to the Twenty-First Century

Arana, R. Victoria, ed., *'Black' British Aesthetics Today* (Newcastle: Cambridge Scholars Publishing, 2009).
Arana, R. Victoria and Lauri Ramey, *Black British Writing* (New York: Palgrave Macmillan, 2004).
Berry, James, ed., *News for Babylon: The Chatto Book of Westindian-British Poetry* (London: Chatto and Windus, 1984).
Chatterjee, Debjani, ed., *The Redbeck Anthology of British Asian Writing* (Bradford: Redbeck Press, 2000).
Dawes, Kwame, 'Black British Poetry: Some Considerations', in *Write Black Write British*, ed. Kadija Sesay (Hertford: Hansib, 2005), pp. 282–99.
ed., *Red: Contemporary Black British Poetry* (Leeds: Peepal Tree Press, 2010).
Donnell, Alison, ed., *Companion to Contemporary Black British Culture* (London and New York: Routledge, 2002).
Donnell, Alison and Sarah Lawson Welsh, eds., *The Routledge Reader in Caribbean Literature* (London and New York: Routledge, 1996).
Evaristo, Bernadine, and Daljit Nagra, eds., *Ten New Poets* (London: Spread the Word, 2010).
Kay, Jackie, James Procter and Gemma Robinson, eds., *Out of Bounds: British Black and Asian Poets* (Newcastle: Bloodaxe, 2012).
Lawson Welsh, Sarah, '(Un)belonging Citizens, Unmapped Territory: Black Immigration and British Identity in the Post-1945 Period', in Stuart Murray, ed., *Not on Any Map: Essays on Postcoloniality and Cultural Nationalism* (Exeter: Exeter University Press, 1997), pp. 43–66.
Markham, E. A., ed., *Hinterland: Caribbean Poetry from the West Indies and Britain* (Newcastle: Bloodaxe, 1989).

McCarthy Woolf, Karen, ed., *Ten: the New Wave* (Newcastle: Bloodaxe, 2014).
Procter, James, ed., *Writing Black Britain: 1948–1998* (Manchester: Manchester University Press, 2000).
Saroukhani, Henghameh, 'Penguinizing Dub: Paratextual Frames for Transnational Protest in Linton Kwesi Johnson's Mi Revalueshanary Fren', *Journal of Postcolonial Writing* 50 (2014): 1–13.

Poetry, Feminism, Gender and Women's Experience

For a comprehensive bibliography of primary and critical works, consult Dowson and Entwistle, *A History of Twentieth Century British Women's* Poetry; for a chronology, see Rees-Jones, *Consorting with Angels*. Details of both books are given under Critical Works below.

Anthologies

Mohin, Lilian, ed., *One Foot on the Mountain: An Anthology of British Feminist Poetry 1969–1979* (London: OnlyWomen Press, 1979).
Rees-Jones, Deryn, ed., *Modern Women Poets* (Tarset: Bloodaxe, 2004).

Critical Works

Acheson, James and Romana Huk, eds., *Contemporary British Poetry: Essays in Theory and Criticism* (Albany: State University of New York Press, 1996.)
Bertram, Vicki *Gendering Poetry: Contemporary Women and Men Poets* (London: Rivers Oram Pandora Press, 2005).
ed., *Kicking Daffodils: Twentieth Century Women Poets* (Edinburgh: Edinburgh University Press, 1997).
Decaires Narain, Denise *Contemporary Caribbean Women's Poetry* (London: Routledge, 2001).
Dowson, Jane, ed., *The Cambridge Companion to Twentieth Century British and Irish Women's Poetry* (Cambridge: Cambridge University Press, 2011).
Dowson, Jane and Alice Entwistle *A History of Twentieth Century British Women's Poetry* (Cambridge: Cambridge University Press, 2005).
Gill, Jo, *Women's Poetry* (Edinburgh: Edinburgh University Press, 2007).
Kinnahan, Linda, *Lyric Interventions: Feminism, Experimental Poetry and Contemporary Discourse* (Iowa City: University of Iowa Press, 2004).
Mark, Alison and Deryn Rees-Jones, eds., *Contemporary Women's Poetry: Reading/ Writing/ Practice* (Basingstoke: Macmillan, 2000).
Montefiore, Jan, *Feminism and Poetry: Language, Experience, Identity in Women's Writing*, (London: Pandora 1987); 2nd edn. (London: Pandora, 1994); 3rd edn., intro. Claire Buck (London: Rivers Oram Pandora, 2003).
Arguments of Heart and Mind: Selected Essays 1977–2000 (Manchester: Manchester University Press, 2002).
Mulford, Wendy, 'Curved … Odd … Irregular: Contemporary Poetry by Women', *Women: A Cultural Review* 1–3 (1990), pp. 261–7.

Rees-Jones, Deryn, *Consorting with Angels: Essays on Modern Women Poets* (Tarset, Bloodaxe Books, 2004).
Riley, Denise, ed., *Poets on Writing: Britain 1970–1991* (London: Macmillan, 1992).
Severin, Laura, *Poetry off the Page: Twentieth Century British Women Poets in Performance* (Farnham: Ashgate, 2004).
Stevenson, Anne, 'Writing as a Woman' in Mary Jacobus, ed., *Women Writing and Writing about Women* (London: Croom Helm, 1979).
Wills, Clair, 'Contemporary Women's Poetry: Experimentalism and the Expressive Voice', *Critical Quarterly* 36.3 (1994), pp. 35–52.
Yorke, Liz *Impertinent Voices: Subversive Strategies in Contemporary Women's Poetry* (London, Routledge 1991).

Ecopoetics and Poetry

Bate, Jonathan, *The Song of the Earth* (London: Picador, 2000).
Bryson, J. Scott, ed., *Ecopoetry: A Critical Introduction* (Salt Lake City: University of Utah Press, 2002).
Buell, Lawrence, *The Future of Environmental Criticism: Environmental Crisis and Literary Imagination* (Oxford: Blackwell, 2005).
Clark, Timothy, *The Cambridge Introduction to Literature and the Environment* (Cambridge: Cambridge University Press, 2011).
Gifford, Terry, *Green Voices: Understanding Contemporary Nature Poetry* (Manchester: Manchester University Press, 1995).
Goodbody, Axel and Kate Rigby, eds., *Ecocritical Theory: New European Approaches* (Virginia: University of Virginia Press, 2011).
Heise, Ursula K., *Sense of Place and Sense of Planet: the Environmental Imagination of the Global* (Oxford and New York: Oxford University Press, 2008).
Kerridge, Richard and Neil Sammells, *Writing the Environment: Ecocriticism and Literature* (London: Zed Books, 1998).
Morton, Timothy, *Ecology without Nature: Rethinking Environmental Aesthetics* (Cambridge, MA and London: Harvard University Press, 2007).
Picot, Edward, *Outcasts from Eden: Ideas of Landscape in British Poetry since 1945* (Liverpool: Liverpool University Press, 1996).
Rosendale, Steven, *The Greening of Literary Scholarship: Literature, Theory and the Environment* (Iowa City: University of Iowa Press, 2002).
Soper, Kate, *What is Nature?* (Oxford and Cambridge, MA: Blackwell, 1995).
Westling, Louise, ed., *The Cambridge Companion to Literature and the Environment* (Cambridge: Cambridge University Press, 2014).

Poetry and the City

Alexander, Neal, and David Cooper, eds., *Poetry and Geography: Space and Place in Post-War Poetry* (Liverpool, Liverpool University Press, 2013).
Barry, Peter, *Contemporary British Poetry and the City* (Manchester: Manchester University Press, 2000).
Bavidge, Jenny, *Theorists of the City: Walter Benjamin, Henri Lefebvre and Michel de Certeau* (London: Routledge, 2009).

Christopher, Nicholas, ed., *Walk on the Wild Side: Urban American Poetry since 1975* (New York: Collier Books, 1994).
Davidson, Ian, and Zoë Skoulding, eds., *Placing Poetry* (Amsterdam: Editions Rodopi B.V., 2013).
Dowson, Jane, ed., *The Cambridge Companion to Twentieth-Century British and Irish Women's Poetry* (Cambridge: Cambridge University Press, 2012).
Feinstein, Elaine, *Cities* (Manchester, Carcanet, 2010).
McNamara, Kevin R., 'Some Versions of Urban Pastoral', in Kevin R. McNamara and Timothy Gray, eds., *The Cambridge Companion to the City in Literature* (Cambridge: Cambridge University Press, 2014), pp. 245–60.
Raban, Jonathan, *Soft City* (London: Hamish Hamilton, 1974).
Rogerson, Barnaby, ed., *London: A Collection of Poetry of Place* (London: Elan Press, 2004).
Skoulding, Zoë, *Contemporary Women's Poetry and Urban Space: Experimental Cities* (Basingstoke: Palgrave Macmillan, 2013).
Soja, Edward W., *Postmetropolis: Critical Studies of Cities and Regions* (Oxford: Blackwell, 2000).

Poetry's Outward Forms

Abse, Dannie, *Goodbye Twentieth Century* (London: Pimlico, 2001).
Acheson, James and Romana Huk, eds, *Contemporary British Poetry: Essays in Theory and Criticism* (Albany, NY: State University of New York Press, 1996).
Alvarez, A., *Beyond All This Fiddle: Essays 1955–1967* (London: The Allen Lane Press, 1968).
Shaping the Spirit (London: Chatto and Windus 1958).
Boland, Eavan, *A Journey With Two Maps: Becoming a Woman Poet* (Manchester: Carcanet, 2011).
Booth, Martin, *British Poetry 1964 to 1984: Driving through the Barricades* (London: Routledge and Kegan Paul, 1985).
Fairfax, John and John Moat, *The Way to Write* (London: Elm Tree Books/Hamish Hamilton, 1981).
Forrest-Thomson, Veronica, *Poetic Artifice* (Manchester: Manchester University Press, 1978).
Fraser, G. S., *The Modern Writer and His World* (London: Derek Verschoyle, 1953); and 3rd revised edition (Harmondworth: Penguin, 1964).
Hall, Donald, *Unpacking the Boxes* (New York: Houghton Mifflin, 2008).
Hobsbaum, Philip, and Edward Lucie-Smith, eds., *A Group Anthology* (London: Oxford University Press, 1963).
Homberger, Eric, *The Art of the Real* (London: J. M. Dent, 1977).
Lucas, John, *Starting to Explain* (Nottingham: Trent Editions, 2003).
McCully, C. B., ed., *The Poet's Voice and Craft* (Manchester: Carcanet, 1994).
Rowbotham, Sheila, *Promise of a Dream* (Harmondsworth: Penguin, 2001).
Rudolf, Anthony, *Silent Conversations* (London, New York; Calcutta: Seagull, 2013).
Spender, Stephen, and Donald Hall, eds., *A Concise Encyclopedia of English and American Poets and Poetry* (London: Hutchinson, 1963).
Schmidt, Michael, and Grevel Lindop, eds., *British Poetry since 1960* (Carcanet: South Hinksey, Oxford, 1972).

Schmidt, Michael and Peter Jones, *British Poetry since 1970: A Critical Survey* (Manchester: Carcanet, 1980).
Silkin, Jon, *The Life of Metrical and Free Verse in Twentieth-Century Poetry* (Basingstoke: Macmillan, 1997).
Wainwright, Jeffrey, *Poetry: The Basics* (London: Routledge, 2004).
Wilmer, Clive, *Poets Talking: The 'Poet of the Month' Interviews from BBC Radio 3* (Manchester: Carcanet, 1994).

INDEX

Cambridge Companions to...

AUTHORS

Edward Albee edited by Stephen J. Bottoms
Margaret Atwood edited by Coral Ann Howells
W. H. Auden edited by Stan Smith
Jane Austen edited by Edward Copeland and Juliet McMaster (second edition)
Beckett edited by John Pilling
Bede edited by Scott DeGregorio
Aphra Behn edited by Derek Hughes and Janet Todd
Walter Benjamin edited by David S. Ferris
William Blake edited by Morris Eaves
Jorge Luis Borges edited by Edwin Williamson
Brecht edited by Peter Thomson and Glendyr Sacks (second edition)
The Brontës edited by Heather Glen
Bunyan edited by Anne Dunan-Page
Frances Burney edited by Peter Sabor
Byron edited by Drummond Bone
Albert Camus edited by Edward J. Hughes
Willa Cather edited by Marilee Lindemann
Cervantes edited by Anthony J. Cascardi
Chaucer edited by Piero Boitani and Jill Mann (second edition)
Chekhov edited by Vera Gottlieb and Paul Allain
Kate Chopin edited by Janet Beer
Caryl Churchill edited by Elaine Aston and Elin Diamond
Cicero edited by Catherine Steel
Coleridge edited by Lucy Newlyn
Wilkie Collins edited by Jenny Bourne Taylor
Joseph Conrad edited by J. H. Stape
H. D. edited by Nephie J. Christodoulides and Polina Mackay
Dante edited by Rachel Jacoff (second edition)
Daniel Defoe edited by John Richetti
Don DeLillo edited by John N. Duvall
Charles Dickens edited by John O. Jordan
Emily Dickinson edited by Wendy Martin
John Donne edited by Achsah Guibbory
Dostoevskii edited by W. J. Leatherbarrow
Theodore Dreiser edited by Leonard Cassuto and Claire Virginia Eby
John Dryden edited by Steven N. Zwicker
W. E. B. Du Bois edited by Shamoon Zamir
George Eliot edited by George Levine
T. S. Eliot edited by A. David Moody
Ralph Ellison edited by Ross Posnock
Ralph Waldo Emerson edited by Joel Porte and Saundra Morris
William Faulkner edited by Philip M. Weinstein
Henry Fielding edited by Claude Rawson
F. Scott Fitzgerald edited by Ruth Prigozy
Flaubert edited by Timothy Unwin
E. M. Forster edited by David Bradshaw
Benjamin Franklin edited by Carla Mulford
Brian Friel edited by Anthony Roche
Robert Frost edited by Robert Faggen
Gabriel García Márquez edited by Philip Swanson
Elizabeth Gaskell edited by Jill L. Matus
Goethe edited by Lesley Sharpe
Günter Grass edited by Stuart Taberner
Thomas Hardy edited by Dale Kramer
David Hare edited by Richard Boon
Nathaniel Hawthorne edited by Richard Millington
Seamus Heaney edited by Bernard O'Donoghue
Ernest Hemingway edited by Scott Donaldson
Homer edited by Robert Fowler
Horace edited by Stephen Harrison
Ted Hughes edited by Terry Gifford
Ibsen edited by James McFarlane
Henry James edited by Jonathan Freedman

Samuel Johnson edited by Greg Clingham
Ben Jonson edited by Richard Harp and Stanley Stewart
James Joyce edited by Derek Attridge (second edition)
Kafka edited by Julian Preece
Keats edited by Susan J. Wolfson
Rudyard Kipling edited by Howard J. Booth
Lacan edited by Jean-Michel Rabaté
D. H. Lawrence edited by Anne Fernihough
Primo Levi edited by Robert Gordon
Mario Vargas Llosa edited by Efrain Kristal and John King
Lucretius edited by Stuart Gillespie and Philip Hardie
Machiavelli edited by John M. Najemy
David Mamet edited by Christopher Bigsby
Thomas Mann edited by Ritchie Robertson
Christopher Marlowe edited by Patrick Cheney
Andrew Marvell edited by Derek Hirst and Steven N. Zwicker
Herman Melville edited by Robert S. Levine
Arthur Miller edited by Christopher Bigsby (second edition)
Milton edited by Dennis Danielson (second edition)
Molière edited by David Bradby and Andrew Calder
Toni Morrison edited by Justine Tally
Nabokov edited by Julian W. Connolly
Nelson Mandela edited by Rita Barnard
Eugene O'Neill edited by Michael Manheim
George Orwell edited by John Rodden
Ovid edited by Philip Hardie
Harold Pinter edited by Peter Raby (second edition)
Sylvia Plath edited by Jo Gill
Edgar Allan Poe edited by Kevin J. Hayes
Alexander Pope edited by Pat Rogers
Ezra Pound edited by Ira B. Nadel
Proust edited by Richard Bales
Pushkin edited by Andrew Kahn
Rabelais edited by John O'Brien
Rilke edited by Karen Leeder and Robert Vilain
Philip Roth edited by Timothy Parrish
Salman Rushdie edited by Abdulrazak Gurnah
Shakespeare edited by Margareta de Grazia and Stanley Wells (second edition)
Shakespearean Comedy edited by Alexander Leggatt
Shakespeare and Contemporary Dramatists edited by Ton Hoenselaars
Shakespeare and Contemporary Dramatists edited by Ton Hoenselaars
Shakespeare and Popular Culture edited by Robert Shaughnessy
Shakespeare edited by Margareta de Grazia and Stanley Wells (second edition)
Shakespeare on Film edited by Russell Jackson (second edition)
Shakespeare on Stage edited by Stanley Wells and Sarah Stanton
Shakespeare's History Plays edited by Michael Hattaway
Shakespeare's Last Plays edited by Catherine M. S. Alexander
Shakespeare's Poetry edited by Patrick Cheney
Shakespearean Comedy edited by Alexander Leggatt
Shakespearean Tragedy edited by Claire McEachern (second edition)
George Bernard Shaw edited by Christopher Innes
Shelley edited by Timothy Morton
Mary Shelley edited by Esther Schor
Sam Shepard edited by Matthew C. Roudané
Spenser edited by Andrew Hadfield
Laurence Sterne edited by Thomas Keymer
Wallace Stevens edited by John N. Serio
Tom Stoppard edited by Katherine E. Kelly
Harriet Beecher Stowe edited by Cindy Weinstein
August Strindberg edited by Michael Robinson

Jonathan Swift edited by Christopher Fox
J. M. Synge edited by P. J. Mathews
Tacitus edited by A. J. Woodman
Henry David Thoreau edited by Joel Myerson
Tolstoy edited by Donna Tussing Orwin
Anthony Trollope edited by Carolyn Dever and Lisa Niles
Mark Twain edited by Forrest G. Robinson
John Updike edited by Stacey Olster
Virgil edited by Charles Martindale
Voltaire edited by Nicholas Cronk
Edith Wharton edited by Millicent Bell
Walt Whitman edited by Ezra Greenspan
Oscar Wilde edited by Peter Raby
Tennessee Williams edited by Matthew C. Roudané
August Wilson edited by Christopher Bigsby
Mary Wollstonecraft edited by Claudia L. Johnson
Virginia Woolf edited by Susan Sellers (second edition)
Wordsworth edited by Stephen Gill
W. B. Yeats edited by Marjorie Howes and John Kelly
Zola edited by Brian Nelson

TOPICS

The Actress edited by Maggie B. Gale and John Stokes
The African American Novel edited by Maryemma Graham
The African American Slave Narrative edited by Audrey A. Fisch
African American Theatre by Harvey Young
Allegory edited by Rita Copeland and Peter Struck
American Crime Fiction edited by Catherine Ross Nickerson
American Modernism edited by Walter Kalaidjian
American Poetry Since 1945 edited by Jennifer Ashton
American Realism and Naturalism edited by Donald Pizer
American Travel Writing edited by Alfred Bendixen and Judith Hamera
American Women Playwrights edited by Brenda Murphy
Ancient Rhetoric edited by Erik Gunderson
Arthurian Legend edited by Elizabeth Archibald and Ad Putter
Australian Literature edited by Elizabeth Webby
Autobiography edited by Maria DiBattista and Emily Wittman
British Literature of the French Revolution edited by Pamela Clemit
British Romanticism edited by Stuart Curran (second edition)
British Romantic Poetry edited by James Chandler and Maureen N. McLane
British Theatre, 1730–1830, edited by Jane Moody and Daniel O'Quinn
Canadian Literature edited by Eva-Marie Kröller
Children's Literature edited by M. O. Grenby and Andrea Immel
The Classic Russian Novel edited by Malcolm V. Jones and Robin Feuer Miller
Contemporary Irish Poetry edited by Matthew Campbell
Creative Writing edited by David Morley and Philip Neilsen
Crime Fiction edited by Martin Priestman
Early Modern Women's Writing edited by Laura Lunger Knoppers
The Eighteenth-Century Novel edited by John Richetti
Eighteenth-Century Poetry edited by John Sitter
English Literature, 1500–1600 edited by Arthur F. Kinney
English Literature, 1650–1740 edited by Steven N. Zwicker
English Literature, 1740-1830 edited by Thomas Keymer and Jon Mee
English Literature, 1830-1914 edited by Joanne Shattock

English Novelists edited by Adrian Poole
English Poetry, Donne to Marvell edited by Thomas N. Corns
English Poets edited by Claude Rawson
English Renaissance Drama, second edition edited by A. R. Braunmuller and Michael Hattaway
English Renaissance Tragedy edited by Emma Smith and Garrett A. Sullivan Jr.
English Restoration Theatre edited by Deborah C. Payne Fisk
The Epic edited by Catherine Bates
European Modernism edited by Pericles Lewis
European Novelists edited by Michael Bell
Fairy Tales edited by Maria Tatar
Fantasy Literature edited by Edward James and Farah Mendlesohn
Feminist Literary Theory edited by Ellen Rooney
Fiction in the Romantic Period edited by Richard Maxwell and Katie Trumpener
The Fin de Siècle edited by Gail Marshall
The French Enlightenment edited by Daniel Brewer
The French Novel: from 1800 to the Present edited by Timothy Unwin
Gay and Lesbian Writing edited by Hugh Stevens
German Romanticism edited by Nicholas Saul
Gothic Fiction edited by Jerrold E. Hogle
The Greek and Roman Novel edited by Tim Whitmarsh
Greek and Roman Theatre edited by Marianne McDonald and J. Michael Walton
Greek Comedy edited by Martin Revermann
Greek Lyric edited by Felix Budelmann
Greek Mythology edited by Roger D. Woodard
Greek Tragedy edited by P. E. Easterling
The Harlem Renaissance edited by George Hutchinson
The History of the Book edited by Leslie Howsam
The Irish Novel edited by John Wilson Foster
The Italian Novel edited by Peter Bondanella and Andrea Ciccarelli
The Italian Renaissance edited by Michael Wyatt
Jewish American Literature edited by Hana Wirth-Nesher and Michael P. Kramer
The Latin American Novel edited by Efraín Kristal
The Literature of the First World War edited by Vincent Sherry
The Literature of London edited by Lawrence Manley
The Literature of Los Angeles edited by Kevin R. McNamara
The Literature of New York edited by Cyrus Patell and Bryan Waterman
The Literature of Paris edited by Anna-Louise Milne
The Literature of World War II edited by Marina MacKay
Literature on Screen edited by Deborah Cartmell and Imelda Whelehan
Medieval English Culture edited by Andrew Galloway
Medieval English Literature edited by Larry Scanlon
Medieval English Mysticism edited by Samuel Fanous and Vincent Gillespie
Medieval English Theatre edited by Richard Beadle and Alan J. Fletcher (second edition)
Medieval French Literature edited by Simon Gaunt and Sarah Kay
Medieval Romance edited by Roberta L. Krueger
Medieval Women's Writing edited by Carolyn Dinshaw and David Wallace
Modern American Culture edited by Christopher Bigsby
Modern British Women Playwrights edited by Elaine Aston and Janelle Reinelt
Modern French Culture edited by Nicholas Hewitt
Modern German Culture edited by Eva Kolinsky and Wilfried van der Will
The Modern German Novel edited by Graham Bartram

The Modern Gothic edited by Jerrold E. Hogle
Modern Irish Culture edited by Joe Cleary and Claire Connolly
Modern Italian Culture edited by Zygmunt G. Baranski and Rebecca J. West
Modern Latin American Culture edited by John King
Modern Russian Culture edited by Nicholas Rzhevsky
Modern Spanish Culture edited by David T. Gies
Modernism edited by Michael Levenson (second edition)
The Modernist Novel edited by Morag Shiach
Modernist Poetry edited by Alex Davis and Lee M. Jenkins
Modernist Women Writers edited by Maren Tova Linett
Narrative edited by David Herman
Native American Literature edited by Joy Porter and Kenneth M. Roemer
Nineteenth-Century American Women's Writing edited by Dale M. Bauer and Philip Gould
Old English Literature edited by Malcolm Godden and Michael Lapidge (second edition)
Paradise Lost edited by Louis Schwartz
Performance Studies edited by Tracy C. Davis
Piers Plowman by Andrew Cole and Andrew Galloway
The Poetry of the First World War edited by Santanu Das
Popular Fiction edited by David Glover and Scott McCracken
Postcolonial Literary Studies edited by Neil Lazarus
Postmodernism edited by Steven Connor
The Pre-Raphaelites edited by Elizabeth Prettejohn
Pride and Prejudice edited by Janet Todd
Renaissance Humanism edited by Jill Kraye
The Roman Historians edited by Andrew Feldherr
Roman Satire edited by Kirk Freudenburg
Science Fiction edited by Edward James and Farah Mendlesohn
Scottish Literature edited by Gerald Carruthers and Liam McIlvanney
Sensation Fiction edited by Andrew Mangham
The Sonnet edited by A. D. Cousins and Peter Howarth
The Spanish Novel: from 1600 to the Present edited by Harriet Turner and Adelaida López de Martínez
Textual Scholarship edited by Neil Fraistat and Julia Flanders
Theatre History by David Wiles and Christine Dymkowski
Travel Writing edited by Peter Hulme and Tim Youngs
Twentieth-Century British and Irish Women's Poetry edited by Jane Dowson
The Twentieth-Century English Novel edited by Robert L. Caserio
Twentieth-Century English Poetry edited by Neil Corcoran
Twentieth-Century Irish Drama edited by Shaun Richards
Twentieth-Century Russian Literature edited by Marina Balina and Evgeny Dobrenko
Utopian Literature edited by Gregory Claeys
Victorian and Edwardian Theatre edited by Kerry Powell
The Victorian Novel edited by Deirdre David (second edition)
Victorian Poetry edited by Joseph Bristow
War Writing edited by Kate McLoughlin
Writing of the English Revolution edited by N. H. Keeble